STAGE, STAKE, AND SCAFFOLD

STAGE, STAKE, AND SCAFFOLD

Humans and Animals in Shakespeare's Theatre

ANDREAS HÖFELE

OXFORD
UNIVERSITY PRESS

*This book has been printed digitally and produced in a standard specification
in order to ensure its continuing availability*

OXFORD
UNIVERSITY PRESS

Great Clarendon Street, Oxford OX2 6DP
United Kingdom

Oxford University Press is a department of the University of Oxford.
It furthers the University's objective of excellence in research, scholarship,
and education by publishing worldwide.
Oxford is a registered trade mark of Oxford University Press in the UK
and in certain other countries

© Andrew Höfele 2011

The moral rights of the author have been asserted

Reprinted 2013

British Library Cataloguing in Publication Data
Data available
Library of Congress Cataloging in Publication Data
Data available
ISBN 978-0-19-956764-5

For Gabriele

Contents

List of Illustrations   viii
Preface   ix
Note on the Text   xiii

Introduction   1
1. 'What beast was't then': Stretching the Boundaries in *Macbeth*   41
2. A Kingdom for a Scaffold   68
3. 'More than a creeping thing': Baiting Coriolanus   92
4. Cannibal–Animal: Figurations of the (In)Human in Montaigne,
   Foxe, and Shakespearean Revenge Tragedy   115
5. 'I'll see their trial first': Law and Disorder in Lear's Animal
   Kingdom   171
6. Revels' End: *The Tempest* and After   229

Bibliography   279
Index   307

List of Illustrations

1. John Norden, *Speculum Britanniae. The first parte. An Historical Chorographical Description of Middlesex* (London, 1593) (detail). © British Library Board. Image-Maps. Crace.1.21 4

2. Map of London in *Civitates Orbis Terrarum*, published by G. Braun and F. Hogenberg (Cologne, 1572) (detail). Reproduced by permission of Corbis 5

3. Wenceslaus Hollar, 'Long View' of London from Southwark, 1647 (detail). Reproduced by permission of Interfoto 8

4. Charles Le Brun, Physiognomical Study ('Conférence sur l'expression des passions', 1668). Reproduced by permission of Corbis 16

5. Skull of a female bear, Dulwich College. Photograph John Hammond 37

6. 'The burning of Thomas Cranmer', in John Foxe, *Actes and Monuments* (1563). © British Library Board. C.37.h.2, 1503 44

7. Carolus Bovillus, 'The anthropological ladder of degree' (1509). Reproduced by permission of the Staats- und Stadtbibliothek, Augsburg 55

8. Frans Snyders, 'The Bear Hunt'. Reproduced by permission of the Bayerische Staatsgemäldesammlungen, Munich. Inv. No. 1267 94

9. Engraving in Jan van der Straet's *Venationes Ferarum* (Antwerp, 1578). Reproduced by permission of the Herzog August Bibliothek, Wolfenbüttel. 39.1 Geom. 2° (1) 96

10. Copper engraving 'The Lambe speaketh. Why do you crucifie me agen' (1553–5). Reproduced by permission of the Herzog August Bibliothek, Wolfenbüttel. 38.25 Aug. 2° fol.259 134

11. Sebastian Münster's *Cosmographei* (Basle, 1550). Reproduced by permission of the Bayerische Staatsbibliothek 170

12. Daniel Nikolaus Chodowiecki, 'The Tempest', in *Goettinger Taschen Calender 1788*. Reproduced by permission of the Bayerische Staatsbibliothek 256

Preface

My interest in what eventually became the subject of this book began with a
bear that lived around the year 1600 and resurfaced in a library some three
hundred years later, where an erudite young man resurrects him in order to
coax his listeners into paying attention to a rather wild story of cuckoldry
and authorship, a story which purports to 'explain' the mystery of *Hamlet*.
The young man is Stephen Dedalus, the place the National Library, Dublin,
the date 16 June 1904, the time three o'clock in the afternoon:

> – It is this hour of a day in mid June, Stephen said, begging with a swift glance
> their hearing. The flag is up on the playhouse by the bankside. The bear
> Sackerson growls in the pit near it, Paris garden. Canvasclimbers who sailed
> with Drake chew their sausages among the groundlings. . . . Shakespeare has
> left the huguenot's house in Silver street and walks by the swanmews along
> the riverbank.[1]

In this short passage of preliminary scene-setting, the bear Sackerson stands
out, the odd specificity of his name proving far more evocative than the
mention of Drake. If there is any energy, any power to 'inwardly work . . . a
stirre of the mynde',[2] in the passage, it issues from Sackerson, the animal
with a human name. Sackerson envelops Shakespeare's walk to work in a
veritable tangle of spectacles and species. This tangle, I will argue, is also
crucially operative in Shakespeare's work itself. With the bear Sackerson
growling in the pit at Paris garden and the groundlings chewing their
sausages in the pit of the neighbouring Globe, the prelude of Stephen's
'psychobiographical' dissertation on Shakespeare introduces the interplay
between two kinds of entertainment, theatre and bear-baiting, and between
two kinds of beings, human and animal.

---

[1] James Joyce, *Ulysses*, ed. Hans Walter Gabler with Wolfgang Steppe and Claus Melchior
(London: The Bodley Head, 1986), 154.
[2] The definition of 'Energia' in George Puttenham, *The Arte of English Poesie*, ed. Gladys
Doidge Willcock and Alice Walker (Cambridge: Cambridge University Press, 1936), 143–4.

Alternative terms might be proposed: 'humans and *non-human* animals'[3] or 'humans and *other* animals'. I have kept to the more conventional 'humans and animals' for two reasons, one historical and one relating to the contemporary debate on what Cary Wolfe has characterized as 'one of the central ethical issues of our time: our moral responsibilities toward nonhuman animals'.[4] 'Humans and animals' emphasizes humanity's specialness. The case for retaining that specialness (which is at bottom a case for the specialness of human responsibility) is forcefully made by Cora Diamond in an early response to the animal-rights activist Peter Singer,[5] entitled 'Eating Meat and Eating People':

> [I]f we appeal to people to prevent suffering, and we, in our appeal, try to obliterate the distinction between human beings and animals and just get people to speak or think of 'different species of animals', there is no footing left from which to tell us what we ought to do. . . . The moral expectations of other human beings demand something of me as other than an animal; and we do something like imaginatively read into animals something like such expectations when we think of vegetarianism as enabling us to meet a cow's eyes. There is nothing wrong with that; there *is* something wrong with trying to keep that response and destroy its foundation.[6]

Reasoning historically, I would argue that if Shakespeare was all too readily identified with exceptionalist humanism in the past, it would be hardly less reductive now to claim him for the opposite camp. The very term 'species' implies specialness, but the 'special specialness'[7] of the human is not some-

---

[3] But, as Marianne Dekoven suggests in a recent article, '[t]he term *nonhuman* itself is' just as 'ideologically loaded' as '[*n*]*onwhite*, *non-European* and *non-Western*'. Marianne Dekoven, 'Guest Column: Why Animals Now?' *PMLA* 124 (2009), 361–9 at 363.

[4] Stanley Cavell, Cora Diamond, John McDowell, Ian Hacking, and Cary Wolfe, *Philosophy and Animal Life* (New York: Columbia University Press, 2008), 3.

[5] Peter Singer, *Animal Liberation: A New Ethics for our Treatment of Animals* (London: Jonathan Cape, 1976). For a balanced critique of the Utilitarian foundations of the animal rights campaign, see also Martha Nussbaum, 'Animal Rights: The Need for a Theoretical Basis', *Harvard Law Review*, 114 (2001), 1506–49 (= review of Steven M. Wise, *Rattling the Cage: Toward Legal Rights for Animals* (Cambridge, Mass.: Perseus Books, 2000)), and ead., 'Facing Animal Complexity', paper given at a panel entitled *Facing Animals*, Harvard University, 24 April 2007, available online at: <http://www.hcs.harvard.edu/~hrp/lecture/facing_animals-nussbaum.pdf> (accessed 23 July 2010).

[6] Cora Diamond, 'Eating Meat and Eating People' (1975–6) in her *The Realistic Spirit: Wittgenstein, Philosophy, and the Mind* (Cambridge, Mass., and London: MIT Press, 1991), 319–34 at 333. The passage is quoted by Cary Wolfe, *Philosophy and Animal Life* (New York: Columbia University Press, 2008), 15. This volume also contains an essay by Diamond that develops her argument further.

[7] Cf. Markus Wild, *Die anthropologische Differenz: Der Geist der Tiere in der frühen Neuzeit bei Montaigne, Descartes und Hume* (Berlin and New York: De Gruyter, 2006), 2–3.

thing that is given up lightly in Shakespeare. His plays may show the superior rank or *dignitas* of 'man' to be questionable and under pressure, even a delusion, but this is the outcome, not the starting point, of a process leading more often than not to painful discovery. Thus for all its agreeableness to present-day sensibilities, the more species-companionable duo 'humans and other animals' would take the edge off this discovery. 'Humans and *other* animals' may indicate the position we find Shakespeare reaching towards or even arriving at, but it would be wrong to flag it as his point of departure. The conflicted nature of human nature in Shakespeare derives from a fundamental sense of difference *and* a fundamental sense of similarity between humans and animals. It is Shakespeare's engagement with this complex doubleness that the following chapters undertake to explore.

In the course of writing I have accumulated a great many debts. I would like to thank, first of all, Ruth Morse for pointing out to me that the gentleman sitting next to me at a lecture in Stratford-upon-Avon in 2006 was Andrew McNeillie of Oxford University Press and that perhaps I would wish to talk to him; Dieter Schulz for reading the whole book in draft and offering sage comments; Stephan Laqué for conversations that brightened and enlightened; Ingeborg Boltz for creating a wonderful working environment at the Munich Shakespeare Library; and Kay Henn and Tom Minnes for expert pruning of my English.

My very special thanks go to Robert Weimann, whose work has been formative in my understanding of Shakespeare's theatre and who responded with wonderfully thoughtful and stimulating advice to the chapters I sent him.

I am deeply grateful to the University of Munich for a research professorship that provided the time for this book to materialize.

I received advice and support from Catherine Belsey, Werner Habicht, Peter Holland, Werner von Koppenfels, Kate McLuskie, Paola Pugliatti, Phyllis Rackin, Johann N. Schmidt, Virginia Vaughan, and Richard Wilson. For opportunities to present work in progress I am grateful to Herbert Grabes and Ansgar Nünning, Tobias Döring and Susanne Rupp, the Heidelberg Academy of Sciences and Humanities, Anne-Julia Zwierlein and Stefan Welz, and Hubert Zapf. Two draft chapters benefited from the scrutiny of the 'Kränzchen', a circle of my Munich colleagues and friends.

An earlier version of Chapter 1 appeared under the title 'Humanity at Stake: Man and Animal in Shakespeare's Theatre', in Peter Holland (ed.), *Shakespeare Survey*, 60 (2007), © Cambridge University Press, reproduced with permission.

I am indebted to Susanne Bayerlipp, Bastian Kuhl, and Markus Ostermair for assistance in preparing the text for publication. Ariane Petit and Kathleen Kerr of Oxford University Press, and Bonnie Blackburn saw the manuscript into print.

My greatest debt of gratitude as always is to my wife. I dedicate this book to her.

Note on the Text

Unless otherwise stated Shakespeare quotations are from *The Complete Works*, ed. Stanley Wells and Gary Taylor (2nd edn., Oxford: Clarendon Press, 2005). F = Folio; Q = Quarto; SD = stage direction.

Introduction

I. Excavation

When the ground in Shakespeare's Elsinore is dug up Hamlet finds the skull of a clown: alas, poor Yorick! When archaeologists dig up the area of the early modern London theatre district what they find are the skulls and bones of mastiff dogs or, occasionally, the skull of a bear.[1] Like the pieces of brick and timber that allow us to trace the layout of the old playhouse, like the odd penny, button, or belt buckle that recalls its long-gone patrons, these bone finds are testimony to what was a common afternoon's entertainment around 1600. Londoners had the choice either to see (or 'hear' as the word often is) the latest play by Shakespeare, Dekker, or Jonson or to watch a bear with a name like Sackerson, Harry Hunks, Nan Stiles, or Bess of Bromley[2] be roped or chained to a stake and set upon by specially trained mastiff dogs. The culture that set the stage for Juliet and her Romeo, for a Falstaff and a Rosalind, also maintained a theatre nearby where animals could be watched tearing each other to pieces. Notable enough in itself, the truly remarkable thing about this is how much more it was than just coexistence. Play-acting and bear-baiting were joined in active collusion. Vying for the attention of the same spectators, they were playing not just side by side or competitively against each other, but also, in the literal sense of Latin *colludere*, together. Like Hamlet's 'old mole' stirring underfoot, the animal bones buried in the

---

[1] A bear skull was found during the excavation of the Rose Theatre in 1989. Christine Eccles, *The Rose Theatre* (London: Routledge, 1990), 230.

[2] '[O]ld Harry Hunks and Sacarson' apparently acquired a celebrity status not unlike that of an actor or prize fighter. Sir John Davies, 'In Publium', *The Poems of Sir John Davies*, ed. Robert Krueger (Oxford: Clarendon Press, 1975), 148–9. There must have been several bears with the name Hunks; a Tom Hunckes (bringing the early modern bear within a vowel's distance of modern Hollywood celebrity) is mentioned as one of the animals 'Burnaby had at the Bear Garden' in 1590. Edmund K. Chambers, *The Elizabethan Stage*, ii (Oxford: Clarendon Press, 1923), 457 n. 8.

foundations of the playhouse furnish the stage of human action with a ghostly double, a silent reminder of the non-verbal sound and fury that accompanied the Shakespearean stage in the cultural work that has been described as 'the invention of the human', but will be explored here as 'the question of the human'.[3] While every new production of a Shakespeare play revives and revises that invention as human performers '[s]uit the action to the word, the word to the action' (*Hamlet*, III. ii. 16–17), in yet another variation, the action of the animals in the baiting ring is for ever lost, their roar for ever silenced.

This book is an attempt to recover their traces in some of the most richly textured literary artefacts in the English language. It aims to substantiate the proposition that the theatre, the bear-garden, and, as a third associate, the spectacle of public execution participated in a powerful semantic exchange and that this exchange between stage, stake, and scaffold crucially informed Shakespeare's explorations into the nature and workings of humanness as a psychological, ethical, and political category. Shakespeare's theatre was physically close to the bear-baiting rings and the scaffolds of public execution, not only resembling them in its basic layout but also sharing a common audience. Though these propinquities have recently received an ever-growing amount of attention,[4] their significance is far from fully explored.

---

[3] Harold Bloom, *Shakespeare: The Invention of the Human* (New York: Riverhead Books, 1998). Although Latin *inventio* primarily means the finding or discovery of something which already exists, the modern sense of creating something new was gaining ground during the Renaissance. In this latter sense, 'invention' logically implies the possibility of modification and reinvention. The title of Bloom's book, rather unlike its overall drift, suggests a radically historicized, constructivist conception of the human, ruling out an essentializing notion of human nature, ontologically determined once and for all.

[4] The most comprehensive study of baiting in early modern England is Christoph Daigl, *'All the world is but a bear-baiting': Das englische Hetztheater im 16. und 17. Jahrhundert* (Berlin: Gesellschaft für Theatergeschichte, 1997). Contemporary documents pertaining to baiting are cited in Chambers, *Elizabethan Stage*, ii. 448–71, and in Gerald Eades Bentley, *The Jacobean and Caroline Stage*, vi (Oxford: Clarendon, 1968), 200–14. Connections between baiting and theatre are discussed by e.g. John Briley, 'Of Stake and Stage', *Shakespeare Survey*, 8 (1955), 106–9; David Wiles, 'William Kemp and Harry Hunks: Play as Game, Actor as Sign—A Theoretical Conclusion', in his *Shakespeare's Clown: Actor and Text in the Elizabethan Playhouse* (Cambridge: Cambridge University Press, 1987), 164–81; Robert F. Willson, Jr., 'Gloucester and Harry Hunks', *Upstart Crow*, 9 (1989), 107–11; Stephen Dickey, 'Shakespeare's Mastiff Comedy', *Shakespeare Quarterly*, 42 (1991), 255–75; Meredith Anne Skura, *Shakespeare the Actor and the Purpose of Playing* (Chicago and London: University of Chicago Press, 1993); Andreas Höfele, 'Sackerson the Bear', in Herbert Grabes (ed.), *Literary History/Cultural History: Force-Fields and Tensions = Yearbook of Research in English and American Literature (REAL)*, 17 (2001), 161–77; Terence Hawkes, 'Harry Hunks, Superstar', in id. (ed.), *Shakespeare in the Present* (London: Routledge, 2002), 83–106; Barbara Ravelhofer, ' "Beasts of Recreacion": Henslowe's White Bears', *English Literary Renaissance*, 32 (2002), 287–323; Jason Scott-Warren, 'When Theatres Were Bear-Gardens; or, What's at Stake in the Comedy of Humours', *Shakespeare Quarterly*, 54 (2003), 63–82.

Situating Shakespearean drama within the material conditions of its early modern media environment, I will argue that the vital spillover (semantic, but also performative, emotive, visceral) from the bear-garden and the scaffolds of execution substantially affects the way Shakespeare models his human characters and his conception of 'human character'[5] in general. His dramatis personae are infused with a degree of animality that a later anthropology, which could be labelled 'modern' or, more specifically, Cartesian, would categorically efface. Such an anthropology undergirds even some readings that would overtly distance themselves from it, readings which reduce Shakespeare's teeming multitude of animal references to a stable marker of moral, social, and ontological difference, 'beast' being everything 'man' is not or ought not to be. By contrast, this book will suggest that the notions of humanity embodied in Shakespeare's dramatis personae rely just as much on inclusion as on exclusion of the animal, more precisely of a whole range of (non-human) animals. Man and beast face each other across the species divide, but the divide proves highly permeable.

II. Setting the Scene: Stage, Stake, and Scaffold

Students of the Elizabethan theatre are aware of the curious substitution that occurs when one tries to trace the public playhouse back to its origins with the help of the extant Tudor maps and panoramas of London. Turning from Norden's *Speculum Britanniae* (1593) (Fig. 1) to the map of London published by Braun and Hogenberg (Cologne, 1572) (Fig. 2) in search of an *Ur*-Globe, a plausible progenitor of James Burbage's Theatre, one finds instead two baiting arenas: odd round structures that look like no other building in the picture but clearly resemble their more elaborate descendants, the theatres and baiting arenas of the 1590s.

'There was an obvious precedent for the amphitheatrical form in the bear and bull rings which preceded the public theatres'[6] wrote Edmund Chambers, and Andrew Gurr concurs: 'Burbage's building...was a wooden, unroofed amphitheatre, close kin to the bear-baiting houses and

---

[5] The term is borrowed from Virginia Woolf's famous dictum that 'on or about December 1910 human character changed'. Virginia Woolf, 'Character in Fiction' (1924), in *Selected Essays*, ed. David Bradshaw (Oxford and New York: Oxford University Press, 2009), 37–54 at 38.

[6] Chambers, *Elizabethan Stage*, ii. 525.

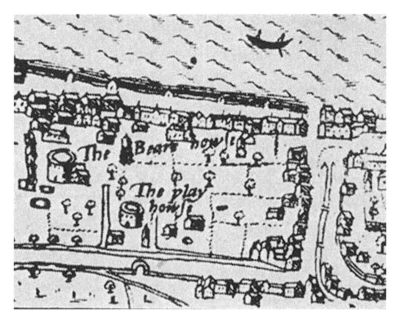

Figure 1. John Norden, *Speculum Britanniae. The first parte. An Historical Chorographical Description of Middlesex* (London, 1593) (detail).

the innyards.'[7] This majority view has not been uncontested. The primitive, corral-like baiting rings depicted in the early maps, Oscar Lee Brownstein maintains, were such a far cry from the splendour of the Elizabethan playhouse as to rule out any direct influence of one on the other.[8] John Orrell, too, denies the baiting rings any part in the genesis of Shakespeare's theatre, contending that the group of London tradesmen and artisans responsible for the building of The Theatre in 1576 disregarded all native precedent and relied wholly on the transmission of Vitruvius' Roman models instead.[9] This highly conjectural hypothesis, one would think,

[7] Andrew Gurr, *The Shakespearean Stage 1574–1642* (2nd edn., Cambridge: Cambridge University Press, 1980), 113. See also Glynne Wickham, *Early English Stages 1300–1660*, ii/1: *1576–1660* (London and Henley: Routledge and Kegan Paul, 1963), 166.

[8] Oscar Lee Brownstein, 'Why Didn't Burbage Lease the Beargarden? A Conjecture in Comparative Architecture', in Herbert Berry (ed.), *The First Public Playhouse* (Montreal: McGill-Queen's University Press, 1979), 81–96. The article is based on Brownstein's unpublished Ph.D. thesis: 'Stake and Stage: The Baiting Ring and the Public Playhouse in Elizabethan England' (University of Iowa, 1963; Microfilm, CDI #64–03353, Ann Arbor, Mich., Microfilms).

[9] John Orrell, *The Human Stage: English Theatre Design, 1567–1640* (Cambridge: Cambridge University Press, 1988). One problem with Vitruvius' *De architectura* is that his precepts for theatre design are far from clear; another, that the Elizabethan playhouses show much less resemblance to the theatres of antiquity than, for example, Andrea Palladio's explicitly Vitruvian Teatro Olimpico in Vicenza (which was not completed until 1585).

Figure 2. Map of London in *Civitates Orbis Terrarum*, published by G. Braun and F. Hogenberg (Cologne, 1572) (detail).

founders on socio-biographical grounds alone.[10] Both scholars are, of course, right in noting the considerable differences between the baiting

---

[10] The level of specialist knowledge among early modern craftsmen and artisans was considerable and their formative role in the history of science and technology is now generally acknowledged. See e.g. Arthur Clegg, 'Craftsmen and the Origin of Science', *Science and Society*, 43 (1979), 186–201; Pamela H. Smith, *The Body of the Artisan: Art and Experience in the Scientific Revolution* (Chicago: University of Chicago Press, 2004). But claims of the kind that Frances A. Yates makes in *Theatre of the World* (Chicago: University of Chicago Press, 1969), turning Burbage and his associates into paragons of humanist book-learning (which their alleged dependence on Vitruvius and his Italian transmission via Leon Battista Alberti would require), seem hardly plausible.

rings of the mid-sixteenth century and the splendidly elaborate playhouses of forty years later. But these differences do not disprove the typological kinship of the buildings. For one thing, there is evidence that at least some early baiting rings cannot have been mere circular scaffolds with spectators looking in from the outside (as the Braun and Hogenberg panorama and the so-called 'Agas' map indicate[11]), but must have had viewing arrangements very much like the roofed galleries of the Globe.[12] Even if those arrangements were more primitive, the difference is one of degree, not of kind, and therefore hardly apt to support Brownstein's main intent: to disaffiliate the Elizabethan theatre from its disreputable cousin. The collapse of the old Bear-Garden in 1583, causing five deaths and injuring many, could hardly have had such a disastrous effect if it had not been of a similar—though obviously more rickety—structure as the solidly built Theatre or Curtain. The fact that these playhouses served as models in the subsequent rebuilding of the Bear-Garden shows that the performance spaces of the two types of entertainment developed in a process of mutual give-and-take. The early bull ring and bear ring on Bankside may not constitute the single architectural 'source' of the Elizabethan playhouse. But they do supply a suggestively plausible link in the development of the English popular theatre from vagrancy to settlement in permanent, purpose-built structures. Moreover, they launch a lasting interplay between the two kinds of entertainment in which each mirrors the other. For Justus Zinzerling, a visitor from Germany, they became one and the same thing. In his Latin account of the sights of London (c.1610), he simply conflates them: 'Theatra comoedorum', he writes, 'in which bears and bulls fight with dogs.'[13]

It is unclear whether Zinzerling actually saw humans and non-humans performing in the same building or whether he simply assumed that they did so. Recent research suggests that the mingling of human actors and baited animals in one venue may indeed have begun as early as 1587, when Philip Henslowe built the Rose, his first theatre on Bankside. The 'key evidence',

---

[11] R. A. Foakes, *Illustrations of the English Stage, 1580–1642* (London: Scolar Press, 1985), 2–4.

[12] This is corroborated by a source from 1576: 'No more than suche as goe to Parisgardein, the Bell Sauage, or some other such common place, to beholde Beare bayting, Enterludes, or Fence playe, can account of any pleasant spectacle vnlesse they first paye one penny at the gate, another at the entrie of the Scaffolde, and the third for a quiet standing.' William Lambarde, *A Perambulation of Kent. . . .Collected and written (for the most part) in the yeare 1570* (London: Ralphe Newberie, 1576), 187–8; quoted in Daigl, 'All the world is but a bear-baiting', 96.

[13] *England as Seen by Foreigners in the Days of Elizabeth and James the First*, ed. William Brenchley Rye (London: John Russell Smith, 1865), 133.

writes Andrew Gurr, 'is the indication that the first stage was tacked on asymmetrically.... Its irregular positioning in the otherwise carefully surveyed groundplan suggests that it must have been built as a temporary structure.'[14] Just such a temporary, removable stage is the salient feature of the dual-purpose Hope theatre which Henslowe, twenty-seven years later, contracted the carpenter Gilbert Katherens to build on the site of the old Bear-Garden: a 'Plaiehouse fitt & convenient in all thinges, bothe for players to playe in, and for the game of Beares and Bulls to be bayted in the same.'[15] What modern business parlance would call the synergies of play-acting and baiting is nowhere more apparent than in the operation of this new theatre, which was to be reserved for 'Stage Playes on Mundayes, Wednesdayes, Fridayes and Saturdayes, And for the Baiting of Beares on Tuesdayes and Thursdayes, the Stage being made to take vp and downe when they please.'[16] 'Difficult though it is for us to imagine,' Gurr concludes wrily, 'it does seem that [Henslowe] always saw bears and players coming close to parity as his tenants.'[17]

At least one player, the famous leading man of the Lord Admiral's troupe, Edward Alleyn, Henslowe's son-in-law and business partner, must have shared this view. Having bought the Bear-Garden in 1594, he remained in the baiting business up to his death in 1626.[18] From 1604 to 1616, Alleyn and Henslowe jointly held the court office of Master and Keeper of Bears, Bulls, and Mastiff Dogs. Not only did theatre and bear-baiting share the same locations and audiences, they were also branches of the same business enterprise.

Despite being predominantly used as a playhouse, the Hope continued to be referred to by its old name, the Bear-Garden. And it is as such that it

[14] Andrew Gurr, 'Bears and Players: Philip Henslowe's Double Acts', *Shakespeare Bulletin*, 22 (2004), 31–41 at 34.

[15] *Henslowe Papers*, ed. W. W. Greg (London: A. H. Bullen, 1907), 19.

[16] In a 1631 continuation of John Stow's *Annales* by E. Howes. Quoted in C. W. W. Wallace, 'The Children of the Chapel at Blackfriars, 1597–1603', *University of Nebraska Studies*, 8 (1908), 103–321 at 147. An acerbic dig at the Tuesday and Thursday occupation of the new playhouse is contained in Ben Jonson's *Bartholomew Fair*, which opened at the Hope in Oct. 1614. The theatre, we are told in the Induction, is quite the right place for the malodorous Fair, 'the place being as dirty as Smithfield and as stinking every whit'. Ben Jonson, 'Bartholomew Fair', in *The Complete Plays of Ben Jonson*, ed. G. A. Wilkes (Oxford: Clarendon Press, 1982), 1–122 at 11, ll. 139–40.

[17] Gurr, 'Bears and Players', 41.

[18] On Alleyn, see S. P. Cerasano, 'Edward Alleyn: 1566–1626', in Aileen Reid and Robert Maniury (eds.), *Edward Alleyn: Elizabethan Actor, Jacobean Gentleman* (London: Dulwich Picture Gallery, 1994), 5–16; cf. also S. P. Cerasano, 'The Master of the Bears in Art and Enterprise', *Medieval and Renaissance Drama in England*, 5 (1991), 195–209.

Figure 3. Wenceslaus Hollar, 'Long View' of London from Southwark, 1647 (detail).

appears in Wenceslaus Hollar's famous 'Long View' of London, where, by a
no less famous mistake, the 'Beere bayting h[ouse]' exchanges names with
the (Second) Globe.[19] (Fig. 3) The theatre thus continues to be haunted by
its family resemblance to the baiting arena. Based on sketches taken on
location in the 1630s and 1640s, Hollar's 'View' was finished in Antwerp in
1647. By that time, the Globe had already been torn down:[20] a case of
posthumously mistaken identity which visibly seals the pact between the
human stage and its animal double for all posterity.

   All these connections are, of course, well known. But the architectural,
economic, or, more generally speaking, socio-cultural overlap[21] of the
two types of entertainment provides only the first step towards an understanding of how they acted upon each other. Looking at the Globe and
'Beere bayting h[ouse]' with Hollar's sharp if confused eye, we are directed

---

   [19] The mistake is so famous that Laurence Olivier alluded to it in the opening sequence of his
1944 film of *Henry V*.
   [20] Bentley, *Jacobean and Caroline Stage*, vi. 200, cites a manuscript note to the effect that the
Globe was torn down on 15 Apr. 1644.
   [21] Theatre and animal-baiting were 'culturally isomorphic events'. Dickey, 'Shakespeare's
Mastiff Comedy', 255.

from the similarity of the 'frames' to the consequences of this similarity for the perception of the 'pictures', from the venues to the shows, from the medium, as it were, to the message.

The pact between the stage and the stake involves a third partner: the scaffold of public execution. The connection between theatre and capital punishment and indeed the idea of capital punishment *as* theatre was firmly rooted in early modern culture, signalled in the public visibility and ritualized demonstrativeness of juridical practice.[22] From the common criminals who might use the opportunity of their 'last dying speeches' for a precarious moment of glory[23] to the Protestant (or Catholic) martyrs who were burnt at the stake before thousands of onlookers, from peers of the realm convicted for treason to doomed Royalty itself going to the block—those who were condemned to die and those who gathered to watch their dying were united by an awareness of the theatricality of the event.[24]

The connection between stage and scaffold links into the exchanges between stage and stake and the human–animal blending these exchanges were liable to produce. For one thing, corporal punishment itself entails an element of animalization. The convict is '[b]rought near to beast' (*King Lear*, II. ii. 172), not only because of the suffering physicality that humans share with other creatures, but also because the protocols of early modern punishment included ceremonies of humiliation such as the pillory or 'whipping at the cart's tail', which signalled the convict's downgrading to a subhuman, 'bestial' status. The fundamental change in the Western penal system, described by Foucault as a withdrawal from public exhibition to invisibilizing confinement, has resulted in the disappearance of the animal

---

[22] The classical study of the topic is Michel Foucault, *Discipline and Punish: The Birth of the Prison*, trans. Alan Sheridan (New York: Vintage, 1995).

[23] J. A. Sharpe, ' "Last Dying Speeches": Religion, Ideology and Public Execution in Seventeenth-Century England', *Past and Present*, 107 (1985), 144–67; Susan Dwyer Amussen, 'Punishment, Discipline, and Power: The Social Meanings of Violence in Early Modern England', *Journal of British Studies*, 34 (1995), 1–34; Catherine Belsey, *The Subject of Tragedy: Identity and Difference in Renaissance Drama* (London: Methuen, 1985), 190: 'The supreme moment to speak was the moment of execution. The requirement for confessions from the scaffold, so that people could see how church and state combined to protect them from the enemies of God and society, paradoxically also offered women a place from which to speak with a hitherto unimagined authority . . .'.

[24] Foxe's Protestant martyrology is a particularly powerful case in point; cf. Andreas Höfele, 'Stages of Martyrdom: John Foxe's *Actes and Monuments*', in Susanne Rupp and Tobias Döring (eds.), *Performances of the Sacred in Late Medieval and Early Modern England* (Amsterdam and New York: Rodopi, 2005), 81–93.

from the scene of punishment, or rather, *with* the scene of punishment.[25] Spectacle is precisely what Enlightenment reformers of the penal system aimed to abolish, fully aware that the performance of punishment in front of an audience not only bestializes the convict but also taints the procedure itself. The reformers usually complain about some particularly gruesome excess of legal 'butchery', but butchery inheres in the normality of the practice itself. The assertion that execution is not slaughter becomes necessary for the very reason that it may all too easily be taken to be just that. Brutus voices the anxiety attending this highly penetrable boundary in his plea: 'Let's be sacrificers, but not butchers' (*Julius Caesar*, II. i. 166). Yet 'butchers' is precisely what he and his fellow conspirators become in Mark Antony's soliloquy over Caesar's dead body: 'O pardon me, thou bleeding piece of earth, / That I am meek and gentle with these butchers' (III. i. 257–8).

If the civilizing process charted by Norbert Elias manifests itself in the effort to suppress 'every characteristic that [people] feel to be "animal"',[26] the staging of corporal punishment is clearly conducive to the opposite effect—and, more often than not, quite intentionally so (as was drastically borne out by the tableaux of abuse in the Abu Ghraib prison photos).

Conversely, the type of entertainment offered at the Bear-Garden was modelled on human punishment, resembling in both form and appeal the attacks on victims of the scaffold, the stocks, the whipping posts, and the pillory, which 'depended for their efficacy on the active participation of the public'.[27] The bear would have been perceived as the more human-like creature,[28] yet it fell to the dogs to execute the violent impulses of the human audience by proxy. This goes for the 'courses' which the dogs fought out with bear or bull, and it also holds true for such sideshows as the baiting of an ape, or monkey, on horseback, which is described in several contemporary accounts: 'Into the same place they brought a pony with an ape fastened on its back, and to see the animal kicking amongst

---

[25] Parallel with the invisibilizing of punishment, the butchering of animals became invisible in Western societies. I will return to this in Ch. 6.

[26] Norbert Elias, *What Is Sociology?*, trans. Stephen Mennell and Grace Morrissey (New York: Columbia University Press, 1978), 120.

[27] J. M. Beattie, 'Violence and Society in Early Modern England', in A. Doob and E. Greenspan (eds.), *Perspectives in Criminal Law* (Aurora, Ont.: Canada Law Books, 1984), quoted in Skura, *Shakespeare the Actor*, 306.

[28] Prior to the arrival of larger primates in Europe, bears were perceived as the animals most similar to humans. Cf. Bernd Brunner, *Bears: A Brief History*, trans. Lori Lantz (New Haven: Yale University Press, 2007), 19–37.

the dogs, with the screams of the ape, beholding the curs hanging from the ears and neck of the pony, is very laughable.'[29] Approved by another witness as 'a fine sight to see'[30], the ape on horseback was apparently meant to provide a kind of light relief to the more serious violence of the main event. Exposing the victim's fear and distress to the audience's derisive laughter, the ape on horseback closely mirrors the charivari or other communal shaming rituals of the period. All extant accounts mention the monkey's screaming; one, a poem by John Taylor, has it wet ('perfume') the saddle.[31] Again, the most human-like animal is cast as victim, its anthropomorphism emphasized by the mock privilege of riding a horse. And again, the dogs are given the role of administering punishment, of acting out the punitive impulses of the watching crowd.

The closest and most obvious approximation between baiting and penal justice, however, occurs in the regularly featured whipping of the blind bear. No longer just watching and cheering, members of the crowd take violence into their own hands. As the German traveller Paul Hentzner reports:

> To this entertainment [the baiting of bears and bulls with dogs] there often follows that of whipping the blinded bear, which is performed by five or six men, standing in a circle with whips, which they exercise upon him without any mercy. Although he cannot escape from them because of his chain, he nevertheless defends himself, vigorously throwing down all who come within his reach and are not active enough to get out of it, tearing the whips out of their hands and breaking them.[32]

A crucial signifier in this scene is the whip, archetypal instrument of animal domestication and a key symbol of man's ascendancy over beast.[33] By

---

[29] The writer is a secretary to the Duke of Nájera, who visited the court of Henry VIII in 1544. His account was translated into English by Frederic Madden, *Archaeologia*, 23 (1831), 344–57 at 354–5.

[30] Giles E. Dawson, 'London's Bull-Baiting and Bear-Baiting Arena in 1562', *Shakespeare Quarterly*, 15 (1964), 97–101, translates the account of a Venetian merchant named Alessandro Magno: 'in which baiting it is a fine sight to see the horse run, kicking and biting, and the monkey grip the saddle tightly and scream, many times being bitten' (p. 99).

[31] 'Which Jacke (his Rider) bravely rides a straddle, / And in his hot Careere perfumes the saddle.' John Taylor, *Bull, Beare, and Horse* (1638), in *The Works of John Taylor the Water Poet Not Included in the Folio Volume of 1630*, iii (Manchester: Spenser Society, 1876), 68.

[32] *Paul Hentzner's Travels in England, during the Reign of Queen Elizabeth*, trans. Horace Walpole (London: Edward Jeffery, 1797), 30.

[33] Niklaus Largier, *In Praise of the Whip: A Cultural History of Arousal*, trans. Graham Harman (New York: Zone Books, 2007).

'tearing the whips out of their hands and breaking them' the bear accomplishes a short-lived reversal of that ascendancy. The state of man, we might say with Brutus, suffers then, if not the nature, then at least the phantom of an insurrection. (*Caesar*, II. i. 67–9) The state of man also comes under attack when 'poore starued wretches' are led, cattle-like, 'to the whipping posts in *London*'.[34] The chain of signification which links baiting and the spectacle of justice operates in a loop: as whipping the blind bear mimics a ritual of corporal punishment inflicted on humans, this ritual in turn is rooted in practices of subjugating, taming, and controlling animals. The humanizing of the mercilessly thrashed animal and the bestializing of the human delinquent emerge as two sides of the same coin.

The salient feature shared by these forms of 'retributive entertainment' is the 'harassment of a centrally displayed figure'.[35] Shakespeare's wooden O, aptly characterized by Meredith Anne Skura as 'the charmed circle in which an audience enshrines or entraps the player',[36] offers a very similar setting and a very similar focus. And it may well be argued, as Terence Hawkes suggests, that the collective gaze of public remonstrance 'presents us with the founding form of what we like to think of as "entertainment" in early modern society, and that some form of "baiting" lies at its source'.[37]

III. Seeing Double: Intermediality and the Habit of Analogical Thinking

Theatre, and Shakespearean theatre in particular, is obviously more complex and more richly textured, and its range of verbal and embodied expression much wider, than to be attributable to its rootedness in the punitive entertainments of its time. But it is my contention that the theatre's family resemblance to animal baiting and the spectacle of punishment bred an ever-ready potential for a transfer of powerfully affective images and meanings. The staging of one of these kinds of performance is always framed by, always grounded in, an awareness of the other two; it always implies their absent-presence, a presence never quite erased and sometimes, indeed, emphatically foregrounded. In the perceptual topography or, to borrow a

---

[34] Thomas Dekker, 'Warres', in *The Non-Dramatic Works of Thomas Dekker*, ed. Alexander B. Grosart, vol. 4 (1885; repr. New York: Russell and Russell, 1963), 99 (italics original).

[35] Hawkes, 'Harry Hunks', 90, drawing on Skura, *Shakespeare the Actor*, 203.

[36] Skura, *Shakespeare the Actor*, 8.   [37] Hawkes, 'Harry Hunks', 90.

term coined by the Russian structuralist Yuri Lotman, the 'semiosphere' of
early modern London,[38] each of the three forms of spectacular performa-
tivity confers on the others its affective energies, its capacity for signification. Without such conferral, Lotman argues, communication is altogether
inconceivable: 'A schema consisting of addresser, addressee and the channel
linking them is not yet a working system. For it to work it has to be
"immersed" in semiotic space.'[39] 'Semiosphere', coined by analogy with
V. I. Vernadsky's concept of the biosphere, indicates how indispensable
such immersion and the exchanges it generates are for the functioning of
semiosis. By way of illustration, Lotman cites the late nineteenth-century
invention of the cinema, which 'made its appearance not alone but along
with a whole procession of traditional and newly invented peep-shows'.[40]
The ensemble of stage, stake, and scaffold, I propose, offers a no less
powerful matrix for semiotic exchanges.

The dynamics of these exchanges may be usefully conceptualized as a
form of 'intermediality', a term which, although it has its roots in 1960s
performance art in the USA,[41] is still less familiar in English than in
Continental criticism, where it has gained wide currency since its emergence in the 1990s.[42] If we regard 'media' as a set of conventions contingent
on specific technical devices, the prefix 'inter-' points to a crossing over
from one such set to another. This can mean turning a novel into a play or a
comic into a film, but such transformations would not in themselves merit
the introduction of a new term, being perfectly well described by an old
one: adaptation. Neither does 'intermediality' seem an indispensable term
when it comes to *ekphrasis* (the description of a piece of visual art in a literary
text) or its musical equivalent (the literary representation of music).[43] But
the concept does become useful when it helps illuminate the dynamics of
in-betweenness itself: the way in which one medium is suffused with and
transformed by the conventions of another when it is enlisted to capture

[38] Yuri Lotman, *Universe of the Mind: A Semiotic Theory of Culture*, trans. Ann Shukman, introd.
Umberto Eco (London and New York: Tauris, 1990), 123–4.
[39] Ibid. 123.
[40] Ibid. 124.
[41] Dick Higgins, 'Intermedia', *Something Else Newsletter*, 1/1 (n.p., 1966); repr. in id., *Horizons:
Poetics and Theory of the Intermedia* (Carbondale: Southern Illinois University Press, 1984), 18–21.
[42] A useful explication of the term in English is Christopher B. Balme, *The Cambridge
Introduction to Theatre Studies* (Cambridge: Cambridge University Press, 2008), 205–8.
[43] Both adaptation and ekphrasis or literary representations of music, however, are now
frequently treated under the rubric of intermediality. See Werner Wolf, *The Musicalization of
Fiction: A Study in the Theory and History of Intermediality* (Amsterdam: Ropopi, 1999).

process instead of just product.[44] In our own time, for instance, we may observe that patterns of cinematic montage reappear in literature and that the aesthetics of computer games together with their concomitant habits of perception encroach on the aesthetics of feature films. Brecht detected such 'intermedial' transfer as early as 1931: 'The film viewer', he wrote, 'reads stories differently. But he who writes stories is also a film viewer. The technification of literary production is irreversible.'[45] Adapting Brecht, we could say that the Elizabethan theatregoer, too, saw plays differently; differently from someone living in a world without bear-baiting and public executions. And, obviously, those Elizabethans who wrote plays were viewers of those spectacles, too. The blood rituals of baiting and criminal justice would inevitably be part of their physical and cultural environment and thus be incorporated in the store of everyday experiences that their imagination drew on.

'Our focus and central concern is *Theatre and Performance in the age of the Intermedial*',[46] the editors of a recent volume state in their introduction. By 'the age of the Intermedial', almost needless to say, they mean the present. But one could equally well class the early modern period as such an age. With the print revolution making an ever larger impact and the theatre being reinvented as professional entertainment and pervasive cultural model, there was a proportionate increase in the possible cross-currents between the various components of this early modern media landscape. There are, moreover, good reasons to assume that early modern perceptions were particularly attuned to such cross-currents. The vast system of analogical relationships which the Renaissance inherited from medieval Scholasticism may, by the late 1500s, have come under severe strain; it may even, as some historians would claim, have entirely forfeited its power to maintain the coherence of a unified cosmic order in the face of radical pluralization. But as a habit of thinking, the forming of analogies remained ubiquitous in all areas of early modern culture.[47] Cut from its moorings in Thomistic

---

[44] Linda Hutcheon thematizes the duality of product and process inherent in the term 'adaptation'. In addressing the process aspect she speaks, not of intermediality, but of re-mediation: Linda Hutcheon, *A Theory of Adaptation* (New York and London: Routledge, 2006), 16.

[45] Bertolt Brecht, *Gesammelte Werke*, vol. 18 (Frankfurt am Main: Suhrkamp, 1967), 156 (trans. Balme, *Cambridge Introduction*, 206).

[46] Freda Chapple and Chiel Kattenbelt (eds.), *Intermediality in Theatre and Performance* (Amsterdam and New York: Rodopi, 2006), 11 (italics original).

[47] Despite critiques of its sweeping periodization, Foucault's *Les Mots et les choses* is still the classic study on the subject. Michel Foucault, *The Order of Things: An Archaeology of Human Sciences*, trans. Alan Sheridan (New York: Pantheon Books, 1970).

ontology, analogizing has a way of inducing as well as arresting movement. Once begun, the exercise was effectively interminable. Just about anything could be seized upon as convertible currency in an open process of exchanges. I argue that the intermedial relationship between the playhouse, the bear-pit, and the place of execution provides a highly productive matrix for precisely such open processes of analogizing between human actors and their animal counterparts.

Analogizing produces more than likeness, though. If Mary Queen of Scots or her grandson Charles are said to act their final scene on the scaffold, it is clear that they, unlike the actor on the playhouse stage, will die in earnest, not in jest. The value of intermedial collusion between stage, stake, and scaffold lies in its foregrounding of what is both like *and* unlike. If the animals performing their 'tragicomedies' at the Bear-Garden and the human players treading the boards of the Globe are seen to resemble each other, this does not mean that they are simply identified with each other. Rather than effacing their difference, the effect could be described as double vision or *syn*opsis, in the literal sense of 'seeing together', of superimposing one image upon the other. What spectators perceived as human or as animal no longer exists in clear-cut separation; it occupies a border zone of blurring distinctions where the animal becomes uncannily familiar and the human disturbingly strange. Epitomizing over a century of Renaissance physiognomy, Charles Le Brun's celebrated man–animal studies of 1668 offer a striking illustration of this disconcerting border zone (see Fig. 4). For all their late seventeenth-century rationalist clarity, these demonstrations of human–animal likeness present a menagerie of troublingly indeterminate creatures. Each of the chimerical specimens facing each other across the species divide is so thoroughly imbricated in its counterpart that it becomes well-nigh impossible to detach what is specifically human from its non-human other.

Shakespeare figures the human in similarly questionable, albeit much less schematic, shape. As Erica Fudge points out, modern criticism has tended to 'ignore the constant presence of animals in early modern writings about the human'.[48] It is the aim of this book to rectify this omission by offering an approach to Shakespearean anthropology which takes full account of its reliance on the presence of animals.

---

[48] Erica Fudge, *Brutal Reasoning: Animals, Rationality, and Humanity in Early Modern England* (Ithaca, NY, and London: Cornell University Press, 2006), 179.

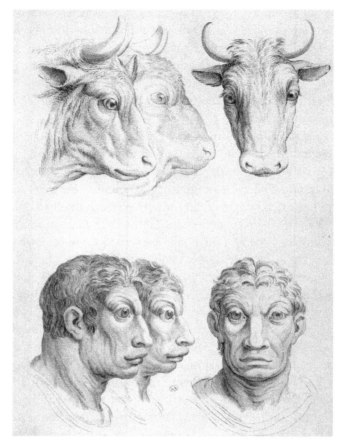

Figure 4. Charles Le Brun, Physiognomical Study ('Conférence sur l'expression des passions', 1668).

IV. Renaissance Anthropology—Shakespearean Animalities

My use of the term 'anthropology' may need some clarification. In the English-speaking world this is commonly understood as the study of human diversity, of peoples and cultures differing from 'our own', Western civilization. Virtually synonymous with 'ethnology', this *'cultural* anthropology' looks at the varieties of the ethnic other. Beginning with Herodotus, its line of descent goes via Marco Polo to the sixteenth-century accounts of the

New World such as Sahagún's *Historia general*.[49] 'Renaissance anthropology', the body of knowledge produced by these accounts, has been exposed as the epistemic arm of militant colonialism, deeply complicit in the atrocities of the European conquest.[50] In this (proto-)anthropology *ánthropos* remains something of a blank encircled by vividly distinct othernesses. Normative, European, humanity is never itself the focus of attention but the implicit vantage point from which this focus is defined.[51]

Contemporary with this charting of human (or allegedly subhuman) othernesses, the term 'anthropology' makes its appearance in learned discourse. But what it denotes is something quite different: an enquiry not into the varieties of non-normative humanity but into universal human nature. This line of enquiry leads to the predominantly continental European tradition of *philosophical* anthropology, which aims at establishing what Otto Casmann, in 1594, called a 'doctrina humanae naturae'. This is flagged by the first recorded use of the term in the title of Magnus Hundt's *Antropologium de hominis dignitate, natura et proprietatibus*, published in 1501, and confirmed by other early examples such as Galeazzo Capella's 1533 *Anthropologia*.[52] If Herodotus is the 'father', or great-grandfather, of

---

[49] Bernardino de Sahagún, *Historia general de las cosas de la Nueva España* (*c*.1540–85), Engl.: Bernardino de Sahagún, *Florentine Codex: General History of the Things of New Spain*, trans. and ed. Charles E. Dibble and Arthur J. O. Anderson, 13 vols. (Santa Fe, NM, and Salt Lake City: School of American Research and University of Utah Press, 1950–82); Miguel León-Portilla, *Bernardino de Sahagún, First Anthropologist*, trans. Mauricio J. Mixco (Norman, Okla.: University of Oklahoma Press, 2002).

[50] See Stephen Greenblatt, *Marvelous Possessions: The Wonder of the New World* (Oxford: Clarendon Press, 1991); François Hartog, *Le Miroir d'Hérodot: Essai sur la représentation de l'autre* (Paris: Gallimard, 1980); Anthony Pagden, *The Fall of Natural Man: The American Indian and the Origins of Comparative Ethnology* (Cambridge: Cambridge University Press, 1982); Margaret Hodgen, *Early Anthropology in the Sixteenth and Seventeenth Centuries* (Philadelphia: University of Pennsylvania Press, 1964); John Howland Rowe, 'The Renaissance Foundations of Anthropology', *American Anthropologist*, 67 (1965), 1–20.

[51] Notable exceptions to this standard point of view are Bartholomé de las Casas and Montaigne, though the extent to which the latter diverges from the ethnocentrically prejudiced 'cosmographers' has been the subject of debate. Cf. Gérard Defaux, 'Un Cannibale en haute de chausses: Montaigne, la différence et la logique de l'identité', *Modern Language Notes*, 97 (1982), 919–57; David Quint, 'A Reconsideration of Montaigne's *Des cannibales*', in Karen Ordahl Kupperman (ed.), *America in European Consciousness, 1493–1750* (Chapel Hill, NC, and London: University of North Carolina Press, 1995), 166–91; Deborah N. Losse, 'Rewriting Culture: Montaigne Recounts New World Ethnography', *Neophilologus*, 83 (1999), 517–28.

[52] Magnus Hundt, *Antropologium de hominis dignitate, natura et proprietatibus, de elementis, partibus et membris humani corporis* (Leipzig: Wolfgang Stöckel, 1501); Galeazzo Capella, *L'anthropologia di Galeazzo Capella secretario dell'illustrissimo signor duca di Milano* (Venice: Aldo Manuzio eredi and Andrea Torresano eredi, 1533). Otto Casmann, *Psychologia anthropologica*, 2 vols. (Hanau: Fischer, 1594–6).

Anglo-American or cultural anthropology, philosophical anthropology
ultimately derives from Aristotle.[53] Direct antecedents to its sixteenth-
century efflorescence are the fifteenth-century treatises on the dignity of
man, a provenance clearly signalled in Hundt's title. These *dignitas* treatises
reacted against the medieval notion of postlapsarian human misery, as set
out by Lottario dei Conti di Segni (Lothar of Segni, later Pope Innocent III)
in his tract *De miseria humanae conditionis* (late twelfth century). Gianozzo
Manetti's *De dignitate et excellentia hominis libri IV* (*c.*1452) was commissioned
as a response to this tract. Giovanni Pico della Mirandola's Preface to his 900
theses is traditionally regarded as the exemplary eulogy of the 'dignity of
man', that 'most fortunate of living things and . . . deserving of all admiration'.[54] 'The nature of all other creatures is defined and restricted within
laws which We have laid down', Pico's God says to Adam, 'you, by
contrast, impeded by no such restrictions, may, by your own free will . . .
trace for yourself the lineaments of your own nature'.[55]

It is in passages like these that Jacob Burckhardt found the bold new
departure and optimism which he identified as the essence of the Italian
Renaissance and 'Renaissance man'.[56] But while it is true that the dignity
tracts extend a promise far beyond the bleakness of Pope Innocent's *miseria*,
the new liberty they celebrate also launches a profound destabilization.
Released from his role as a flawed mimetic reflection of God, Pico's man
is not only free to create himself, but also forced to do so because
he is a 'chameleon', a 'Proteus', a 'creature of indeterminate image'[57] with
no shape of its own, a being without essence. The plight of such a being is
most famously embodied in the strugglings of Shakespeare's Hamlet, who

[53] The relevant works are the *Nicomachean Ethics*, *De Anima*, and *Politics*. For an exposition of
Aristotle's thought on human nature, see Jonathan Lear, *Aristotle: The Desire to Understand*
(Cambridge: Cambridge University Press, 1988), esp. chs. 4 and 5. In a wider sense all philosophical attempts—from Plato to Montaigne and beyond—at specifying the nature of the human can
be classified as 'philosophical anthropology'.

[54] Giovanni Pico della Mirandola, *Oration on the Dignity of Man*, trans. A. Robert Caponigri
(Washington, DC: Regnery Publishing, 1999), 4.

[55] Ibid. 7.

[56] Jacob Burckhardt, *The Civilization of the Renaissance in Italy* (1860), trans. S. G. C. Middlemore (London: Penguin, 2004). For a critique of 19th- and 20th-c. idealizations of Pico see
Brian P. Copenhaver, 'Magic and the Dignity of Man: De-Kanting Pico's Oration', in *The Italian
Renaissance in the Twentieth Century: Acts of an International Conference. Florence, Villa I Tatti, June
9–11, 1999*, ed. Allen J. Grieco, Michael Rocke, and Fiorella Gioffredi Superbi (Florence: Olschki,
2002), 295–320.

[57] Pico della Mirandola, *Oration*, 6.

cites the superlative accolades from the *dignitas* tracts only to deflate them in a shattering anticlimax:[58]

> What a piece of work is a man! How noble in reason, how infinite in faculty, in form and moving how express and admirable, in action how like an angel, in apprehension how like a god—the beauty of the world, the paragon of animals! And yet to me what is this quintessence of dust?   (II. ii. 305–10)

Anthropology has been termed a discipline of crisis, a term prompted by the upsurge of anthropological theory in the troubled years of the First World War.[59] But 'discipline of crisis' is a term just as suited to the emergence of anthropology in the early modern period. For the Renaissance, human nature becomes the object of intense scrutiny precisely because it proves so difficult to define. This difficulty escalates dramatically at the very moment when the human becomes elevated to an infinitely more momentous role in the order of things than it had ever had during the solidly theocentric centuries before. No sooner does man become the centre of attention than this centre begins to show signs of erosion. Instead of substantial identity, there is a Protean non-entity, a chameleon.

The Renaissance did not 'invent' the human. But the period that gave rise to 'humanism' witnessed an unprecedented pluralization of the concept. The doctrines *humanae naturae* proliferate because scholars are searching for common values and discursive norms in situations where authority—religious, epistemic, cultural—finds itself under pressure. This is why attempts at defining humanity in absolute terms were frequently spurred

---

[58] Pico became known in England through John Colet. His biography, written by his nephew Gianfrancesco Pico della Mirandola, was translated by Sir Thomas More: Thomas More, *English Poems, Life of Pico, The Last Things*, ed. Anthony S. G. Edwards, Katherine G. Rogers, and Clarence H. Miller, *Complete Works of St. Thomas More*, i (New Haven and London: Yale University Press, 1997). On More and Pico, see Vittorio Gabrieli, 'Giovanni Pico and Thomas More', *Moreana*, 15–16 (1967), 43–57.

[59] The three major representatives of Philosophical Anthropology in the first half of the 20th c. are Max Scheler (1874–1928), Helmuth Plessner (1892–1985), Arnold Gehlen (1904–76). Gehlen famously defines man as a 'defective being' (*Mängelwesen*) because he lacks the animals' adjustment to his natural environment and needs to develop 'culture' to compensate for this lack. Arnold Gehlen, *Man: His Nature and Place in the World*, trans. Clare McMillan and Karl Pillemer (New York: Columbia University Press, 1988); id., *Man in the Age of Technology*, trans. Patricia Lipscomb (New York: Columbia University Press, 1980). For an introduction to this body of work see Joachim Fischer, 'Exploring the Core Identity of Philosophical Anthropology through the Works of Max Scheler, Helmuth Plessner and Arnold Gehlen', trans. Christina Harrison, in *Iris: European Journal of Philosophy and Public Debate* (Florence: Florence University Press, 2009), 153–70.

by encounters with its seeming other, the bestial and the savage—categories which early modern colonialists habitually ascribed to those who did not fit received European notions of the human. The 'cultural' and 'philosophical' perspectives of early modern anthropological discourse were thus not disjunct but closely connected. The picturing of otherness 'out there' and the picturing of human nature 'as such' inevitably conditioned each other. As Old World stereotypes were projected onto the peoples of the New World, so did the strangeness of those peoples, the 'cultural shock'[60] of their radical difference, put universalist notions of humanity under pressure.

Animality played a prominent and varied part in these negotiations of the human. There was no lack of classical precedent for this. Definitions of the human depending on a differential relation to animals are to be found in both ancestral figures of Renaissance anthropology: in Herodotus' account of the brutish tribes (andróphagoi) on the outer rim of the earth and, crucially, in Aristotle's placing of man's distinctive capacities atop a continuum of common human–animal faculties. 'Thinking with animals' is, of course, not limited to specific historical models. It is a pervasive habit which manifests itself 'in multiple and changing ways'[61] across all of human history. If the Renaissance has such frequent recourse to 'thinking with animals' when it comes to thinking about humans and the human, this just goes to show the perennial usefulness of this habit for stabilizing definitions of the human through exclusion and, alternatively, for typifying human traits through projected analogy. 'The brute creation', Keith Thomas avers for the period 1500–1800, 'provided the most readily-available point of reference for the continuous process of human self-definition.'[62]

But conceptual pragmatism will hardly suffice to account for the massive animal presence in early modern deliberations on the human. Ostensibly serving for convenience of distinction, the very multitude of animals

[60] John H. Elliot, *The Old World and the New, 1492–1650* (Cambridge: Cambridge University Press, 1970), 44. Richard Halpern even speaks of trauma, but that term seems more appropriate in describing the experience of the victims of colonization rather than that of their victimizers. Richard Halpern, ' "The picture of Nobody": White Cannibalism in *The Tempest*', in David Lee Miller, Sharon O'Dair, and Harold Weber (eds.), *The Production of English Renaissance Culture* (Ithaca, NY, London: Cornell University Press, 1994), 262–92 at 287.

[61] Lorraine Daston and Gregg Mitman, 'Introduction: The How and Why of Thinking with Animals', in Daston and Mitman (eds.), *Thinking with Animals: New Perspectives on Anthropomorphism* (New York: Columbia University Press, 2005), 1–14 at 9.

[62] Keith Thomas, *Man and the Natural World: Changing Attitudes in England 1500–1800* (London: Allan Lane, 1983), 40.

crowding the scene of human self-assertion becomes the index of a crisis of distinction,[63] of 'border trouble',[64] a form of encroachment. Instead of serving the ends of 'anthropocentric vanity',[65] the figure of the animal develops an uncontainable power of its own. Michel Foucault describes this power in *Madness and Civilization*:

> In the thought of the Middle Ages, the legions of animals, named once and for all by Adam, symbolically bear the values of humanity. But at the beginning of the Renaissance, the relations with animality are reversed; the beast is set free; it escapes the world of legend and moral illustration to acquire a fantastic nature of its own. And by an astonishing reversal, it is now the animal that will stalk man, capture him, and reveal him to his own truth.[66]

In terms of Foucauldian periodization this reversal clearly pre-dates the advent of an emphatic notion of 'man' which Foucault attributes to the later seventeenth- or eighteenth-century 'classical episteme', 'a linguistic, cultural, and sociopolitical construct of comparatively recent date'.[67] My contention here is that the two actually develop in conjunction, that the unleashing of animality is intricately bound up with the Renaissance ascendancy of 'man'. The 'beast is set free' precisely because of the new urgency of ascertaining the nature of the human.

I am thus proposing an alternative to two diametrically opposed views on early modern notions of human nature. The first of these, taking its cue from Foucault and the sceptical drift in Renaissance thought, credits Shakespeare and his contemporaries with a relentless anti-essentialism; under this description, 'human nature' becomes an untenable concept not only from the vantage point of our own time but according to early modern

---

[63] Manfred Pfister, 'Animal Images in *Coriolanus* and the Early Modern Crisis of Distinction between Man and Beast', *Shakespeare Jahrbuch*, 145 (2009), 141–57; see also his ' "Man's Distinctive Mark": Paradoxical Distinctions between Man and his Bestial Other in Early Modern Texts', in Elmar Lehmann and Bernd Lenz (eds.), *Telling Stories: Studies in Honour of Ulrich Broich on the Occasion of his 60th Birthday* (Amsterdam: Grüner, 1992), 17–33.

[64] Harriet Ritvo, 'Border Trouble: Shifting the Line between People and Other Animals', in Arien Mack (ed.), *Humans and Other Animals* (Columbus, Ohio: Ohio State University Press, 1995), 67–86; Erica Fudge, Ruth Gilbert, and Susan Wiseman (eds.), *At the Borders of the Human: Beasts, Bodies and Natural Philosophy in the Early Modern Period* (Houndmills, Basingstoke: Macmillan, 1999).

[65] Keith Thomas, *Man and the Natural World*, 166, sees anthropocentric vanity as typical of Renaissance humanism.

[66] Michel Foucault, *Madness and Civilization*, trans. Richard Howard (London: Tavistock, 1987), 21.

[67] Diana Fuss, 'Introduction: Human, All Too Human', in ead. (ed.), *Human, All Too Human* (New York and London: Routledge, 1996), 1–7 at 1.

evidence as well. The second asserts that far from denying human nature any substantial reality, the period maintained this notion with great conviction. Again, there is no lack of sources corroborating this view either, the plays of Shakespeare prominent among them.[68] But neither wholesale denial nor confident reassertion seems quite to capture the plays' engagement with the contentious notion of the human. If that notion were already known to be insubstantial and delusory, there would hardly be the need to probe it with such passionate intensity as we find in, say, *Macbeth*. Conversely, this intensity could not be accounted for if human nature were invested with a comfortable sense of stability. By reinserting the animal into the debate about the human, the limitations of both these positions can be overcome. What makes and unmakes 'man' in the drama of the period can best be discerned by looking closely at the edges of the semantic field encompassing the domain of the human. Shakespeare, I will argue, persistently scrutinizes these borderlands, and what his scrutiny inevitably confronts are animals: creatures both alien and all too familiar, creatures not yet categorically cordoned off from humanity through the Cartesian reduction of animals to the status of mere machines.

The present moment seems particularly propitious for this exploration. In recent years, a profound rethinking of human–animal relations has emerged in a wide range of academic disciplines as well as in the cultural and political arena. From biogenetics to ecology, from cognitive science to animal rights, the boundaries between humans and other species have become highly fluid over the last few decades. Even the humanities—'even', because their very name sets a species limit to their catchment area—have discovered our fellow species as a subject within what Alexander Pope famously declared to be 'the proper study of mankind'.[69] Silent and long ignored, animals have at last been conceded a history[70] and a place at the heart of current

---

[68] Robin Headlam Wells, *Shakespeare's Humanism* (Cambridge: Cambridge University Press, 2005); see also Kent Cartwright, *Theatre and Humanism: English Drama in the Sixteenth Century* (Cambridge: Cambridge University Press, 1999).

[69] See Alexander Pope's famous statement: 'the proper study of mankind is man'. Alexander Pope, 'An Essay on Man', in *The Poems of Alexander Pope*, ed. John Butt (London: Methuen, 1963), 501–47 at 516, l. 2.

[70] Published in 1983, Keith Thomas, *Man and the Natural World* is the first major work of historical research in the field. A recent landmark publication is Linda Kalof and Brigitte Resl (eds.), *A Cultural History of Animals*, 6 vols. (Oxford and New York: Berg, 2007); vol. 3 of the series is *A Cultural History of Animals in the Renaissance*, ed. Bruce Boehrer (Oxford and New York: Berg, 2007).

post-humanist discourses.[71] Recently instituted centres and networks for human–animal studies are charting a burgeoning of interdisciplinary explorations, reopening the previously stalemated negotiations between the arts and the sciences.[72]

Having become aware of the suppression and disavowal of animals in Western modernity, we are (or at least should be) more attuned than previous generations of critics to the vast range of human–animal associations in Shakespeare's plays. One discovery to be made here is that animals cannot be reduced either to a single meaning (*the* animal) or to a single function. Previous work on the subject has often tended to do just that, interpreting Shakespeare's animals as vehicles of social or moral—and frequently social *and* moral—discrimination. Animal epithets and comparisons have been mapped onto the hierarchical divisions of class, race, and gender. It almost goes without saying that, in this perspective, 'beast' and 'brute' will invariably be found to be derogatory descriptors of the subaltern, be it women, ethnic minorities, the poor, or the sexually deviant. It is true, of course, that bestialization, the ascription of animal properties to any group or individual considered unworthy of full human status, is one of the perennial strategies of social exclusion. Nor can it be denied that Shakespeare's animal markers often share this practice;[73] but their signifying potential is by no means deployed in this direction alone.

As I will show, Shakespeare's irreducibly plural forms and uses of animality do more than just spell out a moral alphabet in which the hierarchical distinction between man and beast is always already fixed.[74] Animals and animal nature provide Shakespeare not with one semantic possibility but with a whole keyboard of possibilities which he can sound singly or in

---

[71] Giorgio Agamben, *The Open: Man and Animal*, trans. Kevin Attell (Stanford: Stanford University Press, 2004); Donna J. Haraway, *The Companion Species Manifesto: Dogs, People, and Significant Otherness* (Chicago: University of Chicago Press, 2003); Cary Wolfe (ed.), *Zoontologies: The Question of the Animal* (Minneapolis: University of Minnesota Press, 2003); id., *What Is Posthumanism?* (Minneapolis: University of Minnesota Press, 2009).

[72] The mission statement of the New Zealand Centre for Human-Animal Studies (University of Canterbury), for example, names as one of the Centre's objectives: 'developing new paradigms in philosophy, the arts and the sciences for thinking about animals and their relationship to humans' (<http://www.nzchas.canterbury.ac.nz/about.shtml>; accessed 6 December 2010).

[73] For an illuminating study of this particular social dimension of animality in Shakespeare, see Bruce Boehrer, *Shakespeare among the Animals: Nature and Society in the Drama of Early Modern England* (Houndmills, Basingstoke: Palgrave, 2002); also Greta Olson, 'Richard III's Animalistic Animal Body', *Philological Quarterly*, 82 (2003), 301–24.

[74] In this conventional reading, animality 'remains significant only as an essentially negative force against which the human is asserted'. Susan McHugh, 'Literary Animal Agents', *PMLA* 124 (2009), 487–95 at 489.

various chords or discords. The intertwining of sameness and otherness that constitutes the human–animal relationship is anything but a fixed binary; rather it is a swarm of variable oppositions, grouping and regrouping in ever fluid 'fusions, translations, conjoinings'.[75] The dividing line between human and non-human creatures—like that between men and women—is a fundamental structuring principle in Western culture, indeed in all cultures. In the early modern period, a host of enunciations is dedicated to the maintenance of its stability.[76] But as Erica Fudge and others have shown, the very effort is proof of a deeply felt instability.[77] This paradoxical effect can be observed in many of the period's cultural, political, and religious arenas. In all of them we find a dynamic of pluralization paradoxically reinforced by the effort to resist it. Every attempt to stem the tide of noxiously multiplying doctrines, denominations, and world-views by claiming exclusive authority for only one of them, by the very act of doing so acknowledges the claim of all the others: the more insistent the push for the one and only, the more incontrovertible the force of the many.[78]

But over and above this general dynamics of early modern culture, there is a more specific instability built into the very concept of animal, the word 'animal' itself. In Latin, as in Greek zóon, it means 'living being' comprising human and non-human creatures alike. In Aristotle's *scala naturae*, scale of 'ensoulment', the decisive caesura is between *zóa* (humans and beasts) on the one hand and *zónta* (plants, endowed with only a vegetal soul) on the other. Christianity retains the Aristotelian scale but shifts the caesura. Humans alone are now credited with a proper, i.e. immortal, soul.[79] And

---

[75] See Salman Rushdie, *The Satanic Verses* (Dover, Del.: The Consortium, 1992), 8.

[76] Virginia Richter, 'Missing Links: Anthropological Anxiety in British Imperial Discovery Fiction 1870–1930' (postdoctoral thesis, Ludwig-Maximilians-Universität, Munich, 2005; publ. forthcoming), [75].

[77] Erica Fudge, *Perceiving Animals: Humans and Beasts in Early Modern English Culture* (Houndmills, Basingstoke: Macmillan, 2000); Fudge, Gilbert, and Wiseman (eds.), *At the Borders of the Human*.

[78] Unlike our own time, the early modern period shows an almost total lack of a positively valorized concept of 'pluralism'. The age of violent religious schisms regards pluralizing tendencies as a threat, not a promise: something to be tolerated at best, but never actively pursued. Sir Thomas More's much-cited plea for religious toleration in *Utopia*, on closer inspection, turns out to be merely provisional, the peaceful coexistence of several creeds just a passing phase on the road to inevitable Christianization. See Andreas Höfele and Stephan Laqué, 'Introduction', in Andreas Höfele, Stephan Laqué, Enno Ruge, and Gabriela Schmidt (eds.), *Representing Religious Pluralization in Early Modern Europe* (Berlin: Lit, 2007), ix–xviii.

[79] Something like a bridge between Aristotle and the Christian soul is his concept of *nous* (*intellectus*), the rational soul exclusive to man, which Aristotle says might possibly be immortal. *De Anima*, 431[b]. I am grateful to Oliver Primavesi for helping me clarify this point.

paradoxically, those creatures whose very name signals their possession of an *anima* end up in the category that denies them just that. In the amalgamation of classical and Christian doctrine 'animal' becomes a term that both includes and excludes the human. The word that monitors one of the culturally most fundamental demarcation lines is thus one in which that line perpetually collapses.

There is every reason to believe that Shakespeare's time retained a stronger sense of that precariousness than subsequent modernity. Western dualism by no means begins with Descartes, but it is he who laid the foundation for its modern radicalization. Human and animal, just as soul and body, mental and physical, come to be thought of as much more strictly separate, mutually exclusive categories than before. And although much twentieth-century philosophy, as Charles Taylor observes, 'has striven against this dualism', it is still the mode of thought we almost naturally adhere to.[80] Habitually entrapped by it, in looking at Shakespearean animals we must take a step back, seeking to attune ourselves to a mode of thought prior to the rigid Cartesian segregation of man and beast, resisting the temptation to recognize falsely what we see in terms of our own preconceptions.

Even the term 'animal' itself, it has recently been argued, may have to be counted among these misleading preconceptions. Despite the multitude of species crowding Shakespeare's plays, the word 'animal' appears a meagre eight times in the whole canon. According to Laurie Shannon, this shows our 'present idioms . . . that habitually invoke a dualistic logic of human versus/and animal'[81] to be woefully inadequate projections of a post-Cartesian binarism onto a pre-Cartesian episteme. '[B]efore the cogito', Shannon writes,

> there was no such thing as 'the animal'. There were creatures. There were brutes, and there were beasts. There were fish and fowl. There were living things. There were humans, who participated in animal nature . . . None of these classifications line up with the fundamentally modern sense of the animal or animals as humanity's persistent, solitary opposite.[82]

---

[80] 'The onus of argument, the effort, falls to those who want to overcome dualism.' Charles Taylor, *The Sources of the Self: Making of the Modern Identity* (Cambridge, Mass.: Harvard University Press, 1989), 189.

[81] Laurie Shannon, 'The Eight Animals in Shakespeare; or, Before the Human', *PMLA* 124 (2009), 472–9 at 474.

[82] Ibid. 474.

As should be clear from the previous paragraphs, I strongly endorse Shannon's case for the irreducible plurality of early modern orders of species. Yet despite this plurality, and definitely 'before the cogito', I would maintain, there is ample evidence of the kind of dualism which opposes humans to other creatures (including humans whose humanness one is denying). Such dualism, based on Scholastic-Aristotelian rather than Cartesian premisses, provided a well-understood idiom of discrimination. The literary animals of the Renaissance, much like those of earlier and later ages, were frequently (though, as I have argued above, by no means always) 'used to reinforce the denigration of subjugated people'.[83] The point to be made, then, is not that such an idiom was not available to Shakespeare, nor that he did not make use of it (because he did, and liberally so), but that the signifying potential of his animals far exceeds this dualism and the exceptionalist ideology that undergirds it.

'Many men, by reason of their ignorance in the Latine tongue, think that Animal is a beast, whereas it signifieth a living creature.' This caveat from a 1594 translation of La Primaudaye's *French Academy*[84] shows that our modern ignorance (Shannon) has Renaissance precedent. The 'error' would have needed no correction if it had not been entertained by 'many men'. Among those many, Conrad Gesner, the leading sixteenth-century zoologist, is a particularly prominent example. Certainly not ignorant of the Latin tongue, he entitled his magisterial tomes *Historia Animalium*.[85] In Edward Topsell's English translation of 1609, this becomes *The History of Foure-Footed Beasts*.[86] In transit from Continental Latin to English vernacular, *animalia* become beasts and are specified as 'four-footed',[87] which confirms both the pluralizing bent of early modern classification and the rarity of 'animal' in English. Yet rather than indicating the absence of a species dualism, the translation directs us to the term under which this dualism finds its most common early modern expression. Unlike 'animal', the word 'beast', listed with a total of 141 occurrences, is no rarity in the Shakespeare canon. In contrastive conjunction with 'man', it forms a no less normatively charged pair than 'the modern duo of human/animal'.[88]

---

[83] Dekoven, 'Guest Column: Why Animals Now?', 363.
[84] Quoted in Shannon, 'The Eight Animals', 477.
[85] Conrad Gesner, *Historia Animalium*, 4 vols. (Zürich: Froschauer, 1551–8).
[86] Edward Topsell, *The historie of foure-footed beastes . . .* (London: William Jaggard, 1607).
[87] Edward Topsell, *The historie of serpents . . .* (London: William Jaggard, 1608).
[88] Shannon, 'The Eight Animals', 477.

Pre-Cartesian man is animal, but never *just* animal. The force of Lear's epiphanic moment in Act III ('Is man no more than this?') lies precisely in the breakdown of normal and normative distinction. All creatures partake in the 'ensouledness' of nature, but only to the human soul does Christianity from Augustine to Luther grant immortality. This uniquely privileged being is always in danger of lapsing from human to beast.[89] The idea of such lapsing requires both a binary man–beast distinction and a man–beast continuum under a, broadly speaking, Aristotelian dispensation: without this continuum it makes no sense. Cartesian man simply cannot 'become animal' in the way that medieval and early modern writers envisaged it, namely as a form of moral lapsing[90]—but then Cartesianism has obviously never managed to eliminate the culturally pervasive idea of such lapsing.[91]

Inclusion and exclusion are thus inextricably entwined. And so are figurative and literal modes of envisioning human–animal connectedness. This is important for our understanding of the exchanges that took place between the theatres of human and animal performance. Current work on early modern emotions offers useful illumination here. The central insight of this work, as Gail Kern Paster points out, is the extent to which the psychological is embedded in and even identified with the physiology of the humoral body in a cosmological framework of correspondences and analogies:

In this analogical structure, ordinary microcosmic man's flesh is earth and his passions are the seas, because the body itself... is a vessel of liquids.... The passions are like liquid states and forces of the natural world. But the passions—thanks to their close functional relation to the four bodily humors of blood, choler, black bile, and phlegm—had a more than analogical relation to liquid states and forces of nature. In an important sense, the passions actually *were* liquid forces of nature, because, in this cosmology, the stuff of the outside

---

[89] The privilege is also, of course, a burden. Only humans are morally responsible for their actions and thus capable of evil or, under a Christian dispensation, of sin. The 'ethical continuum' between humans and animals, of which much has been written lately, ends where moral choice begins. Without the choice to do evil—a choice few would argue that animals possess—there can be no moral good. Thus when I tell my dog (as I often do) that she is a good dog, I am being blatantly (and unashamedly) anthropomorphic.

[90] Fudge, *Brutal Reasoning*, ch. 3: 'Becoming Animal', 59–83.

[91] The continuing power of this idea is borne out by the rhetoric of abuse which stigmatizes particularly heinous crimes as bestial. 'The association of criminals with animals is common to virtually all periods of history.' 'The animal and the curse of animality... have not disappeared from modern and postmodern discourses.' Mark S. Roberts, *The Mark of the Beast: Animality and Human Oppression* (West Lafayette, Ind.: Purdue University Press, 2008), 159, 177.

world and the stuff of the body were composed of the same elemental materials.[92]

Shakespeare's conception of the relationship between the human and the animal is framed by this great continuum of analogies and physical connectedness. Passions are *like* liquids, but at the same time they *are* liquids. The overlap of figurative and literal meaning that we find in the early modern discourse of the humoral body is equally characteristic of the conceptualization of human–animal relations. Humans are *like* (and in important ways unlike) animals; at the same time they *are* animals. Animal spirits (not animal-*like* spirits) course through the inner channels of man's body, determining his motions and emotions. If human psychology[93] is seen in terms of an economy of body liquids, then it is more than chemistry that people share with beasts: it is mental states, feelings, and affects as well.

One must bear this in mind when engaging with Shakespeare's animal imagery, the metaphors and similes in which human–animal likenesses are expressed. Obviously they are more than just a form of poetical embellishment.[94] Presumably no one today thinks of metaphor as mere decoration. Lakoff and Johnson opened their famous study of 1980 with the observation: 'Metaphor is for most people a device of the poetic imagination and the rhetorical flourish.' Since then, their own counter-proposition that metaphors fundamentally determine '[o]ur ordinary conceptual system', that it is metaphors we actually 'live by', has gained wide acceptance.[95] To

---

[92] Gail Kern Paster, *Humoring the Body: Emotions and the Shakespearean Stage* (Chicago and London: University of Chicago Press, 2004), 4. See also ead., *The Body Embarrassed: Drama and the Disciplines of Shame in Early Modern England* (Ithaca, NY: Cornell University Press, 1993); Susan James, *Passion and Action: The Emotions in Seventeenth-Century Philosophy* (Cambridge: Cambridge University Press, 1997); Gail Kern Paster, Katherine Rowe, and Mary Floyd-Wilson (eds.), *Reading the Early Modern Passions: Essays in the Cultural History of Emotions* (Philadelphia: University of Pennsylvania Press, 2004).

[93] According to the *OED*, the word 'psychology' does not appear until 1654 (in Nicholas Culpeper's *New Method of Physick*).

[94] That such imagery is structurally and semantically at the core of Shakespeare's dramatic art has been incontrovertible since the classical studies of the subject: Caroline F. E. Spurgeon, *Shakespeare's Imagery and what It Tells Us* (Cambridge: Cambridge University Press, 1935); Wolfgang Clemen, *The Development of Shakespeare's Imagery* (London: Methuen, 1951).

[95] George Lakoff and Mark Johnson, *Metaphors We Live By* (Chicago and London: University of Chicago Press, 1980), 3. In the wake of Lakoff and Johnson, Galenic physiology has been discussed in terms of conceptual metaphor in James J. Bono, 'Science, Discourse and Literature: The Role/Rule of Metaphor in Science', in Stuart Peterfreund (ed.), *Literature and Science: Theory and Practice* (Boston: Northeastern University Press, 1990), 59–89 at 78–80; James J. Bono, *The Word of God and the Languages of Man: Interpreting Nature in Early Modern Science and Medicine* (Madison, Wis.: University of Wisconsin Press, 1995); Zoltán Kövecses, *Metaphor and Culture: Universality and Variation* (Cambridge: Cambridge University Press, 2005), 104–105. For a critique

speak of the animals in Shakespeare's plays as '*merely* metaphorical' or '*merely* figurative' would thus grossly underrate what is now generally regarded as the conceptual and cultural power of metaphor.[96]

But the animals 'that will reveal Shakespeare's characters to their own truth'[97] not only exert but also exceed the conceptual power of metaphor. The likeness that enables analogizing presupposes the non-identity of the items analogized. The possibility of a *tertium comparationis* is predicated on the *primum* and the *secundum* of the comparison being distinct. Yet in the human–animal continuum of early modern anthropology this non-identity cannot be guaranteed, and the distinction is all too easily blurred. This is not to deny the metaphorical nature of Shakespearean metaphor. The literary culture of which he was part had, after all, a highly sophisticated understanding of the technical aspects and rhetorical energies of tropes.[98] What I am suggesting, rather, is that the operation of *metaphérein*, of carrying across, straddles a much narrower gap, a much less categorical human–animal divide, than we as modern readers might assume. Or, to use a theatrical image: if metaphor and likening hold the stage, it is the 'fusions and conjoinings' on the species continuum that keep stirring, like Hamlet's old mole, very audibly just below. The proliferation of cross-species likening in Shakespeare's plays thus evinces not so much an emergent awareness of the abysm between words and things that deconstruction has taught us to probe[99] as a fuzziness between material and representational modes of human–animal likeness.

of Lakoff/Johnson and some of the key tenets of cognitive semantics, see Verena Haser, *Metaphor, Metonymy, and Experientialist Philosophy: Challenging Cognitive Semantics* (Berlin and New York: Mouton de Gruyter, 2005).

[96] Coming from a different angle, the philosopher Hans Blumenberg's enquiries into some key metaphors of the medieval and early modern periods make another strong case against regarding imagery as a matter of linguistic surface structure. *The Legitimacy of the Modern Age* (1966), trans. Robert M. Wallace (Cambridge, Mass.: MIT Press, 1983); *The Genesis of the Copernican World* (1970), trans. Robert M. Wallace (Cambridge, Mass.: MIT Press, 1987); *Shipwreck with Spectator: Paradigm of a Metaphor for Existence* (1979), trans. Steven Rendall (Cambridge, Mass.: MIT Press, 1997); *Work on Myth* (1979), trans. Robert M. Wallace (Cambridge, Mass.: MIT Press, 1985). On the 'book of nature', see his *Die Lesbarkeit der Welt* [The Legibility of the World] (Frankfurt am Main: Suhrkamp, 1979).

[97] Cf. Foucault, *Madness and Civilization*, 21.

[98] See e.g. Puttenham, *The Arte of English Poesie*, ed. Willcock and Walker, 142–3, who distinguishes two sorts of effects produced by poetical ornament 'according to the double vertue and efficacie of figures': 'one to satisfie & delight th'eare onely by a goodly outward shew set vpon the matter with words': this 'qualitie the Greeks called Enargia, of this word argos, because it geveth a glorious lustre and light'. The other one, 'Energia of ergon', appeals to the mind 'by certaine intendments or sence of such wordes'—'and figure breedeth them both'.

[99] See e.g. Malcolm Evans, *Signifying Nothing: Truth's True Contents in Shakespeare's Texts* (Hemel Hempstead: Harvester Wheatsheaf, 1989). For a critique of attributing radical linguistic scepticism to Shakespeare see Russ McDonald, *Shakespeare and the Arts of Language* (Oxford: Oxford University Press, 2001), 180–1.

V. Animals Crossing

But what about real animals? Their physical presence on the Shakespearean stage is scanty at best. According to the film *Shakespeare in Love,* Lance's dog Crab was a real creature; and according to a minority vote on *The Winter's Tale,* so was the bear at the end of Act III. As dogs and bears performed the principal parts in the baiting ring, it seems plausible that they would have put in cameo appearances in the neighbouring venue. Though Lance's dog seems a far cry from the 'vaste, huge, stubborne, ougly, . . . terrible, and frightfull'[100] mastiffs which were used for baiting, a stage-trained Crab's canine poker face would have, no doubt, greatly enhanced the comic effect of the scene in which his master gets all tangled up in tearful perplexity and species confusion: 'My mother weeping, my father wailing, . . . our cat wringing her hands, . . . yet did not this cruel-hearted dog shed one tear' (*Two Gentlemen,* II. iii. 6–9). The pun on 'tide' ('Why, he that's tied here, Crab my dog', II. iii. 40) adds likelihood to a real dog's presence.[101]

The case of the bear that occasions Shakespeare's most famous stage direction is far less clear. Whether Antigonus exits pursued by a real bear or by a man in a bearskin (*Winter's Tale,* III. iii. 57) remains a matter for speculation. Sir Arthur Quiller-Couch, baffled by what he considered an egregiously clumsy bit of stage business ('But why introduce a bear?'), voiced the 'private opinion . . . that the Bear-Pit in Southwark . . . had a tame animal to let out, and the Globe management took the opportunity to make a popular hit'.[102] But real bears, Nevill Coghill objects, 'are neither so reliable, so funny, nor so alarming as a man disguised as a bear can be'.[103] The 'beares skyne' in Henslowe's inventory lends further support to the hypothesis of a human bear impersonator, but the case that seemed closed in favour of this view was recently reopened by Barbara Ravelhofer, who sees one of James I's famous white bears as a likely eater of Antigonus: '[A] stage bear which turns out to be genuine would lock into place' in a play which

---

[100] Iohannes Caius, *Of English Dogges,* transl. Abraham Fleming (London: Rychard Johnes, 1576; facs. repr., Amsterdam and New York: Da Capo Press, 1969), 25.

[101] In the parody of stage practice which Quince and company perform in *A Midsummer Night's Dream,* it is generally assumed that Starveling's 'man i'th'moon', despite declaring that 'this dog [is] my dog' (V.i.254), is accompanied by a dummy.

[102] William Shakespeare, *The Winter's Tale,* ed. Sir Arthur Quiller-Couch and John Dover Wilson (Cambridge: Cambridge University Press, 1959), p. xx.

[103] Nevill Coghill, 'Six Points of Stage-Craft in *The Winter's Tale'*, *Shakespeare Survey,* 11 (1958), 31–41 at 34.

'deliberately problematizes the real—old tales become true, a statue that becomes the woman it represents.'[104] Detailing some revoltingly cruel early modern methods of aversive conditioning, Ravelhofer argues that bears could be and were tortured into reliably performing complex routines. None of this, as Ravelhofer herself is ready to admit, amounts to anything like incontrovertible evidence,[105] but even though it seems impossible to decide whether the bear was real or not, the mysterious beast can still tell us something about the relation between real and imaginary animals in Shakespeare's theatre.

The dramaturgy of the bear's entrance is unusual. Shakespeare nearly always prepares for his climaxes by carefully building up our expectations. This is what he does with the oncoming storm: 'The skies look grimly' at line 3, ''Tis like to be loud weather' at line 10, and at line 48 'The storm begins'.[106] The bear, by contrast, is sprung on us by surprise. The Mariner, it is true, makes a general mention of 'creatures of prey' earlier (III. iii. 11–12). But the actual appearance of the beast is curiously underdetermined and abrupt. Antigonus' exclamations, 'A savage clamour!' and 'This is the chase' (ll. 55–6), hardly clarify the situation and have given rise to widely divergent stage directions in modern texts. Is the bear chased by an offstage hunting party, as the Oxford editor's 'Storm, with a sound of dogs barking and hunting horns' suggests?[107] Or is it the bear that clamours savagely and does the chasing, as the Cambridge editors assume?[108] What is most exceptional about the beast, however, is that it does not register at all in the spoken text. As a rule, Shakespeare's dramatic speech is deictically explicit about what we are supposed to see or imagine; the scarcity of explicit stage directions is more than compensated for by the abundance of implicit directions embedded in the characters' speeches.[109] It is the divergence from this rule

---

[104] Ravelhofer, ' "Beasts of Recreacion" ', 307.

[105] Ibid.; for a concise summary of the debate see Susan Snyder and Deborah T. Curren-Aquino, 'Introduction', in their edition of William Shakespeare, *The Winter's Tale* (Cambridge: Cambridge University Press, 2007), 30–3.

[106] Further references to the storm at ll. 53–5.

[107] William Shakespeare, *The Winter's Tale*, ed. Stephen Orgel (Oxford: Oxford University Press, 1996), III. iii. 55 SD.

[108] *The Winter's Tale*, ed. Snyder and Curren-Aquino, 158.

[109] The richness of the text's implicit stage directions enables what Harry Berger, Jr. calls imaginary audition. Harry Berger, Jr., *Imaginary Audition: Shakespeare on Stage and Page* (Berkeley and Los Angeles: University of California Press, 1989). Earlier studies of Shakespeare's texts as performance scores are Bernard Beckerman, *Shakespeare at the Globe 1599–1609* (New York: Macmillan, 1962); John Russell Brown, *Shakespeare's Plays in Performance* (London: Edward Arnold, 1966); Nevill Coghill, *Shakespeare's Professional Skills* (Cambridge: Cambridge University Press, 1964); J. L. Styan, *Shakespeare's Stagecraft* (Cambridge: Cambridge University Press, 1967).

which necessitates Folio's explanatory 'Exit pursued by a bear'. On the page, the animal would simply have no existence without it. On the stage, of course, its presence may be all the more eerily striking for being uncontained by words.

Whether 'real' or 'fake', the bear is a figure of uncertainty,[110] a gatecrasher rushing on and off under the radar, as it were, of discursive clarification. An intruder, speechless and unspoken, he momentarily flashes the raw energies of the neighbouring bear-pit, regardless of whether that is where he actually may have come from, by courtesy of Henslowe and partners. Both scary and crudely comical—and thus fully in keeping with the turning point in Shakespeare's perhaps most intricately tragicomic play[111]—the one moment where a creature from the baiting ring *may* actually have trodden the boards of Shakespeare's Globe offers something like a general emblem of the interaction between stage and stake. For once, the theatre mounts, or at least simulates, a direct invasion of baiting-ring violence.[112] This passes quickly, predator and prey disappear, and speech resumes. Onstage, the bear defies words, offstage he becomes the subject of voluble description, as the clown reports the double disaster, 'by sea and by land', in which the ship's crew and Antigonus are swallowed up 'roaring', a verb that conflates the storm, the bear, and the human victims in a gruesomely funny banqueting inferno:

> O, the most piteous cry of the poor souls! Sometimes to see 'em, and not to see 'em; now the ship boring the moon with her mainmast, and anon swallowed with yeast and froth, as you'd thrust a cork into a hogshead. And then for the land-service, to see how the bear tore out his shoulder-bone, how he cried to me for help, and said his name was Antigonus, a nobleman! But to make an end of the ship—to see how the sea flap-dragoned it! But first, how the poor souls roared, and the sea mocked them, and how the poor gentleman

[110] Daniella Jancsó, *Excitements of Reason: The Presentation of Thought in Shakespeare's Plays and Wittgenstein's Philosophy* (Heidelberg: Winter, 2007).

[111] The tragicomic ambivalence of the bear in the *Winter's Tale* accords with the similarly serio-comic role of bears in 16th-c. Italian pastoral comedy; see Louise G. Clubb, 'The Tragicomic Bear', *Comparative Literature Studies*, 9 (1972), 17–30.

[112] To find oneself, as Antigonus does, pursued by a bear was not altogether unknown at the neighbouring venue, where bears would sometimes break loose and attack spectators. Cf. Slender's boast in *Merry Wives*, I. ii. 234: 'I have seen Sackerson loose, twenty times, and have taken him by the chain.' Occasionally spectators came to serious harm when this happened. Bentley, *Jacobean and Caroline Stage*, vi. 211, quotes an entry from the accounts of St Saviour's, the parish in which the Hope was located: 'Sept. 7. Item, paide for a shrowde to put in the boy that was kilde in the Beargarden, 00-01-06' (1625–6).

roared, and the bear mocked him, both roaring louder than the sea or weather.

(III. iii. 87–99)

In no more than twenty lines of dialogue between Old Shepherd and Clown the verb 'see' occurs no fewer than seven times, its repetitive emphasis reinforced by the homophonic 'sea', the act and object of perception blurring in chaotic fusion.[113] 'I have seen two such sights' (III. iii. 81), the Clown begins his account, and he closes it with: 'I have not winked since I saw these sights. The men are not yet cold under water, nor the bear half dined on the gentleman. He's at it now' (ll. 101–3). The very surfeit of verbalized 'seeing' urges us to (almost) see for ourselves, while at the same time making it clear that this is precisely what we cannot do. As the Prologue of *Henry V* enjoins the audience, we must think, when the actors talk of horses (or the sea or a bear), that we see them.[114] But in the case of the bear we *have* actually just seen him. We too, like the Clown, 'have not winked' since we saw it in the flesh. A virtuoso feat of self-conscious illusionism that easily goes unnoticed in all the simple-minded clowning, the scene thus plays on our sense of an immediacy which is both granted and withheld. Hammering away, as it were, at the partition between onstage and offstage space, it renders this partition so paper-thin as to almost dissolve into transparency. But, of course, only almost, not quite.

In this deft exercise of show-and-hide, the bear of the *Winter's Tale* offers a perfect emblem of the absent-presence that governs the visual economy between theatre and bear-garden. The Clown's 'to see 'em, *and* not to see 'em' captures their 'synoptic' collusion. Just beyond the playgoers' sight, the beasts become an all the more powerful part of their vision. The Bear-Garden as the nearest and most familiar scene-behind-the-scene is the most potent resource of this vision. Its sights are all the more easily absorbed by the human stage because the baiting shows themselves were suffused with elements of human–animal blending.

This is how the German traveller Lupold von Wedel describes his afternoon at the Bear-Garden in August 1584:

On the 23rd we went across the bridge to the above mentioned town [Southwark]. There is a round building three stories high, in which are kept

---

[113] A succession of alliterative sibilants underscores the merging of sea and sky: 'I have *s*een two *s*uch *s*ights, by *s*ea and by land! But I am not to *s*ay it is a *s*ea, for it is now the *s*ky' (III. iii. 81–2).

[114] *Henry V*, Prologue, 26: 'Think, when we talk of horses, that you see them.'

about a hundred large English dogs, with separate wooden kennels for each of them. These dogs were made to fight singly with three bears, the second bear being larger than the first and the third larger than the second. After this a horse was brought in and chased by the dogs, and at last a bull, who defended himself bravely. The next was that a number of men and women came forward from a separate compartment, dancing, conversing and fighting with each other: also a man who threw some white bread among the crowd, that scrambled for it. Right over the middle of the place a rose was fixed, this rose being set on fire by a rocket: suddenly lots of apples and pears fell out of it down upon the people standing below. Whilst the people were scrambling for the apples, some rockets were made to fall down upon them out of the rose, which caused a great fright but amused the spectators. After this, rockets and other fireworks came flying out of all corners, and that was the end of the play.[115]

The recently rebuilt Bear-Garden, now 'three stories high', not only resembles a playhouse, it is one: the entertainment on offer is described as 'the play'.[116] The term hardly seems inappropriate considering the carefully modulated dramaturgy of the show, the size of the bears increasing, in fairy-tale triplicity, from medium to large to extra large, the horse chase inserted for light relief before the climax of the bull fight. The play-likeness of the show becomes even more pronounced with the seamless transition from bears, dogs, and a bull to 'a number of men and women'. 'Dancing, conversing and fighting', these human performers do what actors do: a dance, for example, concluded the performance of *Julius Caesar* witnessed by the Swiss Thomas Platter at the Globe in 1599. But in 'fighting with each other', they are also continuing with another version of what the beasts have done before them. The dogs being released from 'separate wooden kennels' and the humans entering from 'a separate compartment' creates an oddly levelling effect. Further species blending ensues when a man, in the manner of a zookeeper, throws food among the crowd, which responds accordingly and in doing so spills over into the animals' performance space. Confusedly scrambling, showered with more food, and frightened by fireworks, the

---

[115] The text, which is included in Chambers's account of bear-baiting (*Elizabethan Stage*, ii. 455) and frequently cited in subsequent discussions of the topic, was made available in English translation by Gottfried von Bülow, 'Journey through England and Scotland made by Lupold von Wedel in the Years 1584 and 1585', *Transactions of the Royal Historical Society*, NS 9 (1895), 223–70 at 230.

[116] Some caution is called for on this point. The German word used here is *Spil* (modern spelling: *Spiel*), a word with a broader semantic range than 'the play', including 'play(ing)' and 'game': 'damit das Spil ein Ende gehabt'. *Lupold von Wedels Beschreibung seiner Reisen und Kriegser-lebnisse 1561–1606*, ed. Max Bär, Baltische Studien, 45 (Stettin: Gesellschaft für Pommersche Geschichte und Alterthumskunde, 1895), 316.

people who have come to see the beasts are now seen as beasts themselves. 'As downe amongst the dogges and beares [they] go',[117] the species boundary is redrawn between those middle- and upper-class members of the audience who retain the status of spectators and the scrambling rabble, the common herd that becomes the object of their amusement. Visitors to the theatre, the Puritan polemicist John Rainolds alleges, risk turning into dogs.[118] Von Wedel's account demonstrates that such metamorphosis was a fully integral part of the entertainment at the bear-garden in 1584.

Between the easily confusable Globe and 'Beere bayting h[ouse]' (Hollar), a veritable 'intertrafficke of the minde'[119] produced a continuous flow of human–animal, animal–human 'translations'. The term is used to describe the one instance where Shakespeare's human–animal border traffic entails physical transformation, when Bottom the weaver is 'translated' into an ass (*Dream*, III. ii. 113), but it also captures the irreducible doubleness characteristic of that traffic in general. Bottom remains Bottom at the same time as he becomes another. He even becomes more truly Bottom because, re-embodied as an ass, he reveals what he has been all along: becoming animal shows his true character. This 'true character', however, has precious little to do with a real animal; it draws on a stereotype of anthropomorphic projection, a signifying tool, a literary device. Bottom literally changes into an ass, but 'translated' signals both the literary quality of that change and the bifurcation or doubling it entails. Producing a new text without erasing the old, translation creates a relation of two distinct, yet clearly connected, presumptively equivalent versions, as much alike—at least ideally—as they are different. Etymologically a 'carrying across', translation highlights a divide—linguistic, cultural, conceptual—in the very act of bridging that divide. The signifying processes between the human stage and its animal double carry across just such a divide, they are predicated on a representational split, on shades of likeness and difference, of thinking with and meaning by animals.

---

[117] Sir John Davies, 'In Publium', 148–9. Davies satirizes a connoisseur of bear-baiting who is definitely not lower class, but 'an aspiring lawyer from the Inns of Court . . . who regresses to a beast' (Ravelhofer, ' "Beasts of Recreacion" ', 289): 'As downe amongst the dogges and beares he goes, . . . His satten doublet and his velvet hose, / Are all with spittle from above be-spread.'

[118] John Rainolds, *Th'overthrow of stage plays* (Middelburg: Schilders, 1599).

[119] Samuel Daniel, 'To my deere friend M. Iohn Florio, concerning his translation of Montaigne', in *Montaigne's Essays*, trans. John Florio (London: Dent, 1965), i. 13.

VI. The Silence of the Bears

'That skull had a tongue in it, and could sing once', Hamlet broods in the graveyard at Elsinore (V. i. 75–6). The skull of the female bear shown on the next page (Fig. 5) is from the collections of Dulwich College, which was founded by Edward Alleyn, leading man in both the theatre and the bear-baiting business. It, too, had a tongue in it and, although incapable of singing or speaking, could once growl, roar, and howl in wrath or pain. We can foren-sically read the signs of abuse—the cavity from which an incisor was wrenched out, the teeth that were filed down, in order to prolong the 'entertainment'—but no effort at historical empathy will 'put...tongues into those wounds' (*Coriolanus*, II. iii. 7). The bear's suffering is voiceless. It is lost, blotted up, absorbed into the voices of the human actors who have brought and continue to bring Shakespeare's words to life four centuries after their parts were written—in accents then unknown, fraught with meanings then unthinkable.

According to Elaine Scarry, '[p]hysical pain does not simply resist lan-guage but actively destroys it, bringing about an immediate reversion to a state anterior to language, to the sounds and cries a human being makes before language is learned.'[120] In pain, humans lose the attribute that, since time immemorial, has been considered to mark their distinction from all other animals. A silent memento of pain, the bear skull thus signals not just distance but also a most fundamental closeness between man and beast. 'In what sense', Jacques Derrida gropingly asks in his 1997 Cérisy lecture,

> should I say that I am close or *next* to the animal and that I am (following) it
> ...? Being-with it in the sense of being-close-to-it? Being-alongside-it?
> Being-after-it? *Being-after-it* in the sense of the hunt, training, or taming, or
> *being-after-it* in the sense of a succession or inheritance? In all cases, if I am
> (following) *after* it, the animal therefore comes before me, earlier than me....
> The animal is there before me, there close to me, there in front of me—I who
> am (following) after it.[121]

Shakespeare's human stage is 'close to' and 'after' the animal stage of the baiting arena in much the same way as man, according to Derrida, is 'close to' and 'after' the animal, *after* 'in the sense of a succession or inheritance',

    [120] Elaine Scarry, *The Body in Pain: The Making and Unmaking of the World* (Oxford: Oxford University Press, 1985), 4.
    [121] Jacques Derrida, *The Animal that Therefore I Am*, trans. David Wills, ed. Marie-Louise Mallet (New York: Fordham University Press, 2008), 10–11 (italics original).

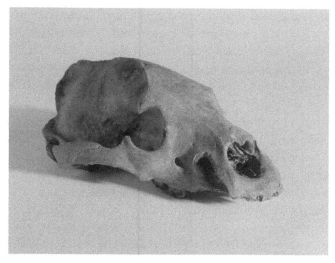

Figure 5. Skull of a female bear, Dulwich College. Photograph John Hammond

but also in the more violent and oppressive sense which is haunted by intimations of persecution and domination, of hunting and taming.

The infliction of pain is described by Scarry as a violent 'Unmaking of the World'. In the bear-garden such unmaking was regularly staged—'and all for . . . foolish pleasure'—as spectators flocked to see, in the words of Phillip Stubbes's *Anatomy of Abuses*, 'to see one poor beast . . . rent, teare, and kill an other'.[122]

The Puritan Stubbes was no less bitterly outraged by the spectacle next door which sublimated the speechlessness of pain into the eloquent world-making of theatre, the 'sweet violence' (Terry Eagleton) of tragic pleasure. '[T]he most crucial fact about pain', Scarry writes, 'is *its presentness*'.[123] When the screaming of the 'dumb beasts' is absorbed into the highly articulate emotion of poetic drama, presentness becomes re-presentation (although, as we will see in the next chapter, Shakespeare's theatre is capable of performatively overcoming this boundary). The representation of violence in Shakespeare's theatre drew on and was enhanced by the calculated savagery of the neighbouring bear-garden, just as the pleasure of watching that savagery was enhanced by a calculated infusion of theatrical human-likeness into the struggle of the beasts.

---

[122] Phillip Stubbes, *The Anatomy of Abuses* (London: William Wright, 1583), sigs. Qv^v–Qvi^r.
[123] Scarry, *Body in Pain*, 9 (italics original).

The exchanges I will explore in the chapters that follow are thus far from innocent. 'Messy entanglements of human and animal agents',[124] to quote Susan McHugh, is a phrase that describes the situation quite well. The violence of the bear-garden resonates through dramatic scores that abundantly resort to animal signifiers in the orchestration of human characters, actions, and predicaments. A case could quite easily be made for an insidious parallel between the physical exploitation of animals in the baiting ring and their symbolic exploitation in the playhouse. But such a view, inevitably centred on the pejoratives of 'anthropocentrism' and 'anthropomorphism', would unduly narrow the perspective and moral scope of Shakespeare's engagement with figures of animality. If we label his vast and varied bestiary 'anthropomorphic' (which in itself would be hardly a blemish),[125] it seems to me crucial to accord equal recognition to the extent to which his portrayals of *ánthropos* are 'theriomorphic'. Arguably, theriomorphism might be considered merely to give anthropomorphism another twist, similar to the double cross-dressing of boy-acts-girl-acting boy in *As You Like It* or *Twelfth Night*: human construed as animal construed as quasi-human. But then this double-crossing of species, like that of gender, has a way of unsettling the categories that are being crossed. If Viola/Cesario and Rosalind/Ganymede offer glimpses of liberating potentialities beyond the strictures of their social and ideological framing, then Shakespeare's zoomorphic[126] blendings open up larger spaces of inclusion beyond the narrowly circumscribed 'borders of the human'. And while the stage cannot remain untainted by its messy company, this very taintedness, this being-close-to the renting, tearing, and killing, also offers a unique platform for mobilizing resistance to it, for evoking sympathy for the suffering fellow creature.

★

[124] McHugh, 'Literary Animal Agents', 490.

[125] Anthropomorphism covers a wide range of attitudes and practices, beneficial as well as damaging. Anthropomorphic 'disneyfication' of animals evinces a parochial speciesism, but without some degree of anthropomorphic projection, empathy with other species would be impossible. Such empathy is regarded as a regrettable (though inescapable) relapse into sentimentality and pre-modern animism by John S. Kennedy, *The New Anthropomorphism* (Cambridge: Cambridge University Press, 1992). His chapter on 'Suffering' makes for interesting—if oddly outmoded—reading in its objection to 'the anthropomorphic bias' (p. 121) in the work of such pioneering animal-rights campaigners as Rollin and Singer.

[126] 'Zoomorphic' is more comprehensive than either 'therio-' (non-human animal) or anthropomorphic (human).

I said at the outset of this introduction that the notions of humanity embodied in Shakespeare's dramatis personae rely just as much on inclusion as on exclusion of the animal, or rather of a whole range of animals. There is a much greater variety of possible roles and zoomorphic blendings than merely those that register a downward mobility on a normative social and/or moral scale. This variety stems from the richness of the Shakespearean scripts, their formal and therefore semantic complexity, their performative power of scenic evocation—in a word, their aesthetic quality. Shakespeare criticism that does not respond to this quality seems to me to be missing the point. What the plays might have to say, both as literary texts and as scores for theatrical performance, is inextricably bound up with how they say it, how they generate the affective energies that have the power to exceed and destabilize any supposed doctrinal content. This richness of meaning and texture has determined the structure of this book. Rather than illustrating points of argument with isolated instances from a wide range of plays, I proceed on the assumption that the complex negotiations of human–animal divisions and blendings will emerge most clearly when traced in the continuum of a single play. Each of the chapters that follow will therefore offer a reading of one Shakespeare play (two in Ch. 4), along with some examination of other, non-Shakespearean textual sources, supplemented by some examples from the visual arts. My aim is not to offer a comprehensive survey but a sequence of exemplary case studies highlighting different, complementary aspects of human–animal border traffic as they emerge in the collusion between stage, stake, and scaffold. For an initial charting of the field, Chapter 1 will centre on *Macbeth*, a play that conducts its probing into what 'may become a man' across a precariously permeable line of species distinction and in doing so compellingly enlists the collaborative forces of the stake and the scaffold. Chapter 2 continues this enquiry with particular focus on stage and scaffold as uncomfortably similar platforms of privileged visibility. Causing an acute anxiety of exposure in King James I's *Basilikon Doron*, this similarity underlies the lethal histrionics of Richard Gloucester, Shakespeare's first full-fledged stage villain, a prototype for the more complex study of villainy in *Macbeth*. Chapter 3 adds hunting as a further frame of reference to the interplay between stage and stake which crucially informs Shakespeare's *Coriolanus*. Bear-baiting constitutes the key metaphor and scenic pattern of a play that pits the body politic against a heroic individual who is both the city's champion and prime antagonist, and who is presented as an animal signally unfit for the *polis*. The common theme linking these three chapters is transgressiveness figured as animality. My contention is that animality, far from being simply condemnatory, can serve as a mark of special, even charismatic distinction that destabilizes commonplace moral certainties and the human–animal binary on which they rely. In Chapter 4, this destabilizing is further explored in the forms of juridical violence which are set up against encroachments of the wild, the barbaric, and the bestial, but turn out to give sway to the very forces they purport to hold in check. Revenge and cannibalism, twin figurations of violent excess, are traced in Montaigne's disquisition on cruelty and his essay on the cannibals, in John Foxe's account of the death of Jan Huss, and in Shakespeare's revenge tragedies *Titus Andronicus* and *Hamlet*. Chapter 5 draws together the various strands pursued thus far in a reading of *King Lear*. Arguably Shakespeare's most searching investigation into the nature of the human, the play also offers his most varied and polysemous zoology. Where older interpretations have seen the play headed towards a telos of redemption in which humanity is purified in suffering and ultimately reclaimed from the abyss of the bestial, my concern will be to show the foundering of such a teleology on the various rocks of un-distinction the play sets up in its staging of order and chaos, the sovereign and the savage, man and beast. Chapter 6 discusses *The Tempest* as Shakespeare's final evocation of the link between stage, stake, and scaffold, the link that was to be broken after the Restoration. The book ends with the severance of the human–animal continuum caused by the ascent of Cartesian rationality and offers a glimpse of what followed, starting with the re-entry of the animal in Nietzsche's critique of anthropocentric humanism and concluding with the afterlife and eventual obsolescence of Renaissance blood sports, which our own time has replaced with industrial regimes of invisibilized violence.

I

'What beast was't then': Stretching the Boundaries in *Macbeth*

I

John Foxe's account of the life of Thomas Cromwell, Lord Chancellor to King Henry VIII, includes an episode which, 'though it be somewhat long, with the circumstances and all',[1] Foxe deems worth our attention. It is the story of how Cromwell helped Cranmer's secretary. In 1540, the twenty-first year of his reign, King Henry pushed the so-called Six Articles through Parliament, 'much agaynst the mind and contrary to the consent of the Archbishop of Canterbury Thomas Cranmer, who had disputed three daies agaynst the same in the Parliament house, with great reasons and authorities' (p. 1185).[2] Henry asked to see Cranmer's objections in writing, presumably without the slightest intention of being swayed by the Archbishop's opinion but because of 'the singular favour which he ever bare to Cranmer, and reverence to his learning'. Whereupon Cranmer 'collecting both his arguments, authorities of Scriptures, and Doctors together, caused his Secretary to write a fayre booke thereof for the king, after his order' (ibid.).

Complications ensue, and with them the story proper begins. Owing to a series of trivial mishaps involving a locked closet, a missing key, and a

---

[1] John Foxe, *Actes and Monuments of Matters Most Speciall and Memorable* (1583), facs. edn. on CD-Rom, ed. David G. Newcombe and Michael Pidd (Oxford: Oxford University Press, 2001), 1185. Page numbers given in the text refer to this edition. Further references are given in text.

[2] These articles, officially titled 'An Act for Abolishing Diversity of Opinions in Certain Articles of Religion', reasserted traditional Catholic doctrine within the English Church and were strongly, though unsuccessfully, opposed by Protestant reformers like Cromwell and Cranmer.

visiting father from the country, the secretary, having failed to deposit the book in a safe place, finds himself in a wherry on the Thames with his precious and, of course, highly incendiary parcel 'thrust . . . under his girdle'. With him in the boat, bound from Westminster Bridge to St Paul's Wharf, are four yeomen of the guard. As it happens, the King himself is in his barge on the river as well, 'with a great number of Barges and boates about him' (ibid.), watching a bear being baited in the water. The guardsmen, over-riding the secretary's wish to make directly for St Paul's Wharf, decide to stop and watch. Using their poleaxes, they manoeuvre the wherry so far into the throng, 'that being compassed with many other whirryes and boates, there was no refuge if the Beare should break loose and come upon them; as in very deede within one pater-noster' the bear does. The guardsmen rather unheroically abandon the boat—'Talle yemen but ill keepers', says the note in the margin—leaving the poor secretary trapped:

> The Beare and the doges so shaked the whirry wherein the Secretary was, that the boate being ful of water, soncke to the ground, and being also as it chanced an ebbing tide, he [the secretary] there sate in the end of the whirry up to the middle in water. To whom came the Beare and all the dogges. The Beare, seking as it were aide and succor of him, came back with his hinder parts upon him and so rushing upon him, the booke was losed from his girdle, and fell into the Thames out of his reach.   (Ibid.)

The King, highly displeased with his pastime turned to mayhem, calls it off: '[A]way away with the Beare, and let us go all hence' (ibid.), he cries.

The secretary's plight, however, is not relieved. '[P]erceiving his booke to fleete away in the Thames, [he] called to the Beareward to take [it] up.' But the bear warden, though a servant of the young princess Elizabeth, is an 'errant Papist'. No sooner does he lay hands on the manuscript than he delivers it to a priest of his own persuasion, who conveniently happens to be 'standing on the bancke'. Before the secretary manages to scramble onto dry land, the priest examines the book, 'made much a doe, and tolde the Beareward, that whosoever claymed the booke, should surely be hanged' (ibid.). When the secretary does claim the book, the bear warden, who 'seemed rather to be a Beare himselfe, than the Maister of the beast' (p. 1186), refuses to hand it over. Not for love nor money can he be dissuaded from wanting to see both the secretary and his master, the Archbishop, hanged.

In the end, after yet further complications, it is only Cromwell's personal intervention that saves the day. 'It is more meter', he tells the bear warden, 'for thee to medle with thy Beares than with such writing and were it not for thy maisters sake, I would set thee fast by the feet, to teach such malapert knaves to meddle with Counceliers matters.' The book restored and the bear warden put in his place, Cromwell and Cranmer exchange amicable jests about the danger now luckily past. 'And so after humble thanks geven to the Lord Cromwell, the said [secretary] departed with his booke, which, when he agayne had fayre written, was delivered to the kinges Maiesty' (ibid.).

<h1 style="text-align:center">II</h1>

Foxe's story pre-dates the Elizabethan theatre by several decades. But the ingredients it draws into the hurly-burly of its central incident look oddly like the parts of a Shakespearean drama assembly kit: a disrupted court entertainment and a king rising in anger; a faithful retainer pursued by a bear and a saucy one put in the stocks (well, almost); a viciously misappropriated object used to ruin its owner and a book (again almost) drowned. Brewed into a plot of potentially fatal consequence, all this is then rerouted into a romance-like denouement of recovery and restoration. So full of quasi-Shakespearean motifs is Foxe's tale that it seems almost impossible, echoing Duke Senior, *not* to find tongues in trees, books in the running brooks, and Shakespeare in everything. But even setting aside such figments of Shakespearean tunnel vision, the story is of interest for its traces of early modern performance.

First, and most obviously, the story provides a record of bear-baiting performed in one of its more unusual forms. This particular variety was thus not new when, eighty-odd years later, it was arranged for the benefit of a distinguished foreign visitor:

> The Spanish ambassador is much delighted in bare-baiting. He was the last weeke at Paris-garden where they shewed him all the pleasure they could both with bull, beare, and horse, besides Jackanapes, and then turned a white beare into the Thames where the dogs baited him swimming, which was the best sport of all.[3]

---

[3] John Chamberlain, in a letter to Sir Dudley Carlton, 12 July 1623, quoted in Bentley, *Jacobean and Caroline Stage*, vi. 211; for discussion, see Ravelhofer, ' "Beasts of Recreacion" ', 291. Whether we must envisage the animals as constantly swimming or able to touch bottom, as Foxe's tale suggests, is hard to say. Swimming would certainly not have been a problem for 'the white swimming Beares, (*Amphibians*)', as John Taylor styles them in *Bull, Beare, and Horse*, 54.

But bear-baiting is not the only public spectacle evoked. The secretary faces the prospect of hanging. Actual execution is averted here but not, of course, in the larger narrative, 'The history concernyng the lyfe, actes, and death of the famous and worthy Counsailour Lord Thomas Cromwell, Earle of Essex'. This history, in which the story of the secretary serves as an illustration of the wit and goodness of the future martyr, has its inexorable *telos* in the final scene on the scaffold. Likewise, Foxe's life of the secretary's master, Archbishop Cranmer, moves towards its inevitable conclusion in the graphic description and indeed graphic illustration of his public burning at the stake in the town ditch at Oxford (Fig. 6). The story, thus fraught with premonition of violent death, serves as a prelude to the horrendous grand final act in which Foxe's lives of Cromwell and Cranmer culminate, as do all his other tales of Protestant martyrdom. Dramatically intersecting with the disrupted spectacle of bear-baiting, the story of the secretary thus forms an episodic conjunction of the lives of two martyrs on their trajectory to spectacular death.

Figure 6. 'The burning of Thomas Cranmer', in John Foxe, *Actes and Monuments* (1563).

In Foxe's Christian world-view, the saint and the beast would seem to be conceivable only as polar opposites, but in drawing them together, the story also hints at the propensity—no less deeply embedded in Christian thinking—for such opposites to converge. Likening his ailing body to a map, his physicians to (map-reading) 'Cosmographers', John Donne *in extremis* envisages his end as a coinciding of contraries:

> As West and East
> In all flatt Maps (and I am one) are one,
> So death doth touch the Resurrection.[4]

The poetic conceit self-reflexively foregrounds its own working principle, a principle very much like that which bridges the extremes of martyr and beast in *Actes and Monuments*. The figure of reversal on which this coincidence of opposites hinges in Foxe's gruesomely veristic death scenes also provides Donne with the 'text', or 'sermon', of his last stanza:

> So, in his purple wrapp'd receive me Lord[5]
> By these his thorns give me his other Crowne;
> And as to other soules I preach'd thy word,
> Be this my Text, my Sermon to mine owne,
> Therefore that he may raise the Lord throws down.

If heretics, like baited bears, were tied to the stake, this would on the one hand signify their demotion below the level of the human. On the other hand, it would also suggest the Christian iconography of the sacrificial Lamb of God, turning the stake into a typological analogue of the cross. Thus Laurence Saunders, being led to the scene of his death on 8 February 1555, converts the apparatus of execution into a religious symbol through a performance of manifest theatricality extolling the conversion of death into life: 'He . . . tooke the stake to which he should be chained, in his arms, and kissed it, saying: "Welcome the crosse of Christ, welcome everlasting life." '[6]

The spectacle of execution and the spectacle of bull- and bear-baiting share the same basic type of performance space: an arena, and a scaffold,

---

[4] John Donne, 'Hymne to God my God, in my sicknesse', in *The Metaphysical Poets*, ed. Helen Gardner (Harmondsworth, Middlesex: Penguin, 1957), 89. 'On a flat map,' Helen Gardner explains, 'before it is pasted on to a globe, the extreme points will be the same.'

[5] '[H]is purple'—Christ's blood.

[6] Foxe, *Actes and Monuments*, 1492. I have discussed the highly theatrical quality of Foxe's 'acts' in more detail in Höfele, 'Stages of Martyrdom', 81–93.

stake, or platform surrounded by spectators. It is the same as that of the
Elizabethan public theatres on the northern outskirts of the city and on
Bankside, the former right next to the gallows at Shoreditch, the latter close
to the Bear-Garden and indeed close to the stretch of river where the bear is
baited in Foxe's story.

In joining martyrs with a bear and thus evoking the spectacle associated
with their respective suffering, Foxe's story traces out a tableau in which the
stage is set for Shakespeare—the wings of a triptych, as it were, in which the
centrepiece remains to be inserted. With the establishment of the public
playhouse, the dyadic interplay between the scapegoating rituals performed
on the bodies of saint and beast becomes a triadic arrangement. To speak
of theatre as the centrepiece in this arrangement is not, I would claim, just
another effect of Shakespearian tunnel vision. The human stage of the
playhouse does indeed mark a middle position between saint and beast.
Horizontally linked with the other contemporary forms of public spectacle
and vertically placed on a sliding scale between heaven and hell,
Shakespeare's stage thrives on an economy of endlessly fungible signifiers
which this symbolic order of space offers. And it is within this economy that
his stage negotiates the place of the human.

III

No story without incident, no incident without a border-crossing: at the
most elementary level, this is, according to Lotman, what defines narrative,
what distinguishes plot from description. The breaking loose of the bear in
Foxe's story is such an incident. It brings about the secretary's plight and
ultimately Cromwell's intervention, from which the story derives its title.
Lotman speaks of 'the shifting of a persona across the borders of a semantic
field'.[7] Although the label 'persona' is usually reserved for humans, it is
curiously apt for the bear in Foxe's story. Crossing the boundary that
separates the stage from the audience and thus guarantees the containment
of the spectacle, the bear invades the space of the spectators. Confusion
ensues, distinctions collapse. Those who had come as safely distanced

[7] Yuri Lotman, *The Structure of the Artistic Text* trans. Gail Lenhoff and Ronald Voon, Department
of Slavic Languages and Literatures (Ann Arbor: University of Michigan, 1977), 233.

spectators to watch an animal show find themselves involuntarily drawn into the show as co-actors thrashing about with the dogs and the bear in the river. But the worst part is obviously that of the secretary, transfixed in panic-stricken dignity as the wherry sinks to the shallow river bottom and the beasts close in. Bear-baiting, it has often been remarked, is an enactment of man's ascendancy. It is a demonstration of wild, brutish nature released but under control and thus, for all its brutal uncouthness, a fitting entertainment for a monarch. Not only Henry VIII and James I, but Elizabeth I too, are reported to have been particularly fond of bear-baiting. At the other end of the social scale, bear-baiting provided the one domain where those at the bottom, those who in their daily lives had to cringe under the whip and scorn of their betters, were given the opportunity to lash out at a creature below even themselves.[8]

The central moment in Foxe's narrative, the moment when human control over animal nature breaks down, is all the more striking because it elides not just the distinction between spectators and actors. When the bear joins the secretary in the swamped boat, the distinction between man and beast all but collapses too. The text registers this in a poignant image, that of '[t]he Beare seking as it were aide and succor of him'. Granting the bear intentionality, the text makes him momentarily indistinguishable in kind from the man in the same boat. Briefly, for the span of half a sentence, an odd, perhaps comical, but also oddly touching companionship in distress is established across the suspended species boundary, bear and man, suddenly fellow creatures. But only for a fleeting moment. Instantly the boundary is re-established through a vanishing act. The bear simply disappears. Unlike the secretary (a footnote in some editions of Foxe's work informs the reader that his name was Morris and that he was alive and well at the time of publication), the bear has neither name nor further story. How many more mastiff attacks he survived we do not know. Nor do we know whether the dogs did not eventually bite or scratch out his eyes so that his only further use to his human masters was to be whipped by their customers in the popular pastime of 'whipping the blind bear'.

---

[8] And, not to be forgotten, bear-baiting offered an ever-ready store of abusive metaphor for the assertion of male dominance over women. Hawkes, 'Harry Hunks', 151 n. 22, quotes Joseph Swetnam's tract *The Arraignment of Lewd, Idle, Froward and Unconstant Women* (London, 1645) for particularly graphic illustration.

Such considerations certainly go against the further drift of Foxe's story, in which the dangerous bear is instantly supplanted by the even more dangerous Papist bear warden, who 'seemed rather to be a bear himself, than the master of the beast'. We can of course swathe the moment of species confusion and category breakdown in layers of contextualization. We could, for instance, relate the humanizing of the bear to the age-old tradition of animal fable, where it is a matter of course that animals think, act, and even speak like humans. Or we could refer to the symbolic zoology of the bestiaries and the *Physiologus* with their perpetual recourse to anthropomorphism. But this would defuse the special strangeness of the moment in which the bear escapes enclosure, the moment in which the order of representation that keeps man and beast apart is overrun by the bear's sheer uncontainable presence. Foxe's story not only marks the precise slot which the theatre in due course filled in the early modern ensemble of semiotically interacting forms of spectacle. Its central incident also highlights a resistance to representational closure which the theatre inherits and shares.

IV

The early modern theatre is an exemplary site of the transition from a culture of presence to a culture of representation, or, as Hans Ulrich Gumbrecht puts it,[9] from a culture of presence to a culture of meaning. Like others before him, Gumbrecht takes the contrast between the medieval, or Catholic, and the early modern, or Protestant, theology of the Eucharist, the contrast between the doctrine of Real Presence and the doctrine of commemorative representation, as a central indicator of this transition.[10] Applying this distinction to the theatre, Gumbrecht writes:

---

[9] Hans Ulrich Gumbrecht, *Production of Presence: What Meaning Cannot Convey* (Stanford: Stanford University Press, 2004).

[10] Gumbrecht's historical watershed closely resembles what Heidegger conceived of as the beginning of 'the age of representation'. According to Heidegger, the Middle Ages did not see objects inherently related to their perception by man. The world was not placed before man, it was not 'pictured', and man did not have to relate to it. Everything in existence was seen as *ens creatum* and had meaning because it was part of creation and because as part of creation it was analogous to the creative cause (*analogia entis*). This axiom, that by virtue of being its creator God was present in everything, rendered the question of representation irrelevant. There was no place, and no need, for further enquiry into the nature of God's presence, let alone for enquiry into the structure of reference or signification. According to Heidegger, modernity (*Neuzeit*) introduced

As the substance of Christ's body and the substance of Christ's blood were being replaced by body and blood as meanings in Protestant theology, so the attention of the spectators at theatrical performances switched from the actors' own bodies to the characters that they embodied.

As dramatic characters reached new levels of complexity, increasingly 'the actors' bodies became removed . . . from the spectators' reach' and 'whatever is tangible, whatever belongs to the materiality of the signifier, becomes secondary, and indeed removed from the early modern signifying scene, as soon as the meaning in question is being deciphered'.[11]

All this is, of course, very sweeping, and in need of differentiation as one comes to look more closely at specific historical texts and their cultural settings. The removal of the actor's physical presence from the signifying scene of *Hamlet*, for example, is clearly more a matter of this character's prolific critical afterlife[12] than of its original scene of signification in Shakespeare's theatre. The transition from presence to representation becomes moment-to-moment 'overlapping or oscillation'[13] in Robert Weimann's pioneering explorations of the interplay between *platea* and *locus* on Shakespeare's open stage.[14] In the scene of Launce and his dog (*Two Gentlemen,* II. iii. 1–32), to give but one example, the doubleness of the player's role and the player's self 'is subjected to an exuberant probing into the limits of dramatic representation in an open space':

> Its openness is such that it suspends the boundaries between the actual site for playing and the imaginary landscape of re-presented departures, romantic vows, and courtly separation. The burlesque version of this doubleness cries out for laughter when finally the dog itself is up against the frontiers of representation—juggled as it is between a symbolic mode of representation and its own nonrepresentable and nonrepresenting physicality in the form, defying all histrionics, of the animal's sheer existence.[15]

the question of *repraesentatio* and created what antiquity and the Middle Ages could not: a world-picture, a sense of the world-as-picture. Martin Heidegger, 'Die Zeit des Weltbildes' in his *Holzwege* (4th edn., Frankfurt am Main: Klostermann, 1963), 69–104.

[11] Both quotations: Gumbrecht, *Production of Presence*, 30.

[12] For a sceptical commentary on this afterlife, see Margreta de Grazia, *Hamlet without Hamlet* (Cambridge: Cambridge University Press, 2007).

[13] Robert Weimann, *Author's Pen and Actor's Voice: Playing and Writing in Shakespeare's Theatre* (Cambridge: Cambridge University Press, 2000), 193.

[14] Robert Weimann, *Shakespeare and the Popular Tradition in the Theater: Studies in the Social Dimension of Dramatic Form and Function* (Baltimore, Md.: Johns Hopkins University Press, 1978).

[15] Weimann, *Author's Pen*, 193.

Positing a historical divide between residually medieval and emergent proto-modern modes of (re)presentation would hardly do justice to the complex interplay of these modes in the early modern English theatre. More important is the recognition of a simultaneity and productive tension between presence effects and meaning effects,[16] and the potential for (quoting Gumbrecht) 'provocative instability and unrest'[17] that this tension generates. Gumbrecht urges that we renew our engagement with the neglected or even repressed aspects of the tangible, the material: that which we experience with our senses before the mind's analytical reflexes kick in. Perennially strong in poetry—'even the most overpowering institutional dominance of the hermeneutic dimension could never fully repress the presence effects of rhyme and alliteration, of verse and stanza'[18]—the tension between presence effects and meaning effects is manifested with particular force in early modern drama. Straddling the divide between conceptual orality and writing, and thriving, as Robert Weimann has shown, on the bifold authority of performance and text, Shakespeare's theatre moves towards the modern regime of representation. But its impact derives from its capacity to disturb this very regime through moments which not only, in Weimann's words, 'exceed the bounds of representational closure'[19] but seem to lie outside it, belonging to a different order altogether.

V

One dog (probably), one bear (less probably)—live animals are extremely rare on Shakespeare's human stage. Their imaginative presence, however, can be overwhelming. The world of Lear, of Timon, or of the *Tempest* virtually teems with them. Can we put this teeming multitude down to 'representation'? Does the Prologue of *Henry V* apply here? Must we think, when we hear of bears, serpents, spaniels, or 'the wolf and owl' (*Lear,* F II. ii. 382), that we see them? The effect of Shakespeare's clusters of animal 'images', I would suggest, is very often not so much mimetic or visual as affective, even visceral. Perhaps it is misleading to speak of animal

---

[16] Gumbrecht, *Production of Presence*, 106–7.
[17] Ibid. 108.   [18] Ibid. 18.   [19] Weimann, *Author's Pen*, 199.

imagery at all. The term seems rather too closely associated with the overconfident assertion of meaning by an older school of criticism, as expressed in the title of Caroline Spurgeon's *Shakespeare's Imagery, and what It Tells Us*. The imaginary range of animals in Shakespeare's plays goes well beyond classifiable signification. Its impact may result precisely from a refusal to tell us what it 'means'. And this is hardly surprising. What is designated as 'animal', 'brute', or 'bestial' in Shakespeare's culture—and, of course, not just in *Shakespeare*'s culture—is a sphere beyond the reach of rational control and discursive order, no less strange and unfathomable than the so-called supernatural, but perhaps even more uncanny because it is closer to us. The *super*-natural lies *outside* nature, whereas man and beast are in it together. The condition of natural being that they share entails a troubling propensity towards convergence. This convergence, which also always undermines the representational order of things, may account for the special affinity of animal nature to presence effects in Shakespearean theatre. This is nowhere more evident than in the first scene of *Macbeth*:

Thunder and lightning. Enter three Witches

FIRST WITCH	When shall we three meet again?
	In thunder, lightning, or in rain?
SECOND WITCH	When the hurly-burly's done,
	When the battle's lost and won.
THIRD WITCH	That will be ere the set of sun.
FIRST WITCH	Where the place?
SECOND WITCH	Upon the heath.
THIRD WITCH	There to meet with Macbeth.
FIRST WITCH	I come, Grimalkin.
SECOND WITCH	Paddock calls.
THIRD WITCH	Anon.
ALL	Fair is foul, and foul is fair,
	Hover through the fog and filthy air.

Exeunt   (I. i. 1–11)

This unique opening addresses the usual questions the exposition of a play is expected to answer: When? Where? Who? But it does so in a way that baffles normal expectation. The here and now of a represented fictitious situation like, for example, that on the battlements of nocturnal Elsinore in the first scene of *Hamlet*, is and is not established at the beginning of *Macbeth*. 'Thunder and lightning', says the stage direction, but thunder, lightning, and rain are at once transported, quoting Lady Macbeth, 'beyond the ignorant present' (I. v. 55–6) so that we are disconcertingly made to feel 'the future in the instant' (I. v. 57). The distinction between present and future, between the place where we are and the place where we will be, is elided, landing us simultaneously in both. Time and place, instead of being reliably fastened down, acquire the hovering indeterminacy of the Weird Sisters themselves. While strongly drawing us into the play, the opening scene does not provide us with a clearly identifiable fictitious *locus*. As representation it remains diffuse. Its presence on the unlocalized *platea*, however, is all the more powerful.

This is largely due to the 'presence effects of rhyme and metre' (Gumbrecht), the incantatory trochaic rhythm. The words register as magically performative, their ritualistic function dominates over the discursive production of sense. The jarring logic of line 4, 'When the battle's lost and won', is driven home by the inexorable cadence of the verse. Some of this strangeness can, no doubt, be defused through rationalization. Battles, some commentators have pointed out, unless they end in a draw, *are* actually lost *and* won, if not by one and the same party.[20] (The line would thus signal not so much the suspension of binary logic as an attitude of indifference.) But, feasible though it may be, such rationalization flattens rather than captures the effect of the scene. The 'or' in line 2 ('In thunder, lightning, or in rain') is arguably even stranger than the 'and' in line 4. By simply exchanging the two words we would be semantically back in the normal world, but the point is precisely that we are not.

The presence effect of the scene is crucially linked with the undoing of distinctions, and the name of Macbeth turns up at the very core of this undoing. After the 'when' and the 'where', the 'who' follows as the necessary third step in a sequence whose end point is made all the more inevitable by the awkward fit of the rhyme, 'heath'/'Macbeth'. But the eerie flow of the witches' chant, once it has closed in on its target, immediately takes off again. The seamless transition to Grimalkin and Paddock in lines 8 and 9 enrols Macbeth in a trinity of bestial familiars. As comrade with the cat and toad, his 'single state of man' (I. iii. 139) is shaken before he even enters the stage.

---

[20] Unless, of course, that party happens to be King Pyrrhus of Epirus.

From the first scene on, the play continues to probe one of the founda-tional distinctions of Western culture, that between man and beast, human and non-human. As Stephen Booth said of *Macbeth*: 'Categories will not define. Words, notably the word man, . . . will not define.'[21] Definition entails separation, the demarcation of a border between A and non-A. But it is in the logic of borders that their very existence generates the impulse to cross them, to smuggle, to transgress. Such border-crossing is at the core of the play's insistent questioning of the human. It surfaces in those instances where terms are shifted across the species boundary, for example, in Lady Macbeth's remark about the messenger: 'The raven himself is hoarse / That croaks the fatal entrance of Duncan / Under my battlements' (I. v. 37–9). Or when the First Murderer's assertion, 'We are men, my liege', triggers Macbeth's casual slip into a taxonomy of dogs whose inflationary differen-tiation of canines elides the much more momentous difference between dog and man:

> Ay, in the catalogue ye go for men,
> As hounds and greyhounds, mongrels, spaniels, curs,
> Shoughs, water-rugs, and demi-wolves are clept
> All by the name of dogs. The valued file
> Distinguishes the swift, the slow, the subtle,
> The housekeeper, the hunter, every one
> According to their gift which bounteous nature
> Hath in him closed; whereby he does receive
> Particular addition from the bill
> That writes them all alike. And so of men.   (III. i. 93–102)

Most horrendously, this shifting of epithets across the species divide shows up in the murder of Lady Macduff and her son. After Macbeth's visionary 'pity, like a naked new-born babe' (I. vii. 21) and the numerous other references to babes in the play, the murderer's 'What, you egg!' (IV. ii. 84), instantly followed by the brutal killing of the boy, is all the more horrifying.

All these instances are orchestrated around the central figure of Macbeth. In him, the questioning of the boundary between human and in-human becomes obsessively intense. It culminates in the agitated dialogue before the killing of Duncan:

---

[21] Stephen Booth, *King Lear, Macbeth, Indefinition and Tragedy* (New Haven: Yale University Press, 1983), 97.

MACBETH   I dare do all that may become a man;
                 Who dares do more is none.
LADY MACBETH   What beast was't then
                 That made you break this enterprise to me?
                 When you durst do it, then you were a man;
                 And to be more than what you were, you would
                 Be so much more the man.   (I. vii. 46–51)

Amid the tense haggling over the proper relation between the terms 'man' and 'more', it is the word 'beast' that catches the ear. The single most strongly stressed syllable in the whole passage, it virtually bursts out from its semantic frame, a suppressed truth finally coming out into the open. The 'beast', these lines declare, is no intruder from outside, but always already lurking within.

'You can degenerate into the lower things, which are brutes', God tells Adam in Pico's *Oration*, but 'you can [also] regenerate, in accordance with your soul's decision, into the higher things, which are divine.'[22] It would be obvious and trivial to say that Macbeth opts for the first possibility; that by degenerating to a lower, brutish level, he forgoes the promise of his spiritual potential. Rather than simply spelling out such a schema of binarisms—upward/downward, divine/brute, good/bad—the radical questioning of Macbeth's 'state of man' parallels the rifts and fissures, the essential lack of essence, which Giorgio Agamben has found at the very core of Pico's text. This ' "manifesto of humanism" ' was celebrated by Jacob Burckhardt as 'one of the noblest of that great age', but its neo-Platonist conception of unlimited human perfectibility is also the record of a fundamental aporia and as such 'anything but edifying'.[23] Rather than giving substance to the notion of man, Agamben argues, it 'verifies the absence of a nature proper to Homo, holding him suspended between a celestial and a terrestrial nature, between animal and human—[a] being always less and more than himself. . . . The humanist discovery of man is that he lacks himself' (pp. 29–30). In placing *homo* not between animal and divine but between 'animal and human', Agamben obviously misreads Pico. But he does so in a way that clarifies rather than distorts.

---

[22] 'Poteris in inferiora quae sunt bruta degenerare; poteris in superiora quae sunt divina ex tui animi sententia regenerari.' Quoted in Agamben, *The Open: Man and Animal*, 29–30.

[23] Both quotations ibid. 29. Further references are given in text.

Figure 7. Carolus Bovillus, 'The anthropological ladder of degree' (1509).

In Pico's *Oration*, the category of the 'human' is not the middle part of a triadic symmetry, equidistant from two poles, but always already predicated on the exclusion of animal nature. As early as Pico man emerges as 'a field of dialectical tensions always already cut by internal caesurae that . . . separate . . . "anthropophorous" animality and the humanity which takes bodily form in it' (p. 12). This is also borne out by Carolus Bovillus' *De Sapiente* (1509), in the words of Ernst Cassirer, 'perhaps the most peculiar and in some respects most characteristic creation of Renaissance philosophy'.[24] Bovillus illustrates his anthropological system with a diagram (Fig. 7) At first glance, it looks reassuringly innocuous—a ladder of degree to please a Tillyard. But the solid-looking architectural symmetry actually enforces a logical paradox: A equals non-A. While the left side distinguishes the mineral, vegetable, and animal stages of existence from man, the right side includes them all within him. The left construes man as a separate

---

[24] Ernst Cassirer, *Individuum und Kosmos in der Philosophie der Renaissance* (1926; Darmstadt: Wissenschaftliche Buchgesellschaft, 1969), 93 (my translation).

entity while the right dissolves this entity, inadvertently revealing (quoting Agamben once more) 'the aporias of this body that is irreducibly drawn and divided between animality and humanity' (p. 12) 'What is man, if he is always the place—and, at the same time, the result—of ceaseless divisions and caesurae?' (p. 16)

VI

An exemplary site of such internal rifting, Macbeth signally fails to achieve what might be called a working wholeness. This is brought out most strikingly in the way his hands and eyes become uncoordinated, even opposed to one another.[25] In his anguished fantasizing he sees what he cannot grasp: 'Is this a dagger which I see before me, / The handle toward my hand?' (II. i. 33–4). But when he braces himself for the murder, it is as if he were trying to overcome this aporetic disjunction by replacing it with his own deliberate dissociation of hand and eye:

> Stars, hide your fires,
> Let not light see my black and deep desires;
> The eye wink at the hand—yet let that be
> Which the eye fears, when it is done, to see.   (I. iv. 50–3)[26]

Since antiquity the hand has ranked high among the distinctive criteria of the human. Anaxagoras held that it was the possession of hands which made humans the most intelligent of animals. Aristotle, conversely, claims that 'it is because they are most intelligent that human beings are given hands'.[27] The hand, it is safe to say, is distinctively human, 'the instrument of instruments',[28] as Aristotle calls it, but an instrument nonetheless in a body

---

[25] On hands and eyes/vision in *Macbeth*, see Kenneth Muir, 'Image and Symbol in *Macbeth*', *Shakespeare Survey*, 19 (1966), 45–54 at 52–3; D. J. Palmer, ' "A New Gorgon": Visual Effects in *Macbeth*', in John Russell Brown (ed.), *Focus on 'Macbeth'* (London: Routledge and Kegan Paul, 1982), 54–69; Huston Diehl, 'Horrid Image, Sorry Sight, Fatal Vision: The Visual Rhetoric of *Macbeth*', *Shakespeare Studies*, 16 (1983), 191–204; Lucy Gent, 'The Self-Cozening Eye', *Review of English Studies*, NS 34 (1983), 419–28; Kathryn L. Lynch, ' "What hands are here?": The Hand as Generative Symbol in *Macbeth*', *Review of English Studies*, 39 (1988), 29–38.

[26] The Oxford editor, Nicholas Brooke, glosses line 52 'let the eye not see what the hand is doing'. *Macbeth*, ed. Nicholas Brooke (Oxford: Oxford University Press, 1990), 110 n. to I. iv. 52.

[27] Aristotle, *On the Parts of Animals*, trans. James G. Lennox (Oxford: Clarendon Press, 2001), 98 (= 687[a]).

[28] Aristotle, *De Anima*, 423[a].

ruled and led by the mind. The eye, on the other hand, is closely associated with the intellective faculty, the prime organ not only of sense perception, but of *insight*. Even if truth, as Augustine avers, 'is not to be seen by bodily eyes but by the pure mind',[29] the eye, since antiquity, has been firmly linked to the idea of human cognition.[30] In seeking to cut the connection between eye and hand, Macbeth is attempting to rid himself of the fetters of human self-perception; he is trying to become an *un*conscious doer of deeds, which is how we first encounter him in the battle report of the 'bloody man' in scene ii, where the grammatical confusion about who unseams whom 'from the nave to th' chops' (I. ii. 22) bestializes both the celebrated butcher and his quarry.

The same severance of doing and seeing recurs in Lady Macbeth's soliloquy in the following scene—evidence of the couple's almost telepathic rapport at this stage. The dissociation is even more extreme when the hand, now 'keen knife', is driven by its own volition and hidden from the view of watchful Heaven:

> Come, thick night,
> And pall thee in the dunnest smoke of hell,
> That my keen knife see not the wound it makes,
> Nor heaven peep through the blanket of the dark
> To cry 'Hold, hold!'   (I. v. 49–53)

Friedrich Engels, founding his anthropology on the centrality of work, turned from the idealist tradition to the materialist Anaxagoras and the hand as the key evolutionary factor in the anthropogenesis of the ape ('Menschwerdung des Affen').[31] The work mentioned in *Macbeth* is of two

---

[29] Augustine, *De vera religione liber unus*, ed. William M. Green (Vienna: Hoelder-Pichler-Tempsky, 1961), nos. 8–10, 4–5.

[30] Cf. St Thomas Aquinas, *Summa Theologiae*, lviii: *The Eucharistic Presence (3a. 73–8)*, trans. and ed. William Barden (London: Blackfriars, 1965), 117: 'There are two kinds of eyes, the eye of the body, properly so called, and the eye of the intelligence, called so by analogy.'

[31] Friedrich Engels, 'Der Antheil der Arbeit an der Menschwerdung des Affen' (= 'The Part Played by Work in the Transition from Ape to Man'), in Karl Marx and Friedrich Engels, *Werke*, xx (Berlin: Dietz, 1962), 444–55 at 444. The hand is also given crucial anthropological importance by Heidegger. The implications of his dictum that 'thinking is a handicraft' and that 'Apes, for example, have organs that can grasp, but they have no hand' are discussed by Jacques Derrida, 'Geschlecht II: Heidegger's Hand', trans. John P. Leavey, Jr., in *Deconstruction and Philosophy: The Texts of Jacques Derrida*, ed. John Sallis (Chicago: University of Chicago Press, 1986), 161–96; Stanley Cavell, *Conditions Handsome and Unhandsome: The Constitution of Emersonian Perfectionism* (Chicago: University of Chicago Press, 1990), 38–9; and Cary Wolfe, 'In the Shadow of Wittgenstein's Lion', in id. (ed.), *Zoontologies*, 1–57 at 20–1.

kinds. It is 'this most bloody piece of work' of which Banquo speaks after the murder of Duncan (II. iii. 127) and the 'work' Macbeth commissions the murderers to perform on Banquo and Fleance (III. i. 135). This is the work where the eye winks at the hand. But there is also the work directed against Macbeth, the campaign expressly ratified by 'Him above' (III. vi. 32), that 'may again / Give to our tables meat, sleep to our nights, / Free from our feasts and banquets bloody knives' (III. vi. 33–5). And even more sharply contrasted with Macbeth's handiwork is the 'most miraculous work in this good King' (IV. iii. 148), the work of 'touching' performed by Edward the Confessor with his healing hands: 'but at his touch, / Such sanctity hath Heaven given his hand, / They presently amend' (IV. iii. 144–6).[32]

VII

By this time in the play (IV. iii), Macbeth's inner dissociation has come to the surface and hardened into an image of total bestialization. While his struggle with himself had revealed the 'mobile border within living man' over which, according to Agamben, 'the very decision of what is human and what is not'[33] is—always inconclusively, always provisionally—fought out, he is now perceived as unambiguously inhuman. What was dual has become single. The play has given us no cause to assume that Macbeth is particularly 'luxurious' or 'avaricious' but in Malcolm's verdict in IV. iii these and all the other 'multiplying villainies of nature ... swarm upon him' (I. ii. 11–12)—all the vices, in fact, which Christianity and humanism classify as bestial:[34]

> I grant him bloody,
> Luxurious, avaricious, false, deceitful,
> Sudden, malicious, smacking of every sin
> That has a name.   (IV. iii. 58–61)

---

[32] See Rebecca Lemon, *Treason by Words: Literature, Law, and Rebellion in Shakespeare's England* (Ithaca, NY, and London: Cornell University Press, 2006), 102; Susanne L. Wofford, 'The Body Unseamed: Shakespeare's Late Tragedies', in ead. (ed.), *Shakespeare's Late Tragedies* (Upper Saddle River, NJ: Prentice Hall, 1996), 3.

[33] Agamben, *The Open*, 15.

[34] An interesting alternative to the humanist position can be detected in Malcolm's rather ambiguous testing of Macduff. It has been argued (Barbara Riebling, 'Virtue's Sacrifice: A Machiavellian Reading of *Macbeth*', *Studies in English Literature 1500–1900*, 31 (1991), 273–86) that Malcolm proves himself a dexterous disciple of the anti-idealist humanism of Machiavelli and his essentially positive view of man's animal capacities.

This radically simplified view of Macbeth is held by his victorious enemies at the end of the play. Macduff's 'Turn, hell-hound, turn' (V. x. 3) sounds an ironic echo to the dog catalogue of Act III which includes, among other breeds, the category of the 'house-keeper'. As 'hell-hound' Macbeth would now register as a 'house-keeper' dog, too, though of a rather dismal kind of abode.

Hell was one of the 'houses' (*mansiones*) of the late medieval mystery cycles. If the opening scene of *Macbeth* casts the Weird Sisters' spell of dislocation over the play, this indeterminate openness of space becomes gradually a more and more claustrophobic enclosure whose name and nature is firmly established in II. iii:

> *Enter a Porter. Knocking within*
>
> PORTER Here's a knocking indeed! If a man were porter of hell-gate he should have old turning the key.   (II. iii. 1–2)

'Based on the miracle plays of the fourteenth century', the Porter's solo performance would have recalled not only the devils in those plays 'happily ushering in the damned',[35] but also the typical setting of hell-mouth imaged as the gaping jaws of a giant beast. Such an image adorned the walls of Holy Trinity Church in Stratford before disappearing under a coat of Reformation whitewash around 1560, but the oral-bestial iconology of hell remained operative for centuries after.[36] Encoded as hell, Macbeth's castle—a castle of grim, unredeemed perseverance—is thus fraught with bestiality and located next door to the infernal bear-pit, where the dramatist Thomas Dekker saw the animals as performing a spectacle of the damned:

> No sooner was I entred [the Bear-Garden] but the very noyse of the place put me in mind of *Hel*: the beare (dragd to the stake) shewed like a black rugged soule, that was Damned and newly committed to the infernall *Charle*, the *Dogges* like so many *Diuels*, inflicting torments vpon it. But when I called to mind, that al their tugging together was but to make sport to the beholders, I held a better and not so damnable an opinion of their beastly doings: for the *Beares*, or the *Buls* fighting with the dogs, was a liuely represe[n]tation (me thought) of poore men going to law with the rich and mightie.

---

[35] Brooke, 'Introduction', in his Oxford edition of *Macbeth*, 1–90 at 79.
[36] See Clifford Davidson and Thomas H. Seiler (eds.), *The Iconography of Hell* (Kalamazoo: Medieval Institute Publications, 1992).

At length a blinde *Beare* was tyed to the stake, and in stead of baiting him with dogges, a company of creatures that had the shapes of men, & faces of christians (being either Colliers, Carters, or watermen) tooke the office of Beadles vpon them, and whipt monsieur *Hunkes*, till the blood ran downe his old shoulders: It was some sport to see Innocence triumph ouer Tyranny, by beholding those vnnecessary tormentors go away w[ith] scratchd hands, or torne legs from a poore Beast, arm'd onely by nature to defend himself against *Violence*: yet me thought this whipping of the blinde *Beare*, moued as much pittie in my breast towards him, as y[e] leading of poore starued wretches to the whipping posts in *London* (when they had more neede to be releeued with foode) ought to moue the hearts of Cittizens, though it be the fashion now to laugh at the punishment.[37]

Dekker's response registers a gradual progress from presence to representation. He is overwhelmed by the sheer impact of the assault on his senses. It 'puts him in mind of Hell'; in other words, it is the spectacle which imposes the presence of hell on him without him being actively engaged in construing this vision. Rational activity, and with it, affective detachment from the terror sets in once Dekker 'calls to mind' what the scene might signify. The progression is similar to that in *Macbeth* where the disconcerting irrational presence of the opening is subsequently absorbed into the representational frame of the dramatic plot, even though in Macbeth's case rational activity does not lead to detachment but creates its own hell, 'the torture of the mind' that keeps him awake 'in restless ecstasy' (III. ii. 23–4). 'Hell is murky' (V. i. 34), says the sleepwalking Lady Macbeth. But it is not so much the blurring of vision as an unrelieved clarity of sight—both awake and in sleeping, both on her part and his—which makes Macbeth's premonition that '[w]e still have judgement here' (I. vii. 8) come true in a veritable hell on earth. The 'dunnest smoke of hell' (I. v. 50) invoked by Lady Macbeth as a screen between hand and eye, doing and knowing, fails to fulfil that function.

Banquo's 'temple-haunting martlet' (I. vi. 4), enveloping the infernal place with an air of sacred hospitality, endorses Duncan's equally deceived 'This castle hath a pleasant seat' (I. vi. 1). A late echo of their collaborative misreading may be heard in the now reckless Macbeth's

> This push
> Will cheer me ever or disseat me now.   (V. iii. 22–3)

---

[37] Dekker, 'Warres', in *Non-Dramatic Works*, 97–9 (italics original).

'Disseat' links his fortune indissolubly to the remaining innermost circle of his shrunken dominion, his anything but pleasant 'seat'. At the same time it sounds the homophone 'deceit', keynote of the action and its logic of reversal. Dis-seating a king by practising satanic deceit ('look like the innocent flower, / But be the serpent under't'; I. v. 64–5), he finds himself deceived as well as dis-seated. In the end, he envisages for himself the same fate that Dekker reports from the neighbouring circle of hell: 'to be baited with the rabble's curse' (V. x. 29).

VIII

If the representational structure of a play such as *Macbeth* is always liable to break up into moments of intense presence and if, under the non-mimetic conditions of a baiting show, blind Monsieur Hunks can become a figure of Aristotelian terror and pity, such slippage between *representational* and *presentational* modes of early modern spectacle reinforces the slippage of species boundaries. Just as blind Monsieur Hunks, blood running down 'his old shoulders', assumes the tragic pathos of a Gloucester, Shakespeare's Gloucester becomes the baited bear. 'I am tied to th'stake', he exclaims, as Goneril, Regan, and Cornwall close in on him, 'and I must stand the course' (*Lear,* III. vii. 52). The words of Gloucester the victim are almost the same as those of the cornered tyrant, Macbeth ('They have tied me to a stake. I cannot fly, / But bear-like I must fight the course'; V. vii. 1–2), and both are echoed by John Taylor in a poem recounting his harassment by an angry crowd at the recently opened, dual-purpose Hope Theatre on 7 October 1614:

> I, like a *Beare* vnto the stake was tide,
> And what they said, or did, I must abide.[38]

Taylor, known as the Water Poet, was one of the more colourful London figures of the period. He had challenged a rival, William Fennor, who styled himself the King's Rhyming Poet, to a public contest of histrionic extem-

---

[38] John Taylor, 'Taylor's Revenge', in *All the Workes of John Taylor the Water Poet* (London: James Boler, 1630), 145. In another poem Taylor casts his antagonist Fennor as a bear to be baited in a 'man-Beare baiting': 'I in thy nose will put an iron ring . . .'. 'A Cast over the VVater by John Taylor', *All the Workes,* 159.

porizing—something like a poetry slam. To publicize the event, he had had a thousand playbills printed. At the appointed hour, the house was crowded, but Fennor failed to show up, which left Taylor stuck with an irate audience demanding their money back and 'in a greater puzzell then the blinde Beare in the midst of all her whip-broth'.[39]

Dekker entering the baiting arena finds himself watching a play. Taylor stepping onto a stage finds himself tied to a stake. Like the baiting of Gloucester and Macbeth, the experiences of Dekker and Taylor are framed by, and thus perceived as, that which they are not, but closely resemble. On entering the Bear-Garden, 'the very noyse of the place' puts Dekker 'in mind of *Hel*'. Similarly, the noise of the tempestuous crowd at the Hope reminds Taylor of '*Purgatorie*'. Dekker's emblematic reading of the torture he is witnessing deftly shifts from hell proper to that hell on earth run by the contemporary penal system,[40] from the 'black rugged soul, that was Damned' to the 'leading of poore starued wretches to the whipping posts in *London*'. In 'Taylor's Revenge', too, the public shaming and punishing rituals of the age—whipping and hanging, the halter and the gallows—are constantly, even obsessively, present, both in the recollection of his tribulation at the Hope and even more so in the imaginary penalty he devises for his adversary. Nothing less than hanging will do for Fennor:

> Then when thou bidst the world thy last good-night
> Squint vpward, and cry, *Gallowes*, claime thy right.
> To whose protection, thy estate I tender,
> And all thy Rights and Titles I surrender,
> Thy Carkas and thy Manners (that are euill)
> To Tyburne, Hangman, and (thy sire) the Deuill.   (pp. 146–7)

Stage, stake, and scaffold, then, are in collusion. Together they define the performance space for spectacular entertainment in early modern England, and together they effect the blurring of species distinctions which this space induces. Dekker's wording is revealing: 'in stead of' dogs, he writes, 'a company of creatures that had the shapes of men, & faces of christians' take 'the office of Beadles vpon them'. In a double replacement similar to the double cross-dressing in Shakespearean comedy where boy (actor) plays girl playing boy, humans act in place of dogs acting in place of humans. By

---

[39] Taylor, 'Taylor's Revenge', 143.   [40] Cf. Foucault, *Discipline and Punish*, 46.

taking the office of 'beadles' upon themselves, the men with the whips not only perform an imitation of juridical practice, but an imitation of the dogs' imitation of that practice at the same time. The result, as noted, is a slippage of species identity which Dekker conveys as his inability to match visual perception with cognitive categorization. Although they have 'the shapes of men, & faces of christians', the nature of the bear's tormentors remains indeterminate: they are 'a company of creatures'. Unlike Hamlet, who knows not 'seems', Dekker can only record 'seeming'. His ability to categorize the 'creatures' goes as far as their professional identity—'(being either Colliers, Carters, or watermen)'—but no further. Their allocation to the category 'human' is conspicuously withheld. The slippage of species distinction is driven to the point of inversion when that which is denied the anonymous tormentors is granted their victim: the personal identity bestowed by a human name, 'monsieur Hunkes'. Consequently, for Dekker, the 'sport' is not to see the bear whipped but 'to see Innocence triumph ouer Tyranny, by beholding those vnnecessary tormentors go away w[ith] scratchd hands, or torne legs from a poore Beast, arm'd onely by nature to defend himself against Violence'.

The 'double vision' that enables Dekker's shifting from baiting to criminal justice and back again with such ease indicates a degree of reciprocity that is premised just as much on the bestialization of the criminal as on the humanization of the baited bear. If the whipping of Monsieur Hunks reminds Dekker of the wretches being led to the whipping posts, the plight of those human wretches can hardly fail to invoke the 'sport' of animal baiting. What clinches the bond between the two kinds of spectacle is the identical audience response they evoke: 'the fashion now to laugh at the punishment'. The hierarchies of class and species coalesce as the members of a 'lower order'—'poore starued wretches' and 'a poore Beast'—become the laughing stock of 'Cittizens'.

'They have tied me to a stake. I cannot fly, / But bear-like I must fight the course' (V. vii. 1–2). Only two steps away from decapitation, Macbeth assumes the role of the bear in a gesture of both self-assertion and self-extinction. All the complications of his earlier moral dilemmas gone, he will ruthlessly fight the course. Conscience, the human capacity to distinguish right from wrong, good from evil, with all its attendant doubts, incertitudes, and hesitations, plays no part any more. By openly declaring his animality, Macbeth also dehumanizes and belittles his attackers. If he is the bear, they have become curs. As Macbeth's scornful address to the murderers made clear earlier on, the step from man to dog is a short one anyway.

The allusions to baiting in Act V are not isolated references, then, but conclude an exploration of 'what may become a man', a probing into the highly questionable nature of humanity. As the bear-tyrant is cornered, the stage of the Globe openly converges with the Bear-Garden. And when, only moments later, Macduff re-enters displaying, as stage tradition has it, the head of the slain Macbeth on a pole, the executioner's scaffold is brought out openly as the third perceptual frame of action. This final image of draconian justice could not possibly have been lost on an audience which, returning to the city after the show, would have to pass a similar display of skewered heads adorning the southern gate of London Bridge.

IX

In exemplary fashion, the last act of Macbeth turns the stage of the public playhouse into the centrepiece of the triptych whose wings are formed by the baiting arena and the gallows. Such a triple vision generates a powerful intermediality, whose most palpable effect is mutual reinforcement. When the playwrights drown the stage in blood, when Shakespeare in *Titus Andronicus* or Webster in *The Duchess of Malfi* contrive sophisticated technologies of physical and psychological torment, such excesses of violence incorporate and are sustained by the competitive co-presence of the other spectacular blood rituals of the period. But catering to the bloodthirsty tastes of an audience accustomed to the spectacular staging of real maiming and killing is only one side of the theatre's engagement with cruelty. The other, as I proposed in the introduction, is its capacity for mobilizing resistance to the very cruelty it exhibits. While the course of action in *Macbeth* follows the relentless snowball logic of violence, the play's focus is, as one critic puts it, on the concomitant 'dissolution of the aggressive organism from inside'.[41]

The baiting references in the last act of *Macbeth* are fully in keeping with how the 'hell-hound' (V. x. 3), the 'rarer monster' (V. x. 25), the 'butcher and his fiend-like queen' (V. xi. 35) are seen by their righteous enemies. But

---

[41] Jürgen Wertheimer, 'Im Blutstrom blättern: Das elisabethanische Theater der Grausamkeit', in Peter Gendolla and Carsten Celle (eds.), *Schönheit und Schrecken: Entsetzen, Gewalt und Tod in alten und neuen Medien* (Heidelberg: Winter, 1990), 39–53 at 52 (my translation).

when the beast is bagged and Macduff presents Macbeth's severed head like a hunting trophy, this final image of defeat and annihilation can hardly capture the lingering unease evoked by the play's two central characters. On the one hand, lopping off Macbeth's head is a drastic reaffirmation of the species boundary, a triumphant gesture of exteriorization. The beast is expelled, the reign of humanity re-established. 'The time is free' (V. xi. 21), and the new king 'will perform in measure, time, and place' (V. xi. 39): after raging excess, due order will 'be planted newly' (V. xi. 31). Yet, on the other hand, though Malcolm says all the right things and gives all the right instructions in his concluding speech,[42] his denunciation of his predecessors seems glibly reductive,[43] because the play has so hauntingly impressed on us a sense of the humanness of the bestial couple. Of all the play's dramatis personae, the Macbeths are the most fully realized individuals. The transgressive 'more' that pushes them beyond the bounds of the human paradoxically also offers us 'more' humanness.

Ironically, much the same could be said of Malcolm. A quietly unremarkable figure, he blooms into full character in out-beasting the bestial Macbeth:

> It is myself I mean, in whom I know
> All the particulars of vice so grafted
> That when they shall be opened black Macbeth
> Will seem as pure as snow, and the poor state
> Esteem him as a lamb, being compared
> With my confineless harms.   (IV. iii. 51–6)

Drawing on himself 'confineless harms', Malcolm places himself in a line of transgression begun with 'the multiplying villainies of nature' that 'swarm upon' the 'merciless Macdonald' (I. ii. 11–12; 9), the play's first villain. Ending up with his head 'fixed . . . upon our battlements' (I. ii. 23), Macdonald prefigures not only Macbeth's villainies, but also the final tableau of Macbeth's end, exhibited 'as our rarer monsters are, / Painted upon a pole, and underwrit / "Here may you see a tyrant" ' (V. x. 25–7).

---

[42] Richard McCoy, ' "The Grace of Grace" and Double-Talk in *Macbeth*', *Shakespeare Survey*, 57 (2004), 27–37, argues that Malcolm pursues a 'canny strategy' throughout the play and proves his fitness to rule with 'the shrewd poise of Machiavelli's prince' (p. 34). Similarly Barbara Riebling, 'Virtue's Sacrifice'. A much more sinister Malcolm emerges in Rebecca Lemon, *Treason by Words*, 79–106.

[43] Howard Felperin, *Shakespearean Representation: Mimesis and Modernity in Elizabethan Tragedy* (Princeton: Princeton University Press, 1977), 136.

The new head of state, standing next to where his precursor's 'cursèd head' now 'stands' (V. xi. 20), balances contrast and parallel. To say that this tableau renders the new ruler thoroughly implicated in the very corruption he claims to have vanquished would reduce the meaning of what, to the very end, remains equivocal. Malcolm's bravura performance in dissimulation (IV. iii) and the gory trophy under which he launches his new feudal order ('Henceforth be earls'; V. xi. 29) do not thwart the hope for 'redress' (IV. iii. 9) that Malcolm promises his 'poor country' (IV. iii. 165). But they do serve as a reminder of the potential that the new king shares with the conquered tyrant, the 'confineless' force to do and be more (and less) than man—to be fox or lion, as Machiavelli counsels, to 'look like the innocent flower, / But be the serpent under't', as Lady Macbeth instructs her husband (I. v. 64–5), or, indeed, to look like the serpent and be the innocent flower, a feat that Malcolm accomplishes so disconcertingly well that it leaves Macduff at a loss for words: 'Why are you silent?' Malcolm asks; and Macduff's puzzled answer embroils the future King of Scotland in the same 'fair is foul' logic that has been the leitmotif of his predecessor's perdition:

> Such welcome and unwelcome things at once
> 'Tis hard to reconcile.   (IV. iii. 138–40)

The potential 'more' which thus passes from Macbeth to Malcolm tellingly omits the God-given charisma which both the woefully defenceless Duncan and his saintly English neighbour, Edward the Confessor, embody. Malcolm marvels at the 'most miraculous work in this good King' (IV. iii. 148), but there is no indication that he aspires to such 'strange virtue' (IV. iii. 157) himself.[44] If Macbeth's crime registers as a 'fall . . . into bestiality',[45] the ending hardly signals a 'regenerat[ion] . . . into the higher things, which are divine'.[46] What we are left with, instead, is a kind of sublation (*Aufhebung*)— albeit one that smacks less of Hegelian idealism than of vigilant *Realpolitik*— in which the 'beast', despite being ritually killed, lives on. What we are left with is a sense of the daunting range and disturbing ambivalence of human– animal potential which an earlier dramatist evoked in the famous opening of a chorus traditionally rendered as:

[44] McCoy, 'Grace of Grace', 30–1.
[45] James L. Calderwood, *If It Were Done: Macbeth and Tragic Action* (Amherst, Mass.: University of Massachusetts Press, 1986), 93.
[46] Pico, *Oration*, as quoted in Agamben, *The Open*, 30.

Wonders are many, and none is more wonderful than man.

But the adjective Sophocles uses is *deinós*, which means terrifying as well as marvellous, awful as well as awesome, dangerous as well as capable, and whose root noun is *deós*, fear. The same line thus also reads:

Terrors are many and nothing more terrible than man.[47]

Just as Sophocles' praise of humanity retains a sense of man's irreducible potential for destructiveness, so the conclusion of *Macbeth* kills and removes the bestial tyrant even as it refuses to oust the beast.

---

[47] Sophocles, *Antigone*, ll. 332–3 (Stasimon 1). The Cambridge editor of the play highlights the fundamental ambiguity of the line: 'Is the view of "Man" . . . predominantly favourable, predominantly unfavourable, mixed, or neutral? (Or, to put it another way, should we translate the key term of the opening line, δεινά, as "wonderful," "terrible," "strange," or "extraordinary"?).' Sophocles, *Antigone*, ed. Mark Griffith (Cambridge: Cambridge University Press, 1999), 179–80.

2

A Kingdom for a Scaffold

I. Heads

During his visit to London in the summer of 1600, Zdeněk, Baron Waldstein, a young nobleman from Bohemia, notes in his diary for 3 July:

> Went to see an English play . . . . On the way back we crossed the bridge; it has very fine buildings on it, and fixed to one of them can still be seen the heads of a number of earls and other noblemen who have been executed for treason.[1]

Such fine buildings, the Baron seems to suggest, deserve no less than earls for toppings.[2] Paul Hentzner, whose account of bear-baiting was quoted in the Introduction, counted 'above thirty' traitors' heads on poles above the bridge, and the Swiss traveller Thomas Platter remarks:

> Their descendants are accustomed to boast of this themselves, even pointing out to one of their ancestors' heads on this same bridge, believing that they will be esteemed the more because their antecedents were of such high descent that they could even covet the crown.[3]

Almost none of the early modern visitors to London failed to make note of the traitors' heads. Like the playhouse and the baiting ring, they were clearly a tourist attraction. In the diaries of von Waldstein, Hentzner, and Platter,

---

[1] *The Diary of Baron Waldstein: A Traveller in Elizabethan England*, trans. and annot. G. W. Groos (London: Thames and Hudson, 1981), 37.

[2] Waldstein himself narrowly escaped the same fate. A leading supporter of the Protestant Frederick of the Palatinate—the unlucky Winter King, James I's son-in-law—he was sentenced to death after the battle of the White Mountain in 1620. His sentence was commuted to life imprisonment, and he died in prison in 1623, aged 42. *The Diary of Baron Waldstein*, 16–17.

[3] Quoted in *The Diary of Baron Waldstein*, 36 n. 35.

stage, stake, and these souvenirs of the scaffold make up an ensemble of sights that defines the typical London experience. This ensemble confers its 'form and pressure' on the very substance of drama itself. In Shakespeare's early quartet of English history plays, the energies of playing, baiting, and beheading, which are dispersed among a clutter of warring factions, eventually converge in a single emblematic figure, the consummate actor, the beast, the traitor who covets nothing but the crown: Richard, hunchbacked son of York. At first just one of many, he carves his way out of the tangle of dynastic rivalry to become the undisputed centre of his own drama, Shakespeare's first tragic, or near-tragic, protagonist. At the opening of the play that will show his eruption from latent malignity into full-blown wickedness he has not yet presented himself as the treacherous villain. But his ambition and his means to attain it are ominously foreshadowed with a *coup de théâtre* of crude but incontestable force:

EDWARD   Lord Stafford's father, Duke of Buckingham,
          Is either slain or wounded dangerous.
          I cleft his beaver with a downright blow.
          That this is true, father, behold his blood.
                    [*He shows a bloody sword*]
MONTAGUE [*To York*] And, brother, here's the Earl of Wiltshire's blood,
          Whom I encountered as the battles joined.
RICHARD   [*To Sommerset's head, which he shows*]
          Speak thou for me, and tell them what I did.   (*3 Henry VI*, I. i. 10–16)

Richard speaks least and does most. Moreover, his father York's applause raises him above both his elder brothers (George, who is absent, as well as the first-born Edward):

YORK   Richard hath best deserved of all my sons.
          [*To the head*] But is your grace dead, my Lord of Somerset?
NORFOLK   Such hap have all the line of John of Gaunt.
YORK   Thus do I hope to shake King Henry's head.
                    [*He holds aloft the head, then throws it down*][4]   (I. i. 17–20)

---

[4] There is some variance among editors as to who does what with the severed head. Michael Hattaway, in his edition of *The Third Part of Henry VI* (Cambridge: Cambridge University Press, 1993), puts the stage direction '[Throwing down the Duke of Somerset's head]' after Richard's 'Speak thou for me, and tell them what I did' (l. 16). This adds to the brute force of Richard's gesture, but leaves open how York then gets hold of the trophy. If Richard throws down the head, his father must take it up to address it and to shake it 'thus'.

Grasping the severed head of a malefactor by the hair and brandishing it at the crowd like a hunting trophy (sometimes with 'comical gestures'[5]) was a routine part of the early modern theatre of punishment. But in Shakespeare's first tetralogy there is no surer way to lose one's head than to triumph over someone else losing theirs. Now mocking his dead enemy, York will be mocked and dead himself before the Act is over. His mounting ambition, traitorous from the Lancastrian point of view, will earn him a traitor's place on a pole, the wordplay on 'gate' invoking the grim exhibits on the gate of London Bridge near this scene of theatrical bloodshed, the capital offenders 'overlooking' the capital:

YORK   Open thy gate of mercy, gracious God—
          My soul flies through these wounds to seek out thee. [*He dies*]
MARGARET Off with his head and set it on York gates—
          So York may overlook the town of York.   (I. iv. 178–81)

And the line does not end here. 'Measure for measure' (II. vi. 55), head for head, the retaliatory logic of the feud demands that York's head be replaced by that of his murderer:

WARWICK   From off the gates of York fetch down the head,
          Your father's head, which Clifford placèd there;
          Instead whereof let this supply the room—   (II. vi. 52–4)

It takes a further whole play, *The Tragedy of Richard the Third: with the Landing of Earle Richmond, and the Battell at Bosworth Field*, in the full Folio title, to bring this killing machine to a halt. As the '[g]rim-visaged war' (*Richard III*, I. i. 9) of Richard's opening soliloquy is supplanted by the 'smooth-faced peace' (V. viii. 33) of Richmond's concluding speech, the chopping off of heads is finally over, '[n]ow civil wounds are stopped' (V. v. 40) and the last decapitation—that of Richard's hostage, young Stanley, who was to '[b]e executed in his father's sight' (V. v. 49)—remains happily unaccomplished.[6] But the scaffold casts its shadow even under the smiling heaven (V.viii. 20) of this hard-won concord and general pardon. Richmond may be a much less ambiguous figure than the Malcolm who takes over at

---

[5] Richard J. Evans, *Rituals of Retribution: Capital Punishment in Germany 1600–1987* (Oxford: Oxford University Press, 1996), 86–7.

[6] The lopping of heads as the play's hallmark was epitomized by the line which David Garrick's performances of Richard made memorable: 'Off with his head, so much for Buckingham.' Once the most famous quotation from *Richard III*, it is not by Shakespeare, but by his adapter Colley Cibber.

the end of *Macbeth*, but for a bringer of unconditional peace, his speech is surprisingly fraught with thoughts of treason—not as a thing of the past, but as a future threat to be averted: 'Abate the edge of traitors, gracious Lord' (V. viii. 35), Richmond entreats, and 'Let them not live . . . / That would with treason wound this fair land's peace' (V. viii. 38–9). Still more remarkable is what he says a few lines earlier:

> Smile, heaven, upon this fair conjunction,
> That long have frowned upon their enmity.
> What traitor hears me and says not 'Amen'?   (V. viii. 20–2)

The intent of Richmond's rhetorical question is clear enough. Like Brutus' challenge to the forum crowd—'Who is here so vile that will not love his country? If any, speak, for him have I offended' (*Caesar*, III. iii. 32–3)—it implies that there is no such person; no traitor to his country, no one who would not honestly say 'Amen' to the reconciliation of York and Lancaster. But the words could also mean exactly the opposite. If the traitor 'hears me' he must already be present and, being a traitor, he will, of course, say 'Amen'. That is precisely what constitutes his treachery. How easily a traitor can give sanctimonious assent has been demonstrated earlier in the play when Richard heartily joins in King Edward's 'blessèd labour' of reconciliation (II. i. 53). The most resounding 'Amen' of the play, after all, is the one that ratifies the arch-traitor's triumph at the end of Act III when Richard is proclaimed king after a virtuoso performance of piety and reluctance (III. vii. 231).

An Elizabethan audience knew, of course, that the dynasty inaugurated by Richmond would in fact prove durable—though not for want of traitors scheming (or allegedly scheming) to overthrow it, as the heads on London Bridge amply attested. Why then undermine the providential moment of stability with such intimations of danger? Evoking the past, Shakespeare's histories speak to the present. It is a very contemporary, Elizabethan fear of treason that is vented in the final words of the Queen's royal ancestor, a fear that passed undiminished from her reign to that of her Scottish successor.[7]

---

[7] On real and imagined threats of treason see Lemon, *Treason by Words*; Curt Breight, '"Treason doth never prosper": *The Tempest* and the Discourse of Treason', *Shakespeare Quarterly*, 41 (1990), 1–28.

II. Acting Royal

'It is a trew old saying, That a King is as one set on a stage, whose smallest actions and gestures, all the people gazingly doe behold.'[8] The observation is commonplace, 'a true old saying'. What makes it remarkable is the emendation it contains. Where we read 'stage' in the second and all subsequent editions of King James's *Basilikon Doron*, his 'royal gift' of advice about statecraft and proper kingship to his eldest son, the first edition had 'skaffold': 'That a King is as one set on a skaffold, whose smallest actions and gestures, all the people gazingly doe behold.'[9] Suppressing ambiguity, the change registers 'the danger James must have felt to be inherent in the royal drama'.[10] For a ruler whose power is constituted, on the one hand, 'in theatrical celebrations of royal glory' and, on the other, in 'theatrical violence visited upon the enemies of that glory',[11] the ambiguous 'scaffold', meaning a platform for play-acting but also one for public executions, suggests the alarming possibility that these two distinct and complementary types of royal theatricality might collapse into one—precisely as they did when James's son and successor Charles was beheld losing his head on a scaffold at Whitehall in 1649, and theatrical violence, instead of being directed against the enemies of royal glory, was visited upon that glory itself:

> That thence the Royal actor borne
> The tragic scaffold might adorn:
> While round the armèd bands
> Did clap their bloody hands.[12]

To credit James, the royal author, with prophetic anticipation of the Royal actor Charles's death scene would be a step too far. But it does seem plausible that James's original choice of word—and his second thoughts about it—may have been suggested by the uncomfortable memory of the scaffold on which his mother, Mary Queen of Scots, lost her life in

[8] King James VI and I, 'Basilikon Doron', in *Selected Writings*, ed. Neil Rhodes, Jennifer Richards, and Joseph Marshall (Aldershot: Ashgate, 2003), 246.

[9] *Basilikon Doron* (Edinburgh, 1599; repr. London: Westheimer, Lea, and Co., 1887).

[10] Stephen Orgel, 'Making Greatness Familiar', *Genre*, 15 (1982), 41–8 at 45.

[11] Stephen Greenblatt, 'Invisible Bullets', in his *Shakespearean Negotiations* (Oxford: Clarendon Press, 1988), 64. Greenblatt's observations refer to Elizabeth I but are equally applicable to her successor.

[12] Andrew Marvell, 'An Horatian Ode upon Cromwell's Return from Ireland', in *The Poems of Andrew Marvell*, ed. Nigel Smith (rev. edn., London: Pearson Longman, 2007), 267–80 at 276, ll. 53–6.

the draughty Great Hall at Fotheringhay Castle in February 1587.[13] This scaffold, too, was a theatre as well as a place of execution. 'I think they are making a scaffold to make me play the last scene of the Tragedy',[14] Mary wrote to the Spanish ambassador when she heard the hammering of the carpenters. Almost four months had elapsed between the passing of the death sentence and its execution because Elizabeth I could not bring herself to give the final order. Urged to action by her parliament, she justified her hesitation by invoking her exposed position: 'We princes are set as it were upon stages, in the sight and view of all the world.'[15]

The discomfort of privileged visibility[16] befalls Shakespeare's Richard Gloucester as soon as he gets what he wants. Finally entitled to play the part he has always coveted, his command of the stage now fails him. Elizabeth and James tellingly use the passive voice to describe their position: princes do not actively occupy the stage, they are 'set upon it'. This is the very condition of their divinely sanctioned authority, the condition which the comedy of Richard's reluctant acceptance of the crown in III. vii is meant to simulate. The ravenous usurper is suddenly all passivity, patience, endurance; no longer the agent, but the object of 'imposition' and 'enforcement' (*Richard III*, III. vii. 222, 223):

> Since you will buckle fortune on my back,
> To bear her burden, whe'er I will or no,
> I must have patience to endure the load.   (III. vii. 218–20)

In Richard's dream, the 'golden yoke of sovereignty' (III. vii. 145)[17] would compensate for and even effectually remove that other load, the 'envious mountain on my back' (*3 Henry VI*, III. ii. 157). But ironically, his dissembling gives an accurate description of what kingship has in store for him.

---

[13] In the light of Carl Schmitt's reading, the whole myth and mystery of Hamlet could be wedged into the rift which James's emendation seeks to paste over: the unspeakable memory of a guilty Queen Mother, the deeply 'disrupted and imperiled' existence of her son the king, who was 'literally from the womb immersed in the schisms of his era'. Carl Schmitt, *Hamlet or Hecuba: The Intrusion of the Time into the Play*, trans. David Pan and Jennifer R. Rust (New York: Telos, 2009), 27.

[14] Antonia Fraser, *Mary Queen of Scots* (10th edn., London: Weidenfeld and Nicolson, 1975), 521.

[15] Ibid. 518. Much as Elizabeth hesitated openly to take responsibility for the death of her royal prisoner, she would apparently have been only too glad to have her liquidated in secret. Her attempt to persuade Sir Amias Paulet, commander of Fotheringhay, to solve the problem in this way is almost reminiscent of Macbeth. Paulet, though a declared enemy of the Catholic Queen of Scots, was horrified at the proposal.

[16] Greenblatt, 'Invisible Bullets', 64.

[17] F, not in Q; listed as 'additional passage' in the Oxford *Complete Works*.

If the crown delivers him from obsessively 'descant[ing] on [his] own deformity' (*Richard III*, I. i. 27), it also seems to drain much of the energy out of his performance. The static institutional charisma of the crown contains and thereby weakens the monstrous charisma of Richard's agility.

A comment in IV. ii registers a decisive shift bearing out James's observation that it is the king's 'smallest actions and gestures, all the people gazingly doe behold'. When Richard appears crowned and 'in pompe' (F) for the first time, and Buckingham, up until now his accomplice, becomes his subject, this brief aside shows not only their immediate estrangement, but also how it is noted:

CATESBY   The King is angry. See, he gnaws his lip.   (IV. ii. 28)

Before, Richard could cloak his betrayals by looking 'cheerfully and smooth' (III. iv. 48). Now that he is 'wear[ing] these glories' (IV. ii. 6) his appearance betrays him. Richard's success was built on his unfailing ability to create suitable stages for his virtuoso performances as seducer, plain-speaking patriot, devout Christian, reluctant heir apparent. It also depended on his equally unfailing ability to turn stage into scaffold. This convertibility now turns against him, making the stage he finds himself 'set upon' dangerously fragile, a kingdom of 'brittle glass' (IV. ii. 63). A 'poor player' (*Macbeth*, V. v. 23), he is reduced to 'fretting' where he used to 'strut'—most exuberantly so in the boasting match with his then still 'other self' (II. ii. 121), Buckingham:

RICHARD   Come, cousin, canst thou quake and change thy colour?
               Murder thy breath in middle of a word,
               And then again begin, and stop again,
               As if thou wert distraught and mad with terror?
BUCKINGHAM Tut, I can counterfeit the deep tragedian,
               Tremble and start at wagging of a straw,
               Speak, and look back, and pry on every side   (III. v. 1–7)

The success of these lethal acting skills is promptly confirmed by the play's hallmark stage prop when Hastings's severed head is brought in, launching Richard into another demonstration of his skills:

So dear I loved the man that I must weep.
I took him for the plainest harmless creature
So smooth he daubed his vice with show of virtue   (III. v. 23–8)

Actors are frequently figured as shadows in Shakespeare. Aptly then, it is 'shadows' that will eventually catch the consummate actor in his own trap, striking a wholly unfeigned 'terror to the soul of Richard' (V. v. 171), making him tremble with real fear ('Cold fearful drops stand on my trembling flesh'; V. v. 135).

The show-off capers of Act III thus anticipate the nocturnal despair in Act V, but they also look back to that primal outburst of self-revelation in *Henry VI*, Part 3, which marks not only the starting point of the Richard who is 'determinèd to prove a villain' (*Richard III*, I. i. 30), but also the first voicing in Shakespeare's oeuvre 'of a fully developed subjectivity', the first instance of 'the characteristically Shakespearean illusion that a stage person has interior being'.[18]

It is no accident that this Shakespearean interiority effect should originate in the stage person of a traitor. The split between 'what a man might play' and 'that within which passeth show' (*Hamlet*, I. ii. 84–5) is the trademark of treason before it can become the enabling condition of the psychological 'depth' we attribute to a character like Hamlet, who is, after all, on the most elementary political level of the play a traitor to his uncle the King. If treason—as the prototypal example of Richard suggests—is the soil in which interiority can take root, then it is hardly surprising that the Shakespearean characters most amply endowed with inner spaces of secrecy tend to know less what, adapting Hamlet, 'denotes them truly' than what denotes them falsely, the various faces of their seeming. Shakespearean subjectivity typically presents itself as an experience not of self-possession, but of the rift through which such possession is for ever withheld. Again Richard offers the model from which Shakespeare's later, more sophisticated representations can be seen to derive. His terrified last soliloquy exposes not so much the inner core of character behind his masks as a frantic search for a role that might serve to patch up what is essentially a void—a self that is nothing but the ensemble of masks it adopts.[19] Such a role does offer itself once the night and its terrors abate and Richard regains composure in a stance of Stoic fortitude.

---

[18] Janet Adelman, *Suffocating Mothers: Fantasies of Maternal Origin in Shakespeare's Plays, 'Hamlet' to 'The Tempest'* (New York and London: Routledge, 1992), 1.

[19] Michael Neill, 'Shakespeare's Halle of Mirrors: Play, Politics, and Psychology in *Richard III*', *Shakespeare Studies*, 8 (1975), 99–129 at 100, speaks of 'the void at the center of [Richard's] being', which means that, 'when the external motives for action are removed, "Richard", literally, disintegrates'.

Richard's bid for the crown involves a twofold plan of action. On the one hand, there is his resolve to 'hew my way out with a bloody axe' (*3 Henry VI*, III. ii. 181), which ties in seamlessly with his previous feats of ruthless violence: the killing of Somerset, the casual abuse of the dead man's skewered head. It is tellingly not the sword, the weapon of chivalric combat, that must serve for this part of his plan, but the cruder and more brutal axe, suggestive of massacre, of butchery, and the chopping off of heads. Carving out his kingship from the flesh of foes, friends and kin, the bloody axe becomes the concrete image of Richard's total self-isolation, his severing of all family ties: 'I had no father, I am like no father; / I have no brother, I am like no brother; . . . I am myself alone' (*3 Henry VI*, V. vi. 80–4). The sign of the axe thus comes to hover over the singular state of a king as conceived by the terms of Richard's radical individualism: it makes the head of state bodiless, severed from the social and dynastic organism that should support it.

But brute force is only one side of Richard's plan. The other side is cunning. The axe is sheathed, as it were, in one smooth rhetorical move, the breathing out of a 'Why'. The course of action now outlined consists in acting:

> Why, I can smile, and murder whiles I smile,
> And cry, 'Content!' to that which grieves my heart,
> And wet my cheeks with artificial tears,
> And frame my face to all occasions.
>
> I can add colours to the chameleon,
> Change shapes with Proteus for advantages,
> And set the murderous Machiavel to school.
> Can I do this, and cannot get a crown?
> Tut, were it farther off, I'll pluck it down.
>
> (*3 Henry VI*, III. ii. 182–95)

Revealing his 'true colour', Richard declares his resolve to change colour. 'Plots have I laid, inductions dangerous' (*Richard III*, I. i. 32), he brags when we re-encounter him at the opening of *Richard III*. Both 'plot' and 'induction' carry a literary as well as conspiratorial meaning, blending play with treason, the stage with the scaffold.

III. Reversals

The anxiety of exposure that *Basilikon Doron* never quite manages to suppress may have been aggravated by James's personal aversion to crowds.

But it is also woven into the fabric of spectacular kingship itself. Claiming absolute sovereignty and considering himself answerable only to God, it is as His deputy that James sees himself treading the boards of the *theatrum mundi*. And it is to God's uniquely privileged spectatorship that his performance is ultimately directed. Ultimately, but by no means exclusively, as the biblical opening of his address to the reader makes clear:

> ... there *is nothing so covered, that shal not be revealed, neither so hidde, that shal not be knowen: and whatsoeuer they haue spoken in darknesse, should be heard in the light: and that which they had spoken in the eare in secret place, should be publikely preached on the tops of the houses.*[20]

The passage James quotes (Luke 12: 2–3) follows Christ's warning to his disciples, 'Beware ye of the leaven of the Pharisees, which is hypocrisy' (12: 1). It serves James to declare his authorial honesty: in what follows the reader will find the King's views frankly expressed. But more importantly, the quotation also furnishes a gloss on how the book came to be published, an outcome the author regards with unconcealed discomfort. Intended only to be 'spoken ... in secret place', James's words of paternal advice to his son Henry will now be 'publikely preached'. Not because the King planned it that way, but because 'false copies ... are alreadie spread'; 'this Booke is now vented, and set forth to the publike view of the world, and consequently subject to every mans censure' (p. 203). The reading public, no different from the audience at a public playhouse, acquires the power to make 'proud majesty a subject'.[21]

The quotation from Luke implies, even if it does not explicitly posit, God as the great discloser of human secrets. James acknowledges this in referring to 'that all-seeing eye ... piercing through the bowels of very darknesse it selfe' (p. 202). But as soon as the royal author turns from the general human condition to a king's specific state of heightened visibility, it is no longer the eye of God that worries him but the myriad-eyed gaze of the crowd. And with this change in perspective the agency of disclosure is relocated, too. The divine prerogative of making public is attributed to the public itself, the active force of the people's irresistible inquisitiveness: 'So as this their great concurrence in curiositie ... hath enforced the un-timous divulging of this Booke, farre contrarie to my intention' (p. 207).

---

[20] King James VI and I, 'Basilikon Doron', 202 (italics original). Further references are given in text.

[21] See the seminal essay by David Scott Kastan, 'Proud Majesty Made a Subject: Shakespeare and the Spectacle of Rule', *Shakespeare Quarterly*, 37 (1986), 459–75.

Thus the passage, which starts from the idea of an all-seeing, all-hearing deity, redirects its focus to a human audience. God can see what happens in private, but the link between king and actor in another variant of the 'true old saying' is that both are exposed to public view: 'for Kings being publike persons, by reason of their office and authority, are as it were set . . . upon a publike stage, in the sight all the people; where all the beholders eyes are attentively bent to looke and pry in the least circumstance of their secretest drift' (p. 202). Relocating the sovereign from the cosmic theatre *of* the world to a public theatre *in* the world, James subjects his performance to the judgement of those subjects to whom his strict line of absolutism—hammered home in *Basilikon Doron* and *The Trew Law of Free Monarchies*—expressly denies any such power. '[E]ver to walke as in the eyes of the Almightie, examining ever so the secretest of my drifts, before I gave them course'— this is how James proposes to prepare himself for the eventuality that these secrets 'might someday bide the touchstone of a publike triall' (p. 202), the eventuality of stage turning scaffold which did arise 'someday', albeit not in his lifetime.

Basilikon Doron betrays a troubled sense of vulnerability about the sphere of public display. Visibility is an indispensable constituent of early modern kingship which must be performatively endorsed by the affirmation of an audience—the court, the people, the world at large. But this audience response can never be safely predicted. How the spectacle of majesty is received by the '*Hydra* of diversly-enclined spectatours' (p. 208) remains ultimately beyond the control of executive authority, even if this authority deploys its sharpest weapon: execution.[22] To decapitate the Hydra is point- less. The serpent monster of rampant plurality will always grow new heads, 'diversly-enclined'.

When James chose his quotation from the Gospel of St Luke he could not fail to register the setting in which Jesus speaks to his disciples, not, as it were, 'in secret place', but where 'there were gathered together an innu- merable multitude of people, insomuch that they trode one upon another' (Luke 12: 1). For a Christian king this is the setting that most vividly evokes the dangerous unpredictability of his audience. From the 'Hosanna' of Palm

---

[22] Thomas W. Laqueur, 'Crowds, Carnival and the State in English Executions, 1604–1868', in A. L. Beier, David Cannadine and James Rosenheim (eds.), *The First Modern Society: Essays in English History in Honour of Lawrence Stone* (Cambridge: Cambridge University Press, 1989), 305–55; V. A. Gatrell, *The Hanging Tree: Execution and the English People 1770–1868* (Oxford: Oxford University Press, 1994), 90–105.

Sunday to the 'Crucify him' of Good Friday, the biblical crowd crammed the scene of Christ's Passion in the street theatre of the Mystery cycles as well as in innumerable altarpieces. It is the crowd that changes from adoration to baiting in a trice, the prototype of the crowd that enshrines and entraps[23] the player king in the circular enclosure of Shakespeare's wooden O.

> And they stripped him, and put about him a skarlet robe, And platted a crowne of thornes, and put it vpon his head, and a reede in his right hand, and bowed their knees before him, and mocked him, saying, God saue thee King of the Iewes, And spitted vpon him, and took a reede, and smote him on the head. (Matthew 27: 28–30, *Geneva*)

A reflection of this Christian *ur*-scene of baiting seeps even into Richard's frenzied imaginings as he launches himself into his deadly hunt for the crown in *3 Henry VI*. Accounting

> this world but hell,
> Until my misshaped trunk that bears this head[24]
> Be round impalèd with a glorious crown
>
> (*3 Henry VI*, III. ii. 169–71)

Richard finds himself 'like one lost in a thorny wood, / That rents the thorns and is rent with the thorns' (III. ii. 174–5). In this 'fluid fantasy', as Janet Adelman has acutely observed, 'the crown and the obstacles to the crown collapse into one another', turning Richard's object of desire into a crown of thorns. Even at the outset of his 'acting career', Richard anticipates the confining enclosure in which his success will eventually trap him. No sooner does he reach 'home' (III. ii. 173) within the palisade of his 'glorious crown' than the pales become 'transformed into the thorns that now impale him'.[25] As 'bear whelp' mothered by a 'dam' (III. ii. 161–2), Richard caught up 'in a thorny wood' strongly suggests a hunted animal as well, struggling to escape, but captured, 'round impaled' much in the way that bears and wild boars were, according to contemporary manuals of hunting.[26]

---

[23] See Skura, *Shakespeare the Actor*, 8, and above, 'Introduction'.

[24] Following Hanmer, Michael Hattaway, the Cambridge editor, emends this to 'Until this head my misshaped trunk does bear'. This obviously makes good sense; but the palpably absurd idea of the crown encircling his whole body arguably brings out more strongly the obsessive urgency of Richard's desire.

[25] Adelman, *Suffocating Mothers*, 2–3.

[26] As illustrated by Jan van der Straet and discussed in Ch. 3 below.

Richard's self-revelation, as Adelman has shown, is dominated by the obsessive idea of a suffocating mother's womb, the origin of his deformity, the enclosure from which he strives 'to hew his way out, giving birth to himself through the rent of a violent caesarian section'.[27] But even as Richard's fantasy hinges on a traumatic maternal matrix, it is equally grounded in a paternal trauma. If Richard himself makes a somewhat unlikely Christ-figure, his father York's death scene all the more pointedly evokes the Passion. The crown within his reach, already seated '[e]ven in the chair of state' (*3 Henry VI*, I. i. 51), York ends up baited by his triumphant enemies, 'round impaled' with a paper crown in a ceremony of mock elevation:

MARGARET Come make him stand upon a molehill here,
　　　　　That wraught at mountains with outstretchèd arms

　　　　　　　　　　　　　　　　　　　　　(*3 Henry VI*, I. iv. 68–9)

Reduced from mountain to molehill, York is enjoined to entertain his tormentors: 'I prithee, grieve, to make me merry, York.... Stamp, rave, and fret, that I may sing and dance' (I. iv. 87–92). In Holinshed, the link to the Passion is made explicit: 'they kneeled down afore him (as the Jews did unto Christ) in scorn, saying to him: "Hail, king without rule..."'.[28] Shakespeare pointedly inflects the biblical model to encompass the plight of the 'poor player', a 'common player' who receives pay (is 'fee'd') for his performance and who cannot do his job unless properly costumed, as Margaret, the stage-manager, declares in mock concern:

　　　Thou wouldst be fee'd, I see, to make me sport.
　　　York cannot speak unless he wear a crown.
　　　[*To her men*] A crown for York, and, lords, bow low to him.
　　　Hold you his hands whilst I do set it on.
　　　[*She puts a paper crown on York's head*]
　　　Ay, marry, sir, now looks he like a king,
　　　Ay, this is he that took King Henry's chair,
　　　And this is he was his adopted heir.

　　　And will you pale your head in Henry's glory,
　　　And rob his temples of the diadem

---

[27] Adelman, *Suffocating Mothers*, 3.

[28] Raphael Holinshed, *Shakespeare's Holinshed: An Edition of Holinshed's Chronicles (1587). Source of Shakespeare's History Plays, King Lear, Cymbeline, and Macbeth*, ed. Richard Hosley (New York: G. P. Putnam's Sons, 1968), 193–4.

Now, in his life, against your holy oath?
O 'tis a fault too, too, unpardonable.
Off with the crown,
> [*She knocks it from his head*]
>> and with the crown his head,   (I. iv. 93–9; 104–8)

The head that York presumed to 'pale' (encompass) in Henry's glory by 'round impaling' it with the crown will soon be impaled on the battlements of the town of York. And the torment of the father's paper crown of thorns will echo in the encircling agony of the son's struggle: 'And I . . . Torment myself to catch the English crown. / And from that torment I will free myself' (III. ii. 174; 179–80).

The mocking of York and the solo performance of his son's self-revelation highlight the entanglement of the stage which kings are set upon with the stage on which they become the subject of dramatic representation. As the playhouse mirrors the pageant of royalty, this mirroring is duplicated both when York, the prince impersonated by a common player, is forced to imitate a common player and when the actor playing Richard shows a Richard who will play the actor to become king.

Nothing, at first glance, could be further removed from the sphere of divinely ordained royalty than the contact zone on the social and topographical margins of the early modern capital[29] where the theatre of punishment rubbed shoulders with the mundane entertainments of the bear-garden and the playhouse. But these scenes tell a different story, one that is corroborated by James's unease about the 'skaffold'. The scene of York's death, in particular, drastically demonstrates that royal distance and the collapse of that distance are stipulated by the same script. Like his mother, who fashioned her ordeal as a Catholic martyr's *imitatio Christi*, James saw his performance on the stage of the world as a mirror of 'Divine Maiestie'.[30] Their keen awareness of being exposed to the gaze of a volatile crowd is intricately bound up with this model and the logic of reversal which it entails. Modelling itself on Christ, kingship comes under the pull of victimization. The King may be seen not only as a possible, but indeed as a first choice for the role of victim, as another royal actor, Richard II, suggests in his litany of royal casualties:

---

[29] On the political and cultural implications of the theatre's marginal or 'heterotopic' location, see Steven Mullaney, *The Place of the Stage: License, Play, and Power in Renaissance England* (Chicago and London: University of Chicago Press, 1988).

[30] King James VI and I, 'Basilikon Doron', 210.

> For God's sake, let us sit upon the ground,
> And tell sad stories of the death of kings—
> How some have been deposed, some slain in war,
> Some haunted by the ghosts they have deposed,
> Some poisoned by their wives, some sleeping killed,
> All murdered. For within the hollow crown
> That rounds the mortal temples of a king
> Keeps Death his court . . .   (*Richard II*, III. ii. 151–8)

The more closely royal authority seeks to attach itself to its divine source, the more closely it associates itself with the figure of the cross, a figure of reversal, or rather double reversal, from glory to humiliation and back, from suffering and death, to resurrection. If it is to drive home the unmatchable greatness of the God-man's sacrifice, the reversal cannot be extreme enough: the deeper the humiliation the greater the glory. This extremity is at the core of the Gospel, crucial to its doctrinal and affective power.

It is also intermedially active between the spectacle of majesty at the top of the social scale and the rituals of retributive entertainment at the bottom. The distance between them is immense, but distance is the very means employed to maintain and intensify the connection. There is a functional link between the highest and the lowest in that neither can be fully realized without the other. Kingly elevation and the abjection of criminal or beast inversely mirror each other in forms of public display that invite synopsis. The visual regime of absolutist kingship is sustained by the gaze that recognizes the distance but also the connection between the display of majesty and the display of the convict on the scaffold, or the bear at the stake. In characterizing the potentially unruly, never to be trusted audience in front of which a king must act his part, King James tellingly uses the same epithet that John Taylor the Water Poet applies to the hostile crowd which baited him at the Hope: 'hydra-headed multitude'.

IV. King of Beasts

Where stage meets scaffold in the royal imagination, symbolic animals—and sometimes real ones—enter the scene of signification. If the Hydra represents 'the many-headed multitude' (*Coriolanus*, II. iii. 16–17) and the lamb signifies Christ's sacrifice, it is the lion, king of beasts, who uniquely embodies the role and attributes of majesty. In England the lion has been the king's heraldic animal since the reign of Henry II.[31] When Henry III received three leopards from the Holy Roman emperor, Frederick II, in 1235, this gift was a flattering allusion to the royal arms of England, which, by then, consisted of three golden leopards or lions,[32] passant gardant, on a red field. This royal gift of live animals was the start of the Tower menagerie, which lasted until 1835.[33] Among the animals caged at the Tower, the lions enjoyed special status in the symbolic representation of kingship. English sovereigns (Elizabeth and James among them) had a lion in captivity named after them, and it 'was believed that the health of monarch and lion were mysteriously linked', so that 'when the monarch fell ill and died, their namesake would do the same in solidarity' (as is supposed to have happened at the death of Charles II).[34]

Their privileged symbolic status notwithstanding, the royal beasts were employed for baiting. In March 1604, Edward Alleyn arranged a lion-baiting for the newly arrived James I in which two mastiffs were killed, while a third survived to receive high praise and dispensation from further combat from the addressee of *Basilikon Doron*, Henry Prince of Wales, who declared 'that he that hath fought with the King of Beasts shall never fight with any inferior creature'. A connoisseur of all blood sports, James had the Lion Tower furnished with a viewing platform, from which he and his guests could watch the lions being baited 'with dogges, beares, bulles, bores etc'.[35]

Not on all these occasions did the animals perform their parts to their master's content. Royal lions might prove diffident rather than valorous or even disappointingly unsuperior when matched against lesser creatures. In one contest James I ordered to be arranged between a lion and a bear, neither animal could be induced to attack, and the King was obliged to retire disappointed.[36] But even if actual behaviour could woefully diverge

---

[31] On the (Plantagenet) origins of the lion in the royal arms of England, see C. W. Scott-Giles, *Shakespeare's Heraldry* (London: Dent, 1950), 2–4 and 42–9. Henry II's single golden lion, rampant, on a red field underwent several metamorphoses, multiplications, and blendings with other motifs, but that did not diminish its symbolic power.

[32] In heraldry, the two species are not distinguished.

[33] Made accessible to a paying public by James I, the menagerie became one of the capital's prime attractions—so much so that 'seeing the lions' came to mean doing the sights of London.

[34] Daniel Hahn, *The Tower Menagerie* (London and Sydney: Simon and Schuster, 2004), 105–6.

[35] Both quotations ibid. 94.

[36] Sometimes when no 'proper' fight ensued, James would settle for the lesser pleasure of sending prey animals such as chickens or sheep into the pit to watch them being torn apart by the lions.

from symbolic status, that status itself was never in doubt. When a bunch of dogs killed one of the king's lions in a fight, Henry VII considered this tantamount to regicide and promptly ordered the perpetrators be put to death.[37]

York, who would be king, and dies mocked as one, is visioned fighting as the king of beasts by his son Richard:

> Methought he bore him in the thickest troop,
> As doth a lion in a herd of neat;   (*3 Henry VI*, II. i. 13–14)

But the royal beast is instantly replaced by the commoner sort of creatures from the baiting ring nearby:

> Or as a bear encompassed round with dogs,
> Who having pinched a few and made them cry,
> The rest stand all aloof and bark at him.
> So fared our father with his enemies;
> So fled his enemies my warlike father.
> Methinks 'tis prize enough to be his son.   (*3 Henry VI*, II. i. 15–20)

The bear-baiting reference underscores the special bond between York and his 'youngest, . . . fiercest, and . . . most intransigently loyal' son,[38] whose misshaped body resembles that of 'an unlicked bear whelp' (*3 Henry VI*, III. ii. 161). At this stage, Richard—unlike Hamlet—cannot be too much 'in the sun/son'. The paternal 'sun of York', however, whose radiance is 'prize enough' for him, has already set, as 'the morning . . . *takes her farewell* of the glorious sun' (*3 Henry VI*, II. i. 21–2; my italics) and, ominously, '*Three suns appear in the air*', as the 1595 octavo text notes:

---

[37] Caius, *Of English Dogges*, 26: 'The force which is in them [the mastiffs] surmounteth all beleefe, the fast holde which they take with their teeth exceedeth all credit, three of them against a Beare, foure against a Lyon are sufficient, both to try masteryes with them and utterly to ouermatch them. Which thing Henry the seventh of that name, King of England (a Prince both politique & warlike) perceauing on a certaine time (as the report runneth) commaunded all such dogges (how many soever they were in number) should be hanged, being deeply displeased, and conceauing great disdaine, that an yll fauoured rascall curre should with such violent villany, assault the valiaunt Lyon king of all beastes. An example for all subiectes worthy remembraunce, to admonishe them that it is no aduantage to them to rebell against the regiment of their ruler, but to keepe them within the limits of Loyaltie.' Cf. also *The European Magazine and London Review*, 42 (July–Dec. 1802), 67: 'This lion baiting was so much of a royal sport, that, perhaps, no King ever disliked it, except Henry VII. He indeed seemed to consider that there was something like Jacobinism in the amusement, and could not brook that a dirty bull-dog should attack the king of beasts.'

[38] Nicholas Grene, *Shakespeare's Serial History Plays* (Cambridge: Cambridge University Press, 2002), 122.

EDWARD Dazzle mine eyes, or do I see three suns?
RICHARD Three glorious suns, each one a perfect sun;
        Not separated with the racking clouds,
        But severed in a pale clear-shining sky.
          [*The three suns begin to join*]
        See, see—they join, embrace, and seem to kiss,
        As if they vowed some league inviolable.
        Now are they but one lamp, one light, one sun.
        In this the heaven figures some event.   (*3 Henry VI*, II. i. 25–32)

Richard's sanguine reading, though not yet marked as intentionally dupli-
citous, is fraught with sinister foreboding.[39] Racking and severing invoke
associations of torture and capital punishment, while embracing and *seeming*
to kiss anticipate the lethal arts of 'seeming' Richard will practise on all those
who stand between him and the solar radiance of the crown. The reunified
sun does indeed turn out to figure an event: the reunion and seemingly
inviolable trinity of brothers at the end of the play, which is sealed by the
three solemn kisses bestowed on Edward's son and heir. But the 'lasting joy'
(V. vii. 46) this ritual is meant to confirm is undermined by Richard's
menacing asides. Having entered the play flourishing a severed head, he
concludes it with the prospect of further decapitation ('I'll blast his harvest,
an your head were laid'; V. vii. 21. 'Work thou the way—and thou shalt
execute'; V. vii. 25) and the confirmation of his role of arch-traitor:

    And that I love the tree from whence thou sprang'st,
    Witness the loving kiss I give the fruit.
        [*He kisses the infant prince*]
    [*Aside*] To say the truth, so Judas kissed his master,
    And cried 'All hail!' whenas he meant all harm.   (V. vii. 31–4)

The cruder combatants from the bear-garden which Richard introduces,
two Acts prior to this finale, in the description of his father's last stand are
also more in keeping than the royal lion with the squalidness of warfare that
we see reaching its nadir in the third part of *Henry VI*. In the tetralogy's
endless cycle of violence and counter-violence words and situations have a
way of echoing from one play into the next, often with a curse-like fatality.
Thus Richard's envisioning his father staked out like a bear recalls the clash

[39] John Dover Wilson notes '[t]he first snarl given to Crook-back' immediately after Edward's
next reply: 'henceforward will I bear / Upon my target three fair-shining suns. RICHARD Nay, bear
three daughters: by your leave I speak it, / You love the breeder better than the male' (II. i. 39–
42). *3 Henry VI*, ed. John Dover Wilson (Cambridge: Cambridge University Press, 1952), 145 n. to
II. i. 41–2.

of the two factions in Act V of the previous play, where scaffold and stake converge as accusations of treason are hurled back and forth and York dares the Lancastrian Clifford to a baiting match:

CLIFFORD   He is a traitor; let him to the Tower,
                  And chop away that factious pate of his.
QUEEN MARGARET He is arrested, but will not obey.

CLIFFORD   Why, what a brood of traitors have we here!
YORK   Look in a glass, and call thy image so.
                  I am thy king, and thou a false-heart traitor.
                  Call hither to the stake my two brave bears,
                  That with the very shaking of their chains,
                  They may astonish these fell-lurking curs.
                  [To an attendant]
                  Bid Salisbury and Warwick come to me. [Exit attendant]

        Enter the Earls of Warwick and Salisbury [with a drummer and soldiers]

CLIFFORD   Are these thy bears? We'll bait thy bears to death,
                  And manacle the bearherd in their chains,
                  If thou dar'st bring them to the baiting place.
RICHARD   Oft have I seen a hot o'erweening cur
                  Run back and bite, because he was withheld;
                  Who, being suffered with the bear's fell paw,
                  Hath clapped his tail between his legs and cried;
                  And such a piece of service will you do,
                  If you oppose yourselves to match Lord Warwick.
                                              (2 Henry VI, V. i. 132–54)

The extended conceit on baiting is sparked by Warwick's crest of 'The rampant bear chained to the ragged staff' (V. i. 201) which visibly presides over the scene because, Warwick says,

                  This day I'll wear [it] aloft my burgonet,
                  As on a mountain top the cedar shows
                  That keeps his leaves in spite of any storm,
                  Even to affright thee with the view thereof.
CLIFFORD   And from thy burgonet I'll rend thy bear,
                  And tread it under foot with all contempt,
                  Despite the bearherd that protects the bear.
                                              (2 Henry VI, V. i. 202–8)

This verbal contest, '[t]he most sustained instance of explicit bearbaiting imagery' in the Shakespearean oeuvre, 'would best be called a draw; the very duration and futility of the exchange enacts in small the military and political stalemate that this play largely dramatizes'.[40] At the same time, the bear-baiting references point up the precarious boundary between feudal order and the savagery which this order is not only incapable of suppressing but indeed keeps generating with every supposedly legitimate new claim to the throne. York, who introduces the bear-baiting trope, reserves for himself the role of the human master or 'bearherd' (V. i. 147 and 208). But the controlled violence of baiting, on one level the emblem of man's rule over brute nature (and of York's royal ascendancy over his allies, Warwick and Salisbury), turns into an image of chaotic, unruly wildness when humans take on the parts of beasts, or, more alarming still, when humans reveal their bestial nature. There is a difference between Warwick's donning his heraldic character of 'rampant bear', which is after all grounded in a chivalric code of honour (a code which is shown to retain some validity in the subsequent fight between York and Clifford), and the more sinister ursine character associated with York's offspring, the misshapen Richard. Addressing him as 'heap of wrath, foul indigested lump' (V. i. 155), young Clifford evokes the 'unlicked bear-whelp' on whom the softening influence of nurture clearly has not been bestowed. While York's call for 'my two brave bears' ostensibly refers to Warwick and Salisbury, it may also be directed at his sons; and the fiercest 'bear' unleashed in this scene is the future Duke of Gloucester and King of England, Richard III. His grim predatory callousness shows in the killing of Somerset which follows (parallel highlighting contrast) immediately upon York's victory over Clifford. While York bids farewell to his dead enemy with a conciliatory 'Peace with his soul' (V. ii. 30), his son Richard parts from his quarry with the chilling exit line: 'Priests pray for enemies, but princes kill' (V. ii. 71).[41] This is not yet the treacherous villain who will suddenly 'speak . . . out in full-throated theatricality the grandeur of his ambition'[42] in the next play. But by Part 2 of the series, he has begun to acquire what we might call an 'animal character'. As Wolfgang Clemen notes, 'the repulsive figure of the hunch-backed Richard as we see it upon the stage is repeatedly transformed into animal bodies conforming to his nature'.[43] But what exactly is his nature?

[40] Dickey, 'Shakespeare's Mastiff Comedy', 265.
[41] I am following F here, as does Roger Warren in his Oxford edition of 2 Henry VI (Oxford: Oxford University Press, 2002).
[42] Grene, Shakespeare's Serial History Plays, 123.
[43] Clemen, The Development of Shakespeare's Imagery, 51.

It is not limited to the ursine, but encompasses a whole bestiary of uncouth creatures: the 'poisonous bunch-back'd toad', 'the wolf', the 'hedgehog', the 'bottled spider', and, most frequently, the bear's canine adversary in the pit. In Queen Margaret's words to Richard's mother:

> From forth the kennel of thy womb hath crept
> A hell-hound that doth hunt us all to death:
> That dog that had his teeth before his eyes,
> To worry lambs and lap their gentle blood;
> That foul defacer of God's handiwork,
> That reigns in gallèd eyes of weeping souls;
> That excellent grand tyrant of the earth
> Thy womb let loose to chase us to our graves.
> O upright, just, and true-disposing God,
> How do I thank thee that this carnal cur
> Preys on the issue of his mother's body,
> And makes her pewfellow with others' moan.
>
> (*Richard III*, IV. iv. 47–58)

Margaret's speech recalls the circular trajectory of Richard's own fantasy of escape and re-entrapment, of hewing his way out only to be 'round impalèd' (*3 Henry VI*, III. ii. 171). Having crept forth from the kennel of the womb, the carnivorous cur returns to prey on that womb's issue, just as in yet another animal persona he has eaten himself into the very entrails of the mother country and her people:

> RICHMOND   The wretched, bloody, and usurping boar,
>   That spoils your summer fields and fruitful vines,
>   Swills your warm blood like wash, and makes his trough
>   In your inbowelled bosoms, this foul swine
>   Lies now even in the centry of this isle, ...
>
> (*Richard III*, V. ii. 7–11)

V. Adding Colours to the Chameleon

The root of all this monstrous, multiform animality is to be found in that womb to which Richard's bestial violence always seems to return him, the womb on which his own fantasy of origin is obsessively centred.[44] The misshaped, unloved child's resentment, the compensatory drive by which,

---

[44] See Adelman, *Suffocating Mothers*, 3.

'since [he] cannot prove a lover', he is 'determined to prove a villain' (*Richard III*, I. i. 28, 30), has furnished critics since Dr Johnson with obvious grounds for psychological explanation. But Richard's long soliloquy in *3 Henry VI* (III. ii. 124–95)—the longest in the whole Shakespearean canon—entwines the aetiology of trauma with another version of beginning. If, on the one hand, Richard's deformity has given him *too much* form—if it has overdetermined his body by adding the protruding 'mountain' on his back, by equipping him with very specifically misshaped extremities (a withered arm, legs of unequal size)—it has, on the other hand, not given him enough form:

> Like to a chaos, or an unlicked bear whelp
> That carries no impression like the dam.
>
> (*3 Henry VI*, III. ii. 161–2)

All three descriptors in these lines denote a lack of shape, a state of incomplete creation, or even a state prior to creation. All three show Richard not so much determined by his shape as enabled to determine it himself. Unlicked and unimpressed or unimprinted with a specific likeness—'I am like no father; . . . I am like no brother' (*3 Henry VI*, V. vi. 80–1)—the chaos that he is allows him, even compels him, to become his own creator. What the soliloquy gives us is a version of (auto-)Genesis, a warped remake of Christian humanist anthropology:

> Oh unsurpassed generosity of God the Father, Oh wondrous and unsurpassable felicity of man, to whom it is granted to have what he chooses, to be what he wills to be! The brutes, from the moment of their birth, bring with them, as Lucilius says, 'from their mother's womb' all that they will ever possess. . . . But upon man, at the moment of his creation, God bestowed seeds pregnant with all possibilities, the germs of every form of life.[45]

The spirit of grateful exultation in which Pico celebrates man's God-given incompleteness, his lack of 'any endowment properly [his] own' (p. 7), could not contrast more sharply with Richard's bitter resentment and savage self-irony. But the condition that triggers these divergent responses and the conclusions drawn from it are remarkably similar. 'Cheated of feature', 'unfinished', 'scarce half made up' (*Richard III*, I. i. 19–21), Richard does after all discover in himself a gift that will go a long way to make up for his deficiencies. It is the same gift, an unlimited potential for self-fashioning, that God bestows on Pico's Adam, and it comes under the same animal label:

---

[45] Pico, *Oration*, 8. Further references are given in text.

Who then will not look with awe upon this our chameleon, or who, at least, will look with greater admiration on any other being? This creature, man, whom Asclepius the Athenian, by reason of his very mutability, this nature capable of transforming itself, quite rightly said was symbolized...by the figure of Proteus. (p. 9)

Who, we might well ask, will not look with awe upon the hunch-backed prodigy as he suddenly bursts from his cocoon of soldierly roughness into the limitless self-multiplication of role play:

> I can add colours to the chameleon,
> Change shapes with Proteus for advantages,
> And set the murderous Machiavel to school.

> (3 Henry VI, III. ii. 191–3)

Though Richard is citing the representative of quite a different, anti-idealist branch of Italian humanism, the humanist matrix of his boasting is unmistakable, just as it is in Machiavelli's own council that the prince 'had need then be a Fox, that he may beware of the snares, and a Lion that he may scare the wolves'.[46]

The plasticity of human character envisioned in these Renaissance texts is significantly linked with notions of metamorphic animality. If in Richard's soliloquy we witness the launching not only of this particular dramatic character, but of a whole new breed of dramatic character—one endowed with a semblance of interiority, the prototype of a Hamlet or Macbeth— then it is important to note that this moment of becoming human is also crucially one of becoming animal. Evolving multiple personalities, Richard branches out into multiple animal personae as well. Proteus and the chameleon are the twin patrons of his self-creation.

The nexus here is thus very similar to what we found in *Macbeth*.[47] In both plays the traversing of human–bestial difference is construed simultaneously as exclusion and inclusion. The transgressive 'more' that propels Macbeth beyond the boundaries of the human is paradoxically also the condition for unfolding a 'more' of humanness. Richard is the

---

[46] 'Nicholas Machiavel's Prince', trans. Edward Dacres (1640), in Niccolò Machiavelli, *The Art of War, 1560* (London: David Nutt, 1905), 322.

[47] This is not to deny the obvious differences between the plays and their protagonists; the difference, for example, in tone and temper between Richard's gleeful exuberance and Macbeth's tortuous hesitation as they take the step into bestiality. 'Richard embraces the bestial difference that sets him apart from and beneath humankind. Macbeth unwillingly falls into bestiality in an effort to attain the regal difference that will raise him above beasts and other men.' Calderwood, *If It Were Done*, 93.

Shakespearean premiere of this paradox and the model for its further exploration. He, too, reveals a wider range of human potential at the very moment when he becomes bestially different.

Or rather, when he decides to make himself so. *Richard III* has been aptly characterized as 'the most stridently theatrical of all of Shakespeare's plays'.[48] The erosion of substantial human identity is already to be found, as I have argued, in Pico's oration on the dignity of man. It is taken to the second power, as it were, in Richard's thoroughly performative, thoroughly histrionic constitution of a self. A born monster, he decides to play the monster:

> The midwife wondered and the women cried
> 'O Jesus bless us, he is born with teeth!'—
> And so I was, which plainly signified
> That I should snarl and bite and *play* the dog.
>
> (*3 Henry VI*, V. vi .74–7; my italics)

One place for the monstrous in early modern culture is the wonder-cabinet or *Wunderkammer*. Strange to us and already dismissed as 'frivolous impostures' by Francis Bacon, these collections exhibited marvels without proper context, or, as Steven Mullaney puts it, 'things on holiday' in an 'order without hierarchy or degree . . . in which kings mingle with clowns, or at least the props of their respective stations do'.[49] Something of a holiday frivolousness attaches to the progress of Shakespeare's most monstrous mingler of king with clown, Richard the ham-actor, the hunch-backed hyperbole, the prancing hellhound who is duly baited and bagged.

But the monster, especially the monstrous birth, is also, as the Latin root of the word (*monere*) indicates, a sign whose purpose it is to remind and admonish, 'a manifestation of God's wrath about the sins of the world'.[50] And it is in this role that Richard, for all his distortion, becomes the perfect mirror for majesty. Hamming it up, out-monstering, as it were, his own monstrosity, he reveals kingship to its own truth: as the precarious theatricality of 'one set on a skaffold, whose smallest actions and gestures, all the people gazingly doe behold'.

---

[48] Neill, 'Shakespeare's Halle of Mirrors', 99.

[49] Mullaney, *Place of the Stage*, 62.

[50] Jan C. Westerhoff, 'A World of Signs: Baroque Pansemioticism, the *Polyhistor* and the Early Modern *Wunderkammer*', *Journal of the History of Ideas*, 62 (2001), 633–50 at 648; see also Lorraine Daston and Katherine Park, *Wonders and the Order of Nature 1150–1750* (New York: Zone Books, 1998).

3

'More than a creeping thing':
Baiting Coriolanus

T he hunt comes first: it precedes 'training or taming' in Derrida's list of
ways in which man may be perceived as 'being-after' the animal.[1]
Images of hunting strongly reinforce the proximity of Shakespeare's human
stage to the animal stage of the baiting arena, a sense of the theatre 'being
after' animals. Both Macbeth and Richard III meet their doom in situations
that evoke hunting as well as baiting.[2] And so does Talbot in *1 Henry VI* as
he makes his last stand against the French:

TALBOT How are we parked and rounded in a pale!—
         A little herd of England's timorous deer
         Mazed with a yelping kennel of French curs.
         If we be English deer, be then in blood,
         Not rascal-like to fall down with a pinch,
         But rather, moody-mad and desperate stags,
         Turn on the bloody hounds with heads of steel
         And make the cowards stand aloof at bay.
         Sell every man his life as dear as mine
         And they shall find dear deer of us, my friends.   (IV. ii. 45–54)

While Talbot employs a straightforward image of the prey resisting the
hunter, he is also exhorting his men to put on a performance much like
those of the bear-pit. The overlap of hunting and baiting is particularly
pronounced in *Coriolanus*. It is closely bound up with the way in which the
play's protagonist emerges as both contained and uncontainable by the

---

[1] Derrida, *The Animal*, 10.
[2] For a discussion of Shakespeare and hunting, see Edward Berry, *Shakespeare and the Hunt*
(Cambridge: Cambridge University Press, 2001).

bounds of common humanity and social order. Like stage and stake, hunting and baiting are joined by what I have called synopsis or double vision. To illustrate this, I will begin this chapter with a look at a hunting scene in a different medium.[3]

I

There is a painting of a bear-hunt in the Bavarian State Collections[4] by the Flemish artist Frans Snyders (1579–1657) (Fig. 8), a disciple of Pieter Brueghel the Younger and contemporary of Rubens who specialized in animals, dead or alive. His opulent still lifes expertly capture the various textures of their feathers and furs. His hunting pieces, praised for being 'done so naturally from life',[5] show the animals 'at their highest pitch and passion'.[6] In the artist's lifetime, they 'were the glory of princely collections',[7] earning him lucrative commissions, even from King Philip IV of Spain. Rubens, the 'prince of painters', employed Snyders to paint animals in some of his own hunting pieces. Snyders, in turn, enlisted the help of colleagues such as Cornelis de Vos, Jan Boeckhorst, or the young van Dyck[8] for human figures—huntsman, kitchen maid, or biblical personage—in his own compositions.

No human extras appear on the canvas of Snyders' *Bear-Hunt*.[9] Unadulterated wildlife, the beasts are left entirely to themselves. Or so it seems. Snyders certainly could have painted the dogs without collars. But he chose not to omit the tag, the sign of their absent master. The wildness of the fight

---

[3] An earlier version of this chapter was presented in a session on 'Defining the Human: Man–Animal Relations in Literature' at the German Anglistentag 2007 in Münster. I would like to thank Stefan Welz and Anne-Julia Zwierlein for inviting me to speak there.

[4] Bayerische Staatsgemäldesammlungen, Munich, Inv. No.1267.

[5] Cornelis de Bie, *Het Gulden Cabinet* (1662), quoted in Susan Koslow, *Frans Snyders: The Noble Estate: Seventeenth-Century Still-Life and Animal Painting in the Southern Netherlands* (Antwerp: Fonds Mercator Paribas, 1995), 219. The standard catalogue raisonné is Hella Robels, *Frans Snyders, Stilleben- und Tiermaler, 1579–1657* (Munich: Deutscher Kunstverlag, 1989).

[6] Arnold Houbraken, *De Groote Schouburgh der Nederlandtsche Konstschilders en Schilderessen* (1719), quoted in Koslow, Frans Snyders, 219.

[7] Koslow, *Frans Snyders*, 219.

[8] The portraits of Frans Snyders and his wife Margareta de Vos are among van Dyck's most impressive early achievements.

[9] David Rosand, 'Rubens's Munich *Lion Hunt*: Its Sources and Significance', *Art Bulletin*, 51 (1969), 29–40 at 39 n. 73, contends that 'Snyders' battles between hounds and boar have all the immediate fascination of a cock fight; they totally lack the heroic spirit of human commitment implicit in all Rubens's hunts'. Koslow, *Frans Snyders*, 252, argues convincingly against this.

Figure 8. Frans Snyders, 'The Bear Hunt'.

is thus discreetly marked as a wildness divided. The dogs may be no less ferocious than the wild bears, but their ferocity is conditional. It is predicated on their tameness, a 'natural' property reinforced and regulated through domestication. The title *Bear-Hunt* leaves no doubt as to who is being hunted, but is less explicit about who is doing the hunting. On the visible face of it, the dogs. Their frenzied assault is presented as an entirely unprompted outburst of what the early modern animal expert Gervase Markham calls their 'natural instinct of enmity'.[10] What we don't see is the hunter who has set the dogs on, the master acting by proxy, unleashing a wildness he has learned to control. Man, though absent, invisibly presides over the scene. He is 'behind it', in the sense of having caused it, just as he is 'before it', the observer for whose benefit the spectacle has been arranged. The painting's evocation of wild nature is thus inscribed in a framework of hierarchical order, endorsing both the ascendancy of man over beast and a stratified society in which hunting was a prerogative of the nobility.[11]

---

[10] Cf. Gervase Markham, *Countrey contentments . . .* (London: R. Jackson, 1615), 3.

[11] Koslow, *Frans Snyders*, 224, points out that interest in the 'noble hunt' was reawakened for political reasons in Brabant in the second decade of the 17th c.: 'Sponsored largely by the archdukes as an element of their policy to restore the splendor of the court and to legitimate an independent state, a romantic evocation of the antiquity of the Netherlands was encouraged. The noble hunt . . . , which suited this policy, was a sign of feudal privilege . . .'. It also provided the new aristocracy with occasions to display its wealth conspicuously and to affiliate itself with the ancient privileged class of knights.

'Stagey' is an adjective much in favour with art critics as a term of abuse. Snyders's *Bear-Hunt* would seem to invite it. There is something undeniably theatrical about its grasp of space, the way the animals are strung across the canvas in a frieze. There is also the fact that there are two bears, not just one. The studied variation of their double act—two virtuoso performers posed side by side—can hardly fail to prompt a sense of contrivedness. The impression of stageyness is compounded when we turn from Snyders's original to a copy from his own workshop in the German Museum of Hunting and Fishing in Munich.[12] The heightened symmetry does not improve the composition. With each bear occupying one-half of the picture it looks almost as though the artist had joined two originally separate studies. The copyist—or, perhaps more likely, an owner who clipped the canvas to make it fit a smaller frame—dispenses with all but the barest traces of landscape. The open meadows and copse that provide some perspectival depth in the left-hand corner of Snyders's original have almost completely disappeared. What remains is a no-place in front of a dull backdrop, a bare shallow stage.

The copy exaggerates, and thereby alerts us to, a theatricality that is perhaps not so much a flaw as an essential quality of the piece. 'Stagey', then, no longer quite works as a term of censure. If the impression of a stage is, as it were, the mould in which the whole composition is cast, it makes little sense to treat it as a fault. To say that the painting quite literally represents a stage would perhaps overstate the case, but only just. The setting may not quite be a stage, but neither is it quite a landscape. The painting merges two frames of reference. And so does the German title of the Munich copy, *Bärenhatz*: the word means both 'bear-hunt' and 'bear-baiting'. In the imagination of the painter and his early modern audience the two would be inextricably entwined.

We find this associative linking of the two corroborated in a pictorial compendium of hunting techniques which another Flemish-born painter, Jan van der Straet (aka Johannes Stradanus or Giovanni Stradano), published in 1578.[13] Stradanus was an important source for seventeenth-century

---

[12] Deutsches Jagd- und Fischereimuseum, Munich, Inv. No. G 82; No. 5027.

[13] Johannes Stradanus, *Venationes Ferarum* (Antwerp, 1578; repr. Hildesheim: Georg Olms, 2000). Born in Bruges in 1523, van der Straet had joined the Antwerp painters' guild of Saint Luke by 1545 (Snyders and Rubens became members later) before permanently moving to Italy, where he lived, mostly in Florence, up to his death in 1605. The *Venationes* reproduce the designs Stradanus had originally executed for a series of tapestries adorning the palace of his patron Cosimo de' Medici at Poggio a Caiano.

Subdit calcar equo pernix venator, acuto
Splendida per campos iactans venabula ferro:

Dum se praecipitem media rotat Ursus arena,
Stridentesq; virum circum se discutit hastas. . 1.

Figure 9. Engraving in Jan van der Straet's *Venationes Ferarum* (Antwerp, 1578).

painters of hunting scenes like Snyders. Four of his fifty-two copperplate engravings show varieties of bear-hunting, and it seems no coincidence that in the Latin captions of two of those (but in no other caption in the whole volume) the term 'arena' appears (Fig. 9).[14] The bear surrounded by hunters and their dogs 'rotates (*rotat*) in the arena' just as he would in a baiting ring.[15]

The spectacle of the hunt almost automatically, it seems, conjures up its theatrical double, just as this double mimics the configuration of a hunt. At least since Roman Antiquity, bears were not only hunted but tormented for entertainment. In England, where huntable bears had become extinct well before the Norman Conquest, the bear-fight had completely replaced the

[14] Only in Stradanus' plate of a bull-fight is hunting completely supplanted by a baiting spectacle.

[15] Translated literally, 'ursus se rotat [in] arena' could be rendered as 'the bear rolls in the sand'. But the theatrical meaning of arena is borne out by the provenance of Stradanus' two-line hexameter:

> Sic capitur gladiis et acutae cuspidis hastis
> Praeceps sanguinea dum se rotat ursus arena.

This is a verbatim quotation from Martial's *Liber spectaculorum,* a book of epigrams written for the inauguration of the Amphitheatrum Flavianum, better known as the Colosseum. I am grateful to Claudia Wiener for her expertise on this point.

bear-hunt. But the memory of their ancient kinship remained culturally active, as in the famous entertainment the Earl of Leicester arranged for the Queen at Kenilworth Castle in 1575, where a day of stag-hunting was followed by a day of bear-baiting, and a lavish masque was to have paid homage to the Queen in the guise of Diana, chaste goddess of the hunt, had not bad weather intervened. 'It was a sport very pleasant of theez beastz', notes the chronicler,

> to see the bear with his pink nyez [= eyes] leering after hiz enmiez approch, the nimblness and wayt of the dog to take hiz avauntage, and the fors and experiens of the bear again to avoid the assauts. If he wear bitten in one place, hoow he woold pynch in an oother to get free: that if he wear taken onez, then what shyft, with byting, with clawying, with roring, tossing and tumbling, he woold work too wynd himself from them: and when he waz lose, to shake his ears twyse or thryse with the blud and the slaver about his fiznamy, was a matter of goodly relief.[16]

What the chronicler so graphically describes in writing translates easily into the pictorial idiom of Snyders's art. The 'goodly relief' registered in the Kenilworth report stems from and appeals to the same mentality that would appreciate Snyders's gorgeously violent hunting scene.

There is a further similarity, perhaps the most crucial one. The painting, as we have remarked, derives its dramatic effect from a vanishing act. Except for the dogs' telltale collars, human agency is invisibilized. The same happens in the report. It begins with the matter-of-fact statement that on '*Thursday, the foourteenth of this July*, and the syxth day of her Majestyez cumming, a great sort of *Bandogs*[17] whear thear tyed in the utter Coourt, and thyrteen *Bearz* in the inner.'[18] That said, a remarkable change occurs. Abruptly—from one sentence to the next—the text unfetters the creatures tied up in the inner and outer courtyards. No longer pieces in a game played by humans, they suddenly seem to pursue an agenda all their own and even, in doing so, acquire a personality:

---

[16]   Robert Laneham, 'A Letter: Whearin, part of the Entertainment, untoo the Queenz Majesty, at Killingworth Castl, in Warwik Sheer, in this Soomerz Progress, 1575, iz signified . . .', in *The Progresses and Public Processions of Queen Elizabeth*, ed. John Nichols, vol. 1 (London: J. Nichols and Son, 1823), 420–84 at 439–40.

[17]   The editor, John Nichols, annotates: 'Bewick describes the Ban-dog as being a variety of the mastiff, but lighter, smaller, and more vigilant; although at the same time not so powerful. . . . The bite of a Ban-dog is keen, and considered dangerous; and its attack is usually made upon the flank. Dogs of this kind are now rarely to be met with.' Bandogs are also described in Caius, *Of Englishe Dogges*, 25–8.

[18]   Laneham, 'A Letter', 438.

A wight of great wizdom and gravitee seemed their [the bears'] forman to be, had it cum to a Jury: but it fell oout that they wear cauzd too appeer thear upon no such matter, but onlie too aunswear too an auncient quarrell between them and the Bandogs, in a cause of controversy that hath long depended, been obstinatly full often debated with sharp and byting arguments a both sydes, and coold never be decided, grown noow too so marveyloous a mallys, that with spitefull obrayds and uncharitabl chaffings alweiz they freat, az far az any whear the ton can heer, see, or smell the toother: and indeed at utterly deadly fohod [enmity].[19]

The text not only naturalizes an antagonism that is stage-managed by humans but, interestingly, also historicizes it. The quarrel is said to be 'ancient'. Bears and bandogs acquire the status of feuding houses breaking from ancient grudge to new mutiny. The narrative relies on troping—double troping, to be precise. In addition to turning animals into quasi-humans, it turns physical violence into a trial in a court of law. The writer palpably delights in his own dexterity at troping as well as in the spectacle thus troped. His obtrusive anthropomorphism operates on the same principle as Snyders's more subtly anthropomorphic *Bear-Hunt*. In the painting as in the text, it is the elision of human agency that allows the animals to become actors in a *theatrum humanum*.

II

In their different media, Snyders's dramatic hunting-piece, the Kenilworth baiting-show, and its textual representation provide stages for animals 'acting as' humans. But the widespread, well-nigh ubiquitous, signifying practice which these examples illustrate is not one-way. With equal ease, actors in the early modern London playhouses negotiated the species crossover in the opposite direction, projecting the creatures from the baiting-ring onto the stage of the wooden O. In *The Tragedy of Coriolanus*, the permeability of the line between man and beast proves crucial to the play's probing of the body politic and the transgressive force of the heroic individual.[20] If *Coriolanus* has been characterized as a debate rather than a tragedy,[21] it is a debate

    [19] Laneham, 'A Letter', 439.
    [20] For an excellent discussion of animal images in *Coriolanus* along similar lines, see Pfister, 'Animal Images'.
    [21] D. J. Enright, '*Coriolanus*: Tragedy or Debate?', *Essays in Criticism*, 4 (1954), 1–19.

that very much resembles the one between the bears and the bandogs in the account of the Kenilworth festivities. Shakepeare's play reverses the anthropomorphism of that account. The controversy between the senate and the people of Rome has also 'long depended, been obstinatly full often debated with sharp and byting arguments a both sydes, and cool never be decided'.[22] But while the Kenilworth chronicler cloaks the animals in mock-humanity, the 'auncient quarrell' in Shakespeare's Rome turns men into beasts:

CORIOLANUS   Are these your herd?
    Must these have voices, that can yield them now
    And straight disclaim their tongues? What are your offices?
    You being their mouths, why rule you not their teeth?
    Have you not set them on?   (III. i. 35–9)

At issue are 'voices', the votes of the people. But in Coriolanus' diatribe the tribunes as the people's spokesmen turn into dog keepers, teeth replacing tongues as organs of oral communication.[23] In Shakespeare's Roman class struggle the mouth is the central organ of the body politic. In a fight over food and votes, the instrument of speech serves equally well for barking and biting. The 'spitefull obrayds and uncharitabl chaffings' that ensue whenever the protagonist encounters his plebeian adversaries are as much instinct-driven and beyond rational control as the behaviour of the bears and the bandogs each time 'the ton can heer, see, or smell the toother'. Three turbulent quarrel scenes mark the opening, the turning point, and the finale of the play (I. iii; III. iii; V. vi). All three are variants of the same basic configuration, showing a single imposing figure pitted against a crowd of opponents: a powerful individual attacked by a pack, or 'cry',[24] of lesser creatures. All three, in other words, replicate the model bear-baiting.[25]

---

[22] Laneham, 'A Letter', 439.

[23] Should Coriolanus become consul, the tribunes warn their clientele, he would 'make them of no more voice / Than dogs that are as often beat for barking / As therefore kept to do so' (II. iii. 215–17). For an illuminating analysis of the use of modals in the play's battle of voices, see Alysia Kolentsis, ' "Mark you / His absolute shall?": Multitudinous Tongues and Contested Words in *Coriolanus*', *Shakespeare Survey*, 62 (2009), 141–50.

[24] The term, now rare, occurs twice in the play: III. iii. 124 'cry of curs'; IV. vi. 155–6, Menenius berating the tribunes: 'You have made good work, / You and your cry.'

[25] Conversely, the baiting show could easily be read as a zoomorphic version of the class struggle in *Coriolanus*: '[T]he torture and killing of animals permitted those who had no rights . . . to demonstrate, often publicly, their strength and dominance. When men who were accustomed to being thrashed and abused could watch the chained bull harried by a pack of dogs,

Menenius' patrician contempt for the starving plebeians finds appropriate expression in the animal most readily associated with the raiding of hoarded-up corn: 'Rome and her rats are at the point of battle' (I. i. 160).[26] But when Martius addresses the people, his term of abuse pushes the scene of battle towards the baiting ring: 'What would you have, you curs' (I. i. 166), and again: 'You common cry of curs' (III. iii. 124). While 'Rome and her rats' suggests numerical balance through alliteration, 'curs' implies one against many. In calling the people 'curs', Coriolanus defines his own role as that of their solitary antagonist. If they are dogs, he must be the bear. By bestializing them he also bestializes himself. 'He is himself alone, / To answer all the city' (I. iv. 22–3), one of the Roman soldiers exclaims when Martius is swallowed up by the gates of Corioli, single-handedly attacking the Volscian army. But the sentence applies equally to his position within his own city. Throughout the play, being outnumbered by the enemy is the defining mark of his heroism, the condition by which he identifies himself. Well before his heroic exploit at Corioli, he threatens to perform a similar single-handed feat inside the walls of Rome:

> Would the nobility lay aside their ruth
> And let me use my sword, I'd make a quarry
> With thousands of these quartered slaves as high
> As I could pitch my lance.   (I. i. 195–8)

Compared with this, his later boast, 'On fair ground / I could beat forty of them' (III. i. 241–2), sounds almost faint-hearted.[27] The final manifestation of heroic self-assertion against impossible odds occurs in the last scene of the play. Surrounded by a hostile crowd of Volscians, who were formerly said

---

it was like seeing the authority of the master torn apart by the mob.' Coral Lansbury, *The Old Brown Dog: Women, Workers and Vivisection in Edwardian England* (Madison, Wis. and London: University of Wisconsin Press, 1985), 32. For this and other social tropings of bear-baiting, see Fudge, *Perceiving Animals*, 15–20.

[26] This is taken up in Martius' cynical remark, later in the scene: 'The Volsces have much corn; take these rats thither / To gnaw their garners' (I. i. 249–50).

[27] The full excess of Coriolanus' self-centred singularity is unleashed when the tribune Sicinius dares to call him traitor:

> Call me their traitor, thou injurious tribune?
> Within thine eyes sat twenty thousand deaths,
> In thy hands clutched as many millions, in
> Thy lying tongue both numbers, I would say
> 'Thou liest' unto thee   (III. iii. 72–6)

to shun him 'As children from a bear' (I. iii. 33), Martius once again performs the part of the baited bear cornered by a pack of hounds. Aufidius, no longer singled out as his alter ego, merges into the crowd. Previously 'a lion' that Coriolanus was 'proud to hunt' (I. i. 235–6), he now becomes 'this cur' (V. vi. 108) and 'False hound' (V. vi. 113). In the teeth of such opposition—the phrase is to be taken almost literally here—Martius utters his ultimate challenge, recalling the deed which earned him the title Coriolanus: 'Alone I did it' (V. vi. 117) The crowd's response could not be more in character: 'Tear him to pieces!' (V. vi. 121) they shout. And the hero's downfall is appropriately ratified in a hunting tableau. As the Folio stage direction has it: '*Auffidius stands on him*'.

III

With so many references to animals, hunting, and baiting, it is perhaps inevitable that the zoomorphism of the play should occasionally rub off on the rhetoric of its critics. Coriolanus, declares G. Wilson Knight, 'is proud as a lion might be proud among jackals', and he adds: 'But that is no reason why jackals should tolerate a lion in their midst.'[28] This was written nearly eighty years ago, and the 'natural' ease with which the critic slips into animal simile has a distinctly dated sound. While confirming Lévi-Strauss's much-quoted dictum that 'animals are good to think with',[29] it also shows that the ways in which we 'think with' animals change considerably over time.[30] Proud lions and ignoble jackals are less likely to be encountered with such blithe assertiveness in critical writing today.[31] Wilson Knight's 'animal kingdom' replicates human class structure and remains contained within undisputed species boundaries. The legitimate form of trade across these

---

[28] G. Wilson Knight, 'The Royal Occupation: An Essay on *Coriolanus*', in his *The Imperial Theme* (1931; repr. London: Methuen, 1963), 154–98 at 184.

[29] Claude Lévi-Strauss, *Totemism*, trans. Rodney Needham (London: Merlin, 1964), 89. Lévi-Strauss formulated this observation with regard to aboriginal society, but as Rod Preece, *Awe for the Tiger, Love for the Lamb: A Chronicle of Sensibility to Animals* (Vancouver and Toronto: University of British Columbia Press, 2002), 364 n. 38, rightly points out, both Christopher Smart in 1720 and Victor Hugo in 1862 expressed the same idea with regard to humanity in general.

[30] Cf. Daston and Mitman, 'Introduction', 1–13.

[31] There is no lack of evidence, however, that this type of emblematic 'thinking with animals' maintains its hold on the popular imagination. Cf. Steve Baker, *Picturing the Beast: Animals, Identity, and Representation* (Urbana, Ill. and Chicago: University of Illinois Press, 1993).

boundaries is allegorical *likening*,[32] simile being the accepted currency between the figurative and the literal. Thus Wilson Knight's lion and jackals
operate under the same rhetorical principle as does the belly in Menenius'
fable:

MENENIUS   The belly answered—
[FIRST] CITIZEN   Well, sir, what answer made the belly?
MENENIUS   Sir, I shall tell you. With a kind of smile,
                     Which ne'er came from the lungs, but even thus—[33]
                     For look you, I may make the belly smile
                     As well as speak—it tauntingly replied
                     To th' discontented members, the mutinous parts
                     That envied his receipt; even so most fitly
                     As you malign our senators for that
                     They are not such as you.   (I. i. 103–12)

Menenius explicates the rules of his language game—quite unnecessarily, as
it turns out. As the second citizen's impatient response shows, his audience
is equally adept at it:

[FIRST] CITIZEN   Your belly's answer—what?
                     The kingly crownèd head, the vigilant eye,
                     The counsellor heart, the arm our soldier,
                     Our steed the leg, the tongue our trumpeter,
                     With other muniments and petty helps
                     In this our fabric, if that they—
MENENIUS   What then?
                     Fore me, this fellow speaks! What then? What then?
SECOND CITIZEN Should by the cormorant belly be restrained
                     Who is the sink o' th' body—   (I. i. 112–19)

The mechanics of likening, of allegorizing body parts as well as animals, is a
recognized technique shared by both parties in this rhetorical contest. It is
part of a common political discourse, part of the *polis*, the *res publica*, and as
such never employed without losing sight of its figurative nature:

MENENIUS   Pray you, who does the wolf love?
SICINIUS   The lamb.
MENENIUS   Ay, to devour him, as the hungry plebeians would the noble
                     Martius.

---

[32] Cf. Robert N. Watson, 'As You Liken It: Simile in the Wilderness', *Shakespeare Survey*, 56
(2003), 79–92.
[33] The deictic 'thus' requires the actor to perform as well as mention this belly smile.

BRUTUS   He's a lamb indeed, that baas like a bear.
MENENIUS He's a bear indeed, that lives like a lamb.   (II. i. 7–12)

This is a thoroughly domesticated animality. Rather than narrowing the categorical gap between the human and the non-human, it is predicated upon that gap and serves to maintain it. But the tragic action transcends the limits of this discourse. The more Coriolanus' uncompromising singularity threatens to disrupt the very fabric of the city, the less the city's customary representational mode of animal troping is able to contain him. His exceptionality pushes him towards a 'zone of indistinction'[34] where man and beast are not categorically segregated but continuous.

Coriolanus' position presents a paradox. He is at the centre of the conflict between patricians and plebeians but at the same time outside it; he is both crucially involved in Rome's political struggle and a figure beyond politics. Two planes of conflict intersect in him. On the political plane, the conflict can be, and is indeed, solved with surprising ease. All that is required is to remove Coriolanus from it. The instant he is banished, peace ensues: 'the world goes well ... Our tradesmen singing in their shops and going / About their functions friendly' (IV. vi. 5–9). The factions have become reconciled to the status quo. Menenius, as Sicinius remarks, 'is grown most kind of late' (IV. vi. 11) and does not hesitate to agree with the tribunes that 'All's well' (IV. vi. 17). Ever the pragmatist, he has come to terms with the system of checks and balances consolidated in the office of the tribunate. That way republican progress lies. There is no such coming to terms with Martius. A deeper divide than that between the two factions alienates him from the city. It flares up in his defiant—and more than just a little ridiculous—response to his expulsion from Rome: 'I banish *you*' (III. iii. 127, my italics). From this moment on, Coriolanus is no longer a member of either party but a stranger to both:

BRUTUS   There's no more to be said, but he is banished
          As enemy to the people and his country.   (III. iii. 121–2)

For once, the tribune, his party bias notwithstanding, is speaking for the republic as a whole, for a Rome in which the time for heroes is irrevocably past. The necessity of expelling the noblest—or at least, the most Roman—

---

[34] See Giorgio Agamben, *Homo Sacer: Sovereign Power and Bare Life*, trans. Daniel Heller-Roazen (Stanford: Stanford University Press, 1998), 181. Agamben speaks of 'the state of exception as zone of indistinction between outside and inside, exclusion and inclusion'. Coriolanus' exceptionality constitutes a very similar coincidence of opposites.

Roman of them all is dictated by a logic of inversion: Coriolanus becomes untenable precisely because he, more than anyone else, embodies *Romanitas*. The force he personifies is both at the root of and opposed to the commonwealth; it is embedded in the very basis of the city but outlawed by civic jurisdiction. His banishment serves to highlight the crucial link between citizenship and human status. Within the city, what is 'human' and what is 'beast' is held apart by an assertion of categorical difference. The political rhetoric of animal analogizing does not undermine but confirms this difference. Assurance of citizenship, the confident discrimination between 'us' and 'them', underwrites the exercise of 'likening'. Once the status of citizenship is revoked, distinctions begin to blur. The banned man is not just *like* an animal but in danger of becoming one.[35] But in Coriolanus' case this slippage, though exacerbated by his expulsion, precedes it. It is not so much caused by as the cause of his banishment. Even when still in Rome and a citizen, he overstrains the measure of civility, the limits of what the city can afford to credit as human.

IV

According to Aristotle, 'someone who cannot live in the community or, because he is sufficient unto himself, has no need of it, is not a member of a state and therefore either a beast or a god'.[36] Aristotle's exclusion of the non-social from the human is the necessary consequence of his definition of man as a *zôon politikón* (an animal fit or meant for the state). It accurately positions Shakespeare's Roman hero. The play presents him not as a political animal, but rather as an animal caught up in politics. 'There was in campe', begins the introduction of Coriolanus in Philemon Holland's English rendering of Livy, 'one *Caius Martius*, a Noble yoong gentleman, right politicke of advise, active besides, and tall of his hands, who afterwards was surnamed *Coriolanus*.'[37] Nothing could be further from Shakespeare's protagonist than the first quality attributed to him in this account. Not only does he

---

[35] Agamben's term 'bare life' entails just that. See Agamben, *Homo Sacer*, 1–12.
[36] Aristotle, *Politics*, 1253[a].
[37] *The Romane Historie Written by T. Livius*, trans. Philemon Holland (1600), quoted in *Narrative and Dramatic Sources of Shakespeare*, v: *The Roman Plays*, ed. Geoffrey Bullough (London: Routledge and Kegan Paul; New York: Columbia University Press, 1964), 498.

conspicuously lack any awareness of political expediency, he is, in a sense, the very antithesis of politics itself. The first mention of his name elicits the comment: 'He's a very dog to the commonalty' (I. i. 27). It is his implacable anti-social fierceness that turns citizens into curs (I. i. 166). His insults contrast sharply with Menenius' 'my countrymen' and 'Why masters, my good friends, mine honest neighbours' (I. i. 53, 60). Though not proving Menenius' 'honesty',[38] these forms of address to the citizens attest his participation in a discourse which makes conflict negotiable and thus integral to the workings of the state. Martius is 'naturally' incapable of this. Perhaps his nature is, as Menenius claims, 'too noble for this world' (III. i. 255). But first and foremost he signally lacks the attribute by which Aristotelian anthropology distinguishes man from beast: reason. His characteristic frame of mind is one of uncontrolled rage. This is the raw energy that bestializes itself and draws its counterforce from a bestialized mob, the monstrous multitude (II. iii. 9–24),[39] the 'Hydra' (III. i. 96), 'the multitudinous tongue' (III. i. 159), the 'herd' (III. i. 34), 'the beast with many heads' (IV. i. 1–2), the 'rats' that, unless kept in check, '[w]ould feed on one another' (I. i. 186), the

> common cry of curs, whose breath I hate
> As reek o' th' rotten fens   (III. iii. 124–5)

In the orchestration of the play, Coriolanus' rage is accompanied by voices of reason—some benign, some wily—figures that assume the role of tamer, keeper or, warden. 'Be calm, be calm' (III. i. 39) is Menenius' characteristic response to one of Coriolanus' outbursts: 'Let's be calm' (III. i. 60) and: 'Not now, not now' (III. i. 66). The first senator concurs: 'Not in this heat, sir, now' (III. i. 67). All these and the many more attempts to placate his anger are, of course, to no avail. Volumnia, another 'keeper' figure, draws a crucial distinction between her own and her son's temper:

> I have a heart as little apt [i.e. yielding, compliant] as yours,
> But yet a brain that leads my use of anger
> To better vantage.   (III. ii. 27–9)

[38] As regards honesty, the play shows that First Citizen couldn't be wider of the mark: 'He [Menenius]'s one honest enough. Would all the rest were so!' (I. i. 51–2).

[39] In this passage, however, the citizens themselves bring up this idea and, by reflecting it, distance themselves from it.

Only his enemies the tribunes, the keepers or 'herdsmen of the beastly plebeians' (II. i. 93), know how to use Coriolanus' anger to advantage and thus assume the part of ringmasters. Untameable, but—precisely because of this—predictable, the hero's wrath is an instinctual reflex, as certain as the bears' response whenever they 'can hear, see, or smell' the bandogs and as easily set off:

BRUTUS   If, as his nature is, he fall in rage
          With their refusal, both observe and answer
          The vantage of his anger.   (II. iii. 258–60)

In Renaissance writing, we are accustomed to find man placed halfway between god and beast on a vertical scale. This seems in full accord with my quotation from Aristotle. But the quotation accords at least as well, if not better, with a scale that places man not *between* but opposite god and beast. Coriolanus is much closer to this scheme than to the vertical scale of the *dignitas* tracts. The god-like and the bestial are inextricably entwined in him. Where he exceeds human limitations he does not move towards anything even remotely like the purified spirituality of neo-Platonic idealism. The divinity ascribed to him rather points to something much more archaic envisaged not as a turning away from but as a turning into the animal:

MENENIUS This Martius is grown from man to dragon. He has wings; he's more
              than a creeping thing....
          When he walks, he moves like an engine, and the ground shrinks
              before his treading....
          He wants nothing of a god but eternity and a heaven to throne in.
                                        (V. iv. 112–14; 18–20; 23–5)

The hero of mythology is typically a slayer of dragons and other monstrous beasts. But by a logic of what we might call totemistic identification the hero also partakes of the beast's nature. Coriolanus' heroism perpetuates some of this archaic bond. There is an inhuman quality to his superhuman exploits. They exalt, but also exclude him, make him strange:

COMINIUS   Who's yonder,
          That does appear as he were flayed? O gods!
          He has the stamp of Martius,   (I. vii. 21–3)

The moment is brief but telling. When Coriolanus is literally most in his element—re-emerging from Corioli 'from face to foot ... a thing of blood' (II. ii. 108–9)—his own general fails to recognize him. He is as alien as he is admirable, a creature so wild even his friends can only talk to him if they tie him up (although Cominius is, of course, joking here):

> If 'gainst yourself you be incensed, we'll put you,
> Like one that means his proper harm, in manacles,
> Then reason safely with you.   (I. x. 55–7)

His very lack of rational control associates Coriolanus with Hercules, whose wrath, as Eugene M. Waith points out, is of a more primitive, more rigorous, and hence more godlike quality than even that of Achilles. 'In Hercules', Waith writes, 'the core of primitive strength, never completely transmuted by the refining power of more civilized ideals, is touched with the strangeness and mystery which belong to a demigod.'[40] Coriolanus is explicitly compared with Hercules in the play.[41] He signally answers Waith's description of the demigod-hero's fundamental ambivalence: 'His exploits are strange mixtures of beneficence and crime, of fabulous quests and shameful betrayals.'[42]

Shakespeare's *Tragedy of Coriolanus* situates itself at the interface between myth and history. The same could be said of his other Roman tragedy, *Julius Caesar*, except that the two plays proceed in opposite directions. In *Julius Caesar* we see history passing into myth—a myth that in turn becomes a crucial factor of historical change—as the stabbing of Caesar's body results in the release and ever-growing momentum of what the play calls Caesar's 'spirit'.[43] In *Coriolanus*, myth as embodied in the figure of the hero comes first; it is residual, a relic of a pre-historic past which is now becoming obsolete. As Rome passes *into* history, the mythical hero, incompatible with the republican order, is passed *over*. In the cold light of rational assessment, his incommensurable exceptionality simply evaporates. Brutus the tribune has an obituary ready which, though it is somewhat premature in Act IV, stands a good chance of eventually becoming the official history-book version:

---

[40] Eugene M. Waith, *The Herculean Hero in Marlowe, Chapman, Shakespeare and Dryden* (London: Chatto and Windus, 1962), 17.

[41] In IV. i. 17 Coriolanus praises his mother as a quasi-Herculean heroine; in IV. vi. 104 Menenius envisages him shaking Rome 'about the ears' 'As Hercules did shake down mellow fruit'. The allusion is to the eleventh of Hercules' labours, the fetching of the golden apples from the garden of the Hesperides, which were guarded by a dragon.

[42] Waith, *Herculean Hero*, 16.

[43] I will return to this point below, Ch. 6.

> Caius Martius was
> A worthy officer i' th' war, but insolent,
> O'ercome with pride, ambitious past all thinking,
> Self-loving   (IV. vi. 31–4)

'A worthy officer' completely demystifies the hero, cutting him down to normal human size, amputating anything smacking of either god or beast, let alone god-and-beast.[44]

While the tribunes represent the new order, Coriolanus evokes foundations. His name, Martius, pays homage to Mars, patron god of the city and progenitor of its founders, Romulus and Remus, the twins suckled by a 'thirsty she-wolf' (*lupa sitiens* in Livy). Something of their fraternal, and fratricidal, bond haunts Martius' relation to Aufidius. Hercules, too, his other 'patron', has a hand in Rome's beginnings. His killing of Cacus inscribes another, even older, murder story in the city's 'book of foundations'. In Michel Serres's sifting of these mythical origins, murder precedes murder as the quintessential founding act of a Rome which ceaselessly repeats its foundation and never stops killing. Passing through Latium with a herd of oxen, Hercules falls asleep. Cacus, a local herdsman, steals the oxen and, pulling them by the tail, leads them backward into his cavern 'so that their tracks are turned only toward the outside'. On awaking, Hercules discovers the theft, reads the tracks, and is fooled by Cacus' trick. But as he is about to leave, the oxen start bellowing. Hercules enters the cave, slays Cacus, and is pardoned by king Evander, a wise man credited with the invention of writing. He recognizes the demigod and builds him an altar. Just as 'Gods pass by before the kings',[45] beasts precede the human and the historical in Serres's account:

> Well before the writing of Evander—of man, of the good man, of historical man, who is accomplished because he writes—the sacred oxen of Hercules left tracks in space; before the language of Evander, the brute beast lends its voice. The first mark on the soft earth, the first bellowing in the tenuous air of dawn, by the beast, before man—prehistory . . . . The voice of the beast leads us back to the origin, back to murder.[46]

---

[44] Bertolt Brecht's adaptation of *Coriolanus* takes its cue from this radically anti-mythological stance.

[45] Michel Serres, *Rome: The Book of Foundations,* trans. Felicia McCarren (Stanford: Stanford University Press, 1991), 10.

[46] Ibid. 12.

Serres's self-admittedly 'liberal' reading of Livy[47] evokes a primordial scene of violence which tends to all but vanish from more conventional inter-pretations. Shakespeare's flawed Roman hero is empowered and disabled by a primordial violence which makes him at once the epitome of *Romanitas*[48] and *un*fit for the state.[49]

V

Coriolanus' unfitness is compounded by his abortive standing for consul. 'Standing' is to be taken quite literally: the citizens whose votes he seeks are 'to come by him where he stands, by ones, by twos, and by threes' (II. iii. 42–4). Preceded and followed by military action—the campaign resulting in the conquest of Corioli and the Volscian advance on Rome—Coriolanus' standing in public marks the turning point of the play. This is not without irony. Incredible feats of valour frame a crisis hinging on a political formal-ity. What would be easy for anyone else—all he has to do, after all, is to stand and 'ask ... kindly' (II. iii. 74)—proves to be too hard for the hero. While his martial exploits are driven by an irresistible dynamism—'he never stood / To ease his breast with panting' (II. ii. 121–2)—civic custom arrests him in unbearable stasis. His urgent pleas to be spared the ceremony sound less like haughtiness than hysteria:

CORIOLANUS   I do beseech you,
            Let me o'erleap that custom, for I cannot
            Put on the gown, stand naked, and entreat them
            For my wounds' sake to give their suffrage. Please you
            That I may pass this doing.   (II. ii. 136–40)

A rite of civic initiation meant to bestow the ultimate stamp of approval by the community results in an eviction: instead of a consul, it produces an outlaw. Rational consideration would tell the candidate that the obligatory

---

[47] Serres's first chapter is prefaced by the note: 'The text that follows is, with some exceptions, a continuous and liberal reading of the first book of Livy's *Ab Urbe Condita*.'

[48] Cominius' praise in II. ii. 83–5 states as much: 'It is held / That valour is the chiefest virtue and / Most dignifies the haver.'

[49] Trevor Saunders's translation of Aristotle's *zôon politikón*: 'an animal fit for a state'. Aristotle, *Politics. Books I and II*, trans. and ed. Trevor J. Saunders (Oxford: Clarendon Press, 1995), 3 (= 1253ᵃ3).

wearing of the 'gown of humility' is not an unreasonable price to pay for the
highest office of state; or perhaps even that, as a customary requirement for
that office, the appurtenances of humility are not really humiliating at all.
But rational consideration is, of course, precisely what the candidate is
incapable of, quite unlike his mother. Taking the socially accepted view,
she cannot wait for her son 'to show the people' the newly received 'large
cicatrices . . . when he shall stand for his place' (II. i. 145–6). For Volumnia
the showing of his wounds—whose exact number and location she gushes
over with Menenius ('One i'th'neck and two i'th'thigh . . . Now it's
twenty-seven' II. i. 148,142)—is part and parcel of her son's triumph,
something not to be dreaded but eagerly to be looked forward to. For all
her suffocatingly tight bond to her son,[50] she is completely out of step with
him on this issue.

The rift between mother and son is the rift between the city as social
system and the hero as anti-social god-beast. Ignorantly glorying in Coriolanus' anticipated exaltation, Volumnia becomes the voice of Rome herself.
The wounds her 'boy Martius' (II. i. 98) has received are nothing if not
public. Unless seen and counted, they are of no account at all. Her (and
Rome's) hero is a hero by public acclaim. His charisma deserves, but also
needs, confirmation by the admiring gaze of the crowd. For Coriolanus, on
the other hand, the 'gown of humility' is truly humiliating. It is unbearable
because, as he says,

> Better it is to die, better to starve,
> Than crave the hire which first we do deserve.
> Why in this wolvish toge should I stand here
> To beg of Hob and Dick that does appear
> Their needless vouches? Custom calls me to't.
> What custom wills, in all things should we do't,
> The dust of antique time would lie unswept
> And mountainous error be too highly heaped
> For truth to o'erpeer. Rather than fool it so,
> Let the high office and the honour go
> To one that would do thus.   (II. iii. 113–23)

---

[50] The major studies of the mother–son relationship in *Coriolanus* are Janet Adelman, 'Escaping
the Matrix: The Construction of Masculinity in *Macbeth and Coriolanus*', in *Suffocating Mothers*,
130–64, and Coppélia Kahn, 'Mother of Battles: Volumnia and her Son in *Coriolanus*', in *Roman
Shakespeare: Warriors, Wounds, and Women* (London and New York: Routledge, 1997), 144–59.

There is both rhyme and reason to this soliloquy, the first of only two for the protagonist in the whole play. Having to beg for what we deserve *is* annoying, and sticking to dusty old customs *can* be stifling. Coriolanus sounds here a bit like Edmund on 'the plague of custom' or Faulconbridge on commodity,[51] only less persuasive than either. But the argument betrays a deeper physical revulsion. We catch a glimpse of it in a textual crux which modern editors have chosen to emend. Folio, our only source text for the play, has 'Why in this Wooluish tongue should I stand heere'. All modern editors consider 'tongue' a compositor's error and emend it to 'toge', and most are agreed that the extraordinary 'wolvish' is indeed correct.[52] Tongues, nevertheless, do haunt the imaginings of the hero's phobic revulsion. They turn up when the citizens discuss the forthcoming election:

THIRD CITIZEN For if he show us his wounds and tell us his deeds, we are to put
tongues into those wounds and speak for them;   (II. iii. 5–7)

What makes the experience so unbearable for Coriolanus is captured in the vividly physical image of tongues being put into his wounds. The humililiation is in his passivity, the exposure of his body to the invasive 'licking' of the 'multitudinous tongue' he so detests: '—at once pluck out / The multitudinous tongue; let them not lick / The sweet which is their poison' (III. i. 158–60). Unlike their exposure, the actual receiving of the wounds is not passive. 'Every gash', Menenius declares, 'was an enemy's grave' (II. i. 152–3).[53]

The idea of the people as many-headed monster was, of course, a commonplace in Shakespeare's day.[54] In a remarkable stroke of irony, it is

---

[51] *King Lear* I. ii; *King John* II. i.

[52] John Dover Wilson (New Shakespeare) replaces it by 'woolyish' and John Jowett (Oxford) by 'womanish'. These emendations strike me as unconvincing (hence my departure from Wells/Taylor in II. iii. 115 above), but 'toge' for 'tongue' seems to me irrefutable.

[53] A most lurid conversion of wounds into organs of active aggression is effected in Volumnia's bloodthirsty hyperbole:

> The breasts of Hecuba,
> When she did suckle Hector looked not lovelier
> Than Hector's forehead when it spit forth blood
> At Grecian sword, contemning.   (I. iii. 42–5)

In Adelman's discussion of the mother–son relationship in *Coriolanus*, this is a key passage. *Suffocating Mothers*, 148–9.

[54] See Ch. 2.

playfully introduced by the 'monster' itself, the citizens, in their discussion of the imminent election:

THIRD CITIZEN Ingratitude is monstrous, and for the multitude to be ingrateful
               were to make a monster of the multitude, of which we, being
               members, should bring ourselves to be monstrous members.
FIRST CITIZEN And to make us no better thought of, a little help will serve; for
               once we stood up about the corn, he himself stuck not to call us
               the many-headed multitude.
THIRD CITIZEN We have been called so of many . . .   (II. iii. 9–18)

Hercules kills the Hydra, but the Hydra also kills Hercules. He steeps his arrows in her poison, and with such an arrow stops the flight of Nessus the centaur, would-be rapist of his wife Deianira. Cunning to the last, the dying Nessus palms off his Hydra-poisoned blood on the gullible spouse, promising her an irresistible aphrodisiac. Hercules, unconquerable by physical strength, is vanquished by guile. His own shirt kills him, sprinkled with the centaur's potion by the jealous Deianira. 'The shirt of Nessus is upon me', cries Antony, Shakespeare's other Herculean hero (*Antony* IV. xii. 43). Although such explicit allusion is missing in *Coriolanus*, the reversal of the hero's fate in the crucial election scenes is deeply if not directly Herculean. No sooner is the hateful ceremony over than he hastens to get rid of the shameful gown in order to 'know . . . myself again' (II. iii. 148). 'May I change these garments?' (II. iii. 147) he appeals.

But for all his aversion to it, the 'wolvish toge' is more perfectly suited to Coriolanus than he realizes. On the one hand, it links him with Rome's mythical beginnings, the nurturing she-wolf, the city's mother. On the other, it identifies him with the mythical shape in which the outcast haunts the wilderness beyond the borders of the city and beyond the borders of the human, in ultimate isolation: the man with the skin of a beast, *lykanthropos*, the werewolf. As Giorgio Agamben points out, this

> monstrous hybrid of human and animal, divided between the forest and the
> city . . . is . . . in its origin the man who has been banned from the city. That
> such a man is defined as a wolf-man and not simply as a wolf . . . is decisive
> here. The life of the bandit, like that of the sacred man, is not a piece of animal
> nature without any relation to law and the city. It is, rather, a threshold of
> indistinction and of passage between animal and man, *physis* and *nomos*,
> exclusion and inclusion: the life of the bandit is the life of the *loup garou*, the

werewolf, who is precisely *neither man nor beast*, and who dwells paradoxically within both while belonging to neither.[55]

Inclusion and exclusion also intersect and merge in the way Coriolanus' 'wolvish toge' represents both an imposition from without and a disclosure of something within. It is obligatory by force of Roman law—in *Coriolanus* emphatically the law of the mother—and at the same time gives expression to the 'wolvish' antisocial energy which will turn Rome's hero into the city's fiercest adversary. Paradoxically, then, what Coriolanus rejects is what reveals him most truly. Putting on the gown *and* standing naked (which is how he puts it in II. ii. 138), at once covered and dis-covered, he anticipates his condition as a stateless 'beast or god':

> I go alone,
> Like to a lonely dragon that his fen
> Makes feared and talked of more than seen   (IV. i. 31–3)

Shakespeare's tragedy takes up and transfigures the ambiguities that trouble the story of Rome's beginnings. If, as Volumnia claims, 'Thy [Coriolanus'] valiantness was mine, thou sucked'st it from me' (III. ii. 129), her son's wolflike qualities derive from the city's lupine patroness herself. The she-wolf in the story of Romulus and Remus, Susan Wiseman writes, 'figure[s] the character of the polis, the establishment and also the cannibalistic or fratricidal falling off of civil government'.[56] In Livy's rendering of the story, Faustulus the herdsman discovers the she-wolf 'licking the twins with her tongue'.[57] Livy also records that the fabulous *lupa* may not have been a real she-wolf at all but a trope casting Larentia, Faustulus' wife, notoriously free with her favours among the herdsmen, as a whore, because that is what the word *lupa* can also mean. Something of this equivocacy survives in Shakespeare's Volumnia. The two-faced nature of the *lupa* manifests itself in that she both nurtures and devours her own offspring. Halfway through the play, Menenius implores:

---

[55] Agamben, *Homo Sacer*, 105.

[56] Susan J. Wiseman, 'Hairy on the Inside: Metamorphosis and Civility in English Werewolf Texts', in Erica Fudge (ed.), *Renaissance Beasts: Of Animals, Humans, and Other Wonderful Creatures* (Urbana, Ill. and Chicago: University of Illinois Press, 2004), 50–69 at 63.

[57] 'lingua lambentem pueros': Livy, *Ab urbe condita libri*, ed. W. Weissenborn and M. Müller (Leipzig: Bibliotheca Teubneriana, 1932), Pars I, Liber I 4, 6. For a thorough discussion of the sources and of modern scholarship, see J. M. Bremmer and N. M. Horsfall, *Roman Myth and Mythography*, Bulletin Supplement 52 (London: University of London, Institute of Classical Studies, 1987), 25–48.

> Now the good gods forbid
> That our renownèd Rome . . .
>   . . . like an unnatural dam
> Should now eat up her own!   (III. i. 291–5)

In the end this is precisely what happens. In preventing her son from 'tearing / His country's bowels out' (V. iii. 103–4), from 'tread[ing] . . . on thy mother's womb / That brought thee to this world' (V. iii. 124–6), Volumnia effectively seals his death. Her triumphant return to Rome confirms her as the city's mother: 'Behold our patroness, the life of Rome!' (V. v. 1). For Rome to live, her son must die or, as the strenuously cheerful rhetoric of Menenius seems to imply, be reincorporated in the mother. Rather than tread on the womb that brought him to the world, he is swallowed up by it.[58]

> Call all your tribes together, praise the gods,
> And make triumphant fires. . . .
> Unshout the noise that banished Martius;
> Repeal him with the welcome of his mother.   (V. v. 2–5)

As far as Rome is concerned, this is it. The killing of Coriolanus, the final baiting scene which ends the play, takes place elsewhere, at Antium. It is left to the Volscians to dispose of a hero who has become untenable. He cannot be Coriolanus anymore; his name is a permanent insult to his new allies. He cannot be 'Romanus' either because in order to gain that title he would have to destroy his native city,[59] winning himself, as Volumnia cautions him, 'such a name / Whose repetition will be dogged with curses' (V. iii. 144–5). History moves on, bearing out Menenius' warning to the plebeians, early in the play, that it is futile to oppose the Roman state, 'whose course', like that of a runaway horse,

>   will on
> The way it takes, cracking ten thousand curbs
> Of more strong link asunder than can ever
> Appear in your impediment.   (I. i. 67–70)

The prediction proves true, only the role of the victim has been reassigned.

---

[58] Cf. Adelman, *Suffocating Mothers*, 158: 'The cannibalistic mother who denies food and yet feeds on the victories of her sweet son stands at the darkest center of the play.'

[59] Kenneth Burke, 'Coriolanus—and the Delights of Faction', in his *Language as Symbolic Action: Essays on Life, Literature, and Method* (Berkeley and Los Angeles: University of California Press, 1966), 91 n.

4

Cannibal–Animal: Figurations of the (In)Human in Montaigne, Foxe, and Shakespearean Revenge Tragedy

I n its grim work of reclamation, the early modern judiciary exorcised crime by bestializing the criminal. But subjecting humans to a treatment that reduced them to animal status entailed a tendency to reflect on the process of the law itself, to bestialize the punishment as well as—or even instead of—the crime. At the same time as it hinged upon human–animal distinction, the spectacle of punishment thus also destabilized this distinction. In this chapter, I propose to explore this instability further by looking at two rather suspect accessories of juridical violence hovering in the wings of the early modern theatre of justice: revenge and cannibalism. Though ostensibly excluded from the order which the law sustains and is sustained by, they are both, I will argue, taking my example from John Foxe, firmly embedded in the signifying processes of punishment. As the law's vengeance demonstratively consumes the body of its victim, revenge and cannibalism are revealed as interdependent rather than just parallel. This interdependence is the sustaining principle of the savagely noble cannibal society beyond the seas which Montaigne presents to his readers as an eye-opener to barbarity at home. It also sustains the performances of revenge on Shakespeare's stage—with drastic literalness in *Titus Andronicus*, more obliquely in *Hamlet*. I come to these plays via 'Des Cannibales', an essay which Shakespeare critics usually bring up in connection with *The Tempest*, owing to my concern here with an intermedial theatre of cruelty in which the borderline figures, cannibal and animal, mark the always questionable limit of the human. Encompassing stage, stake, and scaffold, this theatre extends to such ritual performances of anthropophagy as Montaigne details in his essay and, even more broadly, to any act of violence performed in front of an audience. Thus my first port of call is Montaigne's disquisition on cruelty.

I. Of Cruelty

'No man', Montaigne avers, 'taketh delight to see wild beasts sport and wantonly to make much one of another: Yet all are pleased to see them tugge, mangle, and enterteare one an other.'[1] While copulation offends, 'entertearing' is deemed entertaining. Montaigne may be primarily thinking of the 'violent sport' of hunting (ii. 117), but his observation could equally refer to the 'entertearing' that his contemporaries were pleased to see at the bear-garden. Like any modern critic of media violence, Montaigne is convinced of the detrimental effect of such entertainment: 'After the ancient Romanes had once enured themselves without horror to behold the slaughter of wild beasts in their shewes, they came to the murther of men and Gladiators' (ii. 122).

   Cruelty for Montaigne is the cardinal vice, its abhorrence a—if not *the*—principal ethical concern of the *Essais* as a whole.[2] 'Amongst all other vices', he declares, 'there is none I hate more, than crueltie, both by nature and judgement, as the extremest of all vices' (ii. 117). How deeply, 'by nature', he detests this vice is tellingly exemplified by instances of the killing of animals. Tellingly, too, these instances are crucially linked with watching:

> But it is with such an yearning and faint-heartednesse, that if I see but a chickins necke puld off, or a pigge stickt, I cannot chuce but grieve, and I cannot well endure a seelie dew-bedabbled hare to groane, when she is seized upon by the houndes...   (ii. 117)

The drift here is obvious: the author is claiming an unusual—or, as he would almost seem to admit, exaggerated—sensitivity to even the slightest,

---

[1] 'Of Cruelty', in *Montaigne's Essays*, trans. Florio, ii. 108–25 at 122. Volume and page references to this edition are given in brackets in the text.
[2] See Judith Shklar, *Ordinary Vices* (Cambridge, Mass.: Belknap Press, 1984); cf. also David Lewis Schaefer, *The Political Philosophy of Montaigne* (Ithaca, NY, and London: Cornell University Press, 1990), 227–36.

most everyday instances of cruelty; cruelty that the rest of the world would hardly even recognize as such. In the overall argument of the essay, however, it is not the eccentricity of excessive empathy but the normality of hardened indifference against which Montaigne directs his critique. As it becomes clear that it is the eccentric minority position, rather than the indifferent majority, that sets the ethical norm, animals and humans emerge as fellow victims on a continuum of suffering that bridges the gap between the species. If, as Montaigne maintains, 'There is a kinde of enter-changeable commerce and mutuall bond betweene them and us' (i. 124–5), the most palpable proof of that bond is a shared capacity to feel pain. Throughout the essay, animals recur as particularly pitiable victims of cruelty, and cruelty is inseparable from spectacle. The author's subject position in the text is that of a witness of violent acts, appalled yet unable to look away. The verb repeatedly used to describe this experience is 'see'. Seeing amounts to suffering cruelty; for the sensitive observer, it is an occasion of pain to be endured: 'As for me, I could never so much as endure, without remorse and griefe, to see a poore, sillie, and innocent beast pursued and killed' (ii. 122). At the same time, however, seeing is also conceived as a prime incentive to cruelty, the very cause and driving force of the ultimate abomination— cruelty committed for the sole purpose of watching:

> I could hardly be perswaded, before I had seene it, that the world could have afforded so marble-hearted and savage-minded men, that for the onely pleasure of murther would commit-it; then cut, mangle, and hacke other members in pieces: to rouze and sharpen their wits, to invent unused tortures and unheard-of torments; to devise new and unknowne deaths and that in cold blood, without any gaine or profit; and onely to this end, that they may enjoy the pleasing spectacle of the languishing gestures, pitifull motions, horror-moving yellings, deep fetcht groanes, and lamentable voyces of a dying and drooping man. For, that is the extremest point whereunto the crueltie of man may attaine.   (ii. 121–2)

This passage, its rhetorical intensification marking the climax of the essay, shows remarkable shifts in focus. Beginning with the cruelty of murder, the very acts that exemplify it (cut, mangle, hack) shift our attention from the atrocity of crime to the 'crime of punishment',[3] to those 'unheard-of torments' a resourceful criminal justice never tired of inventing. Not just in 'Of Cruelty' but throughout the *Essais*, the most heinous atrocities are

---

[3] Cf. Karl Menninger, *The Crime of Punishment* (New York: Viking Press, 1968).

committed by figures of authority[4] or 'the authorities'. The 'pleasing spectacle' is thus not a matter of private vice, but implicates all those not so innocent bystanders who, although not directly responsible for the cruelty, endorse it by their mere presence: the crowds of people for whose benefit the early modern judiciary wreaked its 'inhumane outrages and barbarous excesses' (ii. 121)[5] on the bodies of criminal offenders.[6]

Starting out with the committing of atrocities and ending with the enjoyment of watching them, the argument thus proceeds not only from the cruelty of crime to the cruelty of punishment, but also from individual agents to complicit audiences. And although the reality of suffering is never allowed to become invisible, there is also a slide towards something suggestive of theatrical *poesis* and thus of fiction, a slide which connects the real maiming and killing at the stake and on the scaffold with the feigned tragic deaths on page and stage. Just prior to the passage quoted above, the text slips from one to the other in seamless transition as Montaigne deplores the excessive cruelties committed 'through the licentiousnesse of our civill and intestine warres'; 'And read all ancient stories, be they never so tragicall, you shall find none to equall those, we daily see practised' (ii. 121).

As *Moderns* surpass *Ancients* in a macabre *querelle*, the ontological divide between what we see and what we read, between the reality of 'incredible examples of this vice' and 'stories, be they never so tragicall', is elided. The slippage continues: unheard-of torments are invented, new and unknown

---

[4] The opening essay of the whole work ('By Divers Meanes Men Come to a Like End') shows Alexander the Great in a particularly reprehensible case of gratuitous voyeuristic cruelty. Failing to 'see' ('*voyant*' son fier ou obstiné silence'; my italics) signs of submission in Betis, the vanquished enemy commander, the victorious Alexander 'said thus unto himselfe: What? would hee not bend his knee? could he not utter one suppliant voyce? I will assuredly vanquish his silence, and if I cannot wrest a word from him, I will at least make him to sob or groane. And converting his anger into rage, commanded his [Betis's] heeles to be through-pierced, and so all alive with a cord through them be torne, mangled, and dismembred at a carts-tail' (i. 20). Both principal agent and privileged observer, Alexander, that paragon of the ancient world, is thus the archetype of those 'savage-minded men' who inflict torment in order to enjoy their victim's distress.

[5] '*Whatsoever is beyond a simple death, I deeme it to be meere crueltie*' (ii. 119, italics original). Montaigne does not argue against the death penalty as such; what he condemns are the measures that prolong the torment of dying. 'I do not greatly waile for the dead, but rather envie them. Yet doe I much waile and moane the dying.... Let any man be executed by law, how deservedly soever, I cannot behold the execution with an unrelenting eye' (ii. 119).

[6] Foucault, *Discipline and Punish*, 57–8: 'In the ceremonies of the public executions, the main character was the people, whose real and immediate presence was required for the performance ... An execution that was known to be taking place, but which did so in secret, would scarcely have had any meaning.'

deaths are devised 'and only to this end, that they may enjoy the pleasing spectacle of the languishing gestures, pitiful motions, horror-moving yellings, deep fetched groans, and lamentable voices' of the dying—all this is highly theatrical wording. It is also a fairly accurate catalogue of the most riveting and emotionally powerful effects Shakespeare or any other early modern playwright could mobilize to draw their audience into 'pleasing spectacle[s]'. Inventors of new and unknown deaths continue to use similar effects to lure us into their shows to this very day, from *Silence of the Lambs* to the latest feast of fright and gore.[7]

Montaigne's reflections on cruelty, then, though ostensibly not concerned with theatre in the literal sense at all, can help to clarify an inevitable ambivalence in the theatre's attitude to violence, an ambivalence that becomes especially acute in the theatre's relation to the forms of spectacle in which humans or animals are maimed and killed in earnest, not in jest. It would be a pious delusion to construe the playhouse as a critical mirror to the cruelty of baiting and juridical violence, an observation post on an island of 'meta-violence', detached from and uncompromised by the atrocities it exposes. In a culture of spectacle such as early modern England there is no safe haven, no escaping from the circulation of visual energy, the contagious promiscuity of images so suspicious to Puritan advocates of visual abstemiousness.

What we may expect to find in Shakespeare is a searching exposure of the psychological and political sources, motivations, and mechanisms of violence, an unflinching confrontation and indictment of human cruelty. But we can equally expect the cunning plotter of 'new and unknown deaths' to appeal to his audience's irrepressible fascination with the spectacle of violence. His dramaturgy draws on the calculated exploitation of violence as probably the strongest stimulant his medium is capable of. In Shakespeare's theatre (and of course not only there) the representation of violence is inextricably entangled with and contaminated by the violence of representation.[8] And so we, as twenty-first-century witnesses to the carefully crafted outrages and excesses of Shakespearean violence, inevitably become as complicit in them as were our Elizabethan counterparts. Thrilled and

---

[7] On continuity from Shakespearean to postmodern media violence, see Pascale Aebischer, *Shakespeare's Violated Bodies* (Cambridge: Cambridge University Press, 2004). See also R. A. Foakes, *Shakespeare and Violence* (Cambridge: Cambridge University Press, 2003), esp. 61–82.

[8] On this crucial nexus see Elisabeth Bronfen, *Over her Dead Body: Death, Femininity and the Aesthetic* (Manchester: Manchester University Press, 1992), 39–56.

fascinated, we find ourselves, as Hamlet puts it, 'guilty creatures sitting at a play' (II. ii. 591).

II. Noble Others

Montaigne's scene of cruelty is flanked by two figures of the Other, animal and cannibal. In a disquisition on cruelty, one would expect their rhetorical function to be that of marking excess. Excesses of cruelty are displaced onto non-human, non-civilized Others, beast and savage. Epithets like 'brutal', 'brutish', 'bestial' suggest a predatory violence of flesh-rending fangs and claws culminating in the ultimate figure of abhorrence: the beast with a human body that gorges itself on the flesh of its own kind. Herodotus, the 'father' not only of history but of ethnography as well,[9] locates the *andro-phagoi* on the outer rim of the human-inhabited *oikomene*, on the threshold to the deserts where only wild beasts dwell. At the furthest remove from the Mediterranean centre of civilization, the man-eaters represent the zero state of human culture, barely distinguishable from animal nature.[10] In John Mandeville's fourteenth-century travel book, the liminality of the anthro-pophagous 'hippopotami' from 'Bactria' who 'eat men whenever they can get them' is doubly encoded in their amphibious lifestyle—they 'live sometimes on dry land and sometimes in the water'—and in their cen-taur-like body, 'half man and half horse'.[11] The topos of anthropophagy as near-animal primitivism gained new force in the 'Age of Discovery', providing the dominant frame of reference for the representation of New World cannibals. For, as Claude Lévi-Strauss observes, the early European explorers of America 'thought less to discover a new world than to find the past of the Old World confirmed'.[12]

[9] Herodotus, *The History*, trans. David Grene (Chicago: University of Chicago Press, 1987), according to Greenblatt, *Marvellous Possessions*, 122, 'the first great Western representation of otherness'.

[10] James S. Romm, *The Edges of the Earth in Ancient Thought: Geography, Exploration, and Fiction* (Princeton: Princeton University Press, 1992), 32–41.

[11] John Mandeville, *The Travels of Sir John Mandeville*, trans. and ed. C. W. R. D. Moseley (Harmondsworth: Penguin, 1983), 167.

[12] Claude Lévi-Strauss, *Tristes tropiques*, trans. John Weightman and Doreen Weightman (New York: Atheneum Books, 1972).

Montaigne departs from this approach,[13] unsettling the normative distinction which figures of otherness are usually employed to confirm. In their standard normative function, such figures mark the boundary between inclusion and exclusion: in the case of animal and cannibal, the boundary between what is inside and what is outside the category of the human. As categorical opposites to the normative notion of civilized man, animal and cannibal represent an other which is always already known, the other constructed by a colonizing gaze which immunizes itself to recognizing anything but the bestiality of the beast, the savagery of the savage. To this regime, Montaigne brings an epistemology of sceptical defamiliarization, famously exemplified by his question in 'Apology for Raymond Sebond': 'When I am playing with my Cat, who knowes whether she have more sport in dallying with me, than I have in gaming with her?' (ii. 142) Looking closely reveals an unfathomable otherness of which only one thing can be known: that it is looking back. Perceiving the animal looking, Montaigne's observant eye establishes mutuality.[14] In relation to the cannibals, mutuality consists in acknowledging and seeking to understand the other's language, as in the attempted conversation which Montaigne reports to have had with the Brazilian Tupi Indians who disembarked at Rouen in November 1562—though the exchange was hampered by less than perfect comprehension.[15]

The elementary discursive function of animal and cannibal in the production of 'anthropological difference'[16] is used by Montaigne not to confirm but to contest that difference, and in particular to contest the anthropocentric and ethnocentric claims to superiority which animal and cannibal conventionally serve to reinforce. Whatever cruelty may be ascribed to beast or savage, it is surpassed by the unprecedented savagery that 'we daily see practised' (ii. 121). Excesses of violence there most certainly are, but neither animal nor cannibal will serve to deflect them

---

[13] To what extent Montaigne departs from European preconceptions is the subject of ongoing debate. The view of a Montaigne perpetuating ethnocentric stereotypes was argued with particular stringency by Gérard Defaux, 'Un Cannibale en haute de chaussses'. See also Deborah N. Losse, 'Rewriting Culture'.

[14] Montaigne's cat looking back has a late modern revenant in the cat ('a real cat, truly, believe me, *a little cat*') which the naked Jacques Derrida encounters in his bathroom. Jacques Derrida, *The Animal*, 6; italics original.

[15] Peter Hulme, 'Introduction: The Cannibal Scene', in Francis Barker, Peter Hulme, and Margaret Iversen (eds.), *Cannibalism and the Colonial World* (Cambridge: Cambridge University Press, 1998), 5.

[16] Wild, *Die anthropologische Differenz*.

from neighbours and fellow-citizens to the conveniently non-familiar or subhuman. 'Of Cruelty' compares civilized humanity with its Others in a way that shows the 'brute beasts' (ii. 125) as suffering victims rather than allegorical embodiments of 'inhuman' violence, and the allegedly savage cannibal as more humane than Montaigne's own countrymen: 'The Cannibales and savage people do not so much offend me with roasting and eating of dead bodies, as those which torment and persecute the living' (ii. 119).[17] European jurisdiction, he argues, might actually do well to imitate the savages. By unleashing the law's fury not on the living, but, cannibal-like, on the already dead body of the malefactor, the cruelty of punishment would be mitigated without diminishing its intended deterrent effect:

> Were I worthie to give counsell, I would have these examples of rigor, by which superior powers goe about to keep the common people in awe, to be onely exercised on the bodies [i.e. *dead* bodies] of criminall malefactors: For, to see them deprived of christian buriall, to see them haled, disbowelled, parboyled, and quartered, might haply touch the common sort as much, as the paines, they make the living to endure.   (ii. 120)

The relation between stage and scaffold works in two directions here. On the one hand, the scaffold-as-stage caters to the voyeuristic pleasure 'that is the extremest point whereunto the crueltie of man may attaine' (ii. 122).

---

[17] As Peter Hulme ('Introduction', 6) points out, 'At least from Peter Martyr onwards, cannibals have been compared with their describers, comparisons which tend to undermine the strong sense of difference carried by the surface argument.' Thus it became popular in Protestant polemics to denounce the eating of Christ's flesh in Catholic Mass as worse than cannibalism. (See Frank Lestringant, 'Catholiques et cannibales: Le thème du cannibalisme dans le discours protestant au temps des guerres de religion', in Jean-Claude Margolin and Robert Sauzet (eds.), *Pratiques et discours alimentaires à la Renaissance* (Paris: G.-P. Maisonneuve et Larose, 1982), 233–45.

Though by no means the first European to compare New World anthropophagy with Old World customs to the detriment of the latter, Montaigne is more trenchant than most. Jean de Léry, for example, whose report of his voyage to Brazil provides material for Montaigne's cannibal essay, compares Tupinambá eating habits favourably to the practices of European usurers 'who eat everyone alive, especially widows, orphans, and other poor people' (Jean de Léry, *History of a Voyage to the Land of Brazil*, trans. Janet Whatley (Berkeley: University of California Press, 1990), 132). While Montaigne builds on the same dead-versus-alive opposition as his source, he takes Léry's argument a crucial step further by referring directly and unmetaphorically to the physical torment of living bodies. Léry, moreover, was castigating an abuse which, though widely practised, was unanimously condemned by contemporary society at large. Cf. Norman Jones, *God and the Moneylenders* (Oxford: Blackwell, 1989); Eric Kerridge, *Usury, Interest and the Reformation* (Aldershot: Ashgate, 2002); Lloyd Edward Kermode, 'Introduction', in his edition of *Three Renaissance Usury Plays* (Manchester and New York: Manchester University Press, 2009), 1–78. Montaigne's abhorrence aims at the very mainstay of that society, the penal system ordained to ensure civil order, but perverted into begetting 'incredible examples of this vice [i.e. cruelty], through the licentiousnesse of our civill and intestine warres' (ii. 121).

But on the other hand, the cannibal mode of *post mortem* torture leads Montaigne onto a train of thought that reveals theatre not as a means of aggravating but as a way to mitigate the atrocity of juridical violence by bringing the theatre of punishment closer to the condition of theatre proper and thus replacing acts of cruelty with their representation.[18]

If the adjective 'bestial' offloads human cruelty onto man's animal Other, 'barbarous' performs the same operation with regard to the savage. In 'Of Cruelty', and even more forcefully in 'Of the Canniballes', Montaigne consistently refutes this operation: 'I find (as farre as I have beene informed) there is nothing in that nation [the cannibals], that is either barbarous or savage, unlesse men call that barbarisme which is not common to them' (i. 219).[19] 'Barbarisme' is a relative term, and in relation to 'them', the cannibals, it is invariably 'us', the people on an allegedly higher cultural level, that turn out to be more barbarous in Montaigne's reckoning.[20] 'We may then well call them barbarous, in regard of reasons rules, but not in respect of us that exceed them in all kinde of barbarisme' (i. 224). The cannibals are not barbarous, they are natural. So 'neere their originall naturalitie' as to 'exceed all the pictures wherewith licentious Poesie hath proudly imbellished the golden age' (i. 220), these noble savages would seem to corroborate Lévi-Strauss in showing that Montaigne, too, 'thought less to discover a new world than to find the past of the Old World confirmed'.[21] In his idealization of the cannibals, Montaigne replaces one classical template with another: Herodotus' near-animal man-eaters become the heroic innocents of an Ovidian Golden Age.

---

[18] See also 'Of Cruelty', ii. 121: 'Such inhumane outrages and barbarous excesses should be exercised against the rinde, and not practised against the quicke. In a case somewhat like unto this, did *Artaxerxes* asswage and mitigate the sharpnesse of the ancient lawes of *Persia*, appointing that the Lords, which had trespassed in their estate, whereas they were wont to be whipped, they should be stripped naked, and their clothes whipped for them.'

[19] 'Of the Canniballes', *Montaigne's Essays*, i. 215–29.

[20] There is a logical problem here which Montaigne passes over. Exposing the ethnocentric bias of the term 'barbarous', he insists on its irreducible relativity. But at the same time he uses it as a standard of absolute validity, according to which some (we) can be regarded as more barbaric than others (them).

[21] As Michel de Certeau points out in his reading of 'Des cannibales', 'in order to measure the virtue of cannibalism, comparison must be sought among the most heroic examples Greek courage has to offer (King Leonidas or Ischolas); in order to conceive of the generosity implied by polygamy, it is necessary to recall the most lofty female figures of the Bible (Leah, Rachel, Sarah), as well as those of Antiquity (Livia, Stratonice). The finest gold tradition has to offer is used to forge a halo for the cannibals.' Michel de Certeau, *Heterologies: Discourse on the Other*, trans. Brian Massumi (Minneapolis and London: University of Minnesota Press, 1986), 76.

But the picture is more complex and the unspoilt natural virtue of the Brazilian warriors, as David Quint has shown,[22] much closer than appears at first sight, not to a golden European past, but to the troubled present of Montaigne's France. This is connected with a two-sidedness, even incongruity, in Montaigne's account, which ascribes to the cannibals both a total lack of culture *and* a distinct culture of their own. The former is the condition of their unspoilt naturalness; the latter serves as proof of their humanity. The most famous passage of the essay—the passage Gonzalo adapts in *The Tempest*[23]—declares that the cannibals have 'no kinde of traffike, no knowledge of Letters, no name of magistrate, nor of politike superioritie; . . . no contracts, no successions, no partitions, no occupation but idle; . . . no apparell but naturall, no manuring of lands, no use of wine, corne, or mettle' (i. 220), nothing that might intervene between them and 'our great and puissant mother Nature' (i. 219). In short, they have no culture. And because of this, they even lack the words to describe the vices that are the inevitable price of cultural sophistication: 'The very words that import lying, falshood, treason, dissimulations, covetousnes, envie, detraction, and pardon, were never heard amongst them' (i. 220).[24]

The last term, pardon, sits oddly in this list of cultural degeneracies. It is, as Quint notes,[25] 'the sting in the tail' (*venenum in cauda*) of this glowing account of unadulterated simplicity, a first pointer to the darker side of cannibal customs. Given Montaigne's strong approbation of clemency, pardon—'when revenge lies in [the] hands' of those 'we have offended'[26] (i. 17)—is a most unlikely candidate for disapproval. Pardon—more precisely, its absence—forms the link between the culture-free innocence of the cannibals and the very core of what Montaigne is at pains to describe as a culture in its own right. The cannibals, he informs his readers, eat human flesh, 'not as some imagine, to nourish themselves with it, (as anciently the Scithians wont to doe,) but to represent an extreme, and inexpiable revenge' (i. 223).

---

[22] Quint, 'A Reconsideration of Montaigne's *Des cannibales*'.

[23] For significant alterations in Gonzalo's adaptation, see Halpern, ' "The picture of Nobody" '.

[24] The next sentence concludes with emphatic acclamation that the cannibals' polity surpasses even Plato's ideal state: 'How dissonant would hee [Plato] finde his imaginarie commonwealth from this perfection!' (i. 220).

[25] Quint, 'A Reconsideration', 166.

[26] The quotation is from the very first page of the very first of the *Essais*: 'By Divers Meanes Men Come unto a Like End', *Montaigne's Essays*, i. 17.

The remark occurs in a passage of proto-anthropological description which presents cannibal customs with a strong tenor of approval. It is preceded by an account of their 'admirable' 'resolution' in combat, their exemplary treatment of prisoners, and the equally exemplary manner of killing them (quickly, unprolonged by torture). It is followed by an account of how these noble customs deteriorated when the cannibals began imitating the cruelty of the Portuguese. The defining feature of cannibal lifestyle, anthropophagy, is categorically dissociated from the opprobrium of quasi-animal voraciousness in the Herodotian tradition. Not mindlessly gorging themselves with human flesh, but performing an act of *representation*, the cannibals display the defining feature of human culture. But at the same time as this drives a wedge between cannibal and animal, it associates the brave New World natives with the vices, and especially the cruelties, of Old World civilization to which Montaigne's initial encomium of their blissful state of nature places them in such radiant contrast. Revenge—self-perpetuating, retaliatory violence—is the sustaining principle of a warrior society where competitive martial valour—'the meere jelousie of vertue' (i. 224)—is the only means of distinction, where wars are fought 'not for the gaining of new lands' (i. 224), but only for 'glorie, and the advantage to be and remaine superior in valour and vertue', where the victors 'require no other ransome of their prisoners, but an acknowledgement and confession that they are vanquished' (i. 225), but where that acknowledgement is never forthcoming: 'And in a whole age, a man shall not finde one, that doth not rather embrace death, than either by word or countenance remissely to yeeld one jot of an invincible courage' (i. 225). The cannibals' wars may be 'noble and generous, and have as much excuse and beautie, as this humane infirmitie may admit' (i. 224), but wars they nonetheless are, and, what is more, they are perpetual: an unending chain of noble but merciless violence. Warfare is not the state of exception but the normal condition of a society that has no other *raison d'être* than to either be at war or prepare for it.[27] Locked

---

[27] 'All their morall discipline containeth but these two articles; first an undismaied resolution to warre, then an inviolable affection to their wives' (i. 222). Even though this ethical code enjoins the cannibals to make love as well as war, marital love is clearly subsidiary to the purposes of strengthening individual and tribal combat strength, wives being fully factored into the system of competitive male valour. In keeping with this martial mono-culture, the cannibals' prophets predict only war-related issues and are 'hewen in a thousand pieces' if their divination should fail (i. 222).

in a cycle of violence, cannibal society parallels Montaigne's portrayal of ancient Rome,[28] a society which fostered foreign wars to give employment to the nation's military energy ('the over vehement heat of their youth'; ii. 409) rather than risking an eruption of this energy in civil conflict, and which introduced gladiatorial games in order to generate and maintain that very energy which then, in turn, needed to be deflected outwards:

> Surely it was a wonderfull example and of exceeding benefit for the peoples institution, to see dayly one or two hundred, yea sometimes a thousand brace of men armed one against another, in their presence to cut and hacke one another in pieces with so great constancy of courage, that they were never seene to utter one word of faintnes or commiseration, never to turne their backe, nor so much as to shew a motion of demissenesse, to avoide their adversaries blowes . . .   (ii. 411)

This portrayal of Roman courage clearly evokes the prowess of the cannibals, but it also calls to mind the outrages castigated in 'Of Cruelty', particularly the downward spiral of hardening callousness which leads from 'the slaughter of wild beasts in their shewes, . . . to the murther of men and Gladiators' (ii. 122).[29] Since all the excesses of ancient cruelty do not 'equall those, we daily see practised' (ii. 121), this downward slide reaches its all-time low in Montaigne's own present. What separates the noble savages of Brazil from the depravations of war-torn France is thus at the same time the stamp of a deep-rooted kinship: a fanatical fortitude that would rather die than yield an inch. Such heroism, merciless both towards others and towards oneself, is the very curse of a sixteenth-century European country riven by internecine religious conflict.[30] If the cannibals are pure, they are also purely cruel. Where relentless valour is pitted against unflinching constancy and the word pardon has never been heard, there is no way to break the endless cycle of violence and counter-violence, of

---

[28] Book II, ch. 23: 'Of Bad Meanes Emploied to a Good End', ii. 408–12. Cf. Quint, 'A Reconsideration', 176–9.

[29] Immediately following the passage on the pedagogical benefits of gladiatorial violence, a similar moral decline is reported to have prompted the Romans to turn from the disposal of 'their criminals' in the arena to the disposal of 'their innocent servants; yea of their free men . . . : yea of Senators; and Roman Knights, and women also' (ii. 411).

[30] Quint, 'A Reconsideration', 179–86, persuasively suggests a parallel between the fortitude of the cannibals and the neo-Stoic ideal of constancy embraced by French aristocrats and Huguenot martyrs, which Montaigne holds partly responsible for an escalation of violence in contemporary France.

eating and being eaten which 'an extreme, and inexpiable revenge' (i. 223) dictates. This is borne out most graphically by another exhibit from cannibal culture, a poem with which a captured warrior taunts his captors:

> I have a song made by a prisoner, wherein is this clause, Let them boldly come altogether, and flocke in multitudes, to feed on him; for with him they shall feed upon their fathers, and grandfathers, that heretofore have served his body for food and nourishment: These muscles, (saith he) this flesh, and these veines, are your owne; fond men as you are, know you not that the substance of your forefathers limbes is yet tied into ours? Taste them well, for in them shall you finde the relish of your owne flesh. (i. 227)

If this poetic invention, as Montaigne hastens to add, 'hath no shew of barbarisme' (literally: does not *taste* of barbarism; 'ne sent aucunement la barbarie'), this is, for one thing, because it evinces a highly intricate figure of representation: a literary reflection on how the flesh of fathers and grand-fathers is both present in and represented by the flesh of the prisoner, which is about to be consumed in a ritual that 'represent[s] an extreme, and inexpiable revenge'. But it is also because the invention is at least partly Montaigne's own: the final twist, turning self-perpetuating into literally self-consuming violence ('the relish of *your own* flesh'), is his addition, not to be found in his source.[31] And, finally, it is because this inescapable circularity offers a powerful image of the civil wars of religion in which Montaigne's France cannibalized itself—although this last argument risks becoming circular: in Montaigne's view, 'civil' France is actually worse than barbarous itself.

Revenge, in Francis Bacon's famous definition, 'is a kind of wild justice; which the more man's nature runs to, the more ought law to weed it out'.[32] Montaigne's cannibal society, with revenge located at its very heart, confirms the first part of this statement, even though 'wild' in Montaigne's account carries far more positive connotations than it does for Bacon. Where Montaigne and Bacon agree is in the way they both allow us to see the 'wild' enmeshed with the 'civil'. For all his categorical condemnations of revenge, Bacon credits it with a place among anthropological

---

[31] Quint, 'A Reconsideration', 175–6. The source is André Thevet, *Les Singularitez de la France antarctique* (1557), which was translated into English as *The new found vvorlde, or Antarctike . . .* , trans. Thomas Hacket (London: Thomas Hacket, 1568).

[32] Francis Bacon, *The Essays or Counsels Civil and Moral*, ed. Brian Vickers, Oxford World's Classics (Oxford: Oxford University Press, 1999), 10.

fundamentals.[33] Justice, however 'wild', presupposes a uniquely human sense of right and wrong. As an instinctual drive, on the other hand, man's urge to retaliate is also part of that wild nature which it is the law's office to keep in check.[34]

Yet the law itself is founded upon the talionic principle of revenge. Post-Enlightenment legal thinking has sought to remove all traces of this elementary link. Early modern criminal justice, however, has no qualms about openly flourishing it. Public executions were staged as 'rituals of retribution'.[35] 'One sees by the very definition of the law', declares a jurist of the *ancien régime* quoted by Foucault, 'that it tends not only to prohibit, but also to *avenge* contempt for its authority.'[36] 'In the execution of the most ordinary penalty', Foucault comments, 'reign the active forces of revenge.'[37] Both incorporated and excluded by the law, revenge marks a threshold between the civil and the wild, legal order and brute force. It is on this threshold that the force of law can be seen to approach, even to cross into and amalgamate with, cannibalism. A literalized trope, enfleshed in cultural performance, Montaigne's scene of anthropophagous revenge reads back into the procedures of European justice where the *consuming* violence of retributive cruelty feeds on victims who are not even dead yet:

---

[33] Parallel passages confirm this ambivalence. 'Of Nature in Men' (Bacon, *The Essays*, 89–90) defines nature as something man should overcome in himself; the essay offers a whole catalogue of rules of conduct for suppressing, taming, or outwitting one's natural drives. But it also maintains that nature will ultimately defeat any such measures: 'for nature will lay buried a great time, and yet revive upon the occasion or temptation. Like as it was with Aesop's damsel, turned from a cat to a woman, who sat very demurely at the board's end, till a mouse ran before her' (p. 90). The image of weeding out and the irresistible dynamics of 'running to' recur in the attempted closure-by-distinction which the essay offers at the end: 'A man's nature runs either to herbs or weeds; therefore let him seasonably water the one, and destroy the other' (ibid.). Revenge would have to be entered under weeds, but the distinction remains fragile. 'As common laws are to customs in states, such is nature to custom in individuals', declares one of the aphorisms under the headword 'Nature' in Bacon's 'Antitheses of Things' (1623) (*The Essays*, 148). As an argument *pro* nature, the analogy between common law and nature suggests the possibility (though hardly intended by Bacon) to sneak revenge under the umbrella of common law.

[34] What Bacon omits is the cultural—as opposed to natural—dimension of revenge, its normative ethical and social function and its highly coded forms in feudal warrior cultures. But the elimination of residual feudalist obstructions to central state power is nonetheless one of his central concerns.

[35] Cf. Evans, *Rituals of Retribution*.

[36] Pierre-Francois Muyart de Vouglans (1713–91), quoted in Foucault, *Discipline and Punish*, 48 (my italics). For Muyart de Vouglans's role in the late 18th-c. debate about the abolition of torture, see Edward Peters, *Torture* (Philadelphia: University of Pennsylvania Press, 1996), 72–3.

[37] Foucault, *Discipline and Punish*, 48.

I thinke there is more barbarisme in eating men alive, than to feed upon them being dead; to mangle by tortures and torments a body full of lively sense, to roast him in peeces, to make dogges and swine gnaw and teare him in mammockes (as wee have not only read, but seene very lately, yea and in our owne memorie, not amongst ancient enemies, but our neighbours and fellow-citizens; and which is worse, under pretence of pietie and religion) than to roast and eat him after he is dead. (i. 223–4)

III. Consuming Flames: Foxe's Spectacle of Martyrdom

The excesses of cruelty which horrified Montaigne—excesses made all the more appalling for being committed 'under pretence of pietie and religion'—find their most graphic illustration in the accounts of juridical torture gathered in John Foxe's *Acts and Monuments*.[38] Foxe's belligerent Protestantism could not differ more sharply from the spirit of religious moderation and compromise that permeates the *Essais*.[39] But his detailed descriptions of martyrdom—the barbarism of roasting men alive—reveal the same three-tiered representational nexus of justice-as-revenge-as-cannibalism which is so deeply troubling to Montaigne's sense of his own civilization. Here is Foxe's account of the death of John Huss, who was burnt as a heretic at the Council of Constance on 6 July 1415:

> *The martyrdome of blessed Iohn Hus. Precious in the sight of God is the death of hys saintes. The hart of Iohn Hus beaten with staues, and consumed with fire. The ashes of Iohn Hus cast into the riuer of Rheine.*

> Then was the fire kindled, and Iohn Hus began to sing with a loud voice, Iesu Christ the sonne of the liuing God haue mercy vpon me. And when he began

---

[38] Though Foxe is the most prominent and readily available source of 16th-c. accounts of religiously motivated juridical torture, this does not mean that the execution of Catholics followed a different protocol. See Anne Dillon, *The Construction of Martyrdom in the English Catholic Community 1535–1603* (Aldershot: Ashgate, 2002); Susannah B. Monta, *Martyrdom and Literature in Early Modern England* (Cambridge: Cambridge University Press, 2005); Gabriela Schmidt, 'Representing Martyrdom in Post-Reformation England', in Andreas Höfele, Stephan Laqué, Enno Ruge, and Gabriela Schmidt (eds.), *Representing Religious Pluralization in Early Modern Europe* (Berlin: Lit, 2007), 63–90.

[39] However, Foxe had this in common with Montaigne: he too abhorred physical violence to animals, writing that he could 'scarce pass the shambles where beasts are slaughtered, but that my mind recoils with a feeling of pain'. Quoted in William Haller, *Foxe's Book of Martyrs and the Elect Nation* (London: Jonathan Cape, 1963), 56.

to say the same the third time, the winde droue the flame so vpon his face, that it choked him. Yet notwithstanding he mooued a while after, by the space that a man might almost say three times the Lordes prayer. When all the wood was burned and consumed, the vpper parte of the body was left hanging in the chaine, the which they threwe downe stake and all, and making a newe fire burned it, the heade being first cut in small gobbets, that it might the sooner be consumed vnto ashes. The heart, which was founde amongest the bowels, being well beaten with staues and clubbes, was at last pricked vppon a sharpe sticke, and roasted at a fire a parte vntill it was consumed. Then with great diligence gathering the ashes together, they cast them into the riuer of Rhene, that the least remnaunt of the ashes of that man shoulde not be left vppon the earth, whose memorie notwythstanding cannot be abolished out of the minds of the godly, neither by fire, neither by water, neither by anye kinde of torment.

I know very well that these things are very sclenderly wrytten of me as touching the labours of thys most holy Martyr Iohn Hus, with whome the labors of Hercules are not to be compared. For that auncient Hercules slew a few monsters: but this our Hercules with a moste stout and valiant courage hath subdued euen the worlde it selfe, the mother of all monsters and cruell beastes.[40]

Giving rhetorical end weight to the passage, the 'cruel beasts' serve to press home the opposition between the martyr and a corrupt and hostile world. But animality—and cannibalism—are also, if less outspokenly, present in the narration of the event itself, the treatment Huss's mortal remains undergo at the hands of the unnamed 'they'. What strikes a modern observer as an eruption of destructive frenzy is in fact a calculated procedural routine whose grim thoroughness is to make sure that no part of the heretic's body be made into a relic. Step by step this procedure takes Huss down the Aristotelian ladder of being: from articulate human subject to unconscious, barely living body to disposable object and, finally, to a

---

[40] Foxe, *Actes and Monuments*, 625. This event occupies a prominent place in Foxe's grand narrative of the true church of Protestant England. The first edition of *Acts and Monuments* (1563) begins with John Wyclif, who escaped death at the stake, although his bones were burned posthumously, as were his books. This makes Huss, Wyclif's Bohemian follower, the Continental proto-martyr of the English Reformation. In the pictorial narrative of Foxe's work, the place of the English proto-martyr is given to the Lollard William Sawter, whose martyrdom at the stake is the 'first woodcut in *Acts and Monuments* of a person being burnt alive in England'. Tom Betteridge, 'Truth and History in Foxe's *Acts and Monuments*', in Christopher Highley and John N. King (eds.), *John Foxe and his World* (Aldershot: Ashgate, 2002), 145–59 at 145.

quantity of mere matter. Halfway down this scale from man to 'ashes', the text registers a change from human to animal. It occurs at the point where torture turns into butchery, flesh into meat; where the head is 'cut in small gobbets', the heart 'pricked upon a sharp stick, and roasted at a fire'. Gutting, carving, and roasting are basic techniques in the preparation of meat.[41] The use of 'gobbets' reinforces this association with cooking and eating, as does the twice-used verb 'consume'.[42] As the martyr's body is animalized, those officiating at the ceremony are turned into cannibal cooks. While Montaigne is at pains to detach the cannibals from the odium of bestiality, this European representation of 'an extreme, and inexpiable revenge' ('Of the Canniballes', i. 223) draws on the much more conventional imaginary that conceives them as twin variants on a scale of subhuman otherness.

Medieval sources suggest that people harboured 'a deep fear of becoming animal food',[43] of a reversal of the divinely ordained 'natural' food chain in which man must always be the eater but never eaten. This fear attached especially to the wolf—quite in excess of the real danger posed by wolves in the Middle Ages. It manifested itself in a horror at becoming worm food in the grave; and it compounded the terrors of hell, whose inmates were thought to be consumed not only by flames but also by a whole menagerie of dragons, snakes, giant toads, and other voracious monsters.

The spectacle of the heretic's execution presented the on-looking crowd with a graphic anticipation of 'the punishments of the beyond'; it was 'a theatre of hell',[44] just as, conversely, medieval hell presented a phantasmagoric mirror image of criminal justice. This reciprocity reinforces the symbolic cannibalism implied in the treatment of Huss's body. The invisible glutton awaiting this dish of human flesh is very visibly present in both medieval church paintings and the civic mystery cycles where hell's mouth is pictured as the gaping jaws of a giant beast or indeed—narrowing

---

[41] *Carnifex*, 'executioner' in classical Latin, came to acquire the additional meaning 'butcher' in medieval Latin.

[42] 'Consume': *OED* lists 'Senses relating to physical destruction' first, and clearly this sense of 'consume' is the prominent one in Foxe's account. But 'Senses relating to the use or exploitation of resources' as in 'To eat or drink; to ingest' were equally current. The earliest instance cited—quite apposite in our context—is Wyclif *c*.1400.

[43] Joyce E. Salisbury, *The Beast within: Animals in the Middle Ages* (New York: Routledge, 1994), 72.

[44] Cf. Foucault, *Discipline and Punish*, 46.

the gap between animal and cannibal to the point of elision—the Devil himself.[45]

Foxe's text, of course, records the juridical semantics of hellish orality only to triumphantly reverse its bias. Symbolically downgraded to animal status, meat for the jaws of Hell, the tormented heretic reverses his doom, rising from the ashes as a Herculean hero of faith. His mythical predecessor had to take on the Nemean lion, the Hydra, Cerberus the hellhound, and several other monstrous beasts, but Huss achieves the even greater feat of subduing 'the world itself, the mother of all monsters and cruel beasts'. Like redeemed Humankind in a morality play, the slaughtered victim rises above the unholy trinity of World, Flesh, and Beast, *mundus*, *caro*, and *bestia*, in heroic glory.

No such reversal is granted the condemned Huss in the account of one Ulrich von Richenthal, who witnessed the execution.[46] Instead of chanting a pious plea for salvation and, as Foxe's text suggests, silently articulating the Lord's Prayer when 'the flame . . . choked him', Richenthal's Huss perishes screaming.[47] And no sooner is he dead than an evil smell envelops the place of execution. Owing to the heat of the fire, Richenthal explains, the ground burst open and released the smell of a dead mule—formerly the property of Cardinal Pangracius—which happened to have been buried there. In spite of its ostensibly natural cause, the beastly stench rising from below is highly suggestive of the place where the church authorities and, presumably, the

---

[45] In Christian iconology, Satan is at home in humanoid and animal shape alike and is often to be found in a hybridization of the two. His devouring of sinners is thus doubly encoded as both predatory and cannibalistic. The Devil's cannibalistic propensity is still etymologically traceable in his nursery tale descendant, the child-gobbling ogre, the Italian 'ogro' deriving from the Latin Orcus, God of the Underworld. Cf. Marina Warner, 'Fee fie fo fum: The Child in the Jaws of the Story', in Barker, Hulme and Iversen (eds.), *Cannibalism and the Colonial World*, 158–82 at 161. On cannibalism as a feature of the Christian underworld, see Mary Kilgour, *From Communion to Cannibalism: An Anatomy of Metaphors of Incorporation* (Princeton: Princeton University Press, 1990), 65–9.

[46] Foxe's account of the death of Huss draws, via several intermediary stages, on the testimony of one of the reformer's Bohemian friends and followers, Peter von Mladoniovitz (Mladoňovic); an unmistakable sign of this provenance is the time span of Huss's final agony, which is given as 'the space that a man might almost say three times the Lord's Prayer' ('als lang man mocht drey vatter vnser betten'). The text is quoted in Hubert Herkommer, 'Die Geschichte vom Leiden und Sterben des Jan Hus als Ereignis und Erzählung', in Ludger Grenzmann and Karl Stackmann (eds.), *Literatur und Laienbildung im Spätmittelalter und in der Reformationszeit* (Symposium Wolfenbüttel 1981) (Stuttgart: Metzler, 1984), 114–46 at 115.

[47] Richenthal records Huss's agony in a single sentence: 'Do gehůb er sich mit schryen vast übel und was bald verbrunnen' (Then he began screaming hideously and was soon burnt to death). Quoted in Herkommer, 'Die Geschichte vom Leiden', 114.

majority of the spectators, including Richenthal, saw the heretic's soul headed.[48] Again, as in Foxe, animality charges the actual scene of execution with intimations of an infernal orifice; only this time Huss, instead of vanquishing the Beast, is, as it were, of the Beast's party.[49]

The symbolic downgrading of Huss from human to animal corroborates the streak of animalization that we have seen running through the rituals of public shaming, maiming, and killing which the early modern judiciary performed on the bodies of malefactors. But running counter to the affirmative pull of the spectacle there is always the risk of inversion—most markedly in those cases where humans are roasted, as Montaigne protests, 'under pretence of pietie and religion'. At a time when God's one and only Truth had become radically plural, drawing the line between true believer and heretic proved difficult, even as it seemed to become ever more urgent. The very rigour and severity with which religious parties sought to enforce a return to the one and only true path (which could only ever be their own particular, strongly contested version of it), had the unintended but inevitable counter-effect of fostering multiplication instead of containing it, of sharpening rather than eliminating religious schism. If adherence to the wrong faith rather than common felony was to be avenged by the law, the chances were even greater that the legal dismembering of a human being might be perceived to bestialize the executioners instead of the culprit, to turn juridical proceeding into an appalling act of cannibalistic butchery.[50]

In the context of religious persecution, where the severest form of punishment is based on the least stable, most contestable, justification, animality itself is most liable to turn from negative to positive signification. Where human punishment suggests animal slaughter, the slaughtered animal may become fraught with suggestions of human suffering, even, and especially, of martyrdom. Commenting on a seventeenth-century Dutch painting, Joachim Beuckelaer's *Market Scene with Ecce Homo*, Robert Watson

[48] As a cross of horse and ass, the mule (Richenthal: 'roßmul') is an animal fraught with demonic symbolism. Absalon, an exemplary *figura diaboli*, rode to his doom on a mule; the mule combines the horse, *forma hereticorum*, and the ass, the symbol of pride and *immunditia* (uncleanliness). Herkommer, 'Die Geschichte vom Leiden', 120.

[49] The symbolism of the beastly smell was not lost on Huss's Protestant supporters, as is born out by Christoph Walpurger, *Hussus Combustus* (Gera: Andreas Mamitzsch, 1624): the wily cardinal, he claims, had the mule purposely buried at the place of execution in order to denigrate the martyr. See Herkommer, 'Die Geschichte vom Leiden', 130.

[50] Foucault, *Discipline and Punish*, 51.

Figure 10. Copper engraving 'The Lambe speaketh. Why do you crucifie me agen' (1553–5).

observes that 'Jesus in the background is clearly doomed to look very soon like the animal carcasses hung up in the foreground'. From there, Watson continues, 'and from the many depictions of the martyrdom of saints, it is a short leap—though over a scary abyss—to a series of still lifes' which present the carcasses of animals disturbingly like the agonized figures on Calvary.[51] The leap is hardly novel, though, having been anticipated in the popular iconography of sixteenth-century Protestant polemics. For example, in a pictorial broadsheet attacking Marian re-Catholicizing, a lamb hung up by its feet has its throat bitten through by a wolf in cope and mitre who is identified as Bishop Gardiner of Winchester (Fig. 10).[52]

Such movement back and forth between the literal and the symbolic shows the animal to be a veritable figure of inversion, a signifier of high, potentially subversive agility. Even when enlisted to denote subhuman debasement, it has an ever-ready capacity to convert humiliation into glory.[53]

This capacity is closely connected with the semantic ambivalence en-coded in the Latin word *sacer*, which means both 'holy' and 'accursed', and it is a defining feature of the *sacrificium* 'which for the ancients was the sacred experience par excellence'.[54] Animal sacrifice ceased in the West with the victory of Christianity, yet at the core of the Christian civilization that sustained the theatre of punishment stands the execution of Jesus Christ, the sacrificial slaughter of the Word become mortal flesh perennially commem-orated in a symbol of faith that takes its shape from an instrument of torture.

Defying the Church of Rome with nobler-than-Stoic Christian con-stancy, Foxe's martyrs inevitably recall the other, pagan Rome in whose

---

[51] Watson speaks of a 'significant congruence between the way Christians were supposed to identify piteously with the Christ who at once does and does not share their nature as mortal animals, and the way they began to identify piteously with prey animals on the same basis'. Robert N. Watson, *Back to Nature: The Green and the Real in the Late Renaissance* (Philadelphia: University of Pennsylvania Press, 2006), 201.

[52] The copperplate etching with the incipit 'The Lambe speaketh. Why do you crucifie me agen' is reproduced with a critical commentary in *Die Sammlung der Herzog August Bibliothek in Wolfenbüttel*, ed. Wolfgang Harms with Michael Schilling and Andreas Wang, vol. 2 (Munich: Kraus, 1980), 16–17.

[53] As Foucault notes, a similar dynamics is characteristic of the popular literature which records the more sensational cases of early modern crime and punishment: 'There were those for whom glory and abomination were not dissociated, but coexisted in a reversible figure' (*Discipline and Punish*, 67).

[54] Walter Burkert, *Savage Energies: Lessons of Myth and Ritual in Ancient Greece*, trans. Peter Bing (Chicago and London: University of Chicago Press, 2001), 9.

arenas their early Christian predecessors died for their faith. Not only as the headquarters of 'the Romishe Prelates',[55] but also as the site of the persecution of the early Christians, Rome looms large in Foxe's narrative theatre of martyrdom.[56] And so it does in Montaigne's examination of cruelty, where it provides the paramount instance of the interaction between violence and spectacle.[57] The arenas of Imperial Rome have a vivid presence in the cultural memory of the Renaissance. 'These cruel and deadly shows', as Augustine calls them in the *Confessions*,[58] provide a richly evocative frame of reference for the conjunction of spectacle, punishment, and animality which are crucially operative in Shakespeare's theatre. From the first century CE onwards, the increasingly more magnificent and capacious Roman amphitheatres were used for ever more spectacular shows whose 'most distinctive characteristic . . . is that they combined in a single event the execution of criminals or deviants, the slaughter of animals, and prize fights to the death'.[59]

Something like a virtual backdrop, these shows may be seen to hover over the public spectacles of Shakespeare's London in which stage, stake, and scaffold operate separately but, as this book argues, in profound collusion. It is only fitting that Shakespeare's first tragedy of revenge should locate its excesses of wild justice in the city where theatrical entertainment, juridical killing, and human–animal blood-sports took place in a single venue.

---

[55] Cf. the title of the 1563 edition: *Actes and monuments of these latter and perillous dayes touching matters of the Church, wherein ar comprehended and decribed the great persecutions [and] horrible troubles, that haue bene wrought and practised by the Romishe prelates, speciallye in this realme of England and Scotlande, from the yeare of our Lorde a thousande, vnto the tyme nowe present . . .* (London: John Day, 1563).

[56] I have argued elsewhere that, 'If the martyrs regarded their public deaths as a performance, their chronicler Foxe heightens that sense of performance through the use of every means of dramatization available to him . . . Textual representation seeks to literally *re*-present the events it records, striving to approximate as closely as possible the condition of experiential immediacy.' 'Foxe's book strives, as far as its medium will allow, towards the condition and impact of theatre.' Höfele, 'Stages of Martyrdom', 88 and 91.

[57] 'Of Cruelty' (ii. 122); 'Of Bad Meanes Emploied to a Good End' (ii. 411).

[58] St Augustine, *The Confessions of Saint Augustine*, trans. Edward B. Pusey (Teddington, Middlesex: Echo Library, 2006), 60.

[59] W. G. Runciman, 'The Sociologist and the Historian' (= review of Keith Hopkins, *Death and Renewal* (Cambridge: Cambridge University Press, 1983)), *Journal of Roman Studies*, 76 (1986), 259–65 at 259.

IV. Scaffold Theatre and the Dynamics of Revenge: *Titus Andronicus*

At a time when Shakespeare's earliest Roman play was deemed a rather deplorable apprentice piece of the budding Bard—who could be held but partly responsible for it anyway—its Cambridge editor, John Dover Wilson, summarized his condescension thus: 'In a word, *The Most Lamentable Romaine Tragedie of Titus Andronicus* seems to jolt and bump along like some broken-down cart, laden with bleeding corpses from an Elizabethan scaffold, and driven by an executioner from Bedlam dressed in caps and bells.'[60] Scoffing aside, Wilson's comment is not all that wide of the mark. Few plays by Shakespeare or his contemporaries have the collusion of stage and scaffold written all over them as boldly as *Titus Andronicus*. By inter-weaving the spectacle of public punishment with the drama of revenge and by thus eliding the difference between wild and state-authorized justice, the play situates its characters in a space of anthropological liminality. As agents and patients of inseparably public as well as private retribution they under-take and undergo acts of animalization similar to the ones performed in Foxe's account of the death of John Huss. Characteristically, mutilation evokes martyrdom, though not, as we shall see, without important qualifi-cation. From the outset, fundamental lines of distinction between civil and wild, human and animal, are shown to be thoroughly undependable. The initial act of Roman piety reveals a substratum of cannibalism deeply embedded within Roman civilization, not newly begotten but primordially there. The destructive passions and the passion suffered, expressed in cas-cades of recklessly artificial eloquence, have their inevitable telos and emblematic focus in the piteously vulnerable body of the human animal. In this, *Titus Andronicus* proves closely akin to the *theatrum poenarum* detailed with relentless thoroughness in early modern catalogues of the atrocious methods of maiming and killing that a resourceful criminal justice held in store for the delinquent.[61] These manuals share a characteristic mode of

---

[60] John Dover Wilson, 'Introduction: An Essay in Literary Detection' in his edition of *Titus Andronicus* (Cambridge: Cambridge University Press, 1948), p. xii.

[61] The most elaborate and thoroughly methodical of these compilations comes from late 17th-c. Germany: Jacob Döpler, *Theatrum Poenarum, Suppliciorum et Executionum Criminalium, oder Schau-Platz derer Leibes und Lebens-Straffen* (Sondershausen: L. H. Schönermarck, 1693). The table of contents lists over fifty gruesome varieties of legal maiming and killing, each treated in a

objectifying and quantifying the body and its sensations. No longer the physical form of the human individual (literally somebody or something indivisible), the body is treated as an object to be taken to pieces, an assembly of detachable parts: hands, ears, eyes, tongues, bones, throat, head, entrails. Penal justice becomes a system of highly differentiated butchery, a trade of expert meat carvers administering exact doses of pain on an open scale of protracted agony.

This is gruesomely mimicked in *Titus Andronicus*, where a messenger enters with two severed heads and a hand (III. i. 232/3 SD) and where the central image of horror is the silent figure of Lavinia, handless, tongueless, raped. The logic of the system entails infinite intensification, an urge to outwit the finite capability of the human body to endure pain.[62] This urge manifests itself in *Titus Andronicus* when the emperor Saturninus orders Titus' sons Quintus and Martius, falsely accused of murder, to be held in prison 'until we have devised / Some never-heard-of torturing pain for them' (II. iii. 284–5). This is very much the kind of cruelty of which Montaigne is speaking, the cruelty that wants to see its victims suffer and which Montaigne expressly associates with the excesses 'such as Roman Tyrants brought into fashion' (ii. 119).

The play is saturated with the transactions between stage and scaffold; they extend right down to the casual hanging of the play's short-lived clown, who offers a fleeting memento to those estimated 13,000 anonymous men and women who lost their lives on the gallows during the reigns of Elizabeth I and James I.[63]

Almost exactly at mid-point, the play pictures the overthrow of the Andronici, as well as the disintegration of the body politic, in a macabre double allegory of cruelly anatomical justice. Opening Act III, 'the great image of authority' (*King Lear*, IV. v. 154) is mustered in a procession of

separate chapter, for example: '[5.] Of executions with a sword' ('von Hinrichtung mit dem Schwerdt'); '[7.] Of severing the head and neck with a plank, [8.] of ploughing off the head with a ploughshare, [9.] of hitting a sharp nail into the head/eyes/shoulders or knee' ('[7.] von Abstossung des Kopffs und Halses mit einer Dielen [8.] von Abahrung des Halses mit einem Pflug [9.] von Schlagung eines spitzigen Nagels durch den Kopff/Augen/Schultern und Knie'); '[26.] Of tearing human bodies to pieces with iron combs and currycombs' ('von Zerreißung der menschlichen Leiber mit eisernen Kämmen und Striegeln'); '[47.] Of roasting men alive on a spit' ('von Braten der lebendigen Menschen an Spiessen').

[62] The account of the execution of the assassin Damiens in Foucault, *Discipline and Punish*, 3–6, graphically exemplifies this tendency.

[63] Francis Barker, 'Treasures of Culture: *Titus Andronicus* and Death by Hanging', in Miller, O'Dair, and Weber (eds.), *The Production of English Renaissance Culture*, 226–61 at 248.

'*Judges, Tribunes, and Senators with Titus' two sons, Martius and Quintus, bound, passing over the stage to the place of execution*' (III. i. 1 SD). Seeking to halt the march of justice, '*Andronicus lieth down, and the Judges pass by him*' (III. i. 11 SD), leaving him to plead in emblematic futility 'my sorrows to the stones' (III. i. 36). And the scene concludes with a second procession in which carnage meets carnival as the Andronici take up the body parts that justice has dished out to them:

> Come brother, take a head,
> And in this hand the other will I bear.
> And Lavinia, thou shalt be employed.
> Bear thou my hand, sweet wench, between thine arms.
>
> (III. i. 278–81)

Even as the play begins, Rome presents itself in the ominous image of a punished capital offender. Decapitated by the death of its former emperor, the state needs to be, as it were, re-capitated. The victorious Titus is enjoined by his brother, the tribune Marcus Andronicus, to 'help to set a head on headless Rome' (I. i. 186), but declines the offer in a characteristically physical amalgamation of public and private body:

> A better head her glorious body fits
> Than his that shakes for age and feebleness.   (I. i. 187–8)

Though the point here is restoration of wholeness, the line foreshadows the image of the partitionable body that comes to dominate the further course of the action.

But before unleashing its wild justice, the play gives a demonstration of legality and order. Confronted with a state crisis, the constitutional organs prove equal to the challenge of impending civil war between the former emperor's two sons, Saturninus and Bassianus, the one pleading primogeniture, the other his virtue as claim to the title. Ringing with invocations of 'justice' and 'right', the symmetrical—and symmetrically staged—fraternal contest is brought to a temporary conclusion with the prospect of fair arbitration: 'my cause', Bassianus is confident, 'in balance to be weighed' (I. i. 55).

MARCUS Let us entreat by honour of his name
    Whom worthily you would have now succeeded,[64]

---

[64] Both F and QI have 'succeed' here, which makes the referent of 'his' in the previous line unclear. Titus cannot be meant, because the emperor's sons would hardly grant him the succession which each of them wants for himself. The plausible alternative that 'his' refers to the dead emperor himself is made possible by Capell's emendation 'succeeded'.

> And in the Capitol and Senate's right,
> Whom you pretend to honour and adore,
> That you withdraw you and abate your strength,
> Dismiss your followers, and, as suitors should,
> Plead your deserts in peace and humbleness.   (I. i. 39–45)

Senators, tribunes, references to the 'common voice' of 'the people of Rome' (I. i. 12, 41), to the Capitol (I. i. 12, 41) and to the due process of the election ('as suitors should') contribute to the sense of an institutional Rome in reasonably good working order. Armed conflict is forestalled through mediation, even if the mediator, Marcus Andronicus, prevails only because of a third power more strongly armed than either of the quarrelling factions. The announcement of Titus Andronicus' imminent return from war heightens the impression of Roman strength and institutional order. Military force is shown to be answerable to civil authority: SPQR, by order of the Senate and People of Rome, 'He [Titus] by the senate is accited home / From weary wars against the barbarous Goths' (I. i. 27–8). Martial valour, the core element of Roman virtue, maintains and expands the dominion of civilization against the forces of a barbarity which lies strictly and, thanks to Titus, safely outside its boundaries. Fittingly, Rome's champion '[h]ath yoked' (I. i. 30) the barbarous Goths. In the literal sense of the word, he has reduced them to the position of tamed beasts harnessed to draw a plough.[65] Speaking 'fair', Marcus not only manages 'to calm' the hotly ambitious Saturninus' 'thoughts' (I. i. 46), but also to invest the approaching Titus with an aura of venerable *Romanitas*, which is sealed by the mention that he is 'surnamèd *Pius*' (I. i. 23).

After this induction, the lapse that follows registers all the more sharply. Hardly does barbarity seem conquered at the frontier of the empire than it erupts full-fledged at home, not an alien power but embedded in civilization itself, endorsed and executed by the very pillar of Roman society. Returning, the victorious Titus brings back Goth prisoners and a coffin.[66] Of his twenty-five sons ('Half of the number that King Priam had', I. i. 80),

---

[65] The Latin verb *subiugare*-subjugate (*sub iugum agere*/to lead under the yoke) conveys the same idea of human control over a tamed beast.

[66] It is not quite clear how many dead sons Titus is bringing back. The SD (1.1.69/70) speaks of '*a coffin covered with black*', but in his funeral oration speaks of 'These [sons] that I bring unto their latest home' to be given 'burial amongst their ancestors' (I. i. 83–4), which means definitely more than one and perhaps all twenty-one of them.

twenty-one have been killed in action. The triumphal entry is a m
procession; it comes to a halt before the Andronici's tomb. The dea
hovering unburied 'on the dreadful shore of Styx' (I. i. 88), are prom
'silence' and 'peace' (I. i. 90–1). But first their audible, 'groaning' (I. i. 12c,
hunger must be stilled. Not before they have been fed the flesh of their
noblest enemy, Queen Tamora's eldest son Alarbus, can there be 'No noise,
but silence and eternal sleep' (I. i. 155):

LUCIUS   Give us the proudest prisoner of the Goths,
           That we may hew his limbs and on a pile
           Ad manes fratrum sacrifice his flesh
           Before this earthly prison of their bones,
           That so the shadows be not unappeased   (I. i. 96–100)

Deaf to her plea for mercy, Titus informs Tamora that Lucius and his
brothers 'religiously' (I. i. 124) demand no more than what is right and
proper. Retaliatory slaughter is a legitimate act of piety, but, as Tamora is
quick to exclaim, of a 'cruel irreligious piety' (I. i. 130), exceeding the
barbarity of the most notoriously barbaric ancients:

CHIRON   Was never Scythia half so barbarous.
DEMETRIUS   Oppose not Scythia to ambitious Rome.   (I. i. 131–2)

If Titus is 'surnamèd *Pius*' (I. i. 23), this piousness makes cruelty his middle
name—the kind of cruelty 'under pretence of pietie and religion' which
Montaigne holds more appalling than that of 'the Cannibales and savage
people'.

Anthropophagy is deeply ingrained in the fabric of Shakespeare's eclec-
tically composite Rome. In accordance with the play's setting, it does not
feature under its recently acquired transatlantic name,[67] cannibalism, but is
introduced under the label of Scythia, its typological analogue in the ancient
world. The brute force of Rome's voracity breaking the surface of civil
decorum is in the rhetorical contrast between the measured solemnity of
Titus' funeral oration and Lucius' impatient demand for blood, especially his
rapid-fire references to the act of dismemberment itself:

---

[67] Clifford Ronan, *'Antike Romans': Power Symbology and the Roman Play in Early Modern
England, 1585–1635* (Athens, Ga. and London: University of Georgia Press, 1995), 135.

LUCIUS Away with him, and make a fire straight,
      And with our swords upon a pile of wood
      Let's hew his limbs till they be clean consumed.   (I. i. 127–9)

      See, lord and father, how we have performed
      Our Roman rites. Alarbus' limbs are lopped
      And entrails feed the sacrificing fire   (I. i. 142–4)

'Hew' and 'lop', 'consume' and 'feed'—the cannibal nature of 'Our Roman rites' could not be more obvious. That these rites are endorsed with such manifest gusto by Lucius, the only son of Titus to survive the play and Rome's future emperor, underscores their embeddedness in a Rome which has little to do with the idealizations of later white-marble classicism, being all the more in keeping with the deeply ambivalent Elizabethan perception of Rome.[68]

The sacrificial killing of Alarbus, the play's first act of lawful 'man-slaughter', is the source of all the violence to follow, including Titus' Thyestean banquet in Act V. Feeding Alarbus to the dead foreshadows feeding his brothers to their mother, the symbolic cannibalism of the one anticipating the literal cannibalism of the other. Both feedings represent, quoting Montaigne, 'an extreme, and inexpiable revenge' (i. 223). For the play does not begin at the beginning, but opens with the body count of its long prehistory of retaliatory violence, in which Alarbus' death is just one link of a never-ending chain.

The opportunity to cut this chain presents itself when Tamora kneels before Titus, and is missed. Unlike Montaigne's cannibals, Titus knows the word 'pardon' but uses it in a way that, under the circumstances, must seem cruelly witty. Asked for pardon, but granting none, he retorts: 'Patient yourself, madam, and pardon me' (I. i. 121), and wastes no time in having Alarbus dispatched. Having begun with the symmetry of a fraternal tussle for empire, this first confrontation between the Queen of Goths and Rome's general, in which her moving eloquence dispels any presumption of cultural inferiority on the part of the 'barbarians', commences the clash of a pair of much mightier opposites, locked in a scarcely less symmetrical pattern of conflict. She is everything the patriarchal order of Titus' Rome hates, fears, and eventually destroys and expels—a powerful female Other of

---

[68] 'The propensities of the whole civilized/barbaric Roman nation are symbolized in ambivalence and dichotomy'; Ronan, 'Antike Romans' 3.

threatening independence and appetite, both sexual and political.[69] Yet it is
also quite unmistakable how the tie between the play's principal antagonists
is defined by means not only of contrast but also of similarity and corres-
pondence. What her first appeal to Titus makes forcefully clear is something
the play never allows us to lose sight of: the parallels in their respective
situations, how her plight mirrors his and vice versa. The whole point of her
plea for mercy is that Titus recognize this, a recognition impressed on us
once more when Titus pleads prostrate for his sons' life in Act III in very
similar terms of familial sympathy and military valour:[70]

> And if thy sons were ever dear to thee,
> O, think my son to be as dear to me!
>
> But must my sons be slaughtered in the streets
> For valiant doings in their country's cause?
> O, if to fight for king and commonweal
> Were piety in thine, it is in these.   (I. i. 107–8; 112–15)

What unites them more than anything else is the very thing that sets them
asunder: parenthood. If Titus is the archetypal father of the play, Tamora is
its archetypal mother. Though certainly not, as Hamlet quips, 'one flesh'
(*Hamlet* IV. iii. 54), they briefly even have a child together. To the newly
elected emperor Saturninus, Titus is 'father of my life' (I. i. 253) and Tamora
'a mother to his youth' (I. i. 329). Deadly life-givers both, they do not
hesitate to kill *for*, but also kill, their offspring: Titus, the disobedient
Mutius, and the raped Lavinia; Tamora, the new-born child of her illicit
connection with Aaron the Moor. The mother of Titus' sons is as unnamed
and unmentioned, as is the father of hers: Totillius, King of Goths, plays an
important part in the prose *History of Titus Andronicus*, but is non-existent in
Shakespeare's play.[71] The stage is cleared, as it were, of previous spouses for
the consummation, or consumption, of this marriage of revenge.

---

[69] This has been shown, for example, by Marion Wynne-Davies, ' "The Swallowing Womb":
Consumed and Consuming Women in *Titus Andronicus*', in Valerie Wayne (ed.), *The Matter of
Difference: Materialist Feminist Criticism of Shakespeare* (Ithaca, NY, and New York: Cornell
University Press, 1991), 129–51; and Cynthia Marshall, ' "I can interpret all her martyr'd signs":
Titus Andronicus, Feminism, and the Limits of Interpretation', in Carole Levin and Karen Robert-
son (eds.), *Sexuality and Politics in Renaissance Drama* (Lewiston, NY, Queenston, Ont., and
Lampeter, Wales: Edward Mellen Press, 1991), 193–213.

[70] Wynne-Davies, ' "The Swallowing Womb" ', 138.

[71] Cf. Appendix A: 'The Prose History of Titus Andronicus', in *Titus Andronicus*, ed. Eugene
M. Waith (Oxford: Oxford University Press, 1984), 195–8.

Tamora, who enters as Titus' prisoner kneeling before him in a plea for mercy, ends the first scene as empress while he, kneeling, is granted pardon at her behest. In a rush of sudden reversals from outside to centre, from bottom to top, her rise mirrors his equally rapid decline. In a matter of minutes, he who was emperor-elect, in possession of all military and civil power, finds himself a lonely outsider: 'Titus, when wert thou wont to walk alone, / Dishonoured thus and challengèd of wrongs?' (I. i. 336–7). As *pater patriae*, 'father' of both emperor and nation, he had the power of life and death. Now it is Tamora, newly 'incorporate in Rome' (I. i. 459), who has the (maternal) power to 'infuse new life' in Titus (I. i. 458). Counting losses and gains, the scene underscores symmetry as well as contrast in having cost both her and him a son. But the new emperor, prospective son-in-law to Titus, ends up as filial husband under Tamora's maternal sway. Demonstrating his absolute power only to relinquish it, Titus, like King Lear, rushes headlong into disaster, showing a similar lack of judgement and paternal anger control. And like Lear, too, he is suddenly afflicted with the frailty of old age when power escapes him. Though he is the first to allude to his own 'age and feebleness' when turning down the candidacy (I. i. 188), these attributes do not acquire reality until Tamora (not only Rome's new mother, but also '[a] Roman now adopted happily' (I. i. 460), its daughter) enjoins Saturninus to '[t]ake up this good old man, and cheer the heart / That dies in tempest of thy angry frown' (I. i. 454–5). With his power, Titus has also ceded the force of sovereign anger to Saturninus, giving Tamora the opportunity for a demonstratively neat reversal of her initial position: 'By my advice, all humbled on your knees, / You shall ask pardon of his majesty' (I. i. 469–70).

V. The Mouth-Trap

In *A Midsummer Night's Dream* the lovers flee to the forest in order to escape the stern patriarchal law of Athens. In the sheltering woods they undergo a series of metamorphoses which, unsettling though they are, enable them to return to the city and be integrated into society through marriage. *Titus Andronicus* shows the same three-stage movement from city to green world and back,[72] but with fatally different consequences. The forest is visited after

---

[72] For exposition of this basic pattern, see Northrop Frye, 'The Argument of Comedy', in *English Institute Essays, 1948*, ed. D. A. Robertson, Jr. (New York: Columbia University Press, 1949), 58–73; C. L. Barber, *Shakespeare's Festive Comedy* (Cleveland, Ohio, and New York: World Publishing, 1959).

the double wedding of Saturninus to Tamora and Bassianus to Lavinia has taken place and seemingly ended all discord. It becomes the site of unspeakable horrors from which there is no return to the safe haven of civil order. Following the characters back from the wilderness and turning the city itself into 'a wilderness of tigers' (III. i. 53), there is, instead, a wave of further crimes building up to the final bloodbath.

A prelude to the forest scenes of Act II, the dialogue between Tamora's sons Chiron and Demetrius continues the blurring of the boundary between civilization and barbarity initiated by the sacrificial slaughter of Alarbus. The brothers (whose only lines up to this point have expressed shock at the worse than Scythian barbarousness of Roman piety) now enter the scene as rivals for the favour of the adored Lavinia. Longing '[t]o serve, and to deserve my mistress' grace' (II. i. 34), Chiron waxes lyrical over the boundlessness of his love:

> I care not, I, knew she and all the world,
> I love Lavinia more than all the world.   (II. i. 71–2)

This sounds more like Romeo than rape, or indeed more like the Demetrius of *A Midsummer Night's Dream* smitten by the unapproachable Hermia. There is no sense of menace in this quasi-Petrarchan gushing, just as there has been no forewarning of hewing and lopping in Titus' solemn funeral oration. But the shift from high-sounding rhetoric to brutal physicality is equally sudden. Aaron the Moor, something like the evil Puck of this forest, knows what is to be done:

> Why then, it seems some certain snatch or so
> Would serve your turns.   (II. i. 95–6)

No longer the mistress to be served, but the 'snatch' serving 'your turns', Lavinia is downgraded from admired woman to prey animal with chilling casualness. 'Would it offend you then', Aaron asks, 'That both should speed?' (II. i. 100–1). The answer is no, it wouldn't: as hunter-rapists rather than lovers, the brothers do not object to sharing the quarry. But despite its all too obvious drift, this change is more complexly encoded than simply as a lapse from civil to barbaric, humane to bestial. When Demetrius addresses his brother 'Chiron, we hunt not, we, with horse and hound, / But hope to pluck a dainty doe to ground' (II. ii. 25–6) this exposes the pursuit of Lavinia as sexual violence. But at the same time it cloaks the violence in a common metaphorical code of civilized love discourse. The 'violent sport' of hunting, as Montaigne calls it in 'Of Cruelty', immediately evokes an association with 'voluptuousnesse' and 'the thought-confounding violence of that pleasure' (ii. 118). In *Titus Andronicus* this 'sport' occasions the lapse into horrific savagery, but also provides the literary models for aesthetically containing that horror and its transgression of human boundaries. Ovid's Actaeon, the hunter turned stag by a cleverly vengeful goddess and torn to pieces by his own hounds, appropriately inspires the verbal skirmish that sparks off the atrocities:

BASSIANUS   Who have we here? Rome's royal empress,
            Unfurnished of her well-beseeming troop?
            Or is it Dian, habited like her
            Who hath abandonèd her holy groves
            To see the general hunting in this forest?
TAMORA   Saucy controller of my private steps,
            Had I the power that some say Dian had,
            Thy temples should be planted presently
            With horns, as was Actaeon's, and the hounds
            Should drive upon thy new-transformèd limbs,
            Unmannerly intruder as thou art.   (II. iii. 55–65)

If Tamora, invested with a favourite mythical persona of Queen Elizabeth herself,[73] is the goddess presiding over this hunting scene, the central stage symbol of her monstrous regiment is 'this abhorrèd pit' (II. ii. 98), 'this fell devouring receptacle' (II. iii. 235) which first swallows the corpse of Bassianus, then entraps Titus' unsuspecting sons Quintus and Martius, who are promptly found guilty of murdering him.[74] Hellmouth[75], this 'subtle hole … covered with rude-growing briers / Upon whose leaves are drops of new-shed blood' (II. iii. 198–200), combines cannibal voracity with an unmistakable symbolism of sexual aggression. 'Here's Freud aplenty!' rejoyced David Willbern in one of the earliest psychoanalytical

---

[73] Actaeon's encroachment on Diana's privacy offered a readily available template for the Earl of Essex's much commented-on intrusion into the Queen's private chamber on his return from the Irish campaign in Sept. 1599. Cf. Bate, *Shakespeare and Ovid*, 162–6, and James Shapiro, *1599: A Year in the Life of William Shakespeare* (London: Faber and Faber, 2005), 299–302. Once before in the play, at the very moment when she becomes empress of Rome, Tamora is likened to Phoebe/ Diana (I. i. 313).

[74] See Wynne-Davies, ' "The Swallowing Womb" ', 135–6; Marshall, ' "I can interpret all her martyr'd signs" ', 206; and D. J. Palmer, 'The Unspeakable in Pursuit of the Uneatable: Language and Action in *Titus Andronicus*', *Critical Quarterly*, 14 (1972), 320–39 at 327.

[75] 'As hateful as Cocytus' misty mouth' (II. iii. 236); editors are agreed that Cocytus, a river in hell, is used here for hell generally.

readings of the play: ' "The abhorrèd pit" will soon assume its central and over-determined symbolic significance as vagina, womb, tomb, and mouth, and all those "snakes" and "urchins" (hedgehogs or goblins) and "swelling toads" may plausibly be imagined as grotesquely distorted phallic threats.'[76] The phallic threat, however, seems less crucial than the threat posed by this all too obviously female hole. '[B]lood-drinking' (II. iii. 224) as well as blood-stained, it evokes both the man-eating *vagina dentata* of male horror fantasy and the vagina of the rape victim, symbolically uniting the violence done by woman with the violence done to her—perpetrated by Tamora and visited on Lavinia—in one disturbingly overdetermined image. 'The imagery is blatant', writes Marion Wynne-Davies, 'the cave being the vagina, the all-consuming sexual mouth of the feminine earth, which remains outside the patriarchal order of Rome'.[77]

Not entirely outside, though. If the cruel piety of Act I has shown 'that the barbarian is within the gates',[78] then so is the 'swallowing womb' (II. iii. 239). The monument of the Andronici, whose polymorphous symbolism Wynne-Davies reduces to 'the patriarchal vault',[79] clearly centres the action on another 'gaping hole in the stage'.[80] Prefiguring 'the swallowing womb' in the forest, 'the swallowing tomb' in the city suggests a deeper entangle-ment of the destructive paternal forces epitomized by Titus with the destructive maternal power of Tamora. The womb in the forest is also a tomb and a place of human sacrifice where 'Lord Bassianus lies berayed in blood / All on a heap, like to a slaughtered lamb' (II. iii. 222–3) and where the precious ring 'Upon his bloody finger' affords light 'like a taper in some monument' (II. iii. 226–8). The Andronici monument, on the other hand—a blood-stained mouth[81] from which the voices of the dead are 'groaning' for more—is also construed as a womb. Titus addresses it as 'O sacred receptacle of my joys' (I. i. 92), the same noun later applied to 'this

---

[76] David Willbern, 'Rape and Revenge in *Titus Andronicus*', *English Literary Renaissance*, 8 (1978), 159–82 at 169. But 'it obviously needs no Freud to tell Shakespeare what this hole is'. C. L. Barber and Richard P. Wheeler, *The Whole Journey: Shakespeare's Power of Development* (Berkeley: University of California Press, 1986), 142.

[77] Wynne-Davies, ' "The Swallowing Womb" ', 135.

[78] Marshall, ' "I can interpret all her martyr'd signs" ', 196.

[79] Wynne-Davies, ' "The Swallowing Womb" ', 146.

[80] Marshall, ' "I can interpret all her martyr'd signs" ', 206.

[81] Cf. Tamora's plea (I. i. 116): 'Andronicus, stain not thy tomb with blood.'

fell devouring receptacle' in the forest (II. iii. 236). The womb association is reinforced by 'How many sons hast thou of mine in store' (I. i. 94), but the suggestion of fecundity is immediately revoked by the relative clause following: 'That thou wilt never render to me more!' (I. i. 95) This is an inverse womb, one that takes rather than gives life, a fitting symbol for the destructive energies of revenge. The retributive violence of *Titus Andronicus* resembles the cyclical food-chain which David Quint sees in Montaigne's depiction of 'a cannibal society and larger culture that, even as it directs its violence outward in war against its enemy, is literally devouring itself'.[82]

Titus and Tamora, father and mother, contribute to the perpetuation of this consuming revenge in unholy alliance. To the preparation for the final feast she brings the costume ('Revenge'), he brings the knife. And both are conjoined in the ultimate outrage of any play of the period: Lavinia staggers on stage, '*her hands cut off and her tongue cut out, and ravished*' (II. iv SD). The rape of Lavinia, approved and abetted by the mother of her violators, physically consummates the union of the two houses over her invaded, mutilated, silenced body. 'Deflowered'[83] by Chiron and Demetrius, Lavinia becomes Tamora's 'daughter', not in law, but through rape, at the same time as Titus acquires two new 'sons' through the joining of Lavinia's blood with that of her penetrators.[84] In keeping with the Ovidian intertextuality of the scene, Chiron and Demetrius take good care to avoid the mistake that tripped up their literary model, Tereus, who deprived Philomela of speech, but left her with hands to accuse her attacker in writing.[85] 'Write down thy mind', Chiron taunts, 'bewray thy meaning so, / And if thy stumps will let thee play the scribe' (II. iv. 4–5).

The tension between literary representation and stage performance, between linguistic utterance and the silent body in pain, becomes extreme—and to critics of Dover Wilson's generation simply unacceptable[86]—when Marcus' subsequent lyrical description of Lavinia's 'cruel

---

[82] Quint, 'A Reconsideration', 176.

[83] The play insists on 'deflowered' though the deed occurs after her wedding night.

[84] In the economy of the humoral body, blood and semen are convertible. Thomas Laqueur, *Making Sex: Body and Gender from the Greeks to Freud* (Cambridge, Mass., and London: Harvard University Press, 1990), 35, speaks of 'a physiology of fungible fluids and corporeal flux' effectuating '[e]ndless mutations'.

[85] On Ovidian motifs in *Titus*, see Bate, *Shakespeare and Ovid*, esp. 101–17.

[86] Early interventions for a re-evaluation of the play and an appreciation of its aesthetic quality can be found in Palmer, 'The Unspeakable', and Albert H. Tricomi, 'The Aesthetics of Mutilation in *Titus Andronicus*', *Shakespeare Survey*, 27 (1974), 11–19.

metamorphosis'[87] runs disconcertingly alongside her overwhelmingly grim physical presence. Where speech should fail, it becomes floridly—or desperately—articulate instead. Marcus' 'dialogue of one'[88] with his mute niece strains to the utmost the tension between linguistically encoded cultural text and the unspoken and unspeakable otherness of the body—a tension prefigured at the opening of the forest scenes in the complexly ambiguous image of the hunt. Shakespeare translates Ovid from page to stage and then translates Lavinia's literal mutilations back into literary trope, thereby distancing but also deepening the silence of her pain.[89]

Raped 'by the book', Lavinia is also read as Ovidian text. Her very discovery by Marcus, whose entry '*from hunting*' is signalled by the sound of '*Wind horns*' (II. iv. 11 SD), recalls an archetypal Ovidian situation, the maiden pursued by the hunter: 'Who is this—my niece that flies away so fast?' (II. iv. 11) And just like another Daphne, Lavinia is then turned, or at least troped, into a tree as Marcus converts limbs into branches.[90] The verbs leading up to this metamorphosis into metaphor, however, recall in blunt literalness the play's initial act of violence, thus inserting Lavinia's violation into the retaliatory logic of dismemberment launched by the hewing and lopping of Alarbus:

> Speak, gentle niece, what stern ungentle hands
> Hath lopped and hewed and made thy body bare
> Of her two branches   (II. iv. 16–18)

Begun on 'the proudest prisoner of the Goths' (I. i. 96), the continuing work of dismemberment turns 'Rome's rich ornament' (I. i. 52) into a *corpus delicti* made undecipherable through amputation. But, versed in Ovid, Marcus guesses the nature of the crime, if not the identity of the criminals ('But sure some Tereus hath deflowered thee'; II. iv. 26), when he sees Lavinia's bleeding mouth.

The orality of sexual violation and cannibalistic revenge combined in the stage images of tomb and pit continues to pervade the play. Though the rape of Lavinia is not actually committed, as Chiron seems to indicate earlier, *in the abhorred pit itself*—using Bassianus' 'dead trunk [as] pillow to our lust' (II. iii. 130)—the image of the blood-stained hole is projected onto Lavinia's

---

[87] Palmer, 'The Unspeakable', 321.
[88] Marshall, ' "I can interpret all her martyr'd signs" ', 197.
[89] On pain and (non)language, see Scarry, *The Body in Pain*, 4.
[90] Cf. Ovid, *Metamorphoses*, 1. 452–567.

body and simultaneously literalized and re-troped when her bleeding mouth, in jarringly 'beautiful' imagery, gushes forth 'a crimson river of warm blood' which 'Like to a bubbling fountain stirred with wind, / Doth rise and fall between thy rosèd lips' (II. iv. 22–4). Lavinia's tongueless mouth[91] momentarily but momentously regains the power of speech and becomes the instrument of retribution when '*She takes the staff in her mouth, and guides it with her stumps, and writes*' (IV. i. 75/6 SD): '*Stuprum—Chiron— Demetrius*' (IV. i. 77). In a final replication and reversal of what she has suffered, Lavinia holds 'The basin that receives' her violators' 'guilty blood' (V. ii. 182)—an act which again forcefully evokes the orality of sexual violence, human sacrifice, and cannibalism.

In setting the machinery of revenge in motion, Lavinia has been said to gain a degree of agency as an active participant. But in a revenge action which, of necessity, entails her own death, the question of her subject position simply does not arise. 'What shall we do?' (III. i. 133) the disconsolate Titus asks her shortly before her plight moves him to the most poignant speech of the play, in which the father merges with his daughter in a 'coil' of commingling elements:[92]

> When heaven doth weep, doth not the earth o'erflow?
> If the winds rage, doth not the sea wax mad,
> Threat'ning the welkin with his big-swoll'n face?
> And wilt thou have a reason for this coil?
> I am the sea. Hark how her sighs doth blow.
> She is the weeping welkin, I the earth.
> Then must my sea be movèd with her sighs,
> Then must my earth with her continual tears
> Become a deluge overflowed and drowned,
> Forwhy my bowels cannot hide her woes,
> But like a drunkard must I vomit them.   (III. i. 220–30)

At the height of despair, distinctions are 'overflowed and drowned' as the figurehead of the play's patriarchal order identifies with the female fluidity

---

[91] The association of Lavinia's mouth with the other symbolically charged cavities of the play also shows up when Marcus glorifies it as 'that pretty hollow cage / Where, like a sweet melodious bird, it [her tongue] sung / Sweet varied notes, enchanting every ear' (III. i. 84–6). At the same time as this praise extols, it also confines Lavinia's power of speech to the pleasurable warbling of a caged animal. Her tongue is paid a similarly backhanded compliment as 'that delightful engine of her thoughts, / That blabbed them with such pleasing eloquence' (III. i. 82–3).

[92] For a powerful reading of the speech, see Wynne-Davies, ' "The Swallowing Womb" ', 143–4.

of tears, sea, and deluge and with the maternal earth, which will later become the allegorical guise of his female antagonist. Marking the climax of woe, the voracity of revenge is arrested in the image of vomiting. But when the flow is stopped and Titus, having 'not another tear to shed' (III. i. 265), turns his thoughts to revenge, the question of what to do is no longer addressed to Lavinia, not even rhetorically.

As far as her ultimate fate is concerned, it was settled before her violation has even occurred. In order to justify his paternal prerogative to ultimately 'disfigure' his disfigured daughter,[93] Titus quotes the example of Virginius, or rather, he misquotes it, Virginius having in fact killed his daughter to prevent her being raped.[94] As early as Scene i, her brother Lucius proves the more authentic Virginius in the quarrel over Bassianus' abduction of Lavinia, which Saturninus insists on calling 'rape' (I. i. 401). When Titus demands that Lavinia be restored to the emperor, Lucius retorts 'Dead, if you will, but not to be his wife' (I. i. 293). The defenders of female honour, it appears, are as lethal as its attackers. Lavinia may be most 'dear' to her father and the other male members of her family, but once she has been 'martyred' (III. i. 81) her life effectually becomes as 'cheap as beast's' (*King Lear* II. ii. 441). 'Martyred', though resonantly repeated in the next scene when Titus claims that he can 'interpret all her martyred signs' (III. ii. 36), is hardly the right word to describe her plight. Martyrs, as Foxe's case histories amply demonstrate, do not fall victim to sudden, unpredictable violence, but make choices foreseeably leading to that violence. For martyrs, becoming a victim is an assertion of autonomy.[95] It is nothing of the kind for Lavinia. Marcus' hunting simile is much more appropriate:

> O, thus I found her, straying in the park,
> Seeking to hide herself, as doth the deer
> That hath received some unrecuring wound.   (III. i. 88–90)

In identifying her with the same animal as her assailants did ('dainty doe', 'deer'), Marcus captures precisely the nature of the crime and her role as

---

[93] As in Theseus' words to the disobedient Hermia in *A Midsummer Night's Dream* I. i. 47–51: 'To you your father should be as a god, / One that composed your beauties, yea, and one / To whom you are but as a form in wax, / By him imprinted, and within his power / To leave the figure or disfigure it.'

[94] This is how Livy reports the story; in some versions Virginius kills his daughter after she has been raped. Cf. Holger Nørgaard, 'Never Wrong but with Just Cause', *English Studies*, 45 (1964), 137–41 at 139.

[95] Höfele, 'Stages of Martyrdom', 84.

prey. At the same time, the image of the stricken deer proverbially with-drawing to die[96] projects onto her the wish to die, by extension to be killed, as does the diagnosis of her wound as incurable. Marcus, as it were, takes up where the rapists have left off. And it remains for the paternal avenger to complete the work of her violators.[97]

'Of course, in Shakespeare's works no one ever literally eats anyone else', we read in a recent essay on 'Cannibalism and the Act of Revenge in Tudor-Stuart Drama'.[98] This is a somewhat over-confident claim, it would seem, considering that Tamora does precisely that in the final scene of *Titus Andronicus*.[99] Cannibalism, the essay argues, is Revenge's 'obscene supple-ment', 'serving—in the Lacanian sense—as the foreclosed "Real" of . . . re-venge's signification'.[100] 'The consumption of human flesh represents the symbolic order's limit point, a threshold that must not be crossed'[101]—'the word that must not be uttered, the act that must not be realized'.[102] This may well apply as a general rule, but not for *Titus Andronicus*, a play governed by the rule of excess which demands that the threshold be crossed, the unspeakable be spoken, that the act be realized. This is a play that holds

---

[96] See note in *Titus*, ed. Bate, 195.

[97] Though Lavinia's victimization by and within a specifically patriarchal power structure could not be more obvious, it is hard to see at what level of intentionality it makes sense to maintain that 'Lavinia is in effect punished, by rape, for her nascent sexuality and independent voice' (Marshall, ' "I can interpret all her martyr'd signs" ', 194). At the character level, neither the two rapists nor their mother could care less about these things. If Lavinia at this level is 'punished', it is for being her father's daughter. At the level of *intentio auctoris* (the 'patriarchal Bard') or *intentio operis* (the play invested in a patriarchal value system) the evidence for her being *punished* for her sexuality and voice ('lest she evolve into another Tamora', 195) is at best scanty. Lavinia never gets a chance to develop more than trace elements of either, let alone emulate the Queen of Goths. (The one instance where she does display eloquence is when she deploys it to *accuse* Tamora of sexual transgression from the moral high ground of marital righteousness; II. iii. 66–71; 80–4). Wanting to see Lavinia punished can thus only be ascribed to the all-encompassing intentionality of patriarchy at large, the source of a meaning that needs little substantiation in the text of the play to be always already known. By no stretch of the imagination does the society depicted in the play 'allow . . .'—in the sense of 'condone'—'such a violation to occur', as Wynne-Davies suggests in her concluding sentence (' "The Swallowing Womb" ', 148). Whatever the play may be said to support, it is not the claim that Lavinia was asking for it. Bernice Harris, 'Sexuality as a Signifier for Power Relations: Using Lavinia, of Shakespeare's *Titus Andronicus*', *Criticism*, 38 (1996), 383–406 at 383–4, seems nearer the mark when she relates the fate of Lavinia to that of Muslim women raped by Serbs in Bosnia and killed by their own brothers.

[98] Raymond J. Rice, 'Cannibalism and the Act of Revenge in Tudor-Stuart Drama', *Studies in English Language*, 44 (2004), 297–316 at 298.

[99] Rice (ibid. 314 n. 2) claims there is no incontrovertible textual evidence that Tamora actually does eat the pies. But see V. iii. 60: 'Whereof their mother daintily hath fed'.

[100] Rice, 'Cannibalism', 303.   [101] Ibid. 298.   [102] Ibid. 303.

nothing back, that knows no reticence in what it allows to happen and even less reticence in talking about it.[103]

Hence it is only logical that the symbolic cannibalism of revenge is literally acted out in the finale and equally logical for the literal act of anthropophagy to be implanted in the symbolism of the play. In her allegorical disguise as Revenge, Tamora does not actually enter from the stage trap.[104] But both Titus' reference to 'Revenge's cave' (III. i. 269) and Tamora's own statement that 'I am Revenge, sent from below' (V. ii. 3), link her appearance in the play's symbolic topography with the tomb and the pit. As Revenge mounts the stage 'from below', her cannibal double crosses the threshold into visibility. In the play's typical mode of punning, which is a play with both words and objects, the home-baked 'coffin' of Titus' human meat pie mimics the coffin of the opening scene, which also contained the dead flesh of a son:

TITUS   Hark, villains, I will grind your bones to dust,
        And with your blood and it I'll make a paste,
        And of the paste a coffin I will rear,
        And make two pasties of your shameful heads,
        And bid that strumpet, your unhallowed dam,
        Like to the earth swallow her own increase.   (V. ii. 178–90)

At the end of the play as at the beginning, dead sons turn to dust, but with the difference that the repetition of the process reverses the relation between the literal and the figurative. The sons who are figuratively encoffined in a pie are literally eaten (V. iii); the sons resting in literal coffins are figuratively swallowed (I. i)—the latter (Titus' sons) by the earth, figuratively a mother whose 'mouth' is the tomb; the former (Tamora's sons) by their literal mother, who thereby comes to figuratively embody the earth.

---

[103] Among the first critics to take this aesthetics of excess seriously is Tricomi, 'The Aesthetics of Mutilation', 19: 'Whatever our final aesthetic judgement concerning the merits of *Titus Andronicus*, we must understand that we are dealing, not with a paucity of imagination, but with an excess.... However flawed the tragedy may be in other respects, we must grant that the playwright has exploited the language of the stage with inventive brilliance.' The trail for this change in critical opinion was no doubt blazed by actual performance, especially Peter Brook's highly acclaimed 1955 Stratford production.

[104] The dialogue and stage directions make it clear that she calls to Titus, who then enters above, from the platform.

'Eating the flesh that she herself hath bred' (V. iii. 61), Tamora not only consummates Titus' revenge but again personifies Revenge itself, the logic of retaliatory violence—'meed for meed' (V. iii. 65), or indeed meat for meat—as a cycle of ultimately self-consuming cannibalism. Immediately following Titus' disclosure, the final fast-forward turn of retaliation (Tamora stabbed by Titus, Titus stabbed by Saturninus, Saturninus stabbed by Lucius—all within the time-span of four lines of blank verse) presses home this cyclicality with a glut of alliteration and rhyme:

SATURNINUS Die, frantic wretch, for this accursèd deed.
                        [*He kills Titus*]
LUCIUS   Can the son's eye behold his father bleed?
                There's meed for meed, death for a deadly deed.   (V. III. 63–5)

Lucius' 'obituary' characterizes her as a hungry predator, 'that ravenous tiger, Tamora' (V. iii. 194), once more suggesting the voracity of revenge.

The cycle is broken, the self-perpetuating process of eating and being eaten brought to a halt, with a final act of punishment that could not be more cruelly apt; Aaron the Moor is condemned to die of starvation:

LUCIUS   Set him breast-deep in earth and famish him.
                There let him stand, and rave, and cry for food.
                If anyone relieves or pities him,
                For the offence he dies. This is our doom.
                Some stay to see him fastened in the earth.   (V. iii. 178–82)

His avowal to 'heal Rome's harms' (V. iii. 147) and the tearful softness of his 'melt[ing] in showers' (V. iii. 160) notwithstanding, the new emperor Lucius demonstrates in his draconic verdict how little difference there is between the violence of civil and wild justice. The patriarchal order is restored through patrilineal succession. The wheel, as it were, has come full circle. Titus' sole surviving son, himself father of a motherless son, redresses the harm wrought by his father's wrong decision. But this decision, choosing the first-born Saturninus over his worthier brother Bassianus, was based on the very same principle of patrilineal primogeniture. This is not the only irony attached to a finality of closure that could hardly be cast in a more forceful image than that of being 'fastened in the earth'. Aaron, the 'blackest' villain of the play, is also the one and only parent figure showing unconditional attachment to his child. Protecting the new-born first against Tamora, then against Lucius, he ensures the continuance of an alternative black line of succession through the survival of a son who, remembering his father's starvation, may one day discover in himself a hunger for Roman flesh.[105]

> Will't please you eat? Will't please your highness feed?   (V. iii. 53)

VI. 'Not where he eats . . .': Hamlet's fine revolution

For most of the time Hamlet, both the prince and the play, may seem a long way away from this kind of cannibalism. But not always:

> 'Tis now the very witching time of night,
> When churchyards yawn, and hell itself breathes out
> Contagion to this world. Now could I drink hot blood,
> And do such bitter business as the day
> Would quake to look on.   (III. ii. 377–81)

It is night, the jaws of hell agape, and the Prince of Denmark confesses an uncharacteristic craving. For once, in this—his fifth—soliloquy, Hamlet lives up to the part he finds so difficult to play, that of the bloodthirsty avenger. But again all he accomplishes is 'words, words, words', qualifying the 'name of action' with a verb in the conditional. He *could* drink blood and he *could* do such things, but he won't.[106] Saying 'Soft, now to my mother' (III. ii. 381), he softens not only his voice but his resolve. Suppressing forbidden urges with a cautionary reminder of Nero—'Let me be cruel, not unnatural' (III. ii. 384)—Hamlet ends the soliloquy safely returned to the fold of rhetoric: 'I will speak daggers to her, but use none' (III. ii. 385). So it is not as a result of the prince's blood-thirst that this tragedy, too, demonstrates the voracity of revenge with a final banquet of corpses:

---

[105] On the terms in which the play consistently stresses Lucius' Roman virtue, it is unthinkable that he will break his oath 'Even by my god I swear to thee I will' (i.e. 'save [Aaron's] boy, to nurse and bring him up', V. i. 86; 84).

[106] The conditional, as well as the collocation of 'drinking blood' with doing things of an unnaturally cruel sort, seems to argue against the assumption that Hamlet is here calling for a therapeutic dose of blood from the medicine cabinet of humoral healing. But see Paster, *Humoring the Body*, 56–8.

FORTINBRAS This quarry cries on havoc. O proud death,
              What feast is toward in thine eternal cell
              That thou so many princes at a shot
              So bloodily hast struck!   (V. ii. 318–21)

In the manner of a hunter appraising the kill, Fortinbras conceives the remains of Denmark's royal family as so much dead meat. Only seconds before, Horatio had called for 'flights of angels' to sing the 'sweet prince' to his rest (V. ii. 312–13). Now Fortinbras sees bodies ready to be dispatched to an eternal death cell. In its final tableau the play aligns itself with the conventions of the revenge tragedy from which its hesitant protagonist has so often caused it to diverge. And, typically, this final image of wild justice is fraught with intimations of animality and cannibalism.

Indeed, animality and, tied up with it, cannibalism provide a sombre bass note in what to a large extent replaces the actual plotting and performance of revenge: Hamlet's reflections upon the state of his own self, Denmark, and the world at large. Their cue comes—at the earliest possible opportunity—with the first noun in Hamlet's first soliloquy:

              O that this too too solid flesh would melt,
              Thaw, and resolve itself into a dew   (I. ii. 129–30)

No sooner does the prince find himself alone than he begins speaking of flesh. Whether 'solid', 'sallied', or 'sullied'—flesh is the obsessive focus of his thinking.[107] Hamlet's disgust with 'all the uses of the world', even prior to the Ghost's disclosures, is first and foremost a loathing of the flesh as the site, instrument, and object of an appetite which is both lecherous and gluttonous and is consistently denounced as bestial. This abhorrence—occasioned but hardly sufficiently motivated by Gertrude's overhasty remarriage after

---

[107] This has been a frequent theme in *Hamlet* criticism. Janet Adelman, *Suffocating Mothers*, 250 n. 14, speaks of Hamlet's 'hatred of the flesh'; G. Wilson Knight, 'The Embassy of Death: An Essay on *Hamlet*', in his *The Wheel of Fire: Interpretations of Shakespearean Tragedy* (4th edn., London: Methuen, 1962), 17–46 at 23, of Hamlet's 'disgust at the physical body of man'. See also John Hunt, 'A Thing of Nothing: The Catastrophic Body in *Hamlet*', *Shakespeare Quarterly*, 39 (1988), 27–44. The most recent intervention is by David Hillman, who objects that such generalizations fail to take into account important distinctions that 'need to be made between Hamlet's attitudes to bodies which are healthy or sick, open or closed, full or empty, paternal or maternal', and that 'his aversion to the state of corporeality is far less absolute' than deeply ambivalent. David Hillman, *Shakespeare's Entrails: Belief, Scepticism and the Interior of the Body* (Houndmills, Basingstoke: Palgrave Macmillan, 2007), 81–116 at 87.

his father's death[108]—launches a diatribe introduced by a triple expletive of disgust ('Fie on't! ah fie, fie!'; I. ii. 135). Hamlet paints the world a place of 'rank and gross' fertility (I. ii. 136) that finds its half-human, half-animal incarnation in Claudius, a lecherous satyr (I. ii. 140), and in Gertrude, an impious widow. '[A] beast', Hamlet berates her, 'that wants discourse of reason / Would have mourned longer!' (I. ii. 150–1). Gertrude's second marriage is put down to rampantly promiscuous vitality. Strangely but all the more revealingly, Hamlet is unable to suppress his revulsion even at his mother's supposedly ideal first marriage to his father:

> Heaven and earth,
> Must I remember? Why, she would hang on him
> As if increase of appetite had grown
> By what it fed on   (I. ii. 142–5)

'Appetite', which Hamlet identifies as the key to this marital bliss, carries disturbing associations of cannibal gluttony: 'it sounds, as if [Gertrude] were a coffin-worm, and their marriage had been the beginning of King Hamlet's vermiculation. Indeed . . . Hamlet construes Gertrude's marriages as a mindless feeding on her husbands.'[109] The idea of Gertrude's insatiable 'feeding' is made more explicit in the Ghost's complaint that 'lust, though to a radiant angel linked, / Will sate itself in a celestial bed, / And prey on garbage' (I. v. 55–7). The idea recurs in the closet scene, when Hamlet impels her to compare the portraits of her two husbands: 'Could you on this fair mountain leave to feed, / And batten on this moor?' (III. iv. 65–6). Most loathsome of all, the 'one flesh' (IV. iii. 54) born, as he scoffs, from the union of his 'uncle-father' with his 'aunt-mother' (II. ii. 377) agitates his overactive imagination:

> Nay, but to live
> In the rank sweat of an enseamèd bed,
> Stewed in corruption, honeying and making love
> Over the nasty sty—   (III. iv. 81–4)

---

[108] It is this lack of sufficient motivation—an *objective correlative* for Hamlet's emotional state—that T. S. Eliot famously declared to be the play's decisive flaw: 'Hamlet is up against the difficulty that his disgust is occasioned by his mother, but that his mother is not an adequate equivalent for it.' 'Hamlet', in *Selected Prose of T. S. Eliot*, ed. Frank Kermode (London: Faber and Faber, 1975), 45–9 at 48.

[109] Robert N. Watson, *The Rest is Silence: Death as Annihilation in the English Renaissance* (Berkeley, Los Angeles, and London: University of California Press, 1994), 83.

Everything that grows, blooms, and flourishes—everything, in other words, partaking in the life processes of organic nature—becomes an occasion for Hamlet to see filth, defilement, and decay.[110] Cursed with the evil eye, he sees a worm in every bud, foulness and corruption in all that is fair. This is most crassly proved upon the fair Ophelia, whom in his sonneteering past he had elevated beyond the realm of physical nature to the sphere of the 'celestial' (II. ii. 110). Addressing her father Polonius as a seller of easily perishable wares and, implicitly, a pander ('You're a fishmonger', II. ii. 176), he makes her the epitome of a moral corruption that seems almost biologically determined:

HAMLET For if the sun breed maggots in a dead dog, being a good kissing
                carrion—have you a daughter?
POLONIUS I have, my lord.
HAMLET Let her not walk i'th' sun. Conception is a blessing, but not as your
                daughter may conceive. Friend, look to't.[111]

                                                                                        (II. ii. 183–8)

Fertility and decomposition become indistinguishable. Hamlet's obsessive revulsion makes a perfect example of what studies in the phenomenology of disgust have described as its typical dual directedness towards and away from both what is dead as well as what is—too much—alive.[112] If disgust derives its force from a sense of tactile closeness to a revolting object, then 'good kissing carrion' can hardly be surpassed in suggesting the particularly intimate, and hence particularly revolting, touch of lips to lips.[113] The image blends breeding and rotting, but also breeding and feeding, erotic and

---

[110] Cf. Stephen Greenblatt, *Hamlet in Purgatory* (Princeton: Princeton University Press, 2001), 243: 'The play enacts and re-enacts queasy rituals of defilement and revulsion, an obsession with a corporeality that reduces everything to appetite and excretion.'

[111] Hamlet's insinuation only takes up a theme that looms large in the imagination of her male protectors, father and brother: 'Ophelia's body is figured as a set of vulnerable apertures ("too credent ear," "your chaste treasure open") that needs to be protected from Hamlet's "songs" and "importunity." ' Alan Stewart, *Shakespeare's Letters* (Oxford: Oxford University Press, 2008), 249.

[112] The earliest systematic exploration of disgust is by Aurel Kolnai, 'Der Ekel', in *Jahrbuch für Philosophie und phänomenologische Forschung*, ed. Edmund Husserl, vol. 10 (Halle/Saale: Niemeyer, 1929), 515–69; see also William Ian Miller, *The Anatomy of Disgust* (Cambridge, Mass.: Harvard University Press, 1997); Winfried Menninghaus, *Ekel: Theorie und Geschichte einer starken Empfindung* (Frankfurt am Main: Suhrkamp, 1999).

[113] Georges Bataille, *Eroticism, Death and Sensuality*, trans. Mary Dalwood (San Francisco: City Light Books, 1986), 46–7, suggests a similar revulsion from the human corpse which is seen to threaten the living with its contagious touch: 'Death is a danger for those left behind. If they have to bury the corpse it is less in order to keep it safe than to keep themselves safe from its contagion.... We no longer believe in contagious magic, but which of us could be sure of not quailing at the sight of a dead body crawling with maggots?' See also Susan Zimmerman, *The Early Modern Corpse and Shakespeare's Theatre* (Edinburgh: Edinburgh University Press, 2005).

culinary appetite. It makes Ophelia the object but potentially also the subject of such appetite—carrion good for, but also good at kissing, carrion lurking below 'the trappings and the suits' (I. ii. 86), in this case not of woe, but of beauty.[114]

The victim of Hamlet's casual violence, Ophelia is prevented from becoming a 'breeder of sinners' (III. i. 123–4), but not from becoming a corpse that sprouts:[115] 'Lay her i'th' earth', Laertes enjoins, 'And from her fair and unpolluted flesh / May violets spring' (V. i. 234–5). Coming after Hamlet's graveyard disquisition on 'my lady Worm's' (V. i. 86) and Alexander the Great stopping a bung-hole, this brotherly piety may ring as hollow as the ensuing shouting match between Hamlet and Laertes in Ophelia's grave.

Ophelia meets with a 'muddy death' offstage, as Claudius explains, 'Divided from herself and her fair judgement, / Without the which we are pictures or mere beasts' (IV. v. 83–4). Gertrude's word-painting (IV. vii. 138–55) makes this 'liquidation' of Ophelia seem a displacement of Hamlet's own death wish, of his wish for his flesh to melt and dissolve. The burial completes Ophelia's division from herself and also clarifies the alternative between 'picture' and 'mere beast'. While her body—that which in Hamlet's terms is 'mere beast'—is abjected, deposited in the earth with minimum ceremony, the 'picture' of her melting into death has travelled down the centuries in undecaying beauty.[116]

---

[114] John Drakakis, 'Yorick's Skull', paper read at the 'Gothic Renaissance' conference, organized by Beate Neumeier and Elisabeth Bronfen, Cologne, 3–4 Dec. 2009, points to a strikingly similar imaginary of revolting decay in John Donne: 'But for us that dye now and sleepe, in the state of the dead, we must al passe this *posthume* death, this *death* after *death*, nay this death after burial, this *dissolution* after *dissolution*, this *death* of *corruption* and *putrifaction*, of *vermiculation* and *incineration*, of *dissolution* and *dispersion* in and *from* the grave. When those bodies that have beene the *children* of *royall parents*, and the *parents* of *royall children*, must say with *Job*, *to corruption thou art my father*, and *to the Worme thou art my mother and my sister*. *Miserable riddle*, when the *same worme* must bee *my mother*, and *my sister*, and bee both *father* and *mother* to my *owne mother* and my *sister*, and bee both *father* and *mother* to my owne *mother* and *sister*, *beget*, and *beare* that *worme* which is all that miserable *penury*; when my *mouth* shall be *filled* with *dust*, and the *worme* shall *feed*, and *feed sweetly* upon me, when the *ambitious* man shall have no *satisfaction*, if the *poorest alive* tread upon him, nor the *poorest* receive any *contentment* in being made *equall* to *Princes*, for they *shall bee equall* but *in dust*.' *Selected Prose*, ed. Neil Rhodes (Harmondsworth: Penguin, 1987), 317–18; italics original.

[115] Cf. T. S. Eliot, *The Waste Land: A Facsimile and Transcript of the Original Drafts Including the Annotations of Ezra Pound*, ed. Valerie Eliot (London: Faber and Faber, 1971), 9, ll. 125–6: 'That corpse you planted last year in your garden, / Has it begun to sprout . . . ?'

[116] On Ophelia's death in art see e.g. Martha Tuck Rozett, 'Drowning Ophelias and Other Images of Death in Shakespeare's Plays', in Holger Klein and James L. Harner (eds.) *Shakespeare and the Visual Arts* (Lewiston, NY, Queenston, ON, and Lampeter, Wales: Edward Mellen Press,

'Woot drink up eisel, eat a crocodile?' Hamlet challenges Laertes (V. i. 273), but no more would he perform this eating and drinking for 'love' than he would drink hot blood for revenge. Throughout the play, Hamlet is conspicuously exempt from the appetite that he sees running rampant about him. In a world of general gourmandizing, he is almost starving himself. If his father was 'full of bread' when Claudius killed him (III. iii. 80), he himself 'fares . . . of the chameleon's dish', eating 'the air' (III. ii. 89–91). For ever postponing the drinking of hot blood, he 'shows no real *appetite* for revenge'.[117] Refusing food demonstratively sharpens Hamlet's opposition to Claudius and his court, but at the same time it also prevents him from performing the 'bitter business' (III. ii. 380). The allusion to capons, oddly inconsistent after 'I eat the air, promise-crammed'—because capons are certainly not fattened or 'crammed' with air—makes sense in this context because, like the capon, 'a symbol of cowardice', 'he lacks the courage that should enable him to . . . kill his enemy'.[118]

A capon was thought to make good food, '[o]f all tame fowl . . . most best', for it 'maketh little ordure, and much nourishment', while also 'engender[ing] good blood'.[119] If capons, castrated cocks, symbolize cowardice, they also suggest the rich food with which Claudius' court gluttonously crams itself and against which Hamlet revolts. At the same time this rich food he disdains might engender the 'good blood' that would turn him from a bloodless revenger into a bloody one.

This ambivalent encoding of feeding and food refusal also registers in 'A scullion!' (II. ii. 590), the last epithet in Hamlet's litany of self-reproach after the player's speech in II. ii. Following 'whore' and 'drab', 'scullion' has been plausibly suggested to betray Hamlet's sense of himself as effeminized, a reading made even more persuasive by Q2's 'stallyon', which the Arden[119]

2000), 182–96; Alan R. Young, Hamlet *and the Visual Arts, 1709–1900* (Newark, Del.: University of Delaware Press; London: Associated University Presses, 2002), 323–45; Kimberly Rhodes, *Ophelia and Victorian Visual Culture: Representing Body Politics in the Nineteenth Century* (Aldershot: Ashgate, 2008), esp. 73–80, 86–101 and 109–19.

[117] Hillman, *Shakespeare's Entrails*, 101.

[118] Joan Fitzpatrick, 'Apricots, Butter, and Capons: An Early Modern Lexicon of Food', *Shakespeare Jahrbuch*, 145 (2009), 74–90 at 87.

[119] The quotations are (in this order) from Andrew Boorde, *Compendious Regiment or a Dietary of Health* (London: Wyllyam Powell, 1547); Thomas Elyot, *The Castle of Health* (London: T. Berthelet, 1539); and William Bullein, *A New Book Entitled the Government of Health* (London: John Day, 1558). All three are quoted in Fitzpatrick, 'Apricots, Butter, and Capons', 85.

editors gloss as 'male prostitute'.[120] But scullion, according to G. R. Hibbard '[t]he lowest of kitchen servants and employed to do the "dirty work"',[121] also harks back, I would argue, to the conspicuous presence of cooking and eating imagery in the Pyrrhus/Hecuba speech. This line of association is introduced even before the speech itself, when Hamlet asks for a 'taste of your [the actors'] quality' (II. ii. 434), a passionate speech from a play that was 'caviare to the general' (II. ii. 439–40), though 'well digested in the scenes' (II. ii. 442) and 'as wholesome as sweet' (II. ii. 447). The subject of the speech is not the 'death', the 'killing' or 'murder' of Priam, but 'Priam's slaughter', neither particularly wholesome nor sweet, and slaughter is the note on which Hamlet launches into his declamation:

> 'The rugged Pyrrhus, like th'Hyrcanian beast'—
> 'tis not so. It begins with Pyrrhus—
> 'The rugged Pyrrhus, he whose sable arms,
> Black as his purpose, did the night resemble
> When he lay couchèd in the ominous horse,
> Hath now this dread and black complexion smeared
> With heraldry more dismal. Head to foot
> Now is he total gules, horridly tricked
> With blood of fathers, mothers, daughters, sons,
> Baked and impasted with the parching streets,
> That lend a tyrannous and damnèd light
> To their vile murders. Roasted in wrath and fire,
> And thus o'er-sizèd with coagulate gore,
> With eyes like carbuncles the hellish Pyrrhus
> Old grandsire Priam seeks.'
> So, proceed you.   (II. ii. 453–68)

Another mirror in which Hamlet can see 'the image of my cause' reflected in 'the 'portraiture of his' (V. ii. 78–9), Pyrrhus is the play's most bloodthirsty avenger figure. Black as his purpose, he wears the colour of Hamlet's 'customary suits' (I. ii. 78) while lying couchèd, like the prince, in ominous latency, but changes colour as he wreaks his revenge on fathers, mothers, daughters, sons. Covered, head to foot, in the blood of his victims, he becomes 'total gules', coated, that is, in heraldic red. But 'total gules' also means that 'Now is he all gullet, all gluttony'. As John Gower rhymes: 'This

---

[120] Fitzpatrick, 'Apricots, Butter, and Capons', 88: 'Hamlet considers himself effeminized since a male prostitute is economically dependent on the customer and ... servants, because economically dependent, were perceived as sexually available and thus, in the case of male servants, feminized.'

[121] *Hamlet*, ed. G. R. Hibbard (Oxford: Oxford University Press, 1994), 235, n. to II. ii. 576.

vice, which so out of rule / Hath sette ous alle, is clepid Gule.'[122] Or, in the mid-seventeenth-century prose of John Gauden: 'There are many throats so wide and gules so gluttonous in England that they can swallow down goodly Cathedrals.'[123] Pyrrhus is seen as an insatiable orifice constantly guzzling human blood. In a final twist, the scene of horrid voracity converts the feeder himself into food as the burning Troy becomes an infernal oven in which the avenger is 'baked', 'impasted', and 'roasted', terms that recall the Thyestian finale of *Titus*. This may be taken, once more, to suggest the self-consuming circularity of revenge that we found in both Montaigne and *Titus*; but in the context of Hamlet's specific revenger's dilemma Pyrrhus's mutation from feeder to food graphically highlights the knot of attraction and horrified revulsion in which Hamlet finds himself entangled. As the First Player takes over, the feeding imagery does not entirely cease[124] but becomes much less prominent, only to resurface, in full force, in Hamlet's 'I should 'a' fatted all the region kites / With this slave's offal' (II. ii. 581–2) and in his final allusion to the 'dirty work' in the kitchen: 'A scullion!' (II. ii. 590).

Even before the Player does so, Hamlet, too, 'force[s] his soul' to a state of agitation '[b]ut in a fiction, in a dream of passion' (II. ii. 555, 554). Much like the followers of Essex on the eve of their abortive rebellion,[125] he requests a performance that will spur him to action but produces only acting instead. Crucially, the violence of Pyrrhus' cannibalistic revenge is twice removed from actual doing: it is represented in a remembered scene of representation. What Schmitt calls the '*Hamletization of the avenger*'[126] produces a kind of doubly veiled peepshow, in which the hellish Pyrrhus, 'o'ersizèd with coagulate gore, / With eyes like carbuncles' (II. ii. 464–5), plays a tyrant who certainly 'out-Herods Herod' (III. ii. 14). '[N]either having the accents of Christians nor the gait of Christian, pagan, nor no man', he 'so strut[s] and bellow[s]'

---

[122] John Gower, *Confessio Amantis*, ed. Russell A. Peck (Kalamazoo: Medieval Institute Publications, 2004), iii. 209.

[123] John Gauden, *The tears, sighs, complaints, and prayers of the Church of England* (London: Royston, 1659), 323.

[124] See II. ii. 516–17: 'When she saw Pyrrhus make malicious sport / In mincing with his sword her husband's limbs'.

[125] On the command performance of *Richard II* (and its colourful afterlife in Shakespeare criticism), see Leeds Barroll, 'A New History for Shakespeare and his Time', *Shakespeare Quarterly*, 39 (1988), 441–64.

[126] Carl Schmitt, *Hamlet or Hecuba: The Intrusion of the Time into the Play*, trans. David Pan and Jennifer R. Rust (1956; New York: Telos Press, 2009), 21 (italics original).

that I have thought some of nature's journeymen had made men, and not made them well, they imitated humanity so abominably. (III. ii. 30–5)[127]

But in the middle of all the highly theatrical carnage of the Player's speech there occurs a moment when the monstrous—and monstrously overacting—Pyrrhus becomes a suddenly accurate mirror image of the hesitant prince, a moment when representation is raised to yet another level of indirectness by a simile that turns the reported scene into the likeness of a painting. His sword raised, Pyrrhus freezes in what amounts to an anticipatory parody of Hamlet's exemplary moment of hesitation over the praying Claudius in III. iii ('Now might I do it pat'; III. iii. 73):

> For lo, his sword,
> Which was declining on the milky head
> Of reverend Priam, seemed i'th' air to stick.
> So, as a painted tyrant, Pyrrhus stood,
> And, like a neutral to his will and matter,
> Did nothing.   (II. ii. 479–4)

At least part of Hamlet's failure as a cannibal avenger is due to his obsession with the general condition of human existence in this 'mortal coil' (III. i. 69). What 'flesh is heir to' (III. i. 65) extends beyond '[t]he heartache and the thousand natural shocks' (III. i. 64) to the totality of human life in its natural process of growth and decline. But this is normal, says the Queen: 'Thou know'st 'tis common—all that lives must die' (I. ii. 72). And Claudius concurs in the name of nature and reason,

> whose common theme
> Is death of fathers, and who still hath cried
> From the first corpse till he that died today,
> 'This must be so'.   (I. ii. 103–6)

This may be so, yet Hamlet cannot let the matter—nor his father—rest, although, at this point, he does not know that Claudius has biochemically enhanced the process. What troubles him, and will continue to do so even after the Ghost has revealed the exceptional manner of his father's death, is precisely what is 'common':[128] the non-criminal, normal course of organic

---

[127] On Hamlet's advice to the player, see Weimann, *Author's Pen*, 18–28 and 151–79.

[128] Claudius' crime, its exceptionality notwithstanding, is also contained in this common course, motivated as it is by the most common incentives, sexual appetite and the lust for power. Claudius himself implies as much when he refers to the endless succession 'From the first corpse till he that died today', the first corpse being that of Abel slain by his brother.

life. Remodelling his mother's pious notion of 'Passing through nature to eternity' (I. ii. 73), he envisages this 'passing' as an eternal recycling process, a great food-chain of being whose egalitarian digestive regime unites all creatures high and humble in universal cannibalism:

HAMLET	A man may fish with the worm that hath eat of a king, and eat of the fish that hath fed of that worm.
KING	What dost thou mean by this?
HAMLET	Nothing but to show you how a king may go a progress through the guts of a beggar. (IV. iii. 27–31)

'Here's fine revolution,' Hamlet exclaims in the graveyard scene, 'an we had the trick to see't' (V. i. 88–9). This is misleading because Hamlet obviously 'has the trick' even to the point where he can no longer see anything *but* this 'fine revolution': the great revolving door through which kings from Alexander the Great to him 'that died today'[129] must pass en route to 'stopping a bung-hole' (V. i. 200) or furnishing 'baked meats' (I. ii. 179) for another king's table. Halfway through the play, the loquacious Polonius suddenly becomes 'most still, most secret, and most grave'. The rest is silent feeding. No sooner has Hamlet lugged 'the guts into the neighbour room' (III. iv. 186), than his victim is processed in the 'fine revolution':

KING CLAUDIUS	Now, Hamlet, where's Polonius?
HAMLET	At supper.
KING CLAUDIUS	At supper? Where?
HAMLET	Not where he eats, but where a is eaten. A certain convocation of politic worms are e'en at him. Your worm is your only emperor for diet. We fat all creatures else to fat us, and we fat ourselves for maggots. Your fat king and your lean beggar is but variable service—two dishes, but to one table. That's the end. (IV. iii. 17–25)

In Hamlet's thinking, as in Foxe's, the World, the Flesh, and the Beast form an unholy trinity. What Hamlet lacks, however, is Foxe's confident belief in the possibility of overcoming their power. For Hamlet, there is no getting away from what the 'flesh is heir to' (III. i. 65). The peripeteia from ashes to glory which Foxe's martyr achieves is turned upside down in Hamlet's speech on the dignity of man. His mock-humanist eulogy only serves to make the final lapse more devastating:

---

[129] '[H]e that died today' contains a covert reference to Hamlet's father: 'For look you how cheerfully my mother looks, and my father died within's two hours' (III. ii. 120–1).

> What a piece of work is a man! How noble in reason, how infinite in faculty,
> in form and moving how express and admirable, in action how like an angel,
> in apprehension how like a god—the beauty of the world, the paragon of
> animals! And yet to me what is this quintessence of dust? (II. ii. 304–9)

Seeing man as inevitably wedded to dust—*homo* to *humus* according to the
etymology of Isidore of Seville[130]—draws on a commonplace of medieval
thinking. *Homo-humus* in his grave-bound mortality is enjoined to seek his
salvation in what is ultimately detachable from this mortal coil (or indeed
soil): *anima*. The breath that circulates in and out of the animated body
prefigures the soul that escapes when the body expires. From a Christian
perspective, this makes for a stable dualism in which the abhorrent decay
that makes Hamlet's gorge rise (V. i. 183) is always only half the story—and
its ultimately negligeable half at that, contained as it is in a certainty of
transcendence. But Hamlet's investment in human 'dust' is a far cry from
the lofty Christian disdain for the vanity of earthly excellence. Hamlet's
alleged 'hatred of the flesh',[131] David Hillman argues, is shot through with 'a
tenderness towards the facts of mortal embodiment'.[132] Hillman finds the
cue for his rereading in Nietzsche's remark on

> *Misanthropy and Love*:—One speaks of being sick of man only when one can
> no longer digest him and yet has one's stomach full of him. Misanthropy
> comes of an all too greedy love of man and 'cannibalism'; but who asked you
> to swallow men like oysters, Prince Hamlet?[133]

Hamlet's nausea, Nietzsche suggests, is the effect of overeating, of craving
the other to the point of ingestion. The afterglow, or aftertaste, of this all too
greedy love puts the prince's disgust in perspective. It gives a poignancy of
disappointed hope to Hamlet's bitterness. His disgust is a form of lapsed
desire, all the more intense because it is so desperately aware of the betrayed
promise incorporated in the human body. The dualism between man's
animal flesh and angelic, even divine spirit, which Foxe's account presents
and overcomes in teleological sequence, plagues Hamlet in unrelieved
simultaneity. His nauseated vision of universal cannibalism stems from a
philanthropic 'cannibalism' which all too greedily swallows 'men like

---

[130] Isidore of Seville, *Etymologiae*, lib. I, cap. xxvii: 'De orthographia' (10).
[131] Adelman, *Suffocating Mothers*, 250 n. 14.
[132] Hillman, *Shakespeare's Entrails*, 87.
[133] Friedrich Nietzsche, *The Gay Science*, trans. Thomas Common (1882; Mineola, NY: Dover, 2006), 103; italics original.

oysters'.[134] The 'paragon of animals' whose innerworldly perfection could attract such love thus continues to haunt the play. But it is only a memory— only something that was there (or was thought to have been there) but is now 'quite, quite down' (III. i. 157), as in Ophelia's complaint about Hamlet ('O what a noble mind is here o'erthrown!'; III. i. 153–63) or in Hamlet's seeking for his 'noble father in the dust' (I. ii. 71).

Idealizing his father and bestializing his uncle—the one a Hyperion, the other a satyr—Hamlet reproduces the vertical dualism of Pico della Mirandola's seemingly so optimistic Christian humanist anthropology, which gave Adam the choice to either degenerate to the level of beasts or rise to 'the superior orders whose life is divine'.[135] Unlike Pico's Adam or Foxe's heaven-bound martyr-hero, Hamlet finds the route of ascent foreclosed. The extremism of his high–low dichotomy between Hyperion and a satyr allows of no third, middle position.[136] He thus seems to anticipate Giorgio Agamben's reading, which finds Pico's man a being with no substantive 'dignity' or nature, but precariously suspended between 'a celestial and a terrestrial nature . . . always less and more than himself'.[137] Proper humanity would have to exclude the animal. But the human condition is inextricably bound up with and—from the perspective of Hamlet's nauseated humanism—tainted by a mortal animal body.

★

'Presumption', writes Montaigne, 'is our naturall and originall infirmitie. Of all creatures man is the most miserable and fraile, and therewithall the proudest and disdainfullest' (ii. 142). Animal and cannibal serve Montaigne to dampen this presumption in its mutually reinforcing varieties of anthropocentric and ethnocentric arrogance. The animal that is capable of having its own thoughts (if only we knew what they are) and the cannibal, who wears 'no kinde of breeches nor hosen' (i. 229) but is nonetheless in many ways better (nobler, wiser, more reasonable) than 'we' are, reveal the dubiousness of our sense of superiority. Neither *Titus Andronicus* nor *Hamlet* operates on this principle of inverse elevation; in neither of them do we find

---

[134] Hillman explores the image of the oyster as a key to early modern notions of selfhood and psycho-physical interiority. *Shakespeare's Entrails*, 81–3.

[135] Pico, *Oration*, 8.

[136] However, as most critics concur, it does, in the last scene of the play, move towards a state of equanimity or acceptance. But this does not find expression in any newly reached positive insight into human nature or the human condition, but a calm resolve to 'Let be' (V. ii. 170).

[137] Giorgio Agamben, *The Open*, 29.

cannibalism ennobled or animals credited with a potential for reason. What we do find, however, are instances of a very similar dubiousness appearing in figurations of animality and cannibalism. Both cannibal and animal serve as threshold or borderline figures that mark, but also question and infringe the limits of the human, not, as in Montaigne, in the role of 'better humans', but as evidence of the human possibility of inhumanity.

In *Titus Andronicus* this evidence is presented *in actu*, in *Hamlet* it becomes an insistent provocation for thought. The earlier play shows the foundational distinction of political anthropology in dissolution: what is civil can no longer be cordoned off from what is savage, and this state of undecidability persists even when a restitution of order is proclaimed at the end of the play because this restitution is founded on yet another act of vengeful, cannibalistic violence. Though ostensibly banning bestiality once for all, the expulsion of the 'ravenous tiger' Tamora constitutes an at best ambiguous gesture of restoration. Feeding her body to beasts and birds, the decree of the new ruler does not exclude but perpetuates the inclusion of beastliness in the new regime. With his concluding statement the last of the Andronici demonstrates a conspicuous lack of what the grating rhyme of the final couplet invokes, but refuses to grant twice—pity:

LUCIUS As for that ravenous tiger, Tamora,
          No funeral rite, nor man in mourning weed,
          No mournful bell shall ring her burial,
          But throw her forth to beasts and birds to prey:
          Her life was beastly and devoid of pity,
          And being dead, let birds on her take pity.   (V. iii. 194–9)

In *Hamlet* the cannibalism of revenge expands into a bio-anthropology of universal flesh consumption. Rooted though it is in a tradition of Christian *contemptus mundi*, Hamlet's misanthropic world-weariness lacks the compensatory prospect of hope with which medieval disquisitions on the misery of human existence[138] could edify their readers. Cut off from the redemptive certainties of religion, he is equally deprived of those certainties which the philosophy of Descartes would eventually wrest from a process of radical doubt. As cogitating subject (*res cogitans*) Hamlet can regard his bodily substance (*res extensa*) as 'this machine' (II. ii. 123–4)—and according to

---

[138] 'De miseria humanae conditionis'. See Charles E. Trinkaus, *In Our Image and Likeness: Humanity and Divinity in Italian Humanist Thought* (London: Constable, 1970), i, p. xiv.

the *OED* this peculiarly Cartesian-sounding phrase is the first recorded instance in English where 'machine' means 'bodily frame'.[139] But neither from the older body–soul dualism of the Western philosophical and religious tradition—which can only feed, not relieve his disgust—nor from the emergent modern dualism of Descartes, which posits body and mind as separate 'substances', can he draw consolation. For Hamlet any dualism that places man, howsoever noble in reason, above the rest of the animals collapses in the one substance—the quintessence—in which man and beast, eating and being eaten, inevitably unite: dust.

As the earth disgorges skulls and bones in the graveyard scene of Act V, it is left to the clowns to map Hamlet's vision of eternal return onto the localities of juridical and, by extension, theatrical spectacle:

FIRST CLOWN   What is he that builds stronger than either the mason, the
               ship-wright, or the carpenter?
SECOND CLOWN   The gallows-maker; for that frame outlives a thousand tenants.

                                                                        (V. i. 41–4)

Denmark, says Hamlet, is a prison (II. ii. 246), its rotten state sustained by a regime of supervised detention that renders its inmates, most notably the prince himself, '[t]h'observed of all observers' (III. i. 157). Its almost Foucauldian 'panopticism'[140] notwithstanding, this is a pre-modern prison, one that fulfils its purpose in preparation for a final reckoning.[141] 'And where th'offence is, let the great axe fall' (IV. v. 216), says Claudius sending Hamlet to an English executioner's block. Shining through the increasingly frayed pretence of normal court life, the stage behind the stage of *Hamlet* is the scaffold. On the brink of the final showdown, the gravediggers' quip serves to point up the similarity between the two types of building. Both stage and scaffold are for short-term tenants only whose quick succession demonstrates the transitoriness of human life. The playhouse, too, 'outlives' the lives which it snatches from the jaws of oblivion. By re-enacting or—as in the gravediggers' scene—literally excavating them, it becomes an inter-

---

[139] In 16th-c. discussions of Aristotle's *De Anima* the organic or corporeal—as opposed to intellective—soul in humans and animals is sometimes said to work like a 'machine'. Katharine Park in her chapter on 'The Organic Soul' in Charles B. Schmitt, Quentin Skinner, Eckhard Kessler (eds.), *The Cambridge History of Renaissance Philosophy* (Cambridge: Cambridge University Press, 2000), 484, cites instances from Melanchthon and Campanella.

[140] Foucault, *Discipline and Punish*, 195–228.

[141] Yet in making Death's 'eternal cell' (V. ii. 370) the final destination of the play's casualties, Fortinbras's résumé prolongs the condition of claustrophobic confinement to an interminable beyond.

change on the route of all flesh, a gallows in reverse where the dead learn to speak again: almost, it seems, with the voices of the luckless opportunists, Rosencrantz and Guildenstern, whom Hamlet, a humanist not only with inky cloak but also with inky—and bloody—fingers has fed to 'the great axe': ' "Good morrow, sweet lord. How dost thou, good lord?" ' (V. i. 81–2).

★

My theme in this chapter has been the breakdown of distinction between the state theatre of justice and the 'wild justice' of revenge in its 'brutish' and cannibalistic figurations of otherness. Taking my cue from Claudius' 'great axe', I will now close with a final—and, in every sense of the word, marginal—illustration of that breakdown.

Sebastian Münster's *Cosmographei* (1550) takes us back to a genre of writing whose uncritical compilation of the wonders of the earth Montaigne found so hopelessly inadequate. Münster has a chapter entitled 'On the new islands, when and by whom they were found, what they are called and what sort of people live there',[142] which offers a radically truncated account of the discovery of the New World. True to his policy of entertaining the reader with strange and marvellous things ('wunderbarlich ding'), a relatively large part of this account is dedicated to the 'Canibali' or 'leutfressern' (people-eaters) of whom Columbus was told 'how they shipped from their own land to other islands where they caught the people, struck them dead and ate them and treated them no differently from how a tiger or lion does with a tame beast'.[143] Münster's account is supplemented with a woodcut illustration (Fig. 11 left). It shows a man and a woman, both naked, merrily chopping up a human corpse. As in several other cases, Münster—or, rather, his printer—uses the same illustration twice: the image also accompanies his much briefer description of the island of Giava (Java). There, we learn, cannibalism is a measure of social hygiene: when a man 'grows old and no longer wants to work or, if still young, falls desperately ill, he is not left to die, but in time struck dead, cooked and eaten'.[144]

---

[142] Sebastian Münster, *Cosmographei* (1550), ed. Ruthardt Oehme (Amsterdam: Theatrum Orbis Terrarum, 1968), title page: 'von den neüwen inseln / wann und von wem die erfunden / wie sie heissen und was für leüt darin sind'.

[143] Ibid. 1186: 'wie die auß jrem land schiffetē in andere inselen und fiengē die leüt / schlugen sie zu todt fressen sie / und giengen nit anderst mitt jnen umb dan wie ein Tiger oder Löw mit einem zamen thier'.

[144] Ibid. 1179: '[wenn er] alt wirt vnd nit mer arbeiten mag / oder so er iung ist vn in ein verzweifflet kráckheit falt / lat man jn nit selbs sterben sundern schlecht jn zeitlich zu todt / kocht vnd frßt jn'.

But the merry meat-choppers put in a rather unexpected third appearance in Münster's description of Germany ('Von dem Teütschen land'), where they illustrate the history of the town of Lübeck (Fig. 11 right). The text relates how, in the year 1536, during hostilities between the townspeople and the Duke of Mecklenburg, a Lübeck mayor fell into the hands of the enemy, 'was condemned to death and then quartered and, together with his brother and a Danish parson, put on the wheel'.[145] One picture with two similar meanings and one meaning that is radically different: 'floating' would seem too weak a term to describe the mobility of this signifier. The same image serves to represent the extremity of what is seen as subhuman, brutish, and bestial, and the penal system whose task it is to keep the beast at bay.

Is it conceivable that the illustrator or whoever was responsible for the insertion of the image was aware of this coincidence of opposites—that Münster or his publisher actually intended to characterize *iustitia* as cannibalistic? Unlikely as that seems, the miniature picture evinces a certain multicultural touch: the savage's handy little hatchet and the sturdy dissecting table have the solidly crafted look of being 'made in Germany'.[146]

---

[145] Münster, *Cosmographei* (1550) 873: 'zum todt verurtheylet ward / vnnd darnach gefiertheilet / vnnd sampt seinem Bruder vnd einem Dennischenn pfaffen auffs rad gelegt wordenn'.

[146] I have discussed Münster's illustrations in a different context in Andreas Höfele, ' "What have we here—a man or a fish?" ' Animalität und Alterität in Shakespeares *Sturm*', in Christopher Balme (ed.), *Das Theater der Anderen* (Tübingen: Francke, 2001), 55–76.

5

'I'll see their trial first': Law and Disorder in Lear's Animal Kingdom

*K*ing Lear, Shakespeare's arguably most searching investigation into the nature of the human, is conducted under the twin auspices of law and animality. What has been called the 'trial pattern' in *King Lear*[1] is as conspicuously prominent as the multitude of animals crowding its tragic vision. Unsurprisingly, the animal imagery of the play was a favourite subject of New Critical study. Equally unremarkably, it has attracted little interest since. This may be partly because the exhaustiveness of commentators like Wilson Knight, Heilman, and, of course, Spurgeon and Clemen left virtually no animal image unturned,[2] but perhaps also because, to later generations of critics, the topic would appear altogether too much invested in the pieties of an obsolete 'essentialist' humanism, too predictably geared to the orchestration of a questionable narrative of redemption. Humankind,

---

[1] Dorothy C. Hockey, 'The Trial Pattern in *King Lear*', *Shakespeare Quarterly*, 10 (1959), 389–95. Issues of law in *King Lear* are discussed by, among others, C. J. Sisson, 'Justice in *King Lear*', repr. in Frank Kermode (ed.), *Shakespeare: King Lear* (London: Macmillan, 1969), 228–44; Charles Spinoza, '"The name and all th'addition": *King Lear's* Opening Scene and the Common-Law Use', *Shakespeare Studies*, 23 (1995), 146–86; Paul M. Shupack, 'Natural Justice and *King Lear*', *Cardozo Studies in Law and Literature*, 9 (1997) 67–105; B. J. Sokol and Mary Sokol, 'Shakespeare and the English Equity Jurisdiction: *The Merchant of Venice* and the Two Texts of *King Lear*', *Review of English Studies*, 50/200 (1999), 417–39; Paul W. Kahn, *Law and Love: The Trials of 'King Lear'* (New Haven and London: Yale University Press, 2000).

[2] Cf. G. Wilson Knight, *The Wheel of Fire: Interpretations of Shakespearean Tragedy* (London: Methuen, 1962); Robert B. Heilman, *This Great Stage: Image and Structure in* King Lear (Baton Rouge, La.: Louisiana State University Press, 1948); Spurgeon, *Shakespeare's Imagery and What It Tells Us*; Clemen, *The Development of Shakespeare's Imagery*. A single more recent study, Ann and John O. Thompson, *Shakespeare: Meaning and Metaphor* (Brighton: Harvester Press, 1987), deals with the animal imagery in *King Lear* from a more methodological than thematic perspective.

embodied in the suffering Lear, so this narrative goes, may be beset on all sides by predatory bestiality, but in the end it nonetheless emerges tragically vindicated, reasserted, reconciled. Readers like Knight and Heilman manifest an irrepressible urge for this *telos* of ultimate harmony. Both see Lear's 'purgatorial' descent (Knight), his confrontation with a humanity bent on self-destruction in raw bestiality, ultimately ending in redemption. 'The primary persons, good and bad,' says Knight, 'die into love.'[3] Although the course of the play may expose man as an inhuman brute, 'Lear's Nature', Heilman says, eventually prevails over 'Edmund's Nature', the Christian *lex naturalis* over the unscrupulous animal vitalism embodied by Edmund. The deepest 'breach in nature',[4] the most profound violations of cosmic, social, and moral order, in this view, occur only in order to be healed and ultimately forgiven. Lear and Cordelia go under but, going under in love, they lend the human values that they incorporate resilience and universal validity.[5]

Such positive thinking did not go unchallenged even at the height of its proponents' academic renown.[6] After Jan Kott's Beckettian reading of the play[7] and the brilliant theatrical endorsement of this reading by Peter Brook and Paul Scofield,[8] it came to sound hopelessly sentimental or even, from a 1980s, cultural materialist point of view, reactionary, fabricating, as Jonathan Dollimore asserts, 'precisely the kind of essentialist mystification which the play refuses'.[9]

---

[3] Knight, *Wheel of Fire*, 206.

[4] Heilman, *This Great Stage*, ch. 4, 'The Breach in Nature', 89–130.

[5] More emphatically affirmative than Heilman, John F. Danby (*Shakespeare's Doctrine of Nature: A Study of 'King Lear'* (London: Faber and Faber, 1949), 204) finds *King Lear* 'not only our profoundest tragedy, [but] also our profoundest expression of an essentially Christian comment on man's world and society'.

[6] For a particularly strident critique of Heilman, see W. R. Keast, 'The "New Criticism" and *King Lear*', in R. S. Crane (ed.), *Critics and Criticism* (Chicago: University of Chicago Press, 1952), 108–37 at 133–4: 'Heilman's interpretation ... is preposterous. It violates the unmistakable signs of the play's effect which appear in the text.'

[7] Jan Kott, 'King Lear, or Endgame', in his *Shakespeare our Contemporary* (London: Methuen, 1964), 101–37.

[8] Cf. Albert Hunt and Geoffrey Reeves, 'Climbing the Mountain: *King Lear*', in *Peter Brook* (Cambridge: Cambridge University Press, 1995, repr. 1999), 44–56, esp. 52–6.

[9] Jonathan Dollimore, *Radical Tragedy: Religion, Ideology and Power in the Drama of Shakespeare and his Contemporaries* (Brighton: Harvester Press, 1984), 202. In a similar vein Franco Moretti, 'The Great Eclipse: Tragic Form as the Deconsecration of Sovereignty', in his *Signs Taken for Wonders: Essays in the Sociology of Literary Form*, trans. Susan Fischer, David Forgacs, and David Miller (London and New York: Verso, 1988), 42–82; also Kiernan Ryan, *Shakespeare* (Hemel Hempstead and Atlantic Highlands, NJ: Harvester Wheatsheaf, 1989), 44–51 and 66–73.

But the fact that timeless human nature and its alleged moral triumph in *King Lear* stand exposed as unctuous delusions makes a re-examination of the play's animal kingdom all the more timely. Crucial to this task is a realization of the plurality encompassed by the term 'animal' and its cognates. As argued in the introduction, Cartesian anthropology, in its bid to consolidate human exceptionalism, tends to transform animality into mankind's monolithic Other. *King Lear*, by contrast, is an exemplary site of pre-Cartesian diversity, a diversity that erodes rather than reinforces the moral binarism traditionally assumed to ground the animal imagery of the play. Rather than 'the animal', we find various 'animalities'. Bestialization, the notion of a moral decline from properly human conduct to subhuman depravity, from civil order to barbaric wildness, obviously plays a major role. But neither is it quite as tidily restricted to the 'bad' characters as it has often been taken to be, nor does it constitute the dynamic under whose umbrella all of the play's animal signifiers can be subsumed. Drawing on the Aristotelian *scala naturae*, on the signifying systems of the bestiary, fable, and legend, and on the political iconology of chivalric feudalism and early modern sovereignty, the zoology of *King Lear* is polysemous and multifunctional. Animals appear as figures of awesome charisma, as enemies and fellow creatures; they appear as other than *and* indistinguishable from man.

I. Legal Animals

Law and bear-baiting rub shoulders in the public spectacles of criminal justice. The tied-up bear and the human convict on the scaffold, in the pillory, or 'whipped at the cart's tail' reflect each other's ordeal across the species divide. Thomas Dekker visiting the Bear-Garden and Robert Laneham, the chronicler of the Kenilworth baiting show in honour of the Queen, both endorse this mutuality, the one appalled, the other with relish.[10] But neither draws on punishment as the only, nor even as the most prominent, connection between baiting and the law. The dominant trope in both texts is litigation; the play the animals are seen to be performing, a courtroom drama. While the theatre of punishment subjects the human sufferer to a process of animalization, the two narratives reverse

---

[10] See above p. 60 for a discussion of Dekker and pp. 97–8 for a discussion of the Kenilworth report.

that process. Instead of men turning into beasts, beasts turn into men. The struggle of the dogs and bears is not so much a travesty of, as travestied *into*, 'a lively representation of men going to law'. That this travesty should be so readily figured in juridical terms is no great surprise. 'Shakespeare's litigious age'[11] would have been quick to find one of its own pet activities mirrored in the bears' and the dogs' 'beastly doings', their 'tugging together'[12] vividly capturing not just the antagonism but also the inherently theatrical quality of legal dispute.

The connections between law and theatre in early modern London were close and manifold.[13] Theatrical entertainment formed a functional, not merely recreational, part of professional life at the Inns of Court, both as a training ground for the lawyers' rhetorical and histrionic skills and as a means of 'embodying the content of the Ancient Constitution',[14] the quasi-mythical bedrock of Common Law. The courts also provided Londoners with live entertainment, 'a means of recreation, a type of real theater'.[15] Little wonder then that in both Dekker's and the Kenilworth chronicler's accounts the drama of legal contest gives the impression of

---

[11] B. J. Sokol and Mary Sokol, *Shakespeare's Legal Language: A Dictionary* (London and New Brunswick, NJ: Athlone, 2000), 1. Accounts of legal language or themes in Shakespeare typically begin by declaring the law's enormous importance in Elizabethan everyday life. See e.g. E. W. Ives, 'The Law and the Lawyers', *Shakespeare Survey*, 17 (1964), 73–86 at 73; George Keeton, *Shakespeare's Legal and Political Background* (London: Pitman, 1967), 3; A. G. Harmon, *Eternal Bonds, True Contracts: Law and Nature in Shakespeare's Problem Plays* (Albany, NY: State University of New York Press, 2004), 14.

[12] Dekker, 'Warres', in *Non-Dramatic Works*, 98.

[13] Since the rise of Law and Literature Studies in the 1980s they have also become one of the most intensively researched areas of early modern culture. For surveys of the field, see e.g. Patrick Hanafin, Adam Gearey, and Joseph Brooker (eds.), *Law and Literature* (*Journal of Law and Society*, 31/1) (Oxford: Blackwell, 2004); Greta Olson and Martin Kayman, 'From "Law-and-Literature" to "Law, Literature and Language": A Comparative Approach', *European Journal of English Studies*, 11 (2007), 1–15; Lenora Ledwon, *Law and Literature: Text and Theory* (New York: Garland, 1996); Ian Ward, 'Law and Literature: A Continuing Debate', in *Law and Literature: Possibilities and Perspectives*, ed. Ian Ward (Cambridge: Cambridge University Press, 1995), 3–27; R. J. Schoeck, 'Shakespeare and the Law: An Overview', *The Shakespearean International Yearbook* 1999, 219–39.

[14] Paul Raffield, *Images and Cultures of Law in Early Modern England: Justice and Political Power, 1558–1660* (Cambridge: Cambridge University Press, 2004), 124. The masques presented at the Inns, Raffield argues, thus acquired the 'status as legal texts' (ibid.).

[15] Harmon, *Eternal Bonds, True Contracts*, 15. This view has classical precedent in Cicero's *Brutus*, where the oratorical performance of the exemplary lawyer is nothing if not a theatrical event: 'This is what I wish for my orator: when it is reported that he is going to speak let every place on the benches be taken, the judges' tribunal full, the clerks busy and obliging in assigning or giving up places, a listening crowd thronging about, the presiding judge erect and attentive; when the speaker rises the whole throng will give a sign for silence, then expressions of assent, frequent applause; laughter when he wills it, or if he wills, tears; so that a mere passer-by observing from a distance, though quite ignorant of the case in question, will recognize that he is succeeding and that a Roscius is on the stage.' Cicero, *Brutus*, trans. G. L. Henderson (London: William Heinemann; Cambridge,

being the most patently obvious choice when it comes to picturing a show fight between animals. But there is a more fundamental aptness to this choice than either writer may have been aware of.

Travesty (in this case setting up animals as mock-humans) is a game relying on interplay between identity and difference. The more glaringly disparate the ingredients, the more conspicuously witty their enforced match. The classical example poses frogs and mice as Homeric heroes.[16] Baiting-as-litigation works well because the evident fit of the match is spiced with a strong sense of incongruity. Both activities are forms of fighting, but their difference is equally marked, baiting being a physical struggle between animals, litigation a rhetorical one between humans. The difference is blurred, the trope reliteralized, when the Kenilworth account speaks of 'sharp and byting arguments'. In collocation with 'arguments', 'sharp and byting' works figuratively, but also as a literal reference to the fighting creatures' fangs. This momentary collapse of the figurative into the literal foregrounds the very distinction on which the travesty depends, a distinction which contrasts (in order to make conflatable) what is specifically animal with what is specifically human.

Both Dekker and the Kenilworth chronicler capitalize on the incongruity of animals engaging in the unmistakably human *agón* of litigation. Nothing, in fact, could be more specifically and exclusively human than the law.[17] A system of normative distinctions inscribed in any definition of man as a civilized social being, the law is itself constitutive of the distinction between the human and non-human. The line that separates figuratively 'sharp' and 'biting' arguments from literally sharp and biting teeth is thus precisely the line that marks the separation of legality from brute force. Civil order proceeds from drawing and maintaining this line. Every deployment of the law repeats and recalls that separation and thus inevitably evokes (however subliminally and faintly) the absent-presence of what has been and is being excluded by it. As paramount manifestation of civil order, the law is thus trailed by the shadow of the uncivil wildness which it keeps in check. The travesty of animals-as-litigants draws on this buried nexus. No matter

Mass.: Harvard University Press, 1952), lxxxiv, 290 (p. 253). Cicero's aim in *Brutus* is to rebut the so-called Atticists, who argued for a more restrained, unembellished, or, as Cicero puts it, 'pinched and meagre' style of oratory (ibid.). To be truly 'Attic' (i.e. like Pericles or Demosthenes), Cicero asserts, is to be an actor ('a Roscius').

[16] [Homer], *Batrachomyomachia*, ed. T. W. Allen (Oxford: Oxford University Press, 1946).

[17] Picturing animals having dinner at a table produces an arguably lesser degree of incongruity: eating is, after all, an activity that humans share with all other creatures.

how light-hearted its intent, it reveals a more than superficial affinity between the controlled violence of baiting and the controlling violence of the law. If the law puts up a barrier between man and beast, it is inevitably also the threshold where their territories connect. This connectedness is fundamental to *King Lear*; it is also strikingly allegorized in the political philosophy of Thomas Hobbes.

II. Leviathan

Hobbes' great image of authority is a monster. His own ban on 'metaphors, tropes, and other rhetorical figures'[18] notwithstanding, the author of *Leviathan* employs the biblical beast that has 'upon earth . . . not his like' (Job 41: 24) to figure the 'Matter, Forme and Power of a Commonwealth'. The beast continues to puzzle Hobbes's commentators. That the champion of rationality and methodical thinking should choose such an extravagant, infinitely suggestive image[19] is as baffling as the fact that, having chosen it, he makes so little use of its semantic potential. The famous frontispiece of the 1651 edition (most likely based on Hobbes's own design)[20] replaces the biblical sea monster with the figure of a crowned giant, whose body is composed of a crowd of some three hundred human figures, towering over a landscape. This icon is much closer to the Platonic notion of the commonwealth as a *mákros ánthropos* than to the beast from the Book of Job. Of all the possible meanings associated with the Leviathan, only that of hugeness and awesome strength is explicitly invoked; the dark, therio-morphic aspects are toned down to the point of extinction.[21]

But as Hobbes himself would be keenly aware, metaphors tend to exceed their intended signification. According to Carl Schmitt, one of Hobbes's

---

[18] They are listed under 'Causes of absurdity' in ch. 5 of *Leviathan* and 'not to be admitted' 'in reckoning, and seeking of truth'. Thomas Hobbes, *Leviathan, or, The Matter, Forme and Power of a Commonwealth Ecclesiastical and Civil*, ed. Michael Oakeshott (Oxford: Blackwell, 1960), 28.

[19] Thomas Kersting, *Thomas Hobbes* (Hamburg: Junius, 1992), 37.

[20] See Horst Bredekamp, 'Thomas Hobbes's Visual Strategies', in Patricia Springborg (ed.), *The Cambridge Companion to Hobbes's Leviathan* (Cambridge: Cambridge University Press, 2007), 29–60 at 30. The execution of the design has been ascribed to Wenceslaus Hollar (Keith Brown, 'The Artist of the Leviathan Title-Page', *British Library Journal*, 4 (1978), 24–36), but Bredekamp makes a strong case for the Parisian artist Abraham Bosse. Horst Bredekamp, *Thomas Hobbes: Der Leviathan. Das Urbild des modernen Staates und seine Gegenbilder 1651–2001* (Berlin: Akademie Verlag, 2003), 39–55.

[21] Only three times is the Leviathan mentioned in the text. 'Introduction', 5: 'For by art is created that great LEVIATHAN . . . which is but an artificial man.' Ch. 17, p. 117: 'This is the

most incisive twentieth-century readers, this is emphatically true of the
Leviathan: 'In the long history of political theories, a history exceedingly
rich in colorful images and symbols, . . . this leviathan is the strongest and
most powerful image. It shatters the framework of every conceivable theory
or construct.'²² A creature of variable shape, the biblical beast was sometimes rendered as a whale, sometimes as a crocodile, but frequently also as a
serpent or dragon and as such came to be associated, even identified, with
the Antichrist.²³ In Wyclif he figures as 'the vile serpent', in Luther's table
talk as 'that great dragon' ('magnus ille draco'), and in Bodin's *Demonomanie*
as 'Leviathan, that is, the devil, [who] is not satisfied with the body alone but
lays snares for the soul too'. It comes as something of a surprise that Schmitt,
after citing these and many other instances from Christian and Jewish
traditions, roundly declares that 'the essentially demonic content of the
image vanishes between 1500 and 1600' and, by Hobbes's time, has been
replaced 'by a completely nonmythical and nondemonic conception of the
leviathan'.²⁴ But as if these disclaimers ultimately failed to convince him,
Schmitt all but revokes them with a strikingly suggestive image:

> Because of Hobbes' psychological peculiarity, it is possible that behind the
> image of the leviathan is hidden a deeper, symbolic meaning. . . . He said about

generation of that great LEVIATHAN, or rather, to speak more reverently, of that *mortal god*, to
which we owe under the *immortal God*, our peace and defence.' And finally, by way of a delayed
explanation, ch. 28, p. 209: 'Hitherto I have set forth the nature of man . . . together with the great
power of his governor, whom I compared to *Leviathan*, taking that comparison out of the last two
verses of the one-and-fortieth of *Job*; where God having set forth the great power of *Leviathan*,
calleth him King of the Proud. . . . But because he is mortal, and subject to decay, as all other
earthly creatures are; and because there is that in heaven, though not on earth, that he should stand
in fear of, . . . I shall in the next following chapters speak of his diseases.' Hobbes, *Leviathan*. None
of these references betrays a sense of the demonic potential of the image.

²² Carl Schmitt, *The Leviathan in the State Theory of Thomas Hobbes: Meaning and Failure of a
Political Symbol*, trans. George Schwab and Erna Hilfstein (1938; Westport, Conn., and London:
Greenwood Press, 1996), 5.

²³ The variability of the figure goes back to the biblical account itself. The Geneva Bible glosses
the first mention of 'Liviathan' (Job 40: 20) with 'Meaning, the whale', but the subsequent
enumeration of his strengths includes features that are distinctly dragon-like: 'Out of his nostrelles
cometh out smoke, as out of a boyling pot or caldron. His breath maketh the coles burn: for a
flame goeth out of his mouth' (Job 41: 11–12). *The Geneva Bible. A Facsimile of the 1560 Edition*
(Madison, Wis., Milwaukee, and London: University of Wisconsin Press, 1969).

²⁴ Schmitt, *The Leviathan*, 24–5. Schmitt is equally categorical about Shakespeare's references to
the leviathan being 'without any symbolism pointing towards the politico-mythical' (p. 24). At
least with respect to Henry's threatening speech before Harfleur one might well beg to differ:

> We may as bootless spend our vain command
> Upon th'enragèd soldiers in their spoil
> As send precepts to the leviathan
> To come ashore.   (*Henry V*, III. iii. 107–10)

himself that now and then he made 'overtures', but that he revealed his thoughts only in part and that he acted as people do who open a window only for a moment and close it quickly for fear of a storm. The three references to the leviathan that appear in the text of Hobbes' book could symbolically be conceived as three windows opened for a moment.[25]

Following this lead, it seems plausible to propose that, even though Hobbes's book is resoundingly silent about the demonic lineage of its eponymous monster, and although its title page shows a giant man instead of a fearsome beast, the beast and its legacy of menace still haunt the philosopher's rational system of order with its unacknowledged presence—a creature of the fear that commentators from Leo Strauss onward have seen as the mainspring of Hobbes's political thought.[26] Pervasive and all-powerful, fear dominates that pre-social, pre-contractual state of unchecked mutual hostility in which 'the disorders of the present time'[27]—the upheavals of the Civil War, the ruin of the English monarchy—find their nightmare reflection. Pitting force against force, the only possible protection against this fear is the even greater 'counter-fear'[28] instilled by the Leviathan. But before it can be made serviceable as a remedy, the monstrous beast (of whose majesty the mighty are afraid '*and* for feare they faint in them selues', Job 41: 16[29]) is, first and foremost, the terrifying embodiment of fear itself. In its demonic animality, it just as much embodies as it averts the threat of original chaos.

At every step, Hobbes's exposition of civil order sets itself off against a backdrop of primordial anarchy where man was—and, unless properly

---

[25] Schmitt, *The Leviathan*, 26. Schmitt refrains from '[f]urther endeavors to decode the symbolism of Hobbes' leviathan [because that] would lead us into biographical and individual psychological inquiries' (ibid.). But, of course, that symbolism might well be of more than just biographical and psychological relevance. In a diary entry for 8 Mar. 1948, Schmitt notes that Hobbes seems to lack the 'mythical sense' which manifests itself with such force in Bacon and Shakespeare, adding, however, the Hobbes 'probably only repressed it rigorously; for the Leviathan is, after all, a great mythical image.' Carl Schmitt, *Glossarium: Aufzeichnungen der Jahre 1947–1951*, ed. Eberhard Freiherr von Medem (Berlin: Duncker & Humblot, 1991), 111 (my translatin).

[26] Leo Strauss, *The Political Philosophy of Hobbes: Its Basis and its Genesis,* trans. Elsa M. Sinclair (Oxford: Clarendon Press, 1936), 27–8: 'The moral and humanist antithesis of fundamentally unjust vanity and fundamentally just fear of violent death is the basis of Hobbes's political philosophy.' Hobbesian fear has been the subject of widely divergent interpretations; cf. e.g. Norman Jacobson, 'The Strange Case of the Hobbesian Man', *Representations*, 63 (1998), 1–11; Philip Fisher, 'The Aesthetics of Fear', *Raritan*, 18 (1998), 40–72.

[27] Hobbes, *Leviathan*, 467.

[28] Bredekamp, *Thomas Hobbes*, 17.

[29] Quotation from *The Geneva Bible*.

governed, may become again—indistinguishable from beast, relapsing to that original state of war, 'as is of every man, against every man',[30] in which there is 'no society . . . [but] continual fear, and danger of death; and the life of man, solitary, poor, nasty, brutish, and short'.[31] The logic encapsulated in the image of the Leviathan is obvious: it takes a beast to release man from bestiality, to enforce non-bestial law and order. But the image inevitably also intimates the disturbing possibility (which Hobbes all but ignores[32]) that the beast may revert to and act on the untameable impulses of its own bestial nature.

Athens, the exemplary *polis* of the ancient world, personified the interface between civil humanity and bestial wildness in the figure of the mythical city-founder Cecrops: 'He was pictured half man, half dragon,' writes Jacob Spon, a seventeenth-century German traveller to Greece, 'for that he had, so to speak, made the Athenians into tame and reasonable people, who had heretofore, like the wild beasts, dwelt in rocky caves.'[33] Cecrops displays the two halves of his divided nature as simultaneous, but the image of his hybrid body, according to Spon, is intended to illustrate temporal progression, an ascent from animal to human status. There is no guarantee, however, that this duality will always let itself be strung out and defused in a reassuring teleological sequence of before and after. The potentially menacing synchronicity of the division is built into the very foundations of sovereignty, famously defined by Jean Bodin as the authority to change or suspend the laws in a state of exception ('si la nécessité est urgente').[34] For Carl Schmitt this is the crucial feature on which all other attributes of sovereignty are predicated: 'Sovereign is he who decides on the exception.'[35] According to Giorgio Agamben, this means that 'the sovereign is, at the same time, outside and inside the juridical order'.[36] Paradoxically, the ultimate guarantor of this order is legally entitled to suspend, even abolish it. By exercising his lawful right, the sovereign may unleash the very forces the law is meant

[30] Hobbes, *Leviathan*, 82.

[31] Ibid.

[32] Compared with 'the miseries, and horrible calamities, that accompany a civil war', the greatest 'incommodity' caused by a sovereign, Hobbes blandly asserts, would be 'scarce sensible'. *Leviathan*, 120.

[33] Jacob Spon, *Italiänische, Dalmatische, Griechische und Orientalische Reise-Beschreibung* (Nuremberg: Andreas Knorzen, 1681), 2nd part, book 5, p. 21 (my translation).

[34] Jean Bodin, *The Six Bookes of a Commonweale*, trans. Richard Knolles (London: G. Bishop, 1606). Facsimile repr. ed. Kenneth Douglas McRae (Cambridge, Mass.: Harvard University Press, 1962), ch. 8: 'Of Soueraigntie' and ch. 10: 'Of the true markes of Soueraigntie'.

[35] Carl Schmitt, *Political Theology: Four Chapters on the Concept of Sovereignty*, trans. George Schwab (1922; Chicago and London: University of Chicago Press, 2005), 5.

[36] Agamben, *Homo Sacer*, 15.

to control. In Hobbes, too, the sovereign is given unconditional power to restrain the rapacious selfishness of his subjects, while his own nature is under no restraint whatever. To Locke's clear-sighted exasperation, this is the glaring absurdity in the doctrine of absolute rule:

> ... for if it be asked, what security, what fence is there, in such a state, against the violence and oppression of this absolute ruler, the very question can scarce be borne. . . . Betwixt subject and subject, they [the advocates of Hobbes's doctrine] will grant, there must be measures, laws, and judges, for their mutual peace and security; but as for the ruler, he ought to be absolute and is above all circumstances; because he has power to do more hurt and wrong, it is right when he does it. To ask how you may be guarded from harm or injury on that side where the strongest hand is to do it, is presently the voice of faction and rebellion, as if when men, quitting the state of nature, entered into society, they agreed that all of them but one should be under the restraint of laws, but that he should still retain all the liberty of the state of nature, increased with power and made licentious by impunity. This is to think that men are so foolish that they take care to avoid what mischiefs may be done them by polecats or foxes, but are content, nay, think it safety, to be devoured by lions.[37]

An incorporation of the state of nature in society, sovereignty thus presents itself, according to Giorgio Agamben, 'as a state of indistinction between nature and culture, between violence and law, and this very indistinction constitutes specifically sovereign violence.'[38] For Agamben this indistinction is at the root of the biopolitical nightmares of the twentieth century, the totalitarian encroachment of politics on the sphere of 'bare life'. These particular horrors, however, seem too specifically of our own time to be directly applicable to the Renaissance. Too closely bound up with the development of the modern state apparatus, with social engineering and advances in technology, their sophisticated brand of inhumanity hardly warrants being described as simply a relapse into 'barbarism'.[39] But the 'paradox of sovereignty'[40] may also provide the script of an early modern nightmare in which the force of law proves the law's undoing and the sovereign a Cecrops in reverse.

---

[37] John Locke, *The Second Treatise of Government*, ed. Thomas F. Peardon (New York: Liberal Arts Press, 1952), 52–3.

[38] Agamben, *Homo Sacer*, 35.

[39] Theodor Adorno, with Max Horkheimer, *Dialectic of Enlightenment*, trans. Edmund Jephcott (Stanford: Stanford University Press, 2002).

[40] Agamben, *Homo Sacer*, §1, 15–29.

III. Sovereign Wrath

LEAR   But goes this with thy heart?
CORDELIA Ay, good my lord.
LEAR   So young and so untender?
CORDELIA So young, my lord, and true.
LEAR   Well, let it be so. Thy truth then be thy dower;
         For by the sacred radiance of the sun,
         The mysteries of Hecate and the night,
         By all the operation of the orbs
         From whom we do exist and cease to be,
         Here I disclaim all my paternal care,
         Propinquity, and property of blood,
         And as a stranger to my heart and me
         Hold thee from this for ever. The barbarous Scythian,
         Or he that makes his generation
         Messes to gorge his appetite,
         Shall be as well neighboured, pitied, and relieved
         As thou, my sometime daughter.   (i. 97–113; (I. i))[41]

An obvious way to illustrate the nature of sovereignty is to cite the ceremonials of investiture by which it is bestowed. This is Bodin's method of choice. The first of his *Six Books of the Commonwealth* provides a step-by-step account of the protocol observed by the Tartars in appointing their king:

> For the great king of Tartarie beeing dead, the prince and the people to whome the right of election belongeth, make choice of one of the kinsmen of the dead king ... and hauing placed him in a throne of gold, the bishop ... saith thus, Wee pray thee, and charge thee to raigne ouer vs: to whom the king aunswereth, If you will haue me so to doe, you must be readie to performe whatsoeuer I commaund; whomsoeuer I appoint to be slaine, you shall slay him presently, and into my hand you shall commit the whole estate of the king-dome: whereunto the people aunswere, Bee it so: after which the king con-tinuing his speech, saith, My word shall be my sword: whereunto the people giveth great applause.... This so great a power giuen by the people vnto the king, may wel be called absolute and soueraigne, for that it hath no condition annexed thereunto, other than is by the law of God and nature commanded.[42]

---

[41] Quotations from *The History of King Lear* (Oxford *Complete Works*). For ease of orientation I add the more generally used act count based on the Folio text.

[42] Bodin, *The Six Bookes of a Commonweale*, 89.

King Lear, by contrast, reveals the character of sovereignty in the act of abdication. The particular 'paradox of sovereignty' enacted in the opening scene of the play is that Lear pulls out all the stops of regal authority even as he divests himself of the 'sway' (i. 129; (I. i)) to ever enforce that authority again. In a terminal demonstration of majesty's unconditional power, that power liquidates itself.

In contrast to his later cursing of Gonoril (iv. 254–64; (I. iv)), Lear's condemnation of Cordelia is charged with the double force of regal as well as parental wrath. What may strike a modern reader as an incongruous mixing of the familial and the political, both in the love test and in the immediate aftermath of its miscarrying, is fully in keeping with early modern views.[43] Fatherhood and majesty are mutually reinforcing models of unquestionable authority. As Lear's daughter, Cordelia is not only his subject as well, but, as it were, his subject par excellence. Parental authority, unlimited *patria potestas*, is the prototype of sovereign power and as such precedes the exposition of the latter in Bodin.

Basilikon Doron, King James's fatherly advice to his son Henry and the manifesto of his absolutist doctrine, emphatically draws on this nexus. The threat of paternal displeasure which winds up the prefatory address 'To Henry my dearest sonne, and natural successour', exhibits a more than faint resemblance to Lear's 'Better thou hadst not been born than not to have pleased me better' (i. 226; (I. i)):

> To conclude then, I charge you, as ever yee thinke to deserve my Fatherly blessing, to follow and put in practise, as farre as lyeth in you, the praecepts hereafter following. And if yee follow the contrary course, I take the Great GOD to record, that this Booke shall one day bee a witnesse betwixt mee and you; and shall procure to bee ratified in Heaven, the curse that in that case here I give unto you. For I protest before that Great GOD, I had rather not bee a Father, and childlesse, then bee a Father of wicked children.[44]

Paternal wrath is the analogue of God's wrath, the insubordinate child the exemplary instance of disobedience to the great King and Father in Heaven. This ladder of analogy is vividly present in Lear's wrath, too. But it is undercut by a more sinister twist. When, immediately after the torrent of

---

[43] This point is forcefully made in Björn Quiring's excellent reading of *King Lear* in his *Shakespeares Fluch: Die Aporien ritueller Exklusion im Königsdrama der englischen Renaissance* (München: Fink, 2009), 177–96.

[44] King James VI and I, 'Basilikon Doron', 201.

Lear's curse, Kent dares to speak up for the disowned Cordelia, Lear cuts
him short with:

> Peace, Kent. Come not between the dragon and his wrath.
>
> (i. 114; (I. i))

Editors sometimes gloss this with a footnote on heraldry, explaining that the
dragon adorned the coats of arms of Britain's ancient kings. But this does not
begin to capture the force of the line. It is true that the undisputed last entrant
for the category of Britain's 'ancient' kings, the Anglo-Saxon Harold, faced the
conquering Normans at Hastings under a standard bearing a dragon (which
the victorious William subsequently sent to the Pope as a present). But it is
hard to tell how current such historical information would have been around
1600. The heraldic animal more commonly associated with a British king
would have been the lion. And it is indeed in the (anachronistic) company
of heraldic lions that we find Leir and Cordeile in a *Genealogy of the Kings of
England* printed around 1560. Their imaginary portraits are each presided over
by a lion rampant supporting a banner showing two lions passant guardant.[45]
Metrically, 'lion' would have served equally well in Lear's rebuff to Kent.
Semantically, it would have added a touch of royal grandeur[46] to an equally
formidable capacity for wrath.[47] Forming near assonance with the strongly
marked /r/ in 'wrath', 'dragon', however, does seem to have the phonetic
edge over 'lion', adding fierceness to Lear's outburst.

Fierceness rather than royalty stands out as the dominant note in Lear's
reference to the dragon, a fierceness surely much more familiar to Shakespeare's contemporaries than the heraldry of a distant past, because it figures
prominently in the exploits of England's most popular national hero,
St George. Though officially somewhat fallen from grace during the English
Reformation, the (Catholic) saint survived all attempts to oust him and his
fire-breathing escort from village ridings and civic pageants.[48] Reaching new
heights of popularity in the upsurge of Elizabethan patriotism, he was

---

[45] The image is reproduced in Stanley Wells, 'Introduction', in *The History of King Lear*
(Oxford: Clarendon Press, 2000), 1–80 at 18. On the (Plantagenet) origins of the lion in the
royal arms of England, see Scott-Giles, *Shakespeare's Heraldry*, esp. 2–4 and 42–9.

[46] James I was keenly aware of the lion's symbolic association with kingship. See above, Ch. 2.

[47] The lion's proverbial rage is certainly part of Shakespeare's poetical repertoire: see e.g. *Dream*
V. i. 220: 'When lion rough in wildest rage doth roar.' *Richard II*, II. i. 174: 'In war was never lion
raged more fierce.'

[48] For a detailed account of his changeable fate and reputation in the course of the 16th c., see
Mary Ellen Lamb, 'The Red Crosse Knight, St George, and the Appropriation of Popular
Culture', *Spenser Studies*, 18 (2003), 185–208.

equally at home in the highly sophisticated poetry of Spenser's *Faerie Queene* as in Richard Johnson's 'non-elite paean to nation and nationalism',[49] *The Seven Champions of Christendom* (1596/97), where he even acquires a solidly English birthplace, Coventry.[50] In Shakespeare the national saint is regularly invoked before battles throughout the histories,[51] most prominently in the concluding line of Henry V's 'Once more unto the breach' (III. i. 1) harangue when the English troops are rallied with the cry '"God for Harry! England and Saint George!"' (III. i. 34). An established national icon, St George was inseparably associated 'with the dragon he conquers'.[52] Just as he is the archetypal champion of all that is right and good, Christian and English, the dragon is the archetypal embodiment of all that is not: a demonic figure of threatening bestiality, evil, hostile, murderously cruel. 'God himselfe in holy Scripture', writes Edward Topsell, 'doth compare the deuill vnto a dragon.' No wonder there is, as he goes on to point out, 'an ordinary hatred betwixt men and dragons, and therefore in the discourse of their enemies, men must have the first place'.[53]

The very first animal mentioned in the play is none other than the king, and the king is a dragon. If Lear identifies himself neither with the royal English lion nor with the dragon-conquering English patron saint but with—even *as*—the saint's devilish adversary, this is a highly ominous move. The immediate effect of his 'Come not between the dragon and his wrath' is to translate the situation into the iconographic terms of the Saint George legend. As the scene reaches its dramatic climax the king, Kent and Cordelia re-enact the familiar triangle of knight-in-armour, dragon, and virgin—except that the king is playing the wrong role. His

---

[49] Naomi Conn Liebler, 'Bully St George: Richard Johnson's *Seven Champions of Christendom* and the Creation of the Bourgeois National Hero', in ead. (ed.), *Early Modern Prose Fiction: The Cultural Politics of Reading* (New York and London: Routledge, 2007), 115–29 at 115.

[50] According to hagiographic tradition St George was born in Cappadocia, clearly a less desirable location for a hero who was thought of as a slayer not only of dragons but of Turkish infidels.

[51] In *Richard III* both Richard and Richmond invoke St George before the battle at Bosworth (V. v. 224: 'God and Saint George! Richmond and victory!'). Interestingly, Richard departs from his opponent's conventional invocation by (1) not linking St George to God and (2) wanting to borrow the dragon's strength rather than that of the dragon slayer (V. vi. 79–80: 'Our ancient word of courage, fair Saint George, / Inspire us with the spleen of fiery dragons').

[52] Liebler, 'Bully St George', 115.

[53] Topsell, *The historie of serpents*, 155 and 165. While discrediting many dragon-related tales as mere fictions, Topsell is nonetheless convinced that dragons do indeed exist, claiming that 'this which I have written, may be sufficient to satisfie any reasonable man, that there are winged Serpents and dragons in the world'. Ibid. 162.

self-bestialization puts the axe to the very base of that ladder of analogy which ensures the mutually reinforcing authorization of father and king. As the father over his children, the king over his subjects, so reason is set up in command over man's passions. Ophelia's lament over Hamlet's loss of 'that noble and most sovereign reason' (III. i. 160), and Horatio's reference to 'your sovereignty of reason' (I. iv. 54) (again in a situation where that sovereignty is under threat) both attest to the foundational analogy between the constitution of the human *corpus* and the corporation of the state. The king as the head of the body politic rules over his subjects as reason rules over the passions in the 'little kingdom' (*Caesar* II. i. 68) of the human body.

Implied in this analogy is the necessity of self-control. 'He who rules must first rule himself. Reason is both author and result of this analogical command'[54]—both, in other words, the commander and what is being commanded. A poem by Phineas Fletcher postdating *Lear* by nearly three decades dramatizes the same psycho-political complex. 'He' in the first line refers to *ratio*, the king of the 'little kingdom' who is also the 'viceroy' of the ruler of heaven:

> Hence while unsetled here he fighting reignes,
> Shut in a Tower where thousand enemies
> Assault the fort, with wary care and pains
> He guards all entrance, and by divers spies
> Searches into his foes and friends designes:
> For most he fears his subjects wavering mindes.
> This Tower then only falls, when treason undermines.[55]

Fletcher's political economy of the psyche is undiluted Stuart absolutism. With no intermediate level of parliamentary deliberation the prerogative of the ruler is unlimited. All power rests with him—but also the entire burden and hence anxiety of power. With 'wary care and pains' he must be constantly on the alert, constantly (as in Hobbes's state of nature) live in fear of foes and friends alike and, most of all, in fear of his subjects, those irrational forces of passion which—if the metaphor were to be taken at its

---

[54] Rüdiger Campe, 'Der Befehl und die Rede des Souveräns im Schauspiel des 17. Jahrhunderts', in Armin Adam and Martin Stingelin (eds.), *Übertragung und Gesetz: Gründungsmythen, Kriegstheater und Unterwerfungstechniken von Institutionen* (Berlin: Akademie Verlag, 1995), 55–71 at 57 (my translation).

[55] Phineas Fletcher, 'The Purple Island', in Giles and Phineas Fletcher, *Poetical Works*, ed. Frederick S. Boas (Cambridge: Cambridge University Press, 1909), ii. 77.

word—should be mind-less, yet are still possessed of a dangerous mind of their own. The thickest tower walls offer no protection from the greatest threat, which looms, not from without, but from within, as does the civil upheaval in *King Lear* that bursts on the scene under the auspices of the dragon.

It may seem rather excessive to burden a single line, or rather, a single word from that line, with such momentous significance. And so it is, but then excess—the excess of adulation, the excess of absolute power expending itself in its own undoing—is the dominant note of the king's disastrous love trial. Moreover, Lear's dragon does not turn up unprepared for. It is hatched, as it were, in the speech immediately preceding it (the speech quoted at the beginning of this section) and completes the thought process of that speech (i. 97–113). Lear's vow, invoking a distinctly non-Christian cosmic order in which human life is ruled by an impersonal 'operation of the orbs', declares an absolute severance of all personal bonds between father and daughter. Cordelia is to be turned into a complete stranger, and to confirm this estrangement Lear, in fuming hyperbole, cites the strangest, most alien, barely human creature—or creatures—as the measure of his distance from her:

> The barbarous Scythian,
> Or he that makes his generation
> Messes to gorge his appetite,
> Shall be as well neighboured, pitied, and relieved
> As thou, my sometime daughter.   (i. 109–13; (I. i))

Though directed at the accused 'sometime daughter', the words rebound on the judging father. Expelling Cordelia into the wilderness, it is really Lear himself who ends up there. In vowing to treat his own child no better than he would the most brutish savage, he commits himself to acting—and thus becoming—just like such a savage. The cannibalistic drift of Lear's rage once more unwittingly exposes itself in his invitation to his sons-in-law, 'Cornwall and Albany, / With my two daughters' dowers digest this third' (i. 119–20; (I. i)). Lear's intent may be unequivocal, but his words are not: 'this third' offered for digestion could be either the dower or the daughter. Cannibalism, it has been suggested, is universal not because it is or ever was universally practised, but because it is a universal category of radical otherness. The allegation of eating human flesh is a succinct way of stigmatizing 'an individual or group as non-human'.[56] From Lear's inadvertent alliance with the barbarous Scythian and the even more barbarous (and therefore nameless, if not unnameable) cannibal it is only a small—and logical—step to his identification with the dragon.[57]

Lear's lapse from reason into blind 'bestial' rage is a lapse from what is distinctly and thus 'naturally' human. But at the same time it gives vent to the no less natural force of passion, a force which it is the constant 'wary care and pains' of civilizing 'nurture'—the constant vigilance of the law—to tame, to channel, and to suppress. From a theological perspective, this contradiction in the very nature of nature may be unravelled by assigning the unruly force of passion to man's 'fallen' nature—the burden of original sin—and reason to that 'higher' nature which testifies to the possibility of redemption. But the exhibition of the king's rage in the opening scene of *King Lear* makes such tidy partition impossible. Lear's wrath produces a royal monster—a terrible epiphany of indistinction between sovereign order and brute force.[58] It stages a spectacular breakdown of that neat opposition which John Danby's influential study saw maintained through-out *King Lear* in two clearly distinguishable ideas of nature, designated in Danby's chapter headings as 'The Benignant Nature of Bacon, Hooker, and Lear' versus 'The Malignant Nature of Hobbes, Edmund, and the Wicked Daughters'.[59] Lear's self-bestialization at the very outset of the play, his share in those very forces of nature that he will later condemn in the name of nature puts paid to such tidy division.

The savage triad of Scythian, cannibal, and dragon that Lear unleashes in himself will breed and multiply in the actions of his adversaries. Stanley Wells, taking up Winifred Nowottny's observation that 'the play is inexhaustibly patterned',[60] maintains that 'the patterning of its language forms a nervous system for the play, linking all its parts into a single

---

[56] William Arens, *The Man-Eating Myth: Anthropology and Anthropophagy* (Oxford: Oxford University Press, 1979), 140. 'The idea of "others" as cannibals, rather than the act, is the universal phenomenon. The significant question is not why people eat human flesh, but why one group invariably assumes that others do' (ibid. 139). Arens's study raised a storm of protest among anthropologists, but the observations quoted seem incontrovertible.

[57] As pointed out in Ch. 4, the distinction between Scythians and cannibals which Lear seems to draw (line 110: '*Or* he that makes his generation') is tenuous at best because both were thought of as anthropophagous.

[58] This nexus is the subject of Derrida's 2001–2 Paris lectures. Jacques Derrida, *The Beast and the Sovereign*, ed. Michel Lisse, Marie-Louise Mallet, and Ginette Michaud, trans. Geoffrey Bennington (Chicago and London: The University of Chicago Press, 2008).

[59] Danby, *Shakespeare's Doctrine of Nature*, 20 and 31.

[60] Winifred M. Nowottny, 'Lear's Questions', *Shakespeare Survey*, 10 (1957), 90–7 at 90.

intercommunicating organism'.[61] In this aptly so-called 'nervous system', Lear's 'dragon' from Scene i will reverberate in Edmund's sardonic reference to his having been begotten 'under the Dragon's tail' in Scene ii ('so that it follows I am rough and lecherous'; ii. 124–6; (I. ii)); just as Lear's vow to treat Cordelia no differently from the barbarous Scythian or one that feeds on his young will be fulfilled in the treatment he receives at the hands of his daughters Gonoril and Regan, a treatment mockingly sketched in the Fool's song in Scene iv:

> The hedge-sparrow fed the cuckoo so long
> That it had it head bit off by it young;   (iv. 210–11; (I. iv))

IV. Bestialization

The father a witless host bird, the daughters his murderous parasites—the Fool's song registers the breathtaking speed of Lear's reversal of fortune. On his second appearance in the play the mighty dragon has turned into a sparrow. The sovereign violence of father against child is replaced by the as yet half-concealed violence of 'pelican daughters' (xi. 68; (III. iv)) bent on making their parent (as symbolized by Lear's fast-diminishing train of knights) into 'messes' to gorge their appetite.

Humankind at the juncture of flesh and spirit, in the privileged but precarious midway position between animal and angel—these commonplaces of Renaissance thought provided a readily available template for moral didacticism. The majority of animal references in *King Lear* draw on this model, envisaging evil-doing as a descent into subhuman bestiality, and most of these refer to Lear's 'unnatural' daughters: they are the prime instance of this downward moral mobility across the species boundary. The descent begins with the Fool's cuckoo song and continues with Lear's increasingly bitter invectives, first against Gonoril, then against both sisters, heaping upon the pair a veritable bestiary of curses. Gonoril's thanklessness is 'More hideous . . . Than the sea-monster' (iv. 255–6; (I. iv)), 'sharper than a serpent's tooth' (iv. 282), she herself a 'detested kite' (iv. 256). Regan—even when Lear still mistakes her for his ally—is already equipped with claws: 'with her nails / She'll flay thy [Gonoril's] wolvish visage' (iv. 301–2). Gonoril 'hath tied / Sharp-toothed unkindness like a

---

[61] Wells, 'Introduction', 52.

vulture here' (vii. 296–7; (II. ii)) and 'She hath... struck me with her
tongue / Most serpent-like upon the very heart' (vii. 317–19). From parasite
cuckoos, the 'pelican daughters' (xi. 68; (III. iv)) mutate to Lear's 'she-foxes'
(xiii. 18; (III. vi)), Albany's '[t]igers, not daughters' (xvi. 39; (IV. ii)) and
Kent's 'dog-hearted daughters' (xvii. 46; (IV. iii)). But the animal character
most persistently attributed to them is the serpent. Invoked a final time in
the last scene by Albany's reference to his wife as 'This gilded serpent' (xxiv.
82; (V. iii)), it is conclusively endorsed by the manner of their death, as
foreshadowed in Edmund's final soliloquy. Entangled in their mutual
hatred, they are featured as vipers poisoning one another:

> Each jealous of the other as the stung
> Are of the adder.   (xxii. 60–1; (V. i))

As the behaviour of the daughters lends credence to these denigrations, the
ascription of animality becomes an effective means of redirecting sympathy
to the initially vainglorious father-tyrant. He becomes the 'poor, infirm,
weak and despised old man' (ix. 20; (III. ii)), 'more sinned against than
sinning' (ix. 60) now that they have become foxes, vultures, tigers, serpents.

What Heilman, recording these terms of abuse almost in their entirety,[62]
fails to note is the misogynist slant that is all too obvious to a reader today.
Whatever crimes Edmund commits, it is only his own moral account that is
debited. But Gonoril and Regan's deeds are, first, more bestial still and,
second, bankrupt women in general. After the blinding of Gloucester, the
choric commentary of First and Second Servant metes out blame symmetrically to the Cornwall couple, husband and wife (xiv. 97–100; (III. vii)).
But the rhetorical emphasis is clearly on her crime: should Regan be allowed
to get away with it, Second Servant concludes, '[w]omen will all turn
monsters' (xiv. 100).

Does the play, then, heap all the malignancy in nature on the female?[63]
Such a clearly marked gender-division of the (moral) kingdom would
hardly be at odds with the sustaining ideologies of Jacobean culture. It
would, however, oversimplify the play, cutting the vital cord that links
the dethroned patriarch to his 'monstrous' daughters. It is, after all, not the
daughters' disobedience that initially fractures the social and moral order,

---

[62] Heilman, *This Great Stage*, 93–6.
[63] A strong case for such a reading is made by Kathleen McLuskie, 'The Patriarchal Bard:
Feminist Criticism and Shakespeare: *King Lear* and *Measure for Measure*', in Jonathan Dollimore and
Alan Sinfield (eds.), *Political Shakespeare* (Manchester: Manchester University Press, 1985), 88–108.

but the father-king himself. The serpent daughters are born of a dragon father.[64] In the terms of Topsell's *Second Book of Living Creatures*, this makes them smaller specimens from the same family of beasts. In the political zoology of the play, too, Gonoril and Regan are chips off the old block, hatched, as it were, from the dragon's eggs.[65] The sovereign act of juridical violence that empowers them and sentences their 'sometime sister' and the disobedient Kent to exile spawns the violence of their 'monstrous regiment'.[66] If Lear seeks to detach himself from his daughters and from the female in general, the very violence of his denial speaks for an analysis in which the play exposes rather than shares in this effort. The misogyny in King Lear thus has a double edge. Its fervour is unmistakably auto-aggressive, as in Lear's onslaught on Gonoril just prior to his rushing out into the gathering storm:

> Now I prithee, daughter, do not make me mad.
> I will not trouble thee, my child. Farewell,
> We'll no more meet, no more see one another.
> But yet thou art my flesh, my blood, my daughter—
> Or rather a disease that lies within my flesh,
> Which I must needs call mine. Thou art a boil,
> A plague-sore, an embossèd carbuncle
> In my corrupted blood. But I'll not chide thee.
> Let shame come when it will, I do not call it.   (vii. 376–84; (II. ii))

The passage makes for interesting comparison with the disowning of Cordelia, precisely because Lear does not disown her elder sister. While the beloved youngest ends up as an ex-child, 'my sometime daughter' (i. 113; (I. i)), the whole force of Lear's rage goes into declaring Gonoril as inextricably his own. Exiling her—or rather himself from her ('We'll no more meet, no more see one another')—he will nonetheless always carry her with him, even within himself. His bond to her far exceeds the bond described in Cordelia's painstakingly correct 'You have begot me, bred me, loved me. / I return those duties back as are right fit—' (i. 88–9; (I. i)). There is nothing contractual about 'a disease that lies within my flesh', 'A plague-sore, an

---

[64] On the absence—and covert presence—of the mother in this patrilineal succession, see Coppélia Kahn, 'Excavating "those dim Minoan Regions": Maternal Subtexts in Patriarchal Literature', *Diacritics*, 2 (1982), 32–41.

[65] The serpent's egg looms large in Brutus' tortuous auto-suggestive argument for the killing of Caesar (*Caesar* II. i).

[66] John Knox, *The first blast of the trumpet against the monstrous regiment of women* (Geneva: J. Poullain and A. Rebul, 1558).

embossèd carbuncle / In my corrupted blood.' The collapse of the contractual superstructure of familial obligation thus knits father and daughter all the
more tightly together: they are henceforth cursed to remain perpetually
embodied in each other.

This implication of the patriarch in the corruption that he abhors,
especially the corruption of the flesh, culminates in Lear's ultimate image
of female monstrosity:

> Down from the waist
> They're centaurs, though women all above.
> But to the girdle do the gods inherit;
> Beneath is all the fiend's. There's hell, there's darkness,
> There's the sulphury pit, burning, scalding,
> Stench, consummation. Fie, fie, fie; pah, pah!   (xx. 119–24; (IV. v))

The dualism of Christian humanist anthropology is clearly inscribed in this
passage. Woman-as-centaur gives the caesura between God and beast a local
habitation as well as a name. Disjunction is graphically mapped onto the
body, the girdle becoming the demarcation line between heaven and hell,
spirit and flesh. *Tertium non datur:* the extremity of polarization admits of no
third, intermediate position. The 'Link in the Creation', piously evoked in a
late defence of the medieval Great Chain of Being by the anatomist Edward
Tyson (1699),[67] is really a slash: the intermediary domain of the human has
been elided, leaving only God and fiend. 'Centaures', writes Edward
Topsell in *The History of Foure-footed Beasts,*

> are described by the Poets to have their forepart like men, and their hinder
> part like horses, the occasion wherof is thus related by *Pindarus:* that *Centaurus*
> the Sonne of *Ixion*, committed buggery with the mares of *Magnetia*, vnder the
> mountaine *Pelius*, from whence came that monstrous birth in the vpper part
> resembling the father and in the neather the mother. These saith he [were]
> giuen to all manner of Latrociny and Depraedation.[68]

As presented in this passage, the centaur is a monstrous birth of patriarchal
myth-making. 'But to the girdle' does the father 'inherit', reproducing his
own image in the upper, human part, while the mother is 'naturally'

---

[67] '... the Antients were fond of making Brutes to be Men: on the contrary now, most
unphilosophically, the Humour is, to make Men but meer Brutes and Matter. Whereas in truth
Man is part a Brute, part an Angel; and is that Link in the Creation, that joyns them both together.'
Edward Tyson, *Orang-outang: sive Homo-Sylvestris, Or, the Anatomy of a Pygmie: Compared with that
of a Monkey, an Ape, and a Man* (London: Thomas Bennet, 1699), 55.

[68] Topsell, *The historie of foure-footed beastes*, 337.

relegated to 'the neather', 'down from the waist.' A living copula of two species, the centaur presents itself as a literalizing emblem of its own aetiology, a constant reminder of what it took to produce him: copulation; and also a constant reminder of his own *thymós* or purpose in life, form not so much following, as flagging, function. Lear's paroxysm of loathing could hardly hit upon a more appropriate image of lecherous promiscuity[69] ('Let copulation thrive'; xx. III; (IV. v)). But he gives the classical iconology an unorthodox twist by endowing his centaurs with the upper bodies of women and the nether parts of mares: 'the sulphury pit' could not be more graphically gendered. Female centaurs are not entirely unheard of— the famous Athenian artist Zeuxis (4th c. BC) is said to have been the first to paint one[70]—but they are clearly an anomaly in a tradition centring on phallic sexual aggression. Lear thus produces a double monstrosity, a hybridization of hybrids, grafting onto the centaur two images of female cross-species monstrosity: sphinx and siren, both lethally dangerous to their male victims.

Ostensibly, then, Lear's philippic 'presents women as the source of the primal sin of lust'.[71] What seems to me less clear, however, is whether the play, as McLuskie avers, endorses the misogynist rage of its hero. The ambivalence of the tirade's central image resists, I would suggest, such straightforward identification. The force of that image lies at least partly in its being so palpably forced, an effort of displacement, of disassociation. Too strongly rooted in the cultural imagination, the male identity of the centaur will not simply vanish through the operation of a rhetorical sex change. Instead, Lear produces a figure of transvestism, the masculinity of the crossbreed all too visible under a female disguise. 'Though women all above', Lear's centaurs inevitably disclose—in the very act of concealing it—their male provenance 'beneath': reinscribing the mythological palimpsest, they fashion female depravity in the image of the father. In Lear's abhorrence of his daughters '[w]omen will all turn monsters' (xiv. 100; (III. vii)); but instead of severing what bonds there are left between them,

---

[69] Greek mythology knows of only two exceptions to the rule that all centaurs are bibulous, wild, and lecherous: Pholos, gracious host to Heracles, and Chiron, wise teacher of Achilles and many other heroes.

[70] The painting is lost, as is his picture of a family of centaurs of which Lucian gives a description in 'Zeuxis and Antiochus', in *The Works of Lucian of Samosata*, trans. and ed. H. W. Fowler and F. G. Fowler, 4 vols. (Oxford: Clarendon Press, 1905), ii. 94–9 at 95–7.

[71] McLuskie, 'The Patriarchal Bard', 106.

the spectre of monstrous hybridity only serves to lock father and daughters once again in an indissoluble internecine embrace.

The self-punishing circularity of Lear's accusations corresponds to a boomerang logic of justice:

EDGAR   The gods are just, and of our pleasant vices
         Make instruments to scourge us.
         The dark and vicious place where thee he got
         Cost him his eyes.
EDMUND   Thou hast spoken truth.
         The wheel is come full circled. I am here.   (xxiv. 166–70; (V. iii))

Edgar's Sunday school moralizing has won him scant favour with modern critics,[72] but even if his sententiousness seems somewhat flat—and premature in view of what the quite obviously not so 'just' gods still have in store—it nonetheless points to an important structural pattern in the action. Contrary to the suggestion of reassuring moral closure in Edmund's 'full circle', the constitutive circularity of both the Lear and Gloucester plots is one of agonizing repetition, the 'wheel' not a means of transport to some 'promised end' (xxiv. 259; (V. iii)) but an 'instrument . . . to scourge us', as in the Ixion-like torment of Lear's 'but I am bound / Upon a wheel of fire, that mine own tears / Do scald like molten lead' (xxi. 44–6; (IV. vi)).[73]

There is a sinister aptness here: both patriarchs are brought to the lowest depth of their course in situations that cruelly mimic the misjudgement they committed in the full bloom of their paternal and juridical power. A 'justicer' condemned by his own verdict, Gloucester finds himself instantaneously transformed from venerable host into 'the villain Gloucester' (xiv. 3; (III. vi)), 'the traitor Gloucester' (xiv. 21), charged with the same reproaches that he himself poured on his seemingly traitorous son Edgar in a torrent of manic volubility:

O villain, villain—his very opinion in the letter! Abhorred villain, unnatural, detested, brutish villain—worse than brutish! Go, sir, seek him, ay, apprehend him. Abominable villain! Where is he?   (ii. 75–8; (I. 2))

---

[72] It could be argued that the point of Edgar's concluding moral statement is to show how trivial and pointless it is, how it precisely does not capture the truth. Like Albany's (in F: Edgar's) concluding lines of the play it could be read as a demonstration of the inadequacy of language in the face of devastating catastrophe.

[73] For the relevance of Ixion to the play, see Bate, *Shakespeare and Ovid*, 194–6.

Lear, for his part, must perform a farcical replay of his royal dispensation of justice, presiding over a jury of scarecrows in a vain attempt to redress the damage he caused with his first trial. The gods are hardly just, but obviously quite capable of making instruments of torture—and a vicious mockery— 'of our pleasant vices'. Bringing the two old men face to face with their own failings, this retaliatory mechanism moves us straight into the play's 'heart of darkness': Lear's arraignment of his daughters, Gloucester's summary trial and punishment.

V. The Second Time as Nightmare: Lear's Mock Trial

In or around the year 1820, an old fresco showing the public hanging of a pig in man's clothes disappeared under a coat of whitewash in the town church of Falaise, the birthplace of William the Conqueror in Normandy. The painting was the only pictorial record of a legal custom which seems to have originated in northern and eastern France, then spread to the Low Countries, Germany, and Italy and flourished for over five hundred years: the criminal prosecution of animals. The lost Falaise fresco probably commemorated a tragic incident which occurred in 1386. A pig, identified as 'a sow of three years or thereabouts', was found guilty of having 'eaten the face' of a swaddled infant, who subsequently died. Condemned to be dragged and hanged, the offending beast was publicly dispatched by the town executioner.[74]

It is one thing to destroy a dangerous animal in order to prevent future harm. It is quite another formally to indict the animal, arrest, and detain it in a prison cell, ascertain its guilt in a criminal trial involving a judge and several lawyers, and sentence it to public execution at the hands of the local 'master of high works'. This was not 'a kind of wild justice' (Bacon) or, as one writer on the subject would have it, a case of 'the savage in his rage obliterat[ing] all distinctions between man and beast',[75] but a regular legal

---

[74] On animal trials E. P. Evans, *The Criminal Prosecution and Capital Punishment of Animals* (1906; repr. London: Faber and Faber, 1987); Esther Cohen, 'Law, Folklore and Animal Lore', *Past and Present*, 110 (1986), 6–37; Darren Oldridge, *Strange Histories: The Trial of the Pig, the Walking Dead, and Other Matters of Fact from the Medieval and Renaissance Worlds* (London and New York: Routledge, 2005), 40–55.

[75] W. W. Hyde, 'The Prosecution of Animals and Lifeless Things in the Middle Ages and Modern Times', *University of Pennsylvania Law Review*, 64 (1916), 696–730, quoted by Nicholas Humphrey in his foreword to Evans, *The Criminal Prosecution*, p. xvii.

practice observed with all the appurtenances of proper procedure. One judgement speaks of a sow convicted of 'murder flagrantly committed', another, of a pig which had killed with particular 'cruelty and ferocity'. The crime of yet another pig was aggravated by the fact that it had killed a child and eaten his flesh 'although it was Friday'.[76]

King Lear has no hanged pig in human clothes, but it does have the so-called 'mock trial'. Shakespeare's closest approximation to an animal trial, it shows a similar propensity for vanishing as that of the lost fresco of Falaise. Appearing in the quarto *History*, but missing from the folio *Tragedy of King Lear*, the mock trial is one of the play's variables, its most striking instance of textual 'mouvance', and as such has elicited extensive critical debate.

Those who argue for the Folio text being the result of authorial revision need to address the question of why Shakespeare, or indeed, as Gary Taylor puts it, 'why anyone would have wanted to remove a passage which most modern readers regard as an epicentre of the play's meaning'.[77] Taylor's answer is that censorship—one of the usual suspects in such cases—can hardly be held directly responsible for the disappearance of the trial,[78] but may well have intervened in a more indirect way: only too aware of 'the potential sensitivity of the material' (p. 90), Shakespeare anticipated censorship by censoring himself. Understandably dissatisfied with the result of such 'aborting inhibitions' (ibid.), he then decided to omit the scene altogether. There is, as Taylor admits, no proof for this, but that does not prevent him from contemplating what Shakespeare *might* have written if his imagination had been unhampered by political caution. In that case, the scene could have (or, as Taylor leaves us in no doubt, should have) expressed 'two deeply subversive ideas' (ibid.): the idea of 'legal ceremony ... as a theatrical farce', along with the idea that 'the economically and politically powerless, deprived of any resort to real justice, must content themselves

---

[76] Evans, *The Criminal Prosecution*, 157.

[77] Gary Taylor, '*King Lear* and Censorship', in Gary Taylor and Michael Warren (eds.), *The Division of the Kingdoms: Shakespeare's Two Versions of 'King Lear'* (Oxford: Clarendon Press, 1983), 75–119. Further references are given in text.

[78] I agree with Taylor that 'That much, at least, is clear' ('*King Lear* and Censorship', 101). If the censor took umbrage because the scene, representing legal action as a mad farce, was liable to question 'the authority of Authority' (ibid. 88), the blinding of Gloucester (which 'dramatizes a much more damning and objectionable instance of political "legality"'; ibid. 89) and Lear's 'great image of authority' speech in IV. vi would surely have been much more liable to offend. The speech, in particular, offers a critique of legal institutions far more strident and explicit than anything even hinted in the mock trial, yet it is not only retained but expanded in the revised text. Nor is there any evidence that satirical portrayals of justices in other plays of the period were ever curtailed by order of the Master of the Revels.

with fantasies of legal retribution' (ibid.). Explaining in some detail what the
scene might have been, Taylor finds what it actually *is* to be wanting on all
counts:

> To be sure, its dramatic procedure—mute defendants tried on a ridiculous
> charge (kicking a father) before judges who betray a complete inability to stick
> to the point . . . —might to a modern reader sound like something out of
> Genet; but Genet's parodies derive their force from the obsessive verisimili-
> tude of the impersonations. . . . If Shakespeare had dramatized the trial as
> Genet might have done, its structure would be more evident; but by making
> it more evident he might also have made it susceptible to censorship. What he
> has done runs, by contrast, no risk at all of censorship—but some risk of
> obscuring its own structure.   (p. 91)

If the Shakespeare of the mock trial scene is a failed Genet to Gary Taylor,
he is an uncharacteristically inept theatrical craftsman to Roger Warren. The
mock trial, Warren argues, simply never works on stage: 'The whole topsy-
turvy situation seems intended to express Lear's vision of injustice', but no
sooner has the trial begun 'than those whom he has cast as judges go off at
tangents', lapsing 'from their "judicial" roles to the other roles which they
habitually play—Edgar to the Bedlam beggar obsessed by devils, the Fool to
his songs and jibes which bring everything down to earth'.[79] Instead of
achieving 'an elaborate climax', the scene just manages to create 'a generalized sense of chaos' (p. 46). Omitting it, Warren claims, gives a substantial
gain in concentration and dramatic focus, 'which the eccentric digressions
of the mock trial tend to dissipate' (p. 50). Rather than spreading the
important mock-justice theme over two scenes, 'Shakespeare could have
decided to guarantee it maximum impact by concentrating it all in one place
in 4.6' (p. 49). Moving directly from Lear's encounter with Poor Tom to
the atrocity of Gloucester's blinding, the Folio version brings the crises of
suffering undergone by Lear and Gloucester closer together. This, Warren
argues, is a decisive advantage because

> Lear's verbal arraignment of women and justice arises out of the details of their
> [= Lear's and Gloucester's] personal relationship, rather than through the
> elaborate creation of an imaginary courtroom. The reunion of Lear and
> Gloucester in 4.6 is a much simpler, more human scene than 3.6—a major
> reason, I think, for its greater impact in performance.   (p. 50)

[79] Roger Warren, 'The Folio Omission of the Mock Trial: Motives and Consequences' in
Taylor and Warren (ed.), *The Division of the Kingdom*, 45–57 at 46. Further references are given in
text.

Warren's closely argued analysis makes a strong case for Shakespeare having had second thoughts about the mock trial. But not an incontrovertible one. There has been, as Warren himself admits, at least one modern production of *King Lear* that brought the mock trial off with memorable success, a production which, moreover, managed to make the trial directly conducive to an outstanding treatment of the reunion between Lear and the blind Gloucester in IV. v (Q Sc. xx). This was Peter Brook's 1962 Stratford production, frequently acclaimed as perhaps *the* outstanding modern rendering of the play.[80] If ever the word 'suggestive' was appropriate, it is in connection with the mad trial scene, which possesses a seemingly unique capacity for triggering its readers'—perhaps auto-suggestive—imaginings. 'Lear's hallucinations have a terrible reality in the theatre', writes Marvin Rosenberg apropos this scene, citing Granville-Barker and Paul Scofield in Peter Brook's production as evidence.[81] This testimony is not easily dismissed. If, as Gary Taylor writes, 'most modern readers regard [the mock trial] as an epicentre of the play's meaning', Brook's haunting theatrical and subsequent cinematic rendition of the scene gives strong support to this majority opinion. And even those who consider the trial to be flawed would probably concede its essential 'rightness' in the imaginative fabric of the 'Lear world', the overall design of the play.[82] Taylor implicitly acknowledges as much when he calls its omission 'the Folio's most surprising cut'.[83]

This 'rightness' of the mock trial, I feel, may be intricately bound up with what Taylor and Warren identify as its flaws. If 'a generalized sense of chaos' (Warren) does indeed preclude, or detract from, a well-defined satirical message about the absurdities of legal procedure—a message that would readily lend itself to being paraphrased in discursive prose—then perhaps the conveying of such a message should not be assumed to be the primary (unachieved) goal of the scene. Instead one might do well to attempt a reading which seeks to confront rather than elide the chaos in which Lear's broken rite of legal process is conducted. The cue for such a reading could be Gloucester's 'O ruined piece of nature! This great world / Shall so wear out to naught' (xx. 129–30; (IV. v)). Occasioned by his encounter with the

---

[80] Paul Scofield's performance of Lear in Brook's production was voted top Shakespeare performance in a poll conducted among RSC actors in 2004.

[81] Marvin Rosenberg, *The Masks of King Lear* (Berkeley, Los Angeles, and London: University of California Press, 1972), 233.

[82] A valuable discussion of this point is to be found in Paul A. Gottschalk, 'The Universe of Madness in *King Lear*', *Bucknell Review*, 19/3 (1971), 51–68.

[83] Taylor, '*King Lear* and Censorship', 89.

mad Lear, it has a choric resonance well beyond its immediate situational context. Together with the desolate state of the former king, it encompasses the ruin of his realm and thus includes, and is corroborated by, the ruined piece of civil order presented in the mock trial scene. If this scene lacks a coherent structure, so does 'the gored state' (xxiv. 315; (V. iii)), the whole of the social fabric. Lear's sovereign rule depended on clear distinctions of rank and role. In its headlong rush towards 'naught', or nothingness, and 'uncreation',[84] the play undertakes a relentless undoing of these distinctions. The mock trial completes this course, arresting the dynamics of undoing in a tableau of utmost indistinction.

At this point—the zero state, as it were, of the differentiations that sustain any form of social and political order—Lear's arraignment of his absent daughters turns into an animal trial. Not that this idea is pursued with any degree of consistency, but then, as the above-quoted comments by Taylor and Warren have made clear, the scene itself never settles into the clearly fixed shape of a trial. If the contours of the trial as a whole remain blurred, its association with animal justice could be seen as even more tentative—a fleeting evocation at best, sparked off by a single word:

LEAR It shall be done. I will arraign them straight.
    [*To Edgar*] Come, sit thou here, most learnèd justicer.
    [*To Fool*] Thou sapient sir, sit here.—No, you she-foxes—

                                                              (xiii. 16–18; (III. vi))

Breaking off the opening move of the trial, the interjection '—No, you she-foxes—' registers a first disturbance of Lear's juridical proceedings: are the fox-daughters supposed to be putting up some form of verbal resistance, are they already trying to escape? The text offers no explanation. Nor does the next line, spoken by Edgar as Poor Tom, help to clarify what Lear 'sees'. Its meaning is obfuscated by two textual cruces.[85] Q reads: 'Looke where he stands and glars, wanst thou eyes, at tral madam come ore the broome *Bessy* to mee.'[86] In Wells's Oxford edition this becomes: 'Look where he stands and glares. Want'st thou eyes at troll-madam? [*Sings*] Come o'er the burn, Bessy, to me' (xiii. 19–21; (III. vi)). Here's going off at tangents indeed! The undefined 'he' effectively supplants Lear's she-foxes

---

[84] See Edward W. Tayler, '*King Lear* and Negation', *English Literary Renaissance*, 20 (1990), 17–39.
[85] They are discussed in Taylor and Warren, *The Division of the Kingdoms*, 486–8.
[86] *King Lear: 1608 (Pied Bull Quarto)*, Shakespeare Quarto Facsimiles, 1 (Oxford: Clarendon Press, 1964).

with a counter-phantasm all of Tom's own making—perhaps the foul fiend, maybe even Lear, but certainly not the two daughters. The game of troll-madam[87] strays even further from Lear's train of thought. Poor Tom completely disrupts the trial by interposing his own fantasy. But most editors since Theobald have taken Q's 'he' for an error and emended it to 'she'. In combination with Q 2 'triall madam', this reinserts the line into Lear's vision: 'Look where she stands and glares! Want'st thou eyes at trial, madam?' Having Edgar chime in with Lear's imaginings rather than sabotaging them, this version would also tally well with Edgar's behaviour later in the scene when he again supports Lear in setting up his trial: 'Let us deal justly' (xiii. 36).

Considering the amount of interference by snippets of song, the Fool's deflating realism ('Cry you mercy, I took you for a join-stool'; xiii. 47) and Kent's admonishment to stop the whole nonsense, Lear's fantasy trial actually proves remarkably resilient. Though interrupted, it always resurges, and when it finally does disintegrate it is not because of outside interference, but as a direct result of its own inner momentum. Only after Lear has 'seen' the culprits escape and has wound up his inconclusive investigation with the call for anatomizing Regan does Kent prevail upon him to 'lie here a while' (xiii. 76) and rest.

The trial, then, never quite manages to dominate the scene absolutely. Yet though constantly assailed by distractions, its flickering presence is never quite drowned out either. Whether the recurrent animal references—the 'foul fiend . . . in the voice of a nightingale' (xiii. 25–6), the 'sheep' (37), 'the cat' (41)[88] and Lear's 'little dogs and all' (56)—attenuate and subvert or help maintain this presence may be difficult to decide. Arguably, they do both. Although out of place in a conventional court of law, they go well with a trial of 'she-foxes' conducted in what Cordelia later identifies as a pig sty ('And wast thou fain, poor father, / To hovel thee with swine and rogues forlorn / In short and musty straw?' (xxi. 36–8; (IV. vi)). As intimations of animality crowd the fantastical court in the hovel, Lear's royal dispensation of justice recalls the familiar figure of Noble the lion, another 'justicer' who

---

[87] The Oxford editor Stanley Wells cites an explanation from 1572: 'the ladies, gentlewomen, wives and maids may . . . have in the end of a bench eleven holes made, into the which to troll pummets or bowls of lead . . . or also of copper, tin, wood'.

[88] For a possible connection between Edgar's song about the negligent shepherd, his reference to the cat that is proverbially grey, and the overall theme of justice, see Adrienne Lockhart, 'The Cat is Grey: *King Lear's* Mad Trial Scene', *Shakespeare Quarterly*, 26 (1975), 469–71.

cannot prevent a fox from escaping.[89] But beyond the tropes, and the trappings, of the animal epic the scene also suggests the more unsettling strangeness of the juridical hanging of pigs. Completing the downward course of Lear's undoing, the arraignment of 'she-foxes' undoes the most basic distinction of all: that between humans and beasts.

The razing of this particular boundary is no sudden collapse; it has been a long time coming. It starts, as we have seen, at the very outset of the tragedy, even as Lear resolves the first trial of his daughters in a fit of rage that turns him into a dragon. The bizarre human–animal melee in the hovel, then, is no aberration from the overall pattern of the play. Its tragic mockery recalls, and inverts, the self-indulgent display of kingly, paternal, and judicial power with which the play began. If the Lear of the opening scene saw too little, the Lear of the mock trial sees too much. The commands hurled at the disobedient Cordelia and the insubordinate Kent in Scene i—'Hence, and avoid my sight' (i. 116; (I. i)); 'Out of my sight!' (i. 149)—manifest the refusal, on Lear's part, to follow Kent's exhortation to 'see better' (i. 150). By Scene xiii Lear has been brought from lack of sight to an excess of it. Personifying the madman in Theseus' famous comparison of lunatic, lover, and poet, he sees—and hears[90]—'more devils than vast hell can hold' (*Dream* V. i. 9). The babble of voices in the mock trial scene, its very lack of a consistent satirical argument, has the effect of placing us almost inside Lear's troubled mind. Creating a pandemonium of theriomorphic fiends reminiscent of a Bosch, Grünewald, or Bruegel, it projects Lear's hallucinatory inner vision, 'mad as the racked sea' (xviii. 2; (IV. iv)). And just as the late medieval and early modern pictorial tradition that evolved around the Temptation of St Antony has a throng of disturbingly indeterminate creatures crowding in on a white-haired, white-bearded old hermit, the white-haired[91] old Lear is surrounded by phantoms whose exact nature

---

[89]   The trial of Reynard the Fox is the first and best-known (though not the oldest) episode in the sprawling body of tales about Europe's most popular animal trickster-hero, who began his vernacular career in the latter half of the 12th c. The trial of Reynard, it has been argued, holds up a parodic mirror to contemporary judicial procedures, expressing disenchantment with medieval customary law at a time of legal crisis. See Theodore Ziolkowski, *The Mirror of Justice: Literary Reflections of Legal Crisis* (Princeton: Princeton University Press, 1997), 98; Richard W. Kaeuper, 'The King and the Fox: Reactions to the Role of Kingship in Tales of Reynard the Fox', in Anthony Musson (ed.), *Expectations of the Law in the Middle Ages* (Woodbridge: Boydell Press, 2001), 9–21.

[90]   Characteristically, there is no differentiation between seeing and hearing: 'The little dogs and all, / Tray, Blanch, and Sweetheart—see, they bark at me' (xiii. 56–7; (III. vi)).

[91]   Cf. xxi. 28 (IV. vi) where Cordelia refers to 'these white flakes' that should have aroused pity in her sisters.

escapes definition. Who or what is the Gonoril he arraigns first because 'she kicked the poor King her father' (xiii. 43–4; (III. vi))—a woman, a she-fox, a four-legged piece of furniture (joint-stool[92])—or nothing at all?

The mock-trial resumes an investigation begun in the love trial of the first scene. Its focus is defined by the word 'heart'. Cordelia, whose very name contains 'heart' in Latin (*cor*), fails the love trial because she 'cannot heave [her] heart into [her] mouth' (i. 83–4; (I. i)). The king, her father, wants to know: 'But goes this with thy heart?' (i. 97) because '*this*', Cordelia's speech, has been signally lacking the very thing ('heart') that he expected to find in it. The ensuing stichomythic exchange with its resonant stress on the final word of the fourth line sharply reveals the gap between the two semantic units that should, but in Cordelia's speech conspicuously refuse to, form the required alliance:

LEAR   But goes this with thy heart?
CORDELIA Ay, good my Lord
LEAR   So young and so untender?
CORDELIA So young, my lord, and true.   (i. 97–100)

Regan, by contrast, has no trouble joining 'heart' with 'truth'. She heaves her 'true heart' (i. 65) into her mouth with studied ease. Throughout this scene 'heart' is employed rhetorically, an investment to be used as profitably as possible in a verbal transaction (with material consequences) whose rules are stipulated by Lear's insatiable narcissism. 'Heart', as Kent's comment indirectly points out, is no more in this scene than a sound:

> Thy youngest daughter does not love thee least,
> Nor are those empty-hearted whose low sound
> Reverbs no hollowness.   (i. 144–6)

In a trial of 'she-foxes' the accused necessarily lack speech. It is with newly acquired clairvoyance that the mad Lear need only look at Regan (who is, of course, not really there) to see 'What store her heart is made on' (xiii. 49; (III. vi)), the truth which her own profession of 'my true heart' (i. 65) had kept hidden. Lear's probing of hearts proceeds from (falsifying) words to the ocular proof of 'looks', but does not stop there. The face—Regan's

---

[92] There is a curious parallel in the banquet scene in *Macbeth* (III. iv. 66–7), when Lady Macbeth seeks to bring her ghost-struck husband to his senses with 'When all's done / You look but on a stool.'

'warped looks'—may 'proclaim' the heart (xiii. 48; (III. vi)),[93] but the search for ultimate truth has to dig deeper:

LEAR Then let them anatomize Regan; see what breeds about her heart. Is there
      any cause in nature that makes this hardness?   (xiii. 70–2)

Lear's *ultima ratio* of anatomizing is as logical as it is futile. Shakespeare's contemporaries saw the interior of the body, newly exposed in the dissecting theatres of the Renaissance, as the archetypal domain of mystery and revelation, arguably more so than even the newly discovered worlds beyond the horizon.[94] But digging into the innermost secrets of the body will reveal nothing that is not physical, nothing about the particular hardness that has caused Lear's suffering. What Lear, at a loss for a humanly plausible explanation of his daughter's behaviour, seeks to dig out of her body is a 'cause in nature', the physiology rather than the psychology of crime,[95] or, to use Regan's own word, the 'mettle' she is made of.[96]

With 'Then let them anatomize Regan' Lear's jurisdiction once more approaches the condition of an animal trial by endorsing a notion of justice as all-enveloping as the one that enabled, and made sense of, the hanging of a homicidal pig: a notion of 'justice as a universal attribute, applicable to all nature',[97] outreaching even the boundaries of humankind and therefore capable of avenging crime regardless of intention or rational culpability. If

[93] The reliability of physiognomical analysis is an open question in Shakespeare. While Duncan maintains that it is impossible to 'read' faces ('There's no art / To find the mind's construction in the face'; *Macbeth* I. iv. 11–2), Lady Macbeth warns her husband that it is all too easy to do just that: 'Your face, my thane, is as a book where men / May read strange matters' (I. v. 61–2). Cf. Sibylle Baumbach, *Let me behold thy face: Physiognomik und Gesichtslektüren in Shakespeares Tragödien* (Heidelberg: Winter, 2007).

[94] Jonathan Sawday, *The Body Emblazoned: Dissection and the Human Body in Renaissance Culture* (London and New York: Routledge, 1995); Michael Neill, *Issues of Death: Mortality and Identity in English Renaissance Tragedy* (Oxford: Clarendon Press, 1997), 102–40.

[95] The distinction between physiology and psychology is, of course, anything but clear-cut (see above. Introduction, pp. 27–28). A late 17th-c. testimony to their overlap is Thomas Willis, *Two Discourses concerning the Soul of Brutes, Which is that of the Vital and Sensitive of Man*, Englished by S. Pordage (London: Thomas Dring, 1683). In ch. 8, 'Of the Passions or Affections of the Corporeal Soul in General', Willis actually offers 'a cause in nature' for the hardening of the heart, both physiological and moral: 'Hence it is, that Drinking of Wine, Banqueting, and every Kind of Dissolute Life, because they render the Blood lawless, and not able to be restrain'd or bridl'd, are said to make hard the Heart, and to obstruct the Duties of Religion' (p. 47). For the general foundations of such psycho-physical connectedness, see Park, 'The Organic Soul'.

[96] REGAN Sir, I am made / Of that self-same mettle that my sister is, / And prize me at her worth (i. 63–5; (I. i))

[97] Cohen, 'Law, Folklore and Animal Lore', 36.

anatomic dissection is the pursuit of an ever more precisely and minutely differentiated mapping of the human body, the anatomizing of Regan with its strangely literal 'incarnation' of guilt, by contrast, reinforces the sense of a collapse of distinctions.

The line gains additional force through a shift in perception. Regan, hitherto (and again immediately afterwards, in Scene xiv) the perpetrator of violence, is suddenly transformed into its victim. The human corpse stretched out, disembowelled, on the dissecting table is perhaps the most graphic image of the anatomist Edward Tyson's 'Link in the Creation', evoking both the butchered animal and the sacrificial body of Christ. Robert Watson observes a similar overlapping in seventeenth-century Dutch painting, where '[p]alimpsests of both game carcasses in the kitchen and Isaac under the knife are visible in anatomy-theater depictions such as Rembrandt's *Anatomy Lesson of Dr Nicolaes Tulp*'[98] and where in many a still life 'an executed animal takes the place of the sanctified human body'.[99]

But Lear's call for anatomizing Regan also suggests the gory vivisections which the ingenuity of criminal justice conducted on the bodies of its victims. Probing into the flesh of the accused was the customary means of disclosing guilt both in the interrogation process and in the carrying out of the sentence. In this way, Lear's final pronouncement in his chimerical court of law prepares us for what is to follow: the trial and punishment of Gloucester.

Between them, Lear's two trials of his daughters' hearts (Sc. i and Sc. xiii) measure out and delimit the space of the political. Two scenes of law on the brink of the wilderness, of human–animal (con)fusion, they are strategically placed at the very edges of this space, encroaching on it from different, but complementary angles: the one (Sc. i) from above, a position of absolute power, the other (Sc. xiii) from below, a position of absolute powerlessness. Staging rituals of juridical procedure, they highlight what is most characteristic of civilized human order precisely at that liminal moment when this order merges with its very opposite—a state of nature, of primordial anarchy in which, to quote Lear, not Hobbes, this time, 'Man's life is cheap as beast's' (vii. 426; (II. ii)).

---

[98] Watson, *Back to Nature*, 213–14.   [99] Ibid. 211.

VI. The Second Time as Torture: Blinding Gloucester

The trial and blinding of Gloucester, too, harks back to Lear's love trial at the beginning of the play—parallel, as so often in Shakespeare, underlining contrast.[100] While the opening trial had been a grand scene of state (and of grandiloquence), a public display of regal pomp and circumstance, the scene of Gloucester's maiming shows a mode of law enforcement that dispenses with all formality, a mode that is quick and secret rather than decorous and public, and where the dominant impression is one of claustrophobic closeness—a 'closet scene' rather than one in a hall or public chamber. 'This house is little' (vii. 447; (II. ii)), Regan cynically remarks as Lear rushes out into the storm—how stiflingly little does not become apparent until its owner gets trapped in it. Shakespeare's open platform stage has no technical means to distinguish between vast outdoor spaces and crammed interiors, but that does not mean the play is not able to suggest this crucial opposition all the more strongly—as the Prologue of *Henry V* puts it—to our 'imaginary forces'. The valency of the contrast between indoors and outdoors that underlies the storm scenes is abruptly reversed in Scene xiv. Having conducted Lear into the hovel with 'Here is better than the open air' and the promise to 'piece out the comfort with what addition I can' (xiii. 1–3; (III. vi)), Gloucester now finds much worse than discomfort under his own roof, where he ends up 'All dark and comfortless' (xiv. 83; (III. vii)). Nor will 'the gods', as Kent (ever the optimist) wishes, 'deserue' (Q; in the sense of 'require')[101] Gloucester's 'kindness' (xiii. 5). The provider of shelter and 'addition' (a poor remainder—and sad reminder—of 'the additions' (i. 128; (I. i)) that Lear had expected to retain in his retirement) becomes the defenceless victim inside the very doors that his guests had commanded him to 'shut up' against the oncoming storm (vii. 461, 464; (II. ii)).

The scene shows the severance of two fundamental bonds while dubiously invoking an unexpected third. Protesting to his tormentors that 'You are my guests' (xiv. 29; (III. vii)) and 'I am your host' (xiv. 38), Gloucester appeals, first, to the bond of hospitality, and later, after his maiming, to the even stronger bond between father and child when he calls upon Edmund's

---

[100] Lear's 'love trial' does not begin as a trial in a juridical sense, but quickly turns into one.
[101] The Oxford *Complete Works* has the conjectural 'discern', Folio the unequivocal 'reward'.

filial obligation to 'quite this horrid act' (xiv. 84). Both, of course, to no avail. But Cornwall, too, declares himself under an obligation as he ushers Edmund off the scene of the imminent atrocity:

Edmund, keep you our sister company.
The revenges we are bound to take upon your traitorous father are not fit for your
    beholding.   (xiv. 5–7)

The interesting word here is 'bound'. More than just a colloquial warning (as in 'this is bound to get messy'[102]), it endows the gratuitous, merely personal violence of 'revenges' with a higher authority. Loyal to Lear, Gloucester has become a traitor to the regime of his successors. Uncompelled by any *personal* bond such as that which would oblige a 'good son' to seek retribution for his father's injury, Cornwall is 'bound' to take 're-venges' because a capital crime has been committed. His brisk 'Leave him to my displeasure' (xiv. 4) expresses not just the anticipation of a soon to be gratified desire for sadistic pleasure, but also the sovereign will of a reigning prince meting out retribution. Cornwall's 'displeasure' thus echoes the old King's verdict on Cordelia: 'Better thou hadst not been born than not to have pleased me better' (i. 226; (I. i)), mingling personal impulse with public authority in an equally tangled web.

While the mock trial scene creates an inextricable blend of human and animal, the trial of Gloucester makes the rule of law indistinguishable from crime. If revenge, according to Francis Bacon's famous definition, 'is a kind of wild justice',[103] legal punishment is a kind of civilized revenge. While the retaliatory aspect of criminal justice has been all but excised from modern legal thinking, it is spectacularly prominent in the early modern penal system.[104] In punishing Gloucester, Cornwall mimics the Lear of Scene i: he is more brutal, more coldly efficient in his controlled anger, but acts on

---

[102] One of the strengths of Shakespeare's characterization is how Edmund's declarations of filial piety are always demonstratively accepted as true by Cornwall, who is, of course, fully aware that they are pure hypocrisy, just as Edmund is fully aware that Cornwall knows this—and Cornwall knows that Edmund knows he (Cornwall) knows.

[103] Francis Bacon, 'Of Revenge', in *The Essays or Counsels Civil and Moral*, 10–11 at 10.

[104] See Ch. 4. How fundamentally our perceptions have changed shows up in a recent essay by Dympna Callaghan and Chris R. Kyle ('The Wilde Side of Justice in Early Modern England and *Titus Andronicus*', in Constance Jordan and Karen Cunningham (eds.), *The Law in Shakespeare* (Houndmills, Basingstoke: Palgrave, 2007), 38–57). The notorious Elizabethan pursuivant and torturer Richard Topcliffe, the authors write, 'was, to use a contradiction in terms, a kind of legal avenger' (p. 39). But the wide array of sources quoted and astutely analysed in the essay demonstrates that is precisely what this is not: a contradiction in terms.

the strength of the same uncontrolled licence as the displeased king, a
licence that Hobbes would exalt and Locke would condemn:

CORNWALL   Go seek the traitor Gloucester.
              Pinion him like a thief; bring him before us.
                  Exeunt other Servants
              Though we may not pass upon his life
              Without the form of justice, yet our power
              Shall do a curtsy to our wrath, which men
              May blame but not control. Who's there—the traitor?

              Enter the Duke of Gloucester brought in by two or three

REGAN   Ingrateful fox, 'tis he.
CORNWALL (*to Servants*) Bind fast his corky arms.   (xiv. 21–7; (III. vii))

Unlike Lear faced with the recalcitrant Cordelia, Cornwall displays all the
calculating circumspection of the politic Machiavel.[105] Yet the gist of his
statement, carefully hedged by two subordinate clauses, not only describes
what the speaker intends to do, but also recalls what Lear already has done
when 'power did a curtsy to his wrath' in Scene i. Another instance in
which the patterning of the play's language generates something like a
'nervous system' of intercommunicating cues,[106] Cornwall's declaration of
intent ends on the same key word, 'wrath', that Lear used at the crucial
moment when he turned himself into a 'dragon'. Commentators gloss
Cornwall's 'do a curtsy to' as 'yield' (Wells) or 'give way to' (Foakes).[107]
But the point, it seems to me, is not that 'power' (glossed by Wells as 'legal
authority') is to be replaced by wrath, but that power (sovereign power
which includes but is not limited to legal authority) is to be made accessory
to wrath; that power and wrath are to—as is the case in Scene i—operate in
collusion.

   The congruence of law and violence introduced in the opening trial is
carried to its bitter extreme in the trial and blinding of Gloucester. Cornwall
appears as a vicious, scaled-down Lear in a shrunken setting. The parallel, as
well as the difference in scale, is highlighted earlier when Lear, on arrival at
Gloucester's castle, takes offence at his son-in-law's temper. Gloucester's

---

[105] What Machiavellian foresight does not take into account, of course, is that people might
harbour and sometimes even act upon ethical convictions. Ironically, this oversight proves fatal to
the clever duke.
[106] Wells, 'Introduction', 52.
[107] *King Lear*, ed. R. A. Foakes, Arden 3rd ser. (Walton-on-Thames: Thomas Nelson and Sons,
1997).

conciliatory 'You know the fiery quality of the Duke' (vii. 260; (II. ii)) triggers an outburst of that same quality from Lear:

> Vengeance, death, plague, confusion!
> What 'fiery quality'?
> 'Fiery'? The Duke?—tell the hot Duke that Lear—
>
> (vii. 260–1, 266; (II. ii))

Only Lear himself feels entitled to tantrums which others have to put up with. Unbridled display of emotion clearly belongs to the 'additions' of a king; in Cornwall it is presumption, 'mere insolence' (vii. 255).

Scene xiv sees not just Lear's wrath, but also his daughters' adulation recur in gruesome travesty. Gonoril's chillingly brisk 'Pluck out his eyes' (xiv. 4; (III. vii)) recalls her 'Dearer than eyesight, space, or liberty' (i. 51; (I. i)), resoundingly prominent at the beginning of her declaration of love. Pinioned in his own home and blinded, Gloucester loses all three of these essential possessions. The horror of his ordeal is reinforced by an element of childish cruelty:

> GLOUCESTER By the kind gods, 'tis most ignobly done,
> To pluck me by the beard.
> REGAN   So white, and such a traitor!
> GLOUCESTER Naughty lady,
> These hairs which thou dost ravish from my chin
> Will quicken and accuse thee. I am your host.
> With robbers' hands my hospitable favours
> You should not ruffle thus. What will you do?   (xiv. 33–40)

Plucking the prisoner's beard is hardly an appropriate penalty in a case of high treason. It belongs to the sphere of domestic violence and thus contributes to the general impression of a private reprisal, an indulgence of vindictive (dis)pleasure.[108] Eerily consistent with 'the ridiculous charge'[109] of 'kick[ing] the poor King her father' (xiii. 43–4; (III. vi)) in Lear's mock trial, the very silliness of the assault adds to the victim's humiliation, the sequence of 'ravish', 'quicken', and 'accuse' turning the plucking out of facial hair into an act of rape by a 'Naughty lady'. There is a note of hysteria,

---

[108] Beard-plucking and hair-tearing, however, are among the ordeals traditionally associated both with the temptation of St Anthony (as in Matthias Grünewald's Isenheim altarpiece, Colmar 1512–16) and Christ's Passion (as performed in Continental passion plays).

[109] Taylor, '*King Lear* and Censorship', 91.

even a touch of the ridiculous in Gloucester's hair 'quickening' into babies that will accuse their 'mother's' (that is Gloucester's) ravisher.[110] But this deepens rather than deflates the sense of threat: if such gratuitous aggression is allowed to prevail, 'What [else] will you do?' Shakespeare is not quick to produce the answer to this question, preferring to heighten the tension by preparing us for it. In addition to Gonoril's ominous 'Pluck out his eyes' in line 4, Gloucester unwittingly predicts his own fate by envisaging Lear's: 'Because I would not see thy cruel nails / Pluck out his poor old eyes' (xiv. 54–5). The cruelty of the daughters is given a markedly bestial inflection, Regan's 'cruel nails' being paired with Gonoril's 'boarish fangs'. The actual performing of these imagined acts of violence on the body of Gloucester locates the scene in the same human–animal twilight zone as that in which Lear's mock trial plays out. The continuity is emphasized at the opening of the proceedings: in each case the accused are assigned the same animal identity, Lear's 'she-foxes' echoing in Regan's 'Ingrateful fox, 'tis he' (xiv. 27). While the previous scene evokes the strangeness of the historical animal trials, the interrogation and blinding of Gloucester expressly aligns itself with the spectacle of bear-baiting, drawing on both its drastic physicality and its association with the juridical process:

GLOUCESTER I am tied to th' stake, and I must stand the course.   (xiv. 52)

For all the horrors of Webster and the limb-hacking atrocities of *Titus Andronicus*, the blinding of Gloucester with its stomach-turning climax, 'Out, vile jelly!' (xiv. 81), is arguably the most horrendous scene of violence in English Renaissance drama. One effect of enlisting the intermedial support of the Bear-Garden for this ultimate excess of cruelty is reinforcement: it gives the stage a virtual infusion of 'the blud and the slaver'[111] that was abundantly spilt at the neighbouring stake, thereby enhancing the violence of a scene whose visceral impact certainly overshoots the detachment of mere 'representation', but still stops short of real bloodshed. Invoking the violence of the Bear-Garden, Shakespeare's stage colludes with and profits from the raw savagery of baiting. But catering to the bloodthirsty tastes of an audience accustomed to the spectacle of 'live' maiming and killing is only one side of the theatre's engagement with the

---

[110] There is also, again, an element of retributive inversion in that Gloucester, the 'naughty' begetter of a 'whoreson' (i. 24; (I. i)), now finds himself in the position of that whoreson's unnamed ravished mother.

[111] See the account of the Kenilworth bear-baiting cited above, Ch. 3.

cruelty of its animal double. The other is its capacity for mobilizing resistance to the very cruelty it exhibits. It is no accident that the affective force of the Bear-Garden is co-opted in a scene that marks the nadir of human debasement but also releases a counterforce in the intervention of the servant, who refuses to stand by and watch.

The synoptic interplay between the theatre and the bear-garden involves not only the performers but also the site of their performance. As an enclave of wilderness within an urban environment, the bear-pit is a perfect model for the enclosed 'little' (vii. 447; (II. ii)) space of Gloucester's castle-turned-torture-chamber, where violence erupts in the very midst of a domestic setting. What the space of Gloucester's ordeal shares with the scene of animal baiting is its liminal, metamorphic quality. The species divide may be intact as the spectator enters the arena, but will collapse in the course of the show. The spectacle set up to flatter man's sense of exceptionality ends up in a collapse of distinctions when 'a company of creatures that had the shapes of men, & faces of christians' proceed to their sport of whipping blind 'monsieur *Hunkes*',[112] and, handy-dandy, which is the human, which is the beast?[113] Likewise, the tormenting of Gloucester not only inverts the roles of justice and criminal, but, construing both as intersecting versions of animality, crucially complicates the play's tableau of human–animal entanglement.

VII. Comrade with the Wolf and Owl

So far, this chapter has traced a trajectory of bestialization which—from the initial eruption of Lear's wrath to the two trial scenes midway through the play—exposes the ascendancy of brute force over human 'kindness', the disruption of civil order, the regression into a proto-Hobbesian state of nature. From this perspective, bestiality is the marker of a barbaric wildness lurking at the very core of the social order; the force that drives the transgressively active characters of the play: the Lear of the opening scene, Gonoril and Regan, Edmund. But another perspective emerges when Gloucester identifies himself with the baited bear: the bestialization that equips his tormentors with 'boarish fangs' (xiv. 56; (III. vii)) intersects with a

---

[112] Dekker, 'Warres', 98–9.
[113] Cf. *King Lear* xx. 147–8 (IV. v): 'Hark in thy ear: handy-dandy, which is the thief, which is the justice?'

perception of the animal not as an emblem of human degeneracy but as fellow creature.

Sympathy with animals, historians tell us, did not exist in the Renaissance; it was an attitude simply not available in the mindset of the period. But even if this generalization is corroborated by a wealth of quotation from prominent early modern figures such as Luther (and a conspicuous near-absence of evidence to the contrary), this does not mean that the suffering of the 'dumb creatures' went altogether unnoticed or elicited no pity.[114] A degree of empathy is, as I have argued in the introduction, necessary even for the enjoyment of bear-baiting because, without it, there could have been none of the anthropomorphic troping that gave the struggling beasts their mock-human appeal. A higher degree of empathy would diminish that appeal, though not, as witness Thomas Dekker's account of his visit to the Bear-Garden, the degree of anthropomorphism. In Dekker's description the blind bear whipped 'till the blood ran downe his old shoulders'[115] becomes something like an animal version of the tormented Gloucester, just as the theatrical performance of Gloucester's human ordeal draws on, and gains emotive force from, the performance of the unfeigned torment suffered by his animal counterpart in the neighbouring bear-pit. In Dekker's account the role of the bear runs the gamut from overpowering bully to underdog all in one show, 'impersonating' 'the rich and mightie' as convincingly as the 'poore starued wretches',[116] the victim as well as the perpetrator. The stage, accordingly, holds a stake for both the suffering Gloucester and the cornered Macbeth and makes them 'bear' their predicament in almost identical words.

Half a dozen lines into Lear's opening speech, Folio inserts a clause that gives the king's retirement planning a distinctly downbeat spin:[117]

> Know that we have divided
> In three our kingdom, and 'tis our fast intent
> To shake all cares and business from our age,
> Conferring them on younger strengths *while we*
> *Unburdened crawl toward death.*   (I. i. 37–41; my italics)

---

[114] Montaigne is the obvious case in point; John Foxe is another. See Haller, *Foxe's Book of Martyrs*, 56. A fondness for pets was, of course, not unknown, though often sneered at in the period. Women's inordinate love of their lapdogs, for example, was a frequent subject of satirical slurs.

[115] Dekker, 'Warres', 99.

[116] Ibid.

[117] Skipping between the Quarto and Folio texts of *Lear* may be considered a breach of current critical etiquette. In my defence, I would suggest that they present, not different plays, but variant mappings of a single world.

The Folio addition sounds a first faint counterpoint to the zoomorphism of the dragon-king's wrath that will erupt at full blast later in the scene. 'Unburdened', emphasized at the beginning of the line, becomes a leit-motif and signpost for the road Lear will have to travel. But it is 'crawl to death' (readable here still as the genial, almost coquettish self-irony of a spry retiree looking forward to an extended holiday and the solicitude of his pet daughter[118]) that describes more accurately than Lear can know what will follow. 'Crawl' denotes locomotion appropriate to animals, not to grown men;[119] it entails debasement, but a debasement different from that which is triggered by Lear's self-bestializing rage. While this rage feeds on hurt pride, crawling signifies humility, a stepping down from man's biped pre-eminence and its supreme embodiment in the monarch's privilege of towering in solitary uprightness over his bowing subjects. While the dragon's wrath signals a turning away from what is 'properly human', 'crawl toward death' acknowledges the very essence of the human condition: that we are indeed animals, godlike, perhaps, in aspiration (as Renaissance humanists would plead), but most definitely un-godlike in being mortal, creatures of flesh and blood, subject to the processes of physical growth and decay like all else that lives. Instead of signalling the moral debasement entailed by the semantics of 'bestial', Lear's brief nod to mortality hints at the inescapably animal nature of man. His unburdening opens a perspective in which animalization signifies not *de*generation but *re*gener-ation, not a reversion to bestiality, but fraternization with the fellow creature. Quarto does not introduce this theme until Edgar transforms himself into Poor Tom in Scene vii, but from then on this second strand of human–animal rapprochement is as structurally important in the earlier text as it is in the Folio version.

This perspective aligns *Lear* with the pastoral, whose typical progress can be discerned even as the action takes an anti-pastoral course.[120] When the banished Kent takes his leave from court with the words 'Friendship lives hence, and banishment is here' (i. 171; (I. i)),[121] he is expressing the same discontent with civilization, the same escape impulse that drives the hero of

---

[118] This was very much the way Corin Redgrave presented Lear in the opening scene of Bill Alexander's 2004 RSC production in Stratford.

[119] See Clemen, *The Development of Shakespeare's Imagery*, 138.

[120] Maynard Mack developed this idea some decades ago in *King Lear in our Time* (London: Methuen, 1966), 65.

[121] Folio has 'Freedom' instead of 'Friendship'.

the pastoral out and away from the strictures of the courtly world and into the freedom of an Arcadian fraternity with nature.[122] Lear's initial intent also points to the pastoral: a life in field and stream, hunting, relieved of state business. This original direction persists in the actual path of his sufferings: from civilization to the wilderness, but not a *locus amoenus*, instead a grim, forbidding anti-Arcadia. A pitiful travesty of the warbling garlanded shepherd emerges in Cordelia's description of Lear:

> As mad as the racked sea, singing aloud,
> Crowned with rank fumitor and furrow-weeds,
> With burdocks, hemlock, nettles, cuckoo-flowers,
> Darnel, and all the idle weeds that grow
> In our sustaining corn.[123]   (xviii. 2–6; (IV. iv))

Edgar, or rather Poor Tom, is the key figure in the development of this theme, taking the pastoral move towards the simple life beyond all limits. His progress through the play corresponds to the three-stage narrative pattern of departure, initiation, and return described in Joseph Campbell's classic study of comparative mythology, *The Hero with a Thousand Faces*.[124] Typically for that pattern, Edgar's 'road of trials' entails transformation and encounters with ambiguous and fluid forms (though most of these are of his own making).[125] In contrast to, and self-defence against, the (proto-)Hobbesian vitalism of Edmund's materialist creed—'Thou, nature, art my goddess' (ii. 1; (I. ii))—Edgar is thrown back upon nature as a sanctuary, an extraterritorial refuge. Edmund, much like his Shakespearean predecessor, Richard Gloucester, is 'determinèd to prove a villain' (*Richard III*, I. i. 30), in the sense both of being resolved and of having no choice but to prove one.

---

[122] In his next appearance, he is a new man—not a naive shepherd, but nevertheless one whose rough-hewn honesty and bluntness (iv. 31–4; I. iv) mark him as good country folk.

[123] Stage tradition has often followed Q 2's SD (*Enter King Lear mad, crowned with weeds and flowers*) in physically corroborating Cordelia's description. The image of the vexed sea is carried over into the word scenery of the high-grown field, often mistakenly identified as a barren heath, but more accurately associated with the sea-like swaying of high-grown grain stalks before harvest time. Jayne Archer and Richard Marggraf Turley, 'Lear in the "High-grown fields": Landscape, Politics, Performance', paper presented at the autumn meeting of the Deutsche Shakespeare Gesellschaft, Cologne, 27–8 Nov. 2009.

[124] Joseph Campbell, *The Hero with a Thousand Faces* (1949; 2nd rev. edn., Princeton: Princeton University Press, 1968). One of the chief objections to Campbell's (and other comparative mythologists') work is that it allows its mythical-ritual archetypes to be detected too easily in too many stories, thus lacking any specific explanatory value. For an early comment on this problem, see Robert Hapgood, 'Shakespeare and the Ritualists', *Shakespeare Survey*, 15 (1962), 111–24.

[125] Confronted with the mad Lear's demons, Edgar produces a motley crowd of his own.

This makes his nature a much more dominating, not merely poetical, 'goddess' to whose 'law' his services are truly 'bound' (ii. 1–2). Ultimately unable to change, he acknowledges this bondage moments before his final exit, even in the one act that runs counter to it: 'Some good I mean to do, / Despite of my own nature' (xxiv. 239–40; (V. iii)).

While Edmund's 'nature' is the force that drives his self-assertion, the nature to which Edgar turns for shelter is the element in which his self dissolves ('Edgar I nothing am'; vii. 187; (II. ii)). Edgar is no match for his half-brother's agile dissembling in the early scenes of the play, but subsequently proves the much more thoroughly adaptable chameleon of the two. Embracing nature, he performs a vanishing act of protean merging:

EDGAR   I heard myself proclaimed,
         And by the happy hollow of a tree
         Escaped the hunt. No port is free, no place
         That guard and most unusual vigilance
         Does not attend my taking. While I may scape
         I will preserve myself, and am bethought
         To take the basest and most poorest shape
         That ever penury in contempt of man
         Brought near to beast.   (vii. 167–75)

After being expelled from human habitation ('No port . . . no place . . . '), the fugitive resorts to a hiding-place provided by nature in 'the happy [i.e. luckily available] hollow of a tree'. Hunted like an animal, he adopts animal behaviour, surviving on food that is 'unfit for human consumption':[126] 'the swimming frog, the toad, the tadpole, the wall-newt and the water', eating 'cowdung for salads', swallowing 'the old rat and the ditch-dog', drinking 'the green mantle of the standing pool' (xi. 117–21; (III. iv)). His stepping across the culture/nature divide[127] anticipates Lear's later move in the same direction. Reshaping himself into something 'near to beast', Poor Tom prefigures what the self-deposed king will also have to learn: 'To be a comrade with the wolf and owl' (vii. 367; (II. ii)). When Lear, building up towards that 'high rage' (vii. 454) that will propel him out into the fields, invokes this human–animal comradeship, it is still in an attempt to distance

---

[126] Cf. Ruth Morse, 'Unfit for Human Consumption: Shakespeare's Unnatural Food', *Shakespeare Jahrbuch West* (1983), 125–49.

[127] Bruno Latour, *We Have Never Been Modern* (Cambridge, Mass.: Harvard University Press, 1993).

himself from it, a last-ditch effort to maintain 'proper', though all too
obviously crumbling, distinctions:

> Return to her, and fifty men dismissed?
> No, rather I abjure all roofs, and choose
> To be a comrade with the wolf and owl,
> To wage against the enmity of the air,
> Necessity's sharp pinch.[128] Return with her?
> Why, the hot-blood in France that dowerless took
> Our youngest born—I could as well be brought
> To knee his throne and, squire-like, pension beg
> To keep base life afoot. Return with her?
> Persuade me rather to be slave and sumpter
> To this detested groom.   (vii. 365–75; (II. ii))

The Lear of this speech is still clinging to the culture side of the great divide,
but only just. As his 'additions' are cancelled out by wholesale subtraction he
envisages a state of nature in which 'base life' is kept afoot under the dictate
of necessity. Reducing the original hundred to nothing (another instance of
the boomerang logic of justice observed earlier), Regan's final subtraction—
'What needs one?' (vii. 422)—triggers Lear's last affirmation of that ladder of
degree on which he, king of men, claims the highest rung, while necessity
or 'need', the state of base, bare life occupies the lowest, a level on which
the boundary between human and animal is effaced:

> O, reason not the need! Our basest beggars
> Are in the poorest thing superfluous.
> Allow not nature more than nature needs,
> Man's life is cheap as beast's.   (vii. 422–6)

The force that Lear unleashed when he turned himself into a dragon has
passed to others: Gonoril, Regan, and Cornwall, along with Edmund. On
the brink of his exile to the wilderness, Lear in his wrath dwindles from
dragon to 'poor old fellow' (vii. 431), who, instead of spitting hot dry fire,

---

[128] There is debate among editors as to the sequence—and, consequently, exact meaning—of
lines 368–9. Wells notes that he '[s]omewhat tentatively . . . follow[s] Theobald in transposing [the]
lines . . . , taking *wage* to mean wager'. Foakes sees no improvement in this transposition, suggesting that 'Necessity's sharp pinch' be read 'in apposition with, and summing up, Lear's angry and
incoherent choice in the previous three lines'; his (Arden 3) version reads: 'No! Rather I abjure all
roofs and choose / To wage against the enmity o'th'air—/ To be a comrade with the wolf and
owl—/ Necessity's sharp pinch.' Following Wells, I have deviated from the Oxford text by adding
a comma after 'air'. This makes it possible to read 'wage' (with Foakes) as 'struggle, do battle', and
'enmity of the air' and 'Necessity's sharp pinch' as the two parallel objects of 'wage against'.

cannot contain the flow of tears.[129] His dig at Regan's unnecessarily extravagant attire ('Why, nature needs not what thou, gorgeous, wearest, / Which scarcely keeps thee warm'; vii. 428–9) heralds his changing sides. He is soon to take up a position in which he will no longer judge from the vantage point of culture what is lacking. Instead, he will adopt nature's perspective, decrying needless 'pomp' and 'superflux' (xi. 30, 32; (III. iv)). The 'additions' he claimed to be his due become the 'lendings' he is eager to throw off (xi. 99). Lear's and Edgar's tracks converge. The course of human–animal approximation leads to the 'Poor naked wretches' speech (xi. 25–33) and from there to Lear's physical encounter with 'the thing itself' (xi. 97):

> Why, thou wert better in thy grave than to answer with thy uncovered body this extremity of the skies. Is man no more but this? Consider him well. Thou owest the worm no silk, the beast no hide, the sheep no wool, the cat no perfume. Here's three on 's are sophisticated; thou art the thing itself. Unaccommodated man is no more but such a poor, bare, forked animal as thou art. Off, off, you lendings! Come on, be true.   (xi. 92–9)

Watching this moment of truth, we know, of course, that it is founded on make-believe.[130] As Shakespeare scholars, we also know that a good deal of Poor Tom's ravings are picked from Harsnett's case studies of fraudulent demonic possession,[131] which raises the level of pretence to the second power.[132] But as Stephen Greenblatt has argued, *King Lear* manages to do both: it 'loyally confirms' *and* conditionally revokes the Anglican exposure of Catholic fraudulence by 'reconstitut[ing] as theater the demonic principle demystified by Harsnett'.[133] At the heart of this dialectic are the urgencies of Edgar's situation: for Edgar, after all, play-acting is a matter of life and

---

[129] In the gendered terms of Galenic physiology, liquefaction and lowering of temperature indicate feminization.

[130] '[W]hen Lear thinks he has found in Poor Tom "the thing itself"', "unaccommodated man", he has in fact found a man playing a theatrical role.' Stephen Greenblatt, 'Shakespeare and the Exorcists', in his *Shakespearean Negotiations*, 94–128 at 126.

[131] Samuel Harsnett, *A Declaration of egregious Popish Impostures, to withdraw the harts of her Maiesties Subiects from their allegeance, and from the truth of Christian Religion professed in England, vnder the pretense of casting out deuils* (London: James Roberts, 1603). First noted by Lewis Theobald as early as 1733, Shakespeare's appropriation of Harsnett became a central paradigm of New Historicist methodology through its discussion in Greenblatt, 'Shakespeare and the Exorcists'.

[132] To what extent Shakespeare would have been able to count on his audience to know—or indeed not to know—his 'source' is an interesting but probably moot question. The question of whether we should conceive of Edgar—and not just Edgar's author—as a reader of Harsnett is probably best answered by another question: are Romeo and Juliet aware of sharing a sonnet on their first encounter?

[133] Greenblatt, 'Shakespeare and the Exorcists', 127.

death. In this case, as in all the others that the defenders of the theatre have adduced, false identity can work as a true mirror. So even if Edgar's impersonation of Poor Tom confronts us with a kaleidoscope of self-referentiality (an actor playing a lord playing a beggar), his mimicry of 'unaccommodated man' has more to offer than the arid ironies of represen-tation. Beyond the disclosure of nakedness as disguise or costume—and prompted by this disclosure—lies the recognition of costume as barely disguised nakedness. Edgar's cloak of nudity may be pretence, but it is a pretence that exposes silk, hide, wool, and perfume as a specious cloak for the poor, bare, forked human animal.[134]

The Edgar of the early scenes is hardly a character at all, but the object of his brother's scheming. It is through exile and metamorphosis—and crucially through histrionic pretence—that the blank space of a merely functional legitimate brother comes alive as a powerful stage presence. Nothing in Edgar's early appearances comes even close to the experiential intensity of a role that increasingly seems to take possession of him. Eluding the graven fixity of 'character' and the unity implied by the term 'individ-ual', his role-playing creates a plural self that is fluidly shifting between reason and madness and between humanness and animality; a self that encompasses both the possessed beggar and the demons possessing him, a self that becomes quite literally dividable when, in response to the sudden canine invasion of Lear's mock court ('The little dogs and all, / Tray, Blanch, and Sweetheart—see, they bark at me'; xiii. 56–7; (III. vi)), Poor Tom offers to 'throw his head at them' (xiii. 58).

Besides the 'presented nakedness' (vii. 177; (II. ii)) of his 'uncovered body' (xi. 93; (III. iv)), Edgar's performance of Poor Tom exploits the medium of voice and the evocative power of 'words, words, words' (*Hamlet* II. ii. 195). While his body offers ocular proof of human–animal conjunction, his voice projects phantasms of cross-species entanglement. Addressing a phantom horse in human terms of endearment—'Dolphin, my boy, my boy!

---

[134] For a particularly rich contextualization of the passage, see Laurie Shannon, 'Poor, Bare, Forked: Animal Sovereignty, Human Negative Exceptionalism, and the Natural History of *King Lear*', *Shakespeare Quarterly*, 60 (2009), 168–96. The idea that 'man alone is born defenceless and naked' ('solus homo inermis nascitur et nudes'; Hugh of St-Victor, *Didascalicon. De Studio Legendi*, ed. Charles Henry Buttimer (Washington, DC: Catholic University Press, 1939), 17) goes back to Pliny the Elder and is a commonplace in medieval thought. It comes linked with a compensation model of human culture in which man's weakness becomes the source of his strength. Lacking natural armour, he learns to armour himself by artificial means; being a slow runner, he domes-ticates the horse and makes the dog 'a living sword' ('vivum quemdam gladium') for hunting, etc. (William of St-Thierry, *De natura corporis et animae libri duo*, in *Opera Omnia*, iii: *Opera didactica et spiritualia*, ed. Paul Verdeyen (Turnhout: Brepols, 2003), ii, col. 716). Lear, of course, sees only the misery of the human condition (*miseria humanae conditions*, cf. above p. 18), not the incentive it offers to human ingenuity.

Cease, let him trot by' (xi. 90–1)—he gives it the name of both a smaller variety of whale (or leviathan)[135] and a successor to the French throne. What better qualification than this to assist in a trial of a four-footed piece of furniture representing a she-fox who is really a king's daughter ('Cry you mercy, I took you for a join-stool'; xiii. 47; (III. 6))? Perceived as half spirit, half beast on his first appearance,[136] Poor Tom vocally multiplies into a chorus of singing, crying, croaking bird-demons crowding Lear's mock court with chimerical fusions:

> The foul fiend haunts Poor Tom in the voice of a nightingale. Hoppedance cries in Tom's belly for two white herring. Croak not, black angel: I have no food for thee.   (xiii. 25–8)

Theseus, the rationalist Duke of Athens in *A Midsummer Night's Dream*, lumps lunatic, lover, and poet together in what seems a disparagement, but turns out to be a homage to the creative power of the imagination. In Edgar-as-Poor-Tom the lunatic and poet truly converge. Seeing—or pretending to see—as well as making us see 'more devils than vast hell can hold' (*Dream*, V. i. 9) his 'imagination bodies forth / The forms of things unknown', turning 'them to shapes', giving names 'to airy nothing[s]' (*Dream*, V. i. 14–17). A case in point, the abstract 'nightmare' is 'bodied forth' as 'the night mare and her nine foal' (xi. 110; (III. iv)). Madness (whether genuine or not) is a condition close to poetry in its creation of symbiosis, letting (mental) 'copulation thrive'. Imposture may be the name of the game, but that does not diminish the suggestive force of the visions enveloping Lear and his company in distress.

'*Companion*', writes Donna Haraway, 'comes from the Latin *cum panis* [*sic*], 'with bread'. Messmates at table are companions. Comrades are political companions.'[137] Etymologically, comrades are those who share a chamber (Lat. *camera*): housemates. 'To be a comrade with the wolf and owl' is to acknowledge companionship, cohabitation with man's fellow creatures. Outcasts from their society, Lear and Edgar enter into a habitat on the borders of the human, a commonwealth of 'humanimality'.[138] In this perspective, Poor Tom's calling himself 'the poor creature of the earth' (xi. 107–8) sounds temptingly close to Haraway's 'I am a creature of the mud'.[139] But such echoes

---

[135] Shakespeare's contemporaries would hardly have classed the dolphin in the family of whales, but would have subsumed both under the larger category of fish.

[136] FOOL Come not in here, nuncle; here's a spirit (xi. 34); KENT What art thou that dost grumble there in the straw? (xi. 38) The 'grumbling' suggests non-linguistic, animal utterance.

[137] Donna J. Haraway, *When Species Meet* (Minneapolis and London: University of Minnesota Press, 2008), 17.

[138] The term was coined by Michel Surya, *Humanimalité: L'inéliminable animalité de l'homme* (Paris: Néant, 2001).

[139] Haraway, *When Species Meet*, 3.

may be as deceptive as Edgar's appearance: the ascetic earthiness that equates *homo* with *humus* is a far cry from a celebratory proclamation of solidarity with all the other 'critters' 'of the mud' with whom we humans share our 'naturecultures'.[140] Yet in spite of the undeniable historical gap, Haraway's and other 'posthumanist' destabilizations of human–animal boundaries can help us discern to what extent the porosity of these boundaries is implanted in *King Lear*. To read a twenty-first-century utopia of universal 'becoming with' into the endangered enclave in the hovel would be putting an anachronistically cheerful complexion on Shakespeare's early modern landscape of despair. What we are meant to see in the destitute king is forcefully voiced in Gloucester's 'O ruined piece of nature!' (xx. 129; (IV. v)) But at the same time as it is suggested that the abandonment of order, reason, and self, of regal and ultimately human ascendancy portends the world's 'wear[ing] out to naught' (xx. 130), this ruin *of* nature is also presented as an immersion *in* nature, a liminal, heterotopic state of becoming.

VIII. Rites of Readmission

Completing his 'road of trials' with a decisive victory and, in some versions, atonement with a father figure, the hero of Campbell's 'monomyth' returns, fortified, from the wild to the ordinary world, ready to take up his place in society. So too do the lovers in Shakespearean comedy return from a series of unsettling but ultimately salutary tribulations in the green world to the no longer perilous city or court, their wanderings being brought to closure in a dance of life-affirming renewal.[141] The contours of this regenerative cycle are inscribed in the parallel journeys of the exiled father-king and the outcast son. Lear's fortune comes full circle with his awakening to find himself restored to human community in the care of the all-forgiving Cordelia. Edgar's journey reaches its destination with his victory over his bastard brother Edmund. The play musters what could be described as the skeletons of two interlacing rites of passage, two narratives of initiation, but

---

[140] Cf. ibid. 3–42.

[141] The classic expositions of this pattern are Northrop Frye, 'The Argument of Comedy', and Barber, *Shakespeare's Festive Comedy*. For an early comment on ritualistic approaches to Shakespeare, see Hapgood, 'Shakespeare and the Ritualists'. More recent studies include Edward Berry, *Shakespeare's Comic Rites* (Cambridge: Cambridge University Press, 1984), and Rajiva Verma, *Myth, Ritual, and Shakespeare: A Study of Critical Theory and Practice* (New Delhi: Spantech, 1990).

presses on beyond their expected conclusion to a state where there is finally nothing left to be initiated into.

Just prior to the movement towards restitution, Lear's encounter with the blind Gloucester prompts his final verdict on the legal system, enacted in a self-parody of his own role as supreme judge: 'Ay, every inch a king. / When I do stare, see how the subject quakes! / I pardon that man's life' (xx. 105–7; (IV. v)). Authority, which the opening scene figured as an outburst of the dragon's wrath upon the insubordinate Kent, is again conceived in terms of human–animal confrontation, but this time a confrontation that totally deflates the terrible charisma inherent in the image of the royal monster:

LEAR   Thou hast seen a farmer's dog bark at a beggar?
GLOUCESTER Ay, sir.
LEAR   An the creature run from the cur, there thou mightst behold the
            great image of authority. A dog's obeyed in office.[142]   (xx. 149–53)

Bestialization of the criminal is a standard cultural practice. The point of Lear's 'Reason in madness' (xx. 164), confirming what he has already demonstrated *in actu* in the opening scene, is the bestialization of the representative of the law, a reversal of conventional roles which implies that Lear, too, as a king whose word was law, may have been no more than 'a dog obeyed in office'.[143] The question, then, is this: after the scenes in the wilderness, after Lear's recognition of 'how the world goes' (xx. 145–6), what 'restoration of order' can there be that would not simply reproduce the deformities of this great image of authority? And in what manner, what shape could such 'restoration', as distinct from 'repetition' or 'relapse', be achieved? What manner of 'restoration', in other words, would not simply start the destructive cycle all over again?

At the outset of the play, it was not, as we have seen, a violation of law, but the law itself as incarnated in the person of the monarch, that caused the disruption of the social order. The movement towards a restitution of order is staged in protocols that differ from Lear's initial dispensation of justice but

---

[142] Lear's great image of authority is briefly glimpsed again in Edgar's account of how, in his 'madman's rags', he assumed 'a semblance / That very dogs disdained' (xxiv. 184–5; (V. iii))

[143] That editors see fit to gloss 'They [i.e. Gonoril and Regan] flattered me like a dog' (xx. 95–6; (IV. v)) with the explanation that 'like a dog' refers to the fawning daughters, not to the recipient of their fawning, is in itself proof enough of the line's ambiguity—especially when we consider that the subsequent sentence ('When the rain came . . . , there I found them, there I smelt them out'; xx. 99–102) evokes a distinctly canine Lear.

are no less invested in the notion of judgement. While this is obvious in Edgar's case, it also applies to Lear. His awaking is staged as a ritual accompanied by music. The Queen of France, 'this lady...my child, Cordelia' (xxi. 66–7; (IV. vi)) addresses him with the deferential formality of a loyal subject:

CORDELIA How does my royal lord? How fares your majesty?   (xxi. 42)

But Lear sees himself in a situation in which such or any other forms of social protocol fall into abeyance, one in which distinction by rank is superseded by the ultimate distinction that parts the 'soul[s] in bliss' from those remaining unredeemed, 'bound / Upon a wheel of fire' (xxi. 44–5) Waking up, the liminal experience par excellence, is figured as resurrection: 'You do me wrong to take me out o'th' grave' (xxi. 43). Beyond the sway of human law, the dead are raised to face the last judgement. Doomsday, the promised end, has arrived as the delusion of 'a very foolish, fond old man' (xxi. 58).

CORDELIA   Sir, know me.
LEAR   You're a spirit, I know. Where did you die?   (xxi. 46–7)

But Judgement Day dissolves as reality returns. The play, though crowded with intimations of the apocalypse, refuses to offer the finality of apocalyptic resolution at this point, or, for that matter, at any other point later.[144] As Lear is brought back from beyond the grave to a realization of his pre-mortem condition, forms of ceremonial custom are resumed in his daughter's kneeling to him, his kneeling to her. Readmission into the bonds of kin and kind entails a momentary return, and instantaneous rejection, of Lear as judge. No sooner does he enter into measuring up the rights and wrongs of his case ('You have some cause; they have not' (xxi. 72; (IV. vi)), than Cordelia interrupts him with her measureless forgiveness: 'No cause, no cause' (xxi. 72). Recalling and repealing her 'Nothing, my lord' (i. 81; (I. i)), this act of unconditional pardon closes the case, keeping the Lear-type system of measuring or meting out justice in abeyance. But this idyll of

---

[144] Joseph Wittreich, ' "Image of that horror": The Apocalypse in *King Lear*', in C. A. Patrides and Joseph Wittreich (eds.), *The Apocalypse in English Renaissance Thought and Literature: Patterns, Antecedents and Repercussions* (Manchester: Manchester University Press, 1984), 175–206. Wittreich offers an ultimately redemptive reading of the play which is cogently critiqued in Verena Lobsien, 'Multi pertransibunt, oder: das versprochene Ende—Inszenierungen frühneuzeitlicher Apokalyptik in Shakespeares *King Lear*', in Maria Moog-Grünewald and Verena Lobsien (eds.), *Apokalypse: Der Anfang im Ende* (Heidelberg: Winter, 2003), 103–27.

'indemnity and oblivion'[145] barely outlasts its inception. Lear's question 'Am I in France?' (xxi. 73) brings back the politics in which this family reunion is perilously embedded. Kent's answer 'In your own kingdom, sir' (xxi. 74) attests his loyalty, but it is hardly correct, and the next time we see father and daughter, they are prisoners in what is definitely not, at this stage, *his* kingdom.

Edgar's return from exile takes the form of an atavistic juridical ritual, trial by combat, also known as 'wager of battle' or 'judicial duel', the latter term indicating its proximity to the kind of 'wild justice' that early modern state authority sought to eliminate.[146] What Edgar returns to from the wilderness can hardly be called 'society' or 'civilization'. Instead, he exchanges one extraterritorial space for another. It is clear from the defeat of Cordelia's army that the place is definitely not France (or Lear's own kingdom); but just about everything else remains unsettled. The one title that identifies its owner without further epithet or explanation is 'the Queen' (xxiv. 50; (V. iii)), but that refers to the Queen of another country, Cordelia. Internally the situation presents itself not as a state, but something more like Hobbes's state of nature. The power struggle in the British camp repeats the love contest of Scene i; only what is at stake now, besides land, is not the approval of a father but that of a lover. While Albany holds Edmund 'but a subject of this war, / Not as a brother' (xxiv. 59–60), Regan declares him 'My lord and master' (xxiv. 76), a claim that Albany sarcastically bars 'in the interest of my wife. / 'Tis she [Gonoril] is subcontracted to this lord, / And I, her husband, contradict the banns' (xxiv. 83–5). The territorial unity that would warrant being called a realm has dissolved into anarchic indeterminacy. Into this lawless space the challenger advances. Appearing from nowhere, he has no name. More precisely, his name is lost, 'By treason's tooth bare-gnawn' (xxiv. 119) and eaten up by canker-worms. Edgar's restitution, like Lear's, is thus a return from the dead, adding apocalyptic overtones to this scene of judgement. Just prior to Edgar's (re-)entry, the absence of executive power is demonstrated by Albany's attempt to arrest Edmund and Gonoril for capital treason (xxiv. 81), which remains an empty threat

[145] The term is borrowed from the 'Act of Free and General Pardon, Indemnity, and Oblivion' (passed in Aug. 1660), which granted amnesty to members of the jury responsible for the death of Charles I.

[146] Of Germanic origin, trials by combat were customary throughout the Middle Ages, attempts to stop them proving ineffectual. The last such trial under the authority of a British monarch is thought to have taken place in Dublin in 1583. The famous French story of the Dog of Montargis hinges upon a juridical combat between a dog and the man who has killed his master.

because he simply lacks the means to carry out this arrest. Proof of guilt, as in the shape of Gonoril's self-incriminating letter to Edmund, is of no consequence as long as the guilty party can claim possession of the law:

GONORIL   ... the laws are mine, not thine.
           Who shall arraign me for't?
ALBANY   Most monstrous!   (xxiv. 154–5)

With no line of command, no governmental apparatus to enforce any legal measures, each contender has to take justice into his own hands, and the only semblance of order is maintained in the formality of speech observed by the herald and the contestants. In the absence of any other form of law, only 'the law of arms' remains. By this law, Edmund is 'not bound to answer / An unknown opposite' (xxiv. 148–9)[147] but with an air of nonchalance waives his 'right of knighthood' (xxiv. 141), thereby clearing the way to an outcome that Albany describes as 'This justice of the heavens' (xxiv. 226), and Edmund as a triune *Liebestod*: 'I was contracted to them both; all three / Now marry in an instant' (xiv. 223–4).

These deaths bring what Schiller calls 'the jurisdiction of the stage'[148] to a conclusion. The state of internecine power struggle is terminated by a judicial combat which, similarly to a trial by ordeal, counts as an act of God.[149] Albany, the highest-ranking survivor, sets about infusing the state of exception with a modicum of governmental normality. Up to this point, the point before Lear's final entry, the scene is permeated by legal language. Symbiotically linked to this are the last instances in the text in which bestialization serves to brand the criminal: Edmund as 'most toad-spotted traitor' (xiv. 135), Gonoril as 'gilded serpent' (xxiv. 82). But although the wheel may have 'come full circled' (xxiv. 170), it does not cease to wheel on; and if *King Lear* is the 'most final of tragedies',[150] this is precisely because it never stops ending.

---

[147] Just as Edmund, being a bastard, would not be entitled to challenge a brother of legitimate birth.

[148] 'Die Gerichtsbarkeit der Bühne', in 'Was kann eine gute stehende Schaubühne eigentlich wirken', in *Schillers Werke. Nationalausgabe*, xx: *Philosophische Schriften*, ed. Benno von Wiese (Weimar: Böhlau, 1962), 87–100 at 92.

[149] In a typical pledge before a trial by combat the contender would avow not to use any 'enchantment, sorcery or witchcraft where-through the power of God might be strengthened or diminished'.

[150] Watson, *The Rest is Silence*, 45.

IX. Man's work

The last movement of the play carries us beyond the law and, so painfully to Dr Johnson, even beyond justice: 'I was many years ago so shocked by Cordelia's death', he records in a much-quoted note, 'that I know not whether I ever endured to read again the last scenes of the play till I undertook to revise them as an editor.'[151] There is no poetical justice and no observance of the law of genre that demands tragic sacrifice must serve some higher ulterior goal of human religious redemption. Nor is the 'outside' which this last movement constitutes, in relation to a sphere that could be designated as 'inside' the law, quite the same as the outlaw space that offered shelter to the company in the hovel, the comrades 'with the wolf and owl'. Most obviously, it lacks the regenerative potential which the play allows us to glimpse in the undoing of social and species distinctions during the scenes on the heath. Nevertheless, the probing of human–animal boundaries not only continues to the very end of the play, but is given special emphasis in its final moments.

A prelude to this occurs at the beginning of the last scene when Lear and Cordelia are brought on as captives by Edmund and his troops. In a play where opponents never miss a chance to engage in violent verbal altercation, the non-communication between the victor and his prisoners is striking. Edmund speaks of, but not to them. And neither do Lear or Cordelia make any verbal contact with the people surrounding them, their dialogue performatively creating the protective 'cage' that Lear envisions in his fantasy of prison life. Cordelia, to be sure, proposes, or at least shows some inclination, to 'see these daughters and these sisters' (xxiv. 7),[152] but, for once, she unconditionally complies with her father's wish—'No, no. Come, let's away to prison' (xxiv. 8)—leaving without speaking another word.

> Come, let's away to prison.
> We two alone will sing like birds i'th' cage.

(xxiv. 8–9V. iii)

---

[151] *Johnson on Shakespeare*, ed. Arthur Sherbo, The Yale Edition of the Works of Samuel Johnson, 8 (New Haven and London: Yale University Press, 1968), 704.

[152] In Stanley Cavell's reading of the play, Lear's rejection of Cordelia's proposal to 'see' (in the sense of 'confront', 'face up to') Gonoril and Regan is of crucial significance: 'He cannot finally face the thing he has done; and this means what it always does, that he cannot bear being seen.' Stanley Cavell, 'The Avoidance of Love: A Reading of *King Lear*', in his *Disowning Knowledge. In Seven Plays of Shakespeare* (updated edn., Cambridge: Cambridge University Press, 2003), 39–123 at 68.

No sisters, and no intrusive husbands either,[153] are allowed to disturb Lear's escapist prison idyll, which finally accomplishes the complete union between father-child and daughter-mother which lay at the core of his original plan. France—both the country and the man—is a long way away from this womb-like bubble of 'rest' and 'kind nursery'[154] where the blissful moment of *anagnorisis* (xxi. 55–72 (IV. vi)) can be replayed ad infinitum:

> When thou dost ask me blessing, I'll kneel down
> And ask of thee forgiveness; so we'll live,
> And pray, and sing, and tell old tales, and laugh
> At gilded butterflies, and hear poor rogues
> Talk of court news   (xxiv. 10–14; (V. iii))

'As if we were God's spies' (xxiv. 17), Lear and Cordelia assume a vantage point outside human limitations, a position of pure uncorporeal observation. Confinement becomes liberation, and the telling of old tales conjures up a world of 'fairy toys' and 'antique fables' (*Dream* V. i. 3) in which similes are not just poetical decoration but loopholes for magical escape. 'Like birds', the prisoners are simply no longer involved in human affairs. 'Like foxes', they will foil any attempt at detaining them:

> He that parts us shall bring a brand from heaven
> And fire us hence like foxes.   (xxiv. 22–3)

The line is usually annotated with a quotation from Harsnett: '[F]ire him out of his hold, as men smoke out a Foxe out of his burrow.'[155] But while Harsnett refers to a method of trapping a fox, 'firing us *hence*' envisions the foxes' getting away. 'Like birds', 'like foxes'—the lifeline offered by these fantasies is the same: escape through transformation. Both similes could thus be described as Ovidian, not in the sense of alluding to any specific episode in the *Metamorphoses*, but in drawing upon Ovid's metamorphic principle. That foxes should, suddenly and for the first time in the play, not be moralized as animal mirrors of human depravity, but serve as vehicles of

---

[153] There is no reminder of Cordelia's 'untender' objection from Scene i: 'Why have my sisters husbands if they say / They love you all? . . . Sure, I shall never marry like my sisters, / To love my father all' (i. 91–6; (I. i)).

[154] Cf. i. 115–16: 'I loved her most, and thought to set my rest / On her kind nursery.'

[155] Harsnett, *A Declaration of egregious Popish Impostures*, 97. Repr. in F. W. Brownlow, *Shakespeare, Harsnett, and the Devils of Denham* (Newark, Del.: University of Delaware Press, 1993), 278. Another possible source is the three hundred biblical foxes with firebrands tied to their tails that Samson chased into the fields of the Philistines (Judges 15: 4–5); but as far as I can see, to date no one has been able to show the relevance of the Samson episode to the play.

flight,[156] connects them with all the animals (and plants and objects) in Ovid whose forms offer sanctuary to the fugitive. In the moment of utmost distress, Philomela becomes a nightingale, Procne a swallow, Daphne turns into a laurel tree, and Syrinx into a reed. Ovidian metamorphosis offers 'an untragic alternative to death'.[157] This is what the two animal similes on the brink of catastrophe momentarily evoke: an untragic alternative resolution, the possibility that all might somehow end well.

But the tutelary deities whose powers of magic transformation are real enough in the green worlds of comedy are absent from the stage of *King Lear*. And so the Captain whom Edmund commissions to kill the prisoners adds a grim coda to Lear's idyll:

CAPTAIN   I cannot draw a cart,
   Nor eat dried oats. If it be man's work, I'll do't. (xxiv. 37–8(V. iii))

Lear's brief fantasy of flowing borders and refuge in metamorphosis is dispelled with chilling pragmatism and hard-edged indifference. Bestiality is expressly not made responsible for the last crime of the play, the crime that puts paid to any notion of ultimate reconciliation. The murder of Cordelia is clearly 'man's work': not an outburst of 'bestial' rage, but a premeditated act of policy, commissioned in writing, as the text mentions no fewer than three times. And as if this were not enough, the murderer is to 'write "happy" when thou hast done' (xxiv. 35).[158] Writing is an unmistakably and exclusively human skill. And so is the capacity for rational argument, of which Edmund's dialogue with the captain gives a kind of shorthand demonstration:

        if thou dost
  As this instructs thee, thou dost make thy way
  To noble fortunes. Know thou this: that men
  Are as the time is. To be tender-minded
  Does not become a sword. Thy great employment
  Will not bear question. Either say thou'lt do't,
  Or thrive by other means. (xxiv. 28–34)

---

[156] John Danby notes this change of moral valency: 'The good will be "foxes" again. Their strategy will be a cunning superior to the fox-ship of the machiavels' (Danby, *Shakespeare's Doctrine of Nature*, 195). Obviously, the cunning of the 'good' does not really prove superior to 'the fox-ship of the machiavels'.

[157] Karl G. Galinsky, *Ovid's Metamorphoses: An Introduction to the Basic Aspects* (Berkeley: University of California Press, 1975), 61.

[158] The Oxford editor Stanley Wells glosses this with 'write yourself down a happy (fortunate) man'.

In just over half a dozen lines Edmund proposes a condition and the result of its fulfilment, two general maxims with an implied specific application, and finally a choice of two options. He offers logic, not emotion, to which the captain responds in kind. His answer seems less cryptic to me than is sometimes assumed. Because he 'cannot draw a cart, nor eat dried oats'— because, in other words, he is no horse—he will accept employment suitable for a man. Murder being such employment, he will commit it. The captain's exit lines are a syllogism.

The idea of bestialization that we found operative in the initial disruption of civil order is predicated on a vertical distinction between man and beast. Even if the bestial wildness that disrupts the state is located at the very heart of the state itself, this disruption is conceived as a collapse, a fall, a tearing or tumbling down, a triumph of that which is thought of as lower over that which is thought of as higher, or more precisely, over that which is held to be singularly high: human as against the rest of creation; royal as against the rest of humanity. In contrast to this, the captain's distinction between man and beast is radically horizontal. Man is different from beast, but different on a flat scale of species variety. Man, it would be even more correct to say, is different from *other* beasts in specifiable ways—food habits, for example, the ability to write, the inability to draw a cart—but not set above the rest of the animal world in categorical singularity. The casually ominous exit of the captain thus sets the scene for the final tableau of the play.

Lear's entry 'with Cordelia in his arms' is the moment where readings with a Christian bent tend to 'take off'; where the sparse material of what is actually said and done in the scene produces an inversely proportionate amplitude of restorative edification on the part of the critic. Such compensatory fullness takes its cue from the undeniable presence of religious motifs both visual and verbal: the 'secular pietà'[159] of Lear bending over his dead daughter, the Old Testament resonance of Lear's 'Howl, howl, howl, howl!' (xxiv. 253). But, though of religious provenance and fraught with biblical associations, these motifs hardly endorse a pious conclusion. Not once does the father bending over his dead[160] child so much as hint at a

---

[159] The much-quoted phrase is Helen Gardner's (*King Lear. The John Coffin Memorial Lecture 1966* (London: Athlone Press, 1967), 28); Maynard Mack speaks of 'the image of Mary bending over another broken child' (*King Lear in our Time*, 116). Both are quoted in R. A. Foakes's introduction to his Arden (3rd ser.) edition of *King Lear*, 35.

[160] Or, as E. A. J. Honigmann would have it, *dying* rather than already dead: *Myriad-Minded Shakespeare* (Basingstoke: Macmillan, 1989), 91.

Christian hereafter where loss of earthly life may be compensated for by an eternity in heaven. Unconcerned with either soul or salvation, Lear's frantic autopsy has only one object: breath:

> I know when one is dead and when one lives.
> She's dead as earth.
>   Lend me a looking-glass.
> If that her breath will mist or stain the stone,
> Why, then she lives.   (xxiv. 256–9)

Bare physical life is all that matters. Redemption is respiration: if the feather stirs, this 'does redeem all sorrows / That ever I have felt' (xxiv. 262–3).

The howling, too, is redirected from a religious discourse of sin and punishment to a level of elementary physical existence. Its biblical referent is Isaiah 13: 6: 'Howle you, for the day of the Lord is at hand',[161] while the reiteration of the verb also recalls (with a grim twist) the seraphim chanting 'Holy, holy, holy is the Lord of hostes' (Isaiah 6: 3).[162] The apocalyptic note sounded here is reinforced by the halting responses of the three surviving onstage observers:

KENT   Is this the promised end?
EDGAR   Or image of that horror?
ALBANY   Fall and cease.   (xxiv. 258–60)

But if this *is* the promised end it is conspicuously lacking a—if not *the*— crucial ingredient: the promised revelation of God's glory, the meaning in which all seeming meaninglessness will finally converge. For all the felt ultimacy of *King Lear*, this revelation is ultimately deferred.[163] Nor does the quadrupling of the prophet's 'howl' intensify any spirituality the scene may have. Quite the opposite, in fact. More forcefully with each repetition, the verb prescribing a particular kind of utterance becomes that utterance itself: a howl or cry of pain, so elementary as to be trans-semantic, even trans-human.[164] The system of distinctions that makes up human language dissolves into a continuum shared by living beings across species boundaries. 'Howl' is an expression of anguish produced by the voice of human and

---

[161] The imperative 'howl' occurs three more times in Isaiah, and in several others of the Prophets.

[162] Both quotations from *The Geneva Bible*.

[163] *King Lear* taps into a large repertoire of contemporary apocalyptic motifs, but refuses to endorse a consistently apocalyptic vision. See Lobsien, 'Multi pertransibunt'.

[164] For a discussion of 'feeling' speech in Shakespeare, see Gary Taylor, 'Feeling Bodies', in *Shakespeare and the Twentieth Century. The Selected Proceedings of the International Shakespeare Association World Congress, Los Angeles, 1996*, ed. Jonathan Bate, Jill Levenson, and Dieter Mehl (Newark, Del.: University of Delaware Press, 1998), 258–79.

other animals alike, an expulsion and modulation of that without which these animals, become just 'earth': *anima*—breath.

Folio has Lear exclaim 'howl' three times, thereby producing a perfect contrapuntal match to the liturgic triplicity of 'Holy, holy, holy'. Adding one more to the symbolic and rhetorical perfection of three, the four howls of the Quarto version mark a stepping beyond the symbolic order towards arbitrary, potentially endless enumeration. Number four in this case[165] is the odd one out, just as it is in Lear's disconsolate final question:

> Why should a dog, a horse, a rat have life,
> And thou no breath at all?   (xxiv. 301–2)

The dog, the horse, the rat have all appeared in some form in the course of the play, but here they stand as random examples of an infinitely extendable list of animals that have what Lear's daughter has not. At once included in and irrevocably excluded from the register encompassing all living beings, the dead Cordelia confirms the horizontal scale of human–animal relatedness which her murderer asserted in accepting his commission to kill her. But where the Captain's flat scale of species variety marks man as a particularly noxious animal among animals, Lear's animal catalogue presses home the pitiful vulnerability of bare life, his lament ending, as it began, with a fourfold cry of pain: 'O, O, O, O!' (xxiv. 304)

At its most devastating, Shakespeare's theatre does not raze the species divide; it flattens it, as Lear's howl echoes and is echoed by the creatures in the bear-garden.

---

[165] 'In this case' is a necessary qualification here because the number four can obviously be highly symbolic (a symbol of perfection even) in some contexts (architecture, for example).

6

Revels' End: *The Tempest* and After

I. Shipping Mastiffs

The closing of the London playhouses in 1642 marks a watershed in the annals of the English stage. An event that transpired fourteen years later has hardly made it into the footnotes: 'Seuen of Mr. Godfries Beares, by the command of Thomas Pride, then hie Sherife of Surry, were then shot to death, On Saterday the 9 day of February 1655 [=1656], by a Company of Souldiers.'[1] A more detailed account of the incident is preserved in a contemporary diary:

> Feb. [1656] Col. Pride, now Sir Thomas Pride, by reason of some difference between him and the Keeper Godfrey of the Bears in the Bear Garden in Southwark, as a justice of the peace there caused all the bears to be fast tied up by the noses and then valiantly brought some files of musketeers, drew up and gave fire and killed six or more bears in the place (only leaving on[e] white innocent cub), and also all courts [i.e. cocks] of the game.[2]

With the theatres closed and the Globe having been pulled down shortly afterwards in 1644, the Southwark bear massacre marks the final severing of the tie between stage and stake, play-acting and bear-baiting which I have explored in previous chapters.

Both entertainments, to be sure, were back in business before long. But the new playhouses of the Restoration differed crucially from those of the pre-Commonwealth era. Like their predecessors on Bankside, the first

---

[1] Quoted in Joseph Quincy Adams, *Shakespearean Playhouses: A History of English Theatres from the Beginnings to the Restoration* (Boston and New York: Houghton Mifflin, 1917; repr. Gloucester, Mass.: Smith, 1960), 337.

[2] *The Diary of Henry Townsend*, quoted in J. Leslie Hotson, 'Bear Gardens and Bear-baiting during the Commonwealth', *PMLA* 40 (1925), 276–88 at 286.

provisional Restoration theatres were closely linked with sports venues. Only this time the sport was not baiting but tennis,[3] and the architecture had the audience facing the spectacle like a picture rather than encircling it as in an arena. Although acting in the Restoration playhouse still took place *before* the proscenium arch, which did not become a full-fledged 'picture-frame' until the later nineteenth century,[4] there can be no doubt that the visual economy introduced after 1660 differed fundamentally from that of Shakespeare's Globe.

But the difference was not just visual. From the vantage point of a present that considered itself vastly more civilized than the not too distant past, the avid theatregoer Samuel Pepys applauded the sea change in the social and cultural status of theatre: '[T]he stage is now . . . a thousand times better and more glorious than ever heretofore. Now, wax candles, and many of them; then, not above 3 lb. of tallow. Now, all things civil, no rudeness anywhere; then, as in a bear-garden.'[5] With a population of around 200,000 in 1600, London had sustained about half a dozen public theatres, each with a capacity well over a thousand. By 1660–70 the population had almost doubled, with only two licensed acting companies performing in two theatres, Drury Lane (1663) and Dorset Garden (1674), with fewer total seats than the Globe.[6] The civilizing process which had dissociated the stage from the stake and the scaffold in the cultural topography of a refashioned London entailed a narrowing not just in audience size but also in social scope. The exemplary dramatic genre of the period, the Restoration comedy of manners, directs its attention no longer at the frangible borders of the

---

[3] See J. L. Styan, *The English Stage: A History of Drama and Performance* (Cambridge: Cambridge University Press, 1996), 238: 'Davenant assembled the Duke's Men, named for Charles's brother James, Duke of York, and Killigrew the King's Men. Desperately in need of a playhouse, both made temporary use of Tudor tennis courts for theatres: Killigrew working in Gibbons's Tennis Court in Vere Street (1660) and Davenant in Lisle's Tennis Court in Lincoln's Inn Fields (1661). . . . A tennis court had a roof, a surrounding gallery, and had the same sort of intimate dimensions (about 75 by 30 feet overall) the private playhouses had previously enjoyed. If the area was divided at the line of the net, giving half the space to the actors and half to the audience, which would number about four hundred, something of the desirable intimacy of the actor-audience relationship was secured.'

[4] See e.g. Richard Leacroft, *The Development of the English Playhouse* (London: Eyre Methuen, 1973).

[5] *The Diary of Samuel Pepys*, ed. Robert Lanham and William Matthews (Berkeley and Los Angeles: University of California Press, 1970–83), viii. 55–6. See Scott-Warren, 'When Theatres Were Bear-Gardens', 63.

[6] It is commonly assumed that the Globe could hold a maximum of 3,000 spectators.

human but at the jealously guarded entrée to an exclusive urban in-group calling itself 'Society'.[7]

Together with the plebeians themselves, the animals to which they were often likened—'The beast / With many heads' (*Coriolanus* IV. i. 1–2)—were barred from the expensive indoor theatres. No longer were the human actors pursued by their animal doubles; no longer did the howls and shrieks from the bear-pit infringe on the domain of articulate language. An audience now hearing Gloucester's 'I am tied to th' stake, and I must stand the course' (*Lear* xiv. 52) would hardly have seen precisely such a 'course' endured by a roaring, blood-dripping bear just a stone's throw away. With the receding acoustic and visual co-presence of the baiting ring, its 'symbolic energies'[8] faded from the stage. The more Shakespearean drama became detached from its original semiosphere, the more the human–animal correspondences became, in a way they had not been before, *just* figurative.

The 'one white innocent cub'[9] was not the only animal to survive the Southwark bear massacre. 'It is said', the diarist concludes, 'all the mastifs are for to be shipt for Jamaica.'[10] The dogs in the baiting ring, I have argued in the introduction, were given the role of beadles, of acting out the punitive impulses of the onlooking crowd. Trained to perform in these travesties of juridical chastisement, they were also employable for real policing.[11] Their prospective area of work in the Caribbean proceeds from a passage in Richard Ligon's account of Barbados published in 1657. Ligon complains that the islands 'afford no Game to course at', that 'no Stag...has ever set his nimble feet...upon this ground...And then, what use of Hounds?' Very little, save: 'Onely one kinde are usefull here, and those are Liam Hounds, to guide us to runaway Negres, who, as I told you, harbour

---

[7] The Hobbesian bent of these comedies does, of course, endorse a notion of man's 'brutish' nature and the necessity of channelling it into socially acceptable 'manners'. See Michael Neill, 'Heroic Heads and Humble Tails: Sex, Politics, and the Restoration Comic *Rake*', *Literature Criticism from 1400 to 1800*, 140 (2008), 287–301; cf. also Harold Weber, *The Restoration Rake-Hero: Transformations in Sexual Understanding in 17th-Century England* (Madison, Wis.: University of Wisconsin Press, 1986).

[8] Dickey, 'Shakespeare's Mastiff Comedy', 255.

[9] A weakness for white bear cubs must be an anthropological constant. In 2008, the German public was fed daily health bulletins on Knut, a polar bear born in the Berlin zoo whose survival was jeopardized by its indifferent mother. The Knut craze went on for months, abating only when the animal outgrew the cuddly cub phase.

[10] Hotson, 'Bear-Gardens', 286.

[11] On the employment of mastiff dogs trained for bear-baiting in English colonial America, see Mark A. Mastromarino, 'Teaching Old Dogs New Tricks: The English Mastiff and the Anglo-American Experience', *The Historian*, 49 (1986), 10–25.

themselves in Woods and Caves, living upon pillage for many months together.'[12] The mastiffs from the Bear-Garden, lacking the sense of smell of proper bloodhounds, would not have been much use as tracker dogs.[13] But they could well have served to attack and maul the 'runaway Negres', or maroons, whom the retreating Spanish landowners had cast loose when the British, after their failed raid on Hispaniola, landed on the little-defended Jamaica in 1655.[14]

It is not without irony that the canine performers from 'that cruell and lothsome exercise of bayting Beares'[15] which the Puritans never tired of condemning should have been enlisted in the Lord Protector's grand but ill-fated 'Western Design'.[16] Its expansionist purpose—'to strive with the

[12] Richard Ligon, *A true & exact history of the island of Barbados* (London: Humphrey Moseley, 1657), 104–5.

[13] Bloodhounds and mastiffs are quite distinct breeds of dog. Caius, *Of Englishe Dogges*, 5, characterizes the former as 'The greater sort which serue to hunt', i.e. a larger hunting dog used for tracking down game, whose 'singuler specialtie' it is to 'not onely chase the beast whiles it lieth, ... but beying dead also ... hauing in this poynt an assured and infallible guyde, namely, the sent and sauour of the bloud sprinckled heere and there upon the ground.' Mastiffs, on the other hand, 'vaste, huge, stubborne, ougly, and eager ... striking could feare into the hearts of men, but standing in feare of no man' are used as watchdogs and trained up for fighting. The 'liam hounds' mentioned by Ligon are a smaller variety of hunting dogs, a lyam or lyme being a leash. The conflation of the two breeds did not take place until the end of the 18th c., when the slave-hunting bloodhound and the ferocious fighting or war dog (notoriously used by the Spanish conquistadors) converged into the ferocious bloodhound, becoming a salient figure of cruelty in abolitionist discourse. John Campbell, 'The Seminoles, the "Bloodhound War," and Abolitionism, 1796–1865', *Journal of Southern History*, 62 (2006), 259–302.

[14] The slaves set loose by the Spanish at the time of the British conquest, becoming known as Maroons, often proved more than a match for the hapless British occupying forces: 'As for the Negroes, we understand, and to satisfaction, that they, for the most part of them, are at distance from the Spaniards, and live by themselves in several parties, and near our quarters, and do very often, as our men go into the woods to seek provisions, destroy and kill them with their lances. We now and then find one or two of our men killed, stripped, and naked; and these rogues begin to be bold, our English rarely, or seldom, killing any of them.' Letter from Vice Admiral Goodson and Major Sedgwick to Cromwell, Jan. 1656, in *A Collection of the State Papers*, ed. John Thurloe (London, 1742), iv. 154; quoted in Mavis C. Campbell, *The Maroons of Jamaica, 1655–1796: A History of Resistance, Collaboration and Betrayal* (Granby, Mass.: Bergin and Garvey 1988), 18.

[15] John Field, quoted in Chambers, *Elizabethan Stage*, iv. 221.

[16] Thomas Carlyle calls it 'the unsuccessfullest enterprise Oliver Cromwell ever had concern with'. *Oliver Cromwell's Letters and Speeches: With Elucidations*, ed. Thomas Carlyle (London: Chapman and Hall, 1845), iv. 158. Cromwell interpreted the failure of the Caribbean campaign as a 'signal of God's rebuke'; Barry Coward, *Oliver Cromwell* (London and New York: Longman, 2000), 134. '[W]e have cause to be humbled', he wrote, 'for the reproof God gave us at San Domingo upon the account of our sins, as well as others' (letter to Major-General Fortescue at Jamaica, *Cromwell's Letters and Speeches*, iv. 171). In consequence, Cromwell urged the major-generals to combat sinfulness and immorality at home by strictly enforcing 'the Laws against Drunkenness, Blasphemy, and taking of the Name of God in vain, by swearing and cursing, Plays and Interludes, and prophaning of the Lord's day, and such like wickedness and abominations'; *The Writings and Speeches of Oliver Cromwell*, ed. W. C. Abbott (Cambridge, Mass.: Harvard University Press, 1937–47), iii. 845.

Spaniard for the Mastery of all those seas'[17]—was declared subservient to 'enlarging the bounds of the Kingdom of Christ', which, as Cromwell's secretary, John Milton, avers, 'we do not doubt will appear to be the chief end of our late expedition to the West Indies'.[18] English mastiffs may also have played a prior part in spreading the Word to the New World, albeit on the Catholic side. In 1518, Henry VIII had sent four hundred of them to his ally Charles V, Holy Roman emperor and king of Spain, who successfully deployed them against the French at the siege of Valencia.[19] These gift dogs probably arrived too late to have been among those ' "enormous," "tireless," "powerful," and "ferocious" war dogs that attacked and "ate people" '[20] during Cortés's rout of the Aztecs, but they could well be among those mentioned in Bartolomé de las Casas's account of *The Devastation of the Indies* (1552):

> And because all the people who could do so fled to the mountains to escape these inhuman, ruthless, and ferocious acts, the Spanish captains, enemies of the human race, pursued them with the fierce dogs they kept which attacked the Indians, tearing them to pieces and devouring them.[21]

II. Mapping Nowhere

The dual trajectory that detached the theatre from the bear-garden and the mastiff dogs from London to the Caribbean is prefigured in Shakespeare's last play. *The Tempest*, now generally assumed to have been intended for performance at the indoor Blackfriars Theatre,[22] lands us in a remote island

---

[17] *Cromwell's Letters and Speeches*, iv. 170.

[18] 'A Manifesto of the Lord Protector of the Commonwealth of England, Scotland, Ireland, &c. . . . Wherein Is Shown the Reasonableness of the Cause of this Republic against the Depredations of the Spaniards.' This manifesto was written in Latin by Milton in the year 1655 and first translated into English in 1738. The translation is to be found in *The Prose Works of John Milton*, ed. Rufus Wilmot Griswold (Philadelphia: John W. Moore, 1847), ii. 464–77 at 477.

[19] Mastromarino, 'Teaching Old Dogs', 19.

[20] Campbell, 'The Seminoles', 262, quoting from *The Broken Spears: The Aztec Account of the Conquest of Mexico*, ed. Miguel León-Portilla (Boston: Beacon Press, 1962).

[21] Bartolomé de las Casas, *The Devastation of the Indies: A Brief Account*, trans. Herma Briffault (Baltimore, Md.: Johns Hopkins University Press, 1992), 35.

[22] Keith Sturgess, *Jacobean Private Theatres* (London: Routledge and Kegan Paul, 1987), 73–96, though strongly arguing for the Blackfriars, admits that the play would have been equally suitable for the Globe. The earliest recorded performance took place at neither of the King's Men's own theatres but at Whitehall, 1 Nov. ('Hallomas nyght') 1611. E. K. Chambers, *William Shakespeare: A Study of Facts and Problems* (Oxford: Clarendon Press, 1930), ii. 342–3.

setting where a spectral vanguard of the mastiffs shipped to Jamaica in 1656 seems already to be quelling a rebellion headed by 'a savage and deformed slave':[23]

> *A noise of hunters heard. Enter diverse Spirits in shape of dogs and hounds,*
> *hunting them about, Prospero and Ariel setting them on.*
>
> PROSPERO Hey, Mountain, hey!
> ARIEL   Silver! There it goes, Silver!
> PROSPERO Fury, Fury! There, Tyrant, there! Hark, hark!   (IV. i. 255–7)

Transporting us to a distant world of magic and maritime romance, *The Tempest* seems detached from the intermedial triangle of stage, stake, and scaffold. Yet intimations of the familiar spectacles of violence percolate into the seclusion of Shakespeare's enchanted isle, as when short-tempered master meets obstinate slave:

> PROSPERO   Shrugst thou, malice?
> If thou neglect'st, or dost unwillingly
> What I command, I'll rack thee with old cramps,
> Fill all thy bones with aches, make thee roar,
> That beasts shall tremble at thy din.   (I. ii. 368–72)

The torments Prospero threatens to inflict on Caliban sound harsh enough to us, but they may have sounded even worse to a Jacobean audience for whom 'rack' would have had a not just figurative meaning, and 'pinching', mentioned no fewer than seven times in the play, carried sinister overtones of torture, 'more specifically, the contemporary practice of torturing suspected traitors'.[24] Francis Throckmorton, for example, accused of plotting to murder the Queen in 1584, 'was layde upon the [Racke], and somewhat *pinched*, although not much'. And Balthazar Gérard, the assassin of William of Orange, had pieces of flesh 'pinched' from his bones with 'heated pincers of Iron'.[25] Pinching, we recall, also occurred in a baiting context such as at the Kenilworth entertainment, where the bear, '[i]f he wear bitten in one place . . . woold pynch in an oother to get free',[26] or in *3 Henry VI*, where

---

[23] In the Folio list of characters, Caliban is described as 'a savage and deformed slave'.

[24] Breight, ' "Treason doth never prosper" ', 25.

[25] Both quotations from Breight, ' "Treason" ', 25. From his first cursing entry, which sparks Prospero's outburst (I. ii. 329), to his exclamation 'I shall be pinched to death' in the final scene (V. i. 276), Caliban, with his rape attempt on his master's daughter and plot to murder that same master, makes a very plausible traitor—especially, as Breight suggests, of the kind that the Elizabethan state would hatch in order to maintain a politically useful conspiracy paranoia.

[26] Laneham, 'A Letter', 439–40.

York, surrounded by his enemies, is likened to 'a bear encompassed round with dogs, / Who having pinched a few and made them cry, / The rest stand all aloof and bark at him' (3 Henry VI, II. i. 15–17).

Caliban's 'roaring', an animal noise eliciting an animal response ('beasts shall tremble'), evokes a baiting context, which, as we have seen, is intricately bound up with the practices of criminal justice. Beginning with Prospero's threat to deploy pinching and stinging urchins and bees against his rebellious subject (I. ii. 327, 331), The Tempest shows the same close tie between punishment and animality throughout. The shouting contest that ensues when Prospero summons his unruly slave reverberates with anger as unrestrained as the biting, clawing, roaring, tossing, and tumbling which the Kenilworth chronicler finds such 'a matter of goodly relief'.[27] Master and slave are locked in no less fixed a pattern of behaviour than the bears and the bandogs when 'the ton can heer, see, or smell the toother'.[28] As the one 'needs must curse' (II. ii. 4), the other seems equally compulsive in his urge to let not the slightest offence go unpunished:

CALIBAN For every trifle are they [Prospero's spirits] set upon me;
          Sometimes like apes, that mow and chatter at me
          And after bite me; then like hedgehogs, which
          Lie tumbling in my barefoot way and mount
          Their pricks at my footfall; sometime am I
          All wound with adders, who with cloven tounges
          Do hiss me into madness.   (II. ii. 8–14)

Set upon, bitten, pricked, and hissed at, Caliban is subjected to various forms of baiting, which, however fanciful and exotic, retain a family resemblance to contemporary practices of punishment and retributive entertainment. The topicality of such resemblances, however, is no more than hinted at. It will hardly serve to circumscribe the location, epistemic as well as topographical, of a play that situates itself neither in a completely detached world of fantasy nor in a familiar here and now, but rather makes use of an expansive in-between. This location, and dislocation, of the play crucially frames its negotiation of human–animal difference.

Where, then, and what is Prospero's island? More than three decades of postcolonial criticism have left us in no doubt that this island must be located in the West Indies; and yet there can be no doubt that the text

---

[27] Cf. Laneham, 'A Letter', 440.   [28] Ibid. 440.

places it on a route from Tunis to Naples. Rather than attempting to decide the still-vexed question in favour of either alternative, it seems more profitable to construe the play's location as a space encompassing both.

In a eulogy to the boundless power of magic, Prospero's Marlovian predecessor Faustus suggests such a space:

> All things that mooue betweene the quiet poles
> Shalbe at my commaund, Emperours and Kings,
> Are but obeyd in their seuerall prouinces:
> Nor can they raise the winde, or rend the cloudes:
> But his dominion that exceedes in this,
> Stretcheth as farre as doth the minde of man.   (A-text ll. 86–91)[29]

Exceeding the bounds of 'seuerall prouinces', the reach of magic is coextensive with 'the minde of man'. Faustus' aspiration could not be stated more boldly—nor could that boldness more ominously foreshadow his fate. Aiming for omnipotence, he ends up with what one critic has aptly called 'omnimpotence',[30] his dreame of world-empire never attaining a local habitation beyond what it has been confined in from the start: his mind.

Prospero, to be sure, does raise the wind and rend the clouds, but his dominion, too, is not quite of this world—capacious as the human mind, yet sequestered from the 'seuerall prouinces' of a real geography. This may go some way towards accounting for the blending or 'mestizoization' of New World and Old which Richard Halpern has traced in the utopian and counter-utopian strands of *The Tempest*.[31] It may also help elucidate the dialectic of unbounded expanse and cramped confinement which governs the spatial economy of the play.[32] Ranging widely over the Western hemisphere, *The Tempest* crams this scope into the sparsest of time-space frames, stacking 'infinite riches in a little room'.[33] No other Shakespeare play is as compatible with the unities of Renaissance Aristotelianism as *The Tempest*.

---

[29] *Marlowe's Doctor Faustus 1604–1616: Parallel Texts*, ed. W. W. Greg (Oxford: Clarendon Press, 1950).

[30] Constance Brown Kuriyama, *Hammer or Anvil: Psychological Patterns in Christopher Marlowe's Plays* (New Brunswick, NJ: Rutgers University Press, 1980), 95.

[31] Halpern, ' "The Picture of Nobody" '.

[32] This line of enquiry was fruitfully opened by Mary Thomas Crane, *Shakespeare's Brain: Reading with Cognitive Theory* (Princeton and Oxford: Princeton University Press, 2001), 178–209. Also pertinent here is David Hillman, '*Homo Clausus* at the Theatre', in Bryan Reynolds and William N. West (eds.), *Rematerializing Shakespeare: Authority and Representation on the Early Modern English Stage* (Houndmills, Basingstoke: Palgrave Macmillan, 2005), 161–85.

[33] Christopher Marlowe, *The Jew of Malta*, ed. Roma Gill, The Complete Works of Christopher Marlowe, 4 (Oxford: Clarendon Press, 1995), I. i. 37.

Beginning at three in the afternoon, it concludes at six; the action, in the halting verse of the Epilogue, is limited to 'this bare island' (Ep. 8).[34] When all's done you look but on a stage[35] 'of about 30 by 23 feet, with playing space further reduced by the presence of audience members sitting onstage'.[36] Shakespeare's storm-in-a-box offers nothing like the supreme Baroque stage illusion mounted by Gian Lorenzo Bernini during the Roman carnival of 1638, whose spectacular *Inundation of the Tiber* put the audience in fear of drowning.[37] All we see in *The Tempest* is actors simulating a crowded deck on a (quite possibly) crowded stage.[38] The impact of the storm which Prospero raises in this enclosed, 'potentially claustrophobic'[39] space must have been 'largely acoustical',[40] the '*tempestuous noise of thunder and lightning heard*' (I. i. 1 SD) threatening to drown out the dialogue.[41] The storm, like Prospero's island itself is, in other words, all in the mind and, as the insistent metatheatricality of the play suggests, in the mind-space of theatre.

'Cell' is a keyword here. As a marker of location, it precedes Prospero's first mention of 'this island' (I. ii. 171). Introducing himself as 'Prospero, master of a full poor cell' (I. ii. 20), he uses 'cell' to designate not only his place of residence but, metonymically, the whole extent of his dominion. And the same goes for the local deixis of 'before we came unto this cell' a few moments later (I. ii. 39). Entrapment is a condition applying not only to those under Prospero's rule but very much also to the ruler himself, who may finally be released from the confines of the island, only to find himself 'more

[34] Ralph Berry, *Shakespeare and the Awareness of the Audience* (London: Macmillan, 1985), 1–15, argues that Shakespeare frequently conceives of the stage as an 'island'.

[35] Cf. *Macbeth* III. iv. 66–7.

[36] Crane, *Shakespeare's Brain*, 202, drawing on Sturgess, *Jacobean Private Theatres*, 37–44.

[37] A description of this event is in the appendix to Gian Lorenzo Bernini, *Fontana di Trevi*, ed. Cesare d'Onofrio (Rome: Staderini, 1963), 97. On Bernini's artistry see D. A. Beecher, 'Gianlorenzo Bernini's *The Impresario:* The Artist as the Supreme Trickster', *University of Toronto Quarterly*, 53 (1984), 236–47, and Florian Nelle, *Künstliche Paradiese: Vom Barocktheater zum Filmpalast* (Würzburg: Königshausen und Neumann, 2005), 19–20.

[38] Douglas Bruster, 'Local *Tempest:* Shakespeare and the Work of the Early Modern Playhouse', *Journal of Medieval and Renaissance Studies*, 25 (1995), 33–53 at 39, suggests that if the first scene 'is about a ship at sea, it is also about working in a crowded playhouse'.

[39] Crane, *Shakespeare's Brain*, 203.

[40] Sturgess, *Jacobean Private Theatres*, 82; on the specific sound environment of the Blackfriars see Bruce Smith, *The Acoustic World of Early Modern England: Attending to the O-Factor* (Chicago: University of Chicago Press, 1999), 222.

[41] Roger Warren, 'Rough Magic and Heavenly Music: *The Tempest*', in Virginia Mason Vaughan and Alden T. Vaughan (eds.), *Critical Essays on Shakespeare's The Tempest* (New York: Hall, 1998), 152–89 at 152.

inescapably trapped in his own body'.[42] The Arden editors note that '[i]n the early seventeenth century, "cell" did not yet carry implications of imprisonment',[43] but the play's insistent references to the interlinking enclosures of island, stage, and body, make it hard to escape such implications.

A 'cell' is not only a small, confining, 'extremely humble dwelling',[44] it is also the exemplary locus of the contemplative life. Erasmus appropriated the image of St Jerome in his study to endorse his bid for prominence in the humanist republic of letters.[45] The monkish 'cell' in which the painting by Antonello da Messina portrays the Church Father as a biblical scholar is hardly humble or indicative of humility but rather a site of scholarly prestige and knowledge-based authority. But the primary function it signifies is still that of isolating and insulating the scholar from the mundane distractions of the world.[46] Both verbs, isolate and insulate, draw on the meaning of 'island'.[47] Insular seclusion or 'closeness' is an indispensible prerequisite for the pursuit of learning. Thus Prospero—'all dedicated / To closeness and the bettering of my mind' (I. ii. 89–90)—is already islanded and closeted while still in Milan, 'transported' (I. ii. 76) from his physical surroundings even before being physically transported to his island exile. The Tempest is steeped in an epistemic culture that associated the production and storage of knowledge with such cell-like, insular interiors as the study, the library, the cabinet of curiosities (Wunderkammer),[48] the alchemist's kitchen, and, of course, the theatre. The play thus also shares the analogical and topological habits of thought that read these enclosed spaces as emblems of the spatially conceived human mind encased in the cell-like cavity of the skull.[49]

---

[42] Crane, Shakespeare's Brain, 197.

[43] The Tempest, ed. Vaughan and Vaughan, 150 n. to I. ii. 20.

[44] Ibid.

[45] Lisa Jardine, Erasmus, Man of Letters: The Construction of Charisma in Print (Princeton: Princeton University Press, 1993).

[46] With heavy architectural framing in the foreground and windows giving onto a landscape in the background, Antonello da Messina's Saint Jerome in his Study (National Gallery, London) construes the study as a place of both seclusion from and privileged observation of the world.

[47] On insularity/isolation as a fundamental premiss of Western epistemology, see Stephan Laqué's Habilitationsschrift (postdoctoral thesis), The Metaphysics of Isolation: Delimitation, Knowledge and Identity in 20th-Century Literature (Munich, 2009).

[48] On Wunderkammern see Arthur MacGregor, Curiosity and Enlightenment: Collectors and Collections from the Sixteenth to the Nineteenth Century (New Haven and London: Yale University Press, 2007); R. J. W. Evans and Alexander Marr (eds.), Curiosity and Wonder from the Renaissance to the Enlightenment (Aldershot, Burlington: Ashgate, 2006); Mullaney, Place of the Stage, 60–87.

[49] Cognitivist critics have thus only rediscovered what the Renaissance already knew, that 'the relationship between places and systems of knowledge is complex and reciprocal'; Crane, Shakespeare's Brain, 209.

The theatres of memory explored by Frances Yates were the first such mind or knowledge spaces to be brought to the attention of Shakespeare studies.[50] As Prospero underwent a critical transformation from benevolent magus-artist (and wistful author-double) to heavy-handed colonizer, such theatre (together with the attendant reverence for the arcana of neo-Platonic hermeticism) faded from relevance.[51] But attention to the play's manifest engagement with repressive power structures is no reason to disregard its embeddedness in late Renaissance knowledge cultures, if only because knowledge, after all, is the means of maintaining those structures. Attempts to clarify and classify this knowledge—if magic, what type, if art, in what sense, if science, how modern?—have proved no more conclusive than the search for the exact location of Prospero's island.[52] What the play gives us is a composite fictional picture of an epistemic order that is both perplexingly different from ours and, to complicate matters more, in the process of radical reconfiguration.[53] Something of this conglomerate quality is captured in Elizabeth Spiller's characterization of Prospero's island:

> At the close of the first scene, Gonzalo confronts the possibility that he might drown and wishes for 'an acre of barren ground' (1.1.66). *The Tempest*'s island is the acre that human imagination has called up: it and everything that happens in that space is in some way an invented construct. Like the alchemist's crucible, William Gilbert's magnetic terrella, or Francis Bacon's idea for experiments that use the 'vexations of art' to reveal the 'secrets of nature', the island is a small world in which Prospero seeks to use art to control nature and, in doing so, create different forms of knowledge.[54]

---

[50] Frances Yates, *Shakespeare's Last Plays* (London: Routledge, 1975); ead., 'Magic in Shakespeare's Last Plays—On *The Tempest*', *Encounter*, 44 (1975), 14–22.

[51] Barbara Mowat, 'Prospero, Agrippa, and Hocus Pocus', *English Literary Renaissance*, 11 (1981), 281–303, indicates a shift in critical mood. 'Hocus pocus' is a term that would never have occurred to Yates.

[52] Cf. Barbara Mowat, 'Prospero's Book', *Shakespeare Quarterly*, 52 (2001), 1–33, who usefully distinguishes different types of magicians as well as the different types of books they used, but concludes that these distinctions ultimately collapse into the composite picture of a Prospero who is 'simultaneously (or perhaps alternately) a serious master of spirits and a stage-or-romance wizard who also reminds us ... of a Renaissance magus and a Jacobean street magician' (p. 29).

[53] For an illuminating summary see Katharine Park and Lorraine Daston, 'Introduction: The Age of the New', in *The Cambridge History of Science*, iii: *Early Modern Science*, ed. Katharine Park and Lorraine Daston (Cambridge: Cambridge University Press, 2006), 1–17.

[54] Elizabeth Spiller, 'Shakespeare and the Making of Early Modern Science: Resituating Prospero's Art', *South Central Review*, 26 (2009), 24–41 at 26.

As a place of artificially created wonders, a site of knowledge production, Prospero's island is also a theatre, at a time when 'theatre' meant encyclopedia as well as playhouse, when, in fact, it meant encyclopedia *before* it meant playhouse.[55] Humanists may have deemed the vulgar playhouses unworthy of this lofty name, but the common players asserted their right to it by naming London's first purpose-built playhouse The Theatre. A theatre detractor yet deeply fascinated by its power, Francis Bacon put theatre at the very centre of his scientific utopia. Salomon's House, described as 'the very eye of this kingdom', i.e. the New Atlantis, is not just a place for research and development but also, crucially, one for creating and watching spectacles:

> We have also great and spacious houses, where we imitate and demonstrate meteors—as snow, hail, rain, some artificial rains of bodies and not of water, thunders, lightnings; also generations of bodies in air—as frogs, flies, and divers others.[56]

The Tempest, for all its fanciful magic, would seem just the play to put on in one of the theatre laboratories on Bacon's imaginary Pacific island. Under the laboratory conditions of insular abstraction, it instantiates not only 'the colonialist imperative of emergent science',[57] but, more generally, the knowledge-power nexus at the heart of the Baconian project. If 'Prospero seeks to use art to control nature and, in doing so, create different forms of knowledge',[58] the principal use he makes of that knowledge is to control people. Although 'cell' was unlikely to trigger thoughts of prison when *The Tempest* was written, imprisonment is nonetheless a key aspect of the play, the condition of virtually all its characters. Apart from associations with the study, the theatre, the mind, and the laboratory, Prospero's enclosed dominion is also very manifestly a place of punishment—a colony, but more specifically a penal colony. Even '[t]hese our actors' (IV. i. 148), the spirits conjured to perform the felicitations of the wedding masque, have to be released 'from their confines' (IV. i. 121).

[55] William N. West, *Theatres and Encyclopedias in Early Modern Europe* (Cambridge: Cambridge University Press, 2002), gives an excellent account of the complex relations between theatres and encyclopedias, of how '[i]n early modern Europe, the ideas of these two institutions were used to define one another' (p. 1).

[56] Francis Bacon, 'The New Atlantis', in *Francis Bacon: A Critical Edition of the Major Works*, ed. Brian Vickers (Oxford: Oxford University Press, 1996), 457–89 at 481.

[57] Denise Albanese, *New Science, New World* (Durham, NC, and London: Duke University Press, 1996), 57.

[58] Spiller, 'Shakespeare and the Making of Early Modern Science', 26.

This returns us to the historical realities of public violence reverberating through the insulation of Prospero's exile. It projects these realities into an abstract space of Protean indeterminacy which presents a different appearance to each beholder: utopian or dystopian, lush or barren. This indeterminacy aligns the island with 'the baseless fabric of this vision', the 'insubstantial pageant' of the masque which Prospero dismisses as a mere 'trick' or 'vanity of mine art' (IV. i. 37; 40) but whose very insubstantiality makes it a perfect model of 'the great globe itself' and of 'our little life', which is no more than just another island, 'rounded with a sleep' (IV. i. 151–8).[59] Drawn into a vortex of dissolution, this island world, somewhat like the Cheshire cat in *Alice in Wonderland*, manages to disappear but leave its grin. A trace of the island's penal practices lingers in the very denial of traces: 'Like this insubstantial pageant faded', it shall leave 'not a *rack* behind' (IV. i. 156).

III. Imagining Nobody

The indeterminacy of *The Tempest*'s setting tallies with the indeterminate nature of its native inhabitant. 'What have we here, a man or a fish?' (II. ii. 24–5) asks Trinculo on his first encounter with Caliban. According to the Folio list of characters Trinculo is only 'a jester', and a none too bright one at that. But learned commentators have shared his puzzlement. Morton Luce, in the introduction of his 1901 Arden edition of the play, sees a quandary: 'If all the suggestions as to Caliban's form and feature and endowments that are thrown out in the play are collected, it will be found that one half renders the other half impossible.'[60] If 'tortoise', 'fish', 'mooncalf', 'freckled whelp', 'cat', or simply 'beast Caliban' (IV. i. 140) are all taken as literal descriptions, then indeed a veritable cocktail of species ensues, a chimera of the kind that, according to old Gonzalo, has migrated from fable to fact in his own lifetime:

---

[59] In Derek Jarman's film version of *The Tempest* (1979), the whole of the action is, as it were, 'rounded with a sleep'. 'When *The Tempest* begins, we see a figure in bed who is clearly dreaming the storm. The storm itself is rendered immediately as part of an imaginary world...'. Steven Dillon, *Derek Jarman and Lyric Film: The Mirror and the Sea* (Austin, Tex.: University of Texas Press, 2004), 90–9 at 91.
[60] *The Tempest*, ed. Morton Luce (London: Methuen, 1901), p. xxxv.

> When we were boys,
> Who would believe that there were mountaineers
> Dewlapped like bulls, whose throats had hanging at 'em
> Wallets of flesh? Or that there were such men
> Whose heads stood in their breasts? Which now we find
> Each putter-out of five for one will bring us
> Good warrant of?[61]   (III. iii. 43–9)

A wonder among the other wonders of the isle, Caliban is clearly part of the colonial imaginary which this passage evokes. But, interwoven with the markers of his alienness and monstrosity, the text offers clear enough evidence that the nature of the monster is understood to be human. Prospero's account of his arrival is unmistakable on this point:

> Then was this island
> —Save for the son that she did litter here,
> A freckled whelp, hag-born—not honoured with
> A human shape.
> ARIEL   Yes, Caliban, her son.   (I. ii. 282–4)

On closer inspection, Trinculo comes to the same conclusion: 'Legged like a man and his fins like arms', the creature he has found 'is no fish, but an islander' (II. ii. 32–3). However, far from settling the question of Caliban's 'nature', this clarification makes it all the more remarkable that his human-ness is constantly under attack, strafed with a veritable barrage of animal epithets. What 'human shape' concedes, 'litter' and 'freckled whelp' take away. Caliban may be human, but only, as it were, on probation, and under Prospero's regime of *surveiller et punir*, he never stops violating his probation. For ever hovering on the brink of humanity, he is never quite admitted into its fold, but neither can he be safely relegated to a stable order of the non-human. If Prospero is confined to an island, Caliban is 'stied' in a rock ('and here you sty me / In this hard rock';[62] I. ii. 43–4); but if Caliban is

---

[61] Gonzalo's opinion closely resembles Raleigh's view of the Ewaipoma, 'a nation of people, whose heads appear not above their shoulders; which though it may be thought a meere fable, yet for mine owne part I am resolved it is true, because every childe in the provinces of Arromaia and Canuri affirme the same: they are reported to have their eyes in their breasts, and that a long traine of haire groweth backward betweene their shoulders.... Such a nation was written of by Mandeville, whose reports were holden for fables many yeeres, and yet since the East Indies were discovered, we find his relations true of such things as heretofore were held incredible.' *Hakluyt's Voyages*, vii: *The Principal Navigations, Voyages, Traffiques & Discoveries of the English Nation*, ed. John Masefield (London: Dent, 1927), 328–9.

[62] The Arden editors note that this is the first occurrence of the verb registered in the *OED* v.[2] 1b. See *The Tempest*, ed. Virginia Mason Vaughan and Alden T. Vaughan, Arden 3rd ser. (Walton-on-thames: Thomas Nelson and Sons, 1999).

capable of categorizing his treatment as bestialization, this excludes him from the category to which this treatment seeks to demote him.

Shakespeare's liminal figure par excellence, Caliban not only highlights the contact zone between European civilization and its non-European Other, but also embodies the fluid threshold of human–animal distinction.

For some decades critics have tended to see the latter almost exclusively in terms of the former: bestialization as an ideological tool of colonialism. Take away the demonized animality and Caliban emerges as the subaltern whose humanity asserts itself despite, or precisely because of, being constantly denied. In his powerful discussion of the play, Stephen Greenblatt states the case concisely. *The Tempest*, he argues,

> utterly rejects the uniformitarian view of the human race, the view that would later triumph in the Enlightenment and prevail in the West to this day. All men, the play seems to suggest, are *not* alike; strip away the adornments of culture and you will *not* reach a single human essence. If anything, *The Tempest* seems closer in spirit to the attitude of the present-day inhabitants of Java who, according to Clifford Geertz, quite flatly say, 'To be human is to be Javanese.'
>
> And yet out of the midst of this attitude Caliban wins a momentary victory that is, quite simply, an assertion of inconsolable human pain and bitterness. And out of the midst of this attitude Prospero comes, at the end of the play, to say of Caliban, 'this thing of darkness/I acknowledge mine' (V. i. 275–76).[63]

What this reading and those that have followed suit take for granted is the play's investment in a firm ethnocentric notion of normative humanity: 'To be human is to be a white European.' Even if Caliban is granted a momentary victory and Prospero is made to acknowledge a bond with him, these exceptional moments do not shake that notion. All they do is temporarily suspend the off-limits sign guarding white European exclusivity.

Yet it might be argued that Prospero's acknowledgement of a bond with the 'thing of darkness' works in the other direction as well; that Caliban is not just a foil but a constant challenge to Prospero's sense of his own self, a challenge to the very notion of humanness to which he lays claim and which his island rule is committed to enforcing. Caliban's 'darkness' rubs off on Prospero; and it is not—or not necessarily, though this is often taken for granted—a darkness of skin. The Folio list of characters classifies Caliban as 'a savage and deformed slave', and although most likely concocted by the

---

[63] Stephen Greenblatt, *Learning to Curse: Essays in Early Modern Culture* (New York and London: Routledge, 1990), 26.

scrivener Ralph Crane, not by Shakespeare, it may well reflect contemporary stage practice.[64] A manifestly reasonable antidote to all those ape-shaped or even reptile Calibans which *The Tempest* hatched in the overactive imagination of eighteenth- and nineteenth-century readers, Crane's description now sometimes tends to be taken as the final word on what Caliban 'really' is and, consequently, what we are supposed to think that he looks like. And so, just as the Victorians opted for Caliban as a Darwinian primate, we rush to the conclusion that he must be an oppressed person of colour. But can he be 'freckled' if his skin is brown? Deliberating this may engender the same kind of contortions which Caliban's blue-eyed Algerian mother occasioned in earlier textual commentaries.[65] Yet even if 'freckled' should turn out to be just another word for 'tawny' in Jacobean English (which it does not), or if it were discovered that a blue-eyed North African lived two doors from Shakespeare's lodgings in Silver Street around 1610, such documentary evidence would ultimately fail to resolve what the play's deliberately crossed signals make unresolvable.

The desire to clarify 'what we have here' and what this creature looks like presupposes a normative idea of closed representation. The Chorus in *Henry V* enjoins the audience to 'Think, when we talk of horses, that you see them' (Prologue, 26)—unnecessarily, for this is the standard contract between players and patrons in Shakespeare's wooden O. But what is the audience supposed to think that it sees when players talk of horses that bark and have fins? More than any other character in the Shakespearean canon, Caliban exemplifies a characteristic quality of the playtext: its resistance to closed representation. What goes for *The Tempest*'s peculiarly shifting verbal scenery, of which there are as many different descriptions as there are speakers describing it, also goes for Caliban, the character most intimately linked with that scenery, 'Shakespeare's changeling'.[66] The dialogue inundates him with a veritable glut of descriptors that refuse to add up to any recognizable form or shape, be it human or animal. Rather than furnishing the closure of a 'rounded picture', such overdetermination reflects upon itself, foregrounding not the product but the productivity of ascription.

---

[64] Cf. *The Tempest*, ed. Vaughan and Vaughan, 141.

[65] For a brilliant exposition of these critical manoeuvres see Leah S. Marcus, 'Introduction: The Blue-Eyed Witch', in her *Unediting the Renaissance: Shakespeare, Marlowe, Milton* (London and New York: Routledge, 1996), 1–37.

[66] Alden T. Vaughan and Virginia Mason Vaughan, *Shakespeare's Caliban: A Cultural History* (Cambridge: Cambridge University Press, 1991), 7.

The strange and varied pictorial history of Caliban attests to both the force of this productivity and the ceaseless effort to contain it by moulding radical indeterminacy into concrete shape. Reductive if not downright absurd as many of these endeavours may appear, the theatre must renew the effort with every new production of the play. Inhabiting the body of an actor, Caliban is circumscribed by the physical specificity of that body and the performance choices that go into the making of his 'character'. He may seem a far cry from the complexity of a Hamlet and the choices that complexity entails for the actor. But while not as subtly nuanced as the script for Hamlet, the script for Caliban challenges the theatre with a perhaps even more fundamental openness. This has often been obscured by the convention that envisions the comic as lively but flat. The more exuberantly *funny* the comic, the more it becomes stereotyped, sustained by a single dominant mannerism or humour. It is this approach that made the actor Frank Benson, preparing for the part in 1891, spend 'many hours watching monkeys and baboons in the zoo, in order to get the movements and postures in keeping with his "make-up"', which his wife described as 'half monkey, half coco-nut'. Benson then 'delighted in swarming up a tree on the stage and hanging from the branches head downwards while he gibbered at "Trinculo"'.[67]

Dressing or, as here, overdressing the part domesticates alterity by exaggerating it. The play itself anticipates this strategy by letting us witness how Caliban's strangeness is coopted into the conceptual frameworks of his observers. Trinculo's response is exemplary: he has never seen anything like this 'strange beast' but immediately knows what it is good for:

> Were I in England now (as once I was) and had but this fish painted, not a holiday fool there but would give a piece of silver. There would this monster make a man; any strange beast there makes a man. When they will not give a doit to relieve a lame beggar, they will lay out ten to see a dead Indian.
>
> (II. ii. 27–32)

No less promptly than Trinculo, Antonio asserts that this 'plain fish', however doubtful his appearance, is 'no doubt marketable' (V. i. 266). That it is the play's unreclaimed villain who endorses Trinculo's entrepreneurial fantasy seems no accident. If *The Tempest* itself provides the kind of 'holiday' which an audience will lay out ten doits to see and thus partakes in

---

[67] Quoted in Vaughan and Vaughan, *Caliban*, 185.

the commodification of wonder which was integral to the colonial enterprise, it also exposes this commodification for what it is. Where the colonial gaze asserts its 'natural' right of possession by assigning animal attributes, the text registers an uncontrollable ambiguity: at the same time as these attributes confer the stamp of possessive recognition (subjecting the other to one's own preconception), they signal a residue of incommensurable otherness which eludes appropriation.

Both human and animal but fully at home in neither category, an object of commodification but also a subject with a protesting voice of his own, Caliban in his defiance of classification, Julia Lupton argues, suggests the term 'creature' and the openness it entails. *Creatura*, the Latin suffix *-ura* indicating a permanent state of becoming, of ongoing creation, captures the 'indeterminacy at the heart of Caliban',[68] his 'oddly faceless and featureless being, caught at the perpetually flooded border between metamorphic mud and mere life' (p. 8). The term neither clearly grants, nor clearly denies Caliban humanity, which 'remains a question rather than a given in the play' (p. 13). Suspended in a condition of emergence, 'Creature . . . measures the difference between the human and the inhuman while refusing to take up residence in either category' (p. 5).

Offering her reading as a 'political theology of the Creature' (p. 3), Lupton draws on Carl Schmitt and his postmodern exegete Giorgio Agamben, but also on a less obvious reader of the rightist Schmitt, the early Walter Benjamin. For Benjamin, in his *Origin of the German Tragic Drama*, '[t]he Creature represents the flip side of the political theology of absolute sovereignty'. In Schmitt's analysis the king 'is like God in the creative-destructive potential of his decisive word' and 'his subjects are his creatures' (p. 5). Benjamin maintains that 'the sovereign, unlike God, is himself a creature' (p. 6). '[H]owever highly he is enthroned over subject and state,' he writes, 'his status is confined to the world of creation; he is the lord of creatures, but he remains a creature.'[69] If Lupton's excellent analysis is to be faulted for anything, it would be for not pursuing this Benjaminian line of thinking further. Convincingly as she demonstrates Caliban's primeval Adamic connection to the earth as a hallmark of his creaturely status, the extent to which

---

[68] Julia Reinhard Lupton, 'Creature Caliban', *Shakespeare Quarterly*, 51 (2000), 1–23 at 2. Further references are given in text.

[69] Walter Benjamin, *The Origin of the German Tragic Drama*, trans. John Osborne (London: New Left Books, 1977), 85.

Prospero shares this status remains largely unexplored. Much in the play bolsters the opposition between the master of the island and his subject: 'Sun and moon, Prospero and Caliban, Creator and Creature, king and subject' (p. 9). 'Caliban is Mere Creature, a creature separate (like Adam) from the Creator but (unlike Adam) not reflected back to the Creator as His image' (p. 8). I would suggest that this creature *does* reflect back to his creator, more specifically to the creator surrogate the play offers in the figure of Prospero.

If his for ever incomplete humanity makes Caliban 'radically singular', 'a lonely monster rather than the representative of a nation or a race, a strange exception born in a state of emerg-ency' (p. 20), we may well ask why he should worry his sovereign 'creator' as much as he obviously does, or indeed why this creator should have any need of him in the first place. The text hardly accounts for the intensity of Prospero's engage-ment with his creature. Not for a moment does Caliban's conspiracy pose any real threat; and the explanation that 'We cannot miss him; he does make our fire' (I. ii. 312) is of the kind we are given in fairy tales and are therefore not supposed to question. But surely someone who has 'given fire' 'to the dread-rattling thunder . . . and rifted Jove's stout oak / With his own bolt' (V. i. 45–6) would have other means to keep his cell heated. Caliban himself knows best what he is really needed for, as has often been noted:

> For I am all the subjects that you have,
> Which first was mine own king,   (I. ii. 343–4)

To be absolute master, Prospero needs Caliban as absolute slave. While Ariel's service is based on contract (though certainly not on a contract between equals), Caliban's is based on force and expropriation. His political advantage exponentially increased by magic, Prospero has every conceiv-able instrument of power at his disposal. This should make him tower in unassailable superiority over his '[a]bhorred slave' (I. ii. 352), but the fierce altercation that ensues on each of his encounters with the creature that is, or should be, 'all subject' as well as 'all the subjects that he has', tells a different story. Caliban is and remains defiantly insubordinate, a constant thorn in the flesh of his master. Though 'rack[ed] . . . with old cramps' (I. ii. 370), he remains stubbornly unregenerate, answering the charge of attempted rape with an oddly gleeful regret for having failed:

O ho, O ho! Would't had been done!
Thou didst prevent me; I had peopled else
This isle with Calibans.   (I. ii. 351–3)

The contrast with Prospero's civilizational and dynastic project could not be more pronounced. Drawing on a language not learned from his educator, Caliban's 'O ho, O ho!' launches a counter-history, an alternative pagan myth of violent beginning opposed to Prospero's analogue of an Eden lost through sexual transgression. By continuing to punish the offender, Prospero keeps re-presenting, reiterating the offence. By continuing to be punished, Caliban continues in readiness to transgress and transgress again. What ostensibly confirms Prospero's absolute rule—'I must obey,' says Caliban, 'his art is of such power' (I. ii. 373)—can thus become a constant reminder of a rule that fails, a constant reminder also of a creation that fails and whose failure reflects on the creator. The 'felt singularity'[70] of a creature 'on whose nature / Nurture can never stick' (IV. i. 188–9) does not prevent this nature from infiltrating, or rather from always already inhabiting, the human order Prospero seeks to create. Caliban persists as an irritant to the civility and humanness from which his freakish singularity for ever excludes him.

IV. Mastermind Slavebody

Colonization and culture derive etymologically from the same Latin verb *colere*, whose primary meaning is to till or cultivate the soil. Prospero, it has been said, is not really a colonizer because he abandons the island as soon as his dynastic goal is achieved. But his colonial-cultural project is not primarily conceivable in terms of territorial expansion. It is directed not so much at a plot of foreign earth as at the earth creature that he finds dwelling there. 'Caliban', Lupton writes, 'appears as a *thing* made of *earth*', his 'earthen core recalls the first fashioning of conscious life out of an inert yet infinitely malleable substance, as if the very plasticity of mud prompted the idea of conscious life in the Creator'.[71] Prospero's project has come to an impasse, pitting the far from infinitely malleable creature in bitter opposition to his creator-colonizer. Yet it cannot simply be abandoned. If Caliban's nature resists nurture, this hints at the possibility of a more pervasive failing of the

---

[70] Lupton, 'Creature Caliban', 19.   [71] Ibid. 8.

civilizing effort. Rather than illustrating the humanist belief in upward mobility, Caliban exemplifies the gravitational counterforce to that mobility, a bit of naggingly unfinished business persisting even to the final tableau of the play. The force which his physical maturation emblematizes ('And, as with age his body uglier grows, / So his mind cankers'; IV. i. 191–2) is present, if hidden under a veneer of civility, in the unrelenting Antonio and Sebastian. And even the well-mannered Ferdinand, whose forced labour makes him Caliban's parodic double, is suspected of being imbued with it. Prospero sharply cautions him against what would be a repetition of Caliban's sexual offence:

> Look thou be true. Do not give dalliance
> Too much the rein. The strongest oaths are straw
> To th' fire i' th' blood. Be more abstemious
> Or else, good night your vow.   (IV. i. 51–4)

What the conquistadors and the chroniclers of their exploits thought they had found in the New World was a version of the historical, or pre-historical, past of their own culture. What Prospero finds in Caliban is the unreclaimed nature of the old Adam, a creatureliness not culturally disciplined into full humanity. His worry about 'the beast Caliban' (IV. i. 140) derives from the suspicion that his beastliness may be lurking, for ever uncontrollable, under the brittle surface of normative civility, that the thing of darkness is not a thing out there but a thing within. Although Caliban is denied humanity, humanity somehow always seems to be at stake in him. Hence Prospero's inordinately agitated outburst over his failure to make a passable man of his 'brutish' ward: 'on whom my pains / Humanely taken—all, all lost, quite lost!' (IV. i. 189–90), which uncannily echoes the mariners' drowning cries, 'All lost! To prayers, to prayers! All lost!' (I. i. 50) Such agitation would hardly be warranted if Prospero had never expected more of the 'freckled whelp' than that he be trainable to fetch wood. The fierce, almost hysterically intense energy of abhorrence which the failed educator expends on the 'Hag-seed', the 'born devil', 'savage', 'Filth' betrays a deep bond between master and slave which neither is able to undo, and which denial, however violent, only serves to confirm.

The clash of this unequal, antagonistic and yet inseparable pair is Shake-speare's last engagement with the question of the human, played out in the abstract space of *The Tempest*'s nowhere island. Ensconced in the cranial cavity of his book-lined cell, Prospero, the mastermind of the island, exerts his sovereign power in feats that accomplish a spectacular convergence of magic and the utopian aspirations of Baconian science. Commanding the elements, he wields the prerogatives of 'a glorious God that maketh . . . the blustering tempests and whirlwinds', as Reginald Scot asserts in refutation of those who (like King James) ascribed such power to witches and de- mons.[72] He is the 'god of power' (I. ii. 10) whom Miranda, in terror and pity, invokes as the King of Naples's ship goes under, the god who '[p]ut the wild waters in this roar' and can just as easily 'allay them' (I. ii. 1–2). Prospero's magical exploits anticipate what Francis Bacon expected from knowledge of the workings of nature. Besides such items as the 'prolonga- tion of life' and the '[m]aking of new species', his list of 'Magnalia Naturae', appended to the first edition of the *New Atlantis* (1627), also includes ' [i]mpressions of the air, and raising of tempests'.[73] Dedication to 'the bettering of my mind' (I. ii. 90) has given Prospero what Faustus could only dream of, the power to 'raise the winde, or rend the cloudes', a dominion that '[s]tretcheth as farre as doth the minde of man'.

There is a circularity in this phantasm of omnipotence, with the mind conceived both as the agent and the domain, or object, of human power. The power of human thought working undisturbed on a world of its own making—this ultimate wish-fulfilment of the humanist imagination can only be realized through magic or in the magic circle of the theatre, the laboratory enclosure of Prospero's island where 'the mind of man' becomes coextensive with the notion of the human itself. In this regime of mind- as-master, Caliban can only be allocated a 'sty' or else be made an exhibit in the wonder-cabinet of learned (or not so learned) curiosity. Alive or dead, he is an object at man's (or mind's) disposal, the 'base', bare life which it is the rational mind's task to bring under control. If Prospero is mind, Caliban is body. In terms of the humanist *dignitas* of man, Prospero represents the human, while Caliban remains the 'anthropophorous',[74] or carrier animal, in whom *ánthropos* remains for ever unrealized.

It is this dualism that energizes *The Tempest*. Implanted in the urgency of Prospero's tour de force undertaking to right the wrongs of many years within three hours, it accounts for his nervous flare-up at the least sign of

[72] Reginald Scot, *The Discoverie of Witchcraft* (1584) (Arundel: Centaur Press, 1964), 25. King James I, *Daemonologie* (1597). *Newes from Scotland* (1591), ed. G. B. Harrison (London: John Lane, The Bodley Head; New York: E. P. Dutton, 1924).

[73] Bacon, 'New Atlantis', 488–9.

[74] Agamben, *The Open*, 12.

obstruction and, perhaps most of all, for his constant state of treason alert. The ascendancy of the spiritual, the rational, the good, the human or 'humane' over the base, the dark, the evil, the bestial is never securely established. It is an embattled fortress or a tower like that described in Phineas Fletcher's poeticized treatise on statecraft, which was cited in the previous chapter. Prospero, unlike Lear,

> . . . guards all entrance, and by divers spies
> Searches into his foes and friends designes:
> For most he fears his subjects wavering mindes.
> This Tower then only falls, when treason undermines.[75]

Ratio, head of state, head of the body politic, Prospero watches everyone (or has them watched 'by divers spies') but most of all he watches Caliban. 'His spirits hear me' (II. ii. 3) describes a state of permanent invigilation. Nothing escapes the master's punitive attention, and nothing fails to offend: 'For every trifle are they [Prospero's spirits] set upon me' (II. ii. 8). Fletcher regards the little commonwealth of man's body and the macro-body of the state as linked in one-to-one correlation. Shakespeare's island kingdom, a monarchy literally in granting the one ruler exactly *one* subject (I. ii. 342), marks the limit of this macro–micro, state–body analogy. Tied to each other, Caliban and Prospero are so entangled in their obsessive mutuality as to almost become two halves of a single being, a unity of irrepressible difference. Unlike the two halves in Plato's myth of eros, whose 'role is to restore us to our ancient state by trying to make unity out of duality and to heal our human condition',[76] *The Tempest*'s antagonistic pair are not spurred on by a nostalgic longing for a lost union. Rather, they are held together by the force of the rift itself, the contested line of distinction where the creature is always not only in the process of emerging but also threatening to re-emerge. The drama played out here, then, is that of creature Caliban and creature Prospero as well, and it is about the reversal Foucault mentions when he speaks of 'the animal that will stalk man, capture him, and reveal him to his own truth'.[77] If the proud creator shared Bacon's dream of the 'making of new species', the fading of that dream confronts Prospero not only with the unreclaimed Caliban (and the unreclaimed, though civilly

---

[75] Fletcher, 'The Purple Island', 77.
[76] Plato, *The Symposium*, trans. M. C. Howatson, ed. M. C. Howatson and Frisbee C. C. Sheffield (Cambridge: Cambridge University Press, 2008), 24.
[77] Foucault, *Madness and Civilization*, 21.

cloaked predators Antonio and Sebastian) but, in a halting epilogue of Benjaminian melancholy, with his own limitations: no longer 'the lord of creatures, . . . he remains a creature'.[78]

Prospero's final speech, hovering indecisively between the play world and the world of the audience,[79] sounds a curiously despondent note. The power is gone, the god-like magus reduced to his own strength, '[w]hich is most faint' (Ep. 3). The descent that has brought him this low can be traced in his abjuration speech earlier in Act V. Beginning with the noontide sun and ending with drowning—if only the drowning of 'my book'—the speech reinscribes the trajectory of Icarus' fall (V. i. 33–57). But, contrary to the classical hubris pattern, Prospero's fall is self-induced, resulting from what could perhaps be described as a state of existential vertigo, a *mise en abîme* extending well beyond artistic self-reference, which plunges 'the great globe itself' into the void. Prospero's address to the audience reinforces the play's pervasive sense of confinement, but with the difference that he himself is the prisoner now, 'confined . . . In this bare island' (Epilogue 4 and 8), begging to be released. The mind-powered ascendancy of human aspiration (of human presumption, as Montaigne would say) comes under a dizzying spell of unreality in the latter part of the play. Our little human life is 'rounded with a sleep' (IV. i. 158). In the play's opposition of civilization and wilderness, human and animal, it is also something like a clearing rounded with a forest, and the effort to maintain this clearing is always confronted with its own futility, always in danger of folding back upon itself, as in the threats of punishment that Prospero heaps on Caliban:

> If thou neglect'st or dost unwillingly
> What I command, I'll rack thee with old cramps,
> Fill all thy bones with aches, make thee roar
> That beasts shall tremble at thy din.   (I. ii. 370–3)

Punitive discipline unleashes the beast it seeks to repress. If Caliban's 'beast-like nature is the justification for the torments', these torments, Mary Crane observes, are 'relentlessly imagined as turning him into a beast . . . Prospero's persistent linking of pain that he causes with animal noises breaks down the distinctions between human and animal or savage that he insists upon'.[80]

---

[78] Benjamin, *The Origin of the German Tragic Drama*, 85.
[79] See Weimann, *Author's Pen and Actor's Voice*, 224, for discussion of the in-between status of the epilogue.
[80] Crane, *Shakespeare's Brain*, 188 and 186.

The isle is indeed 'full of noises', and not just those 'that give delight and hurt not' (III. ii. 135–6). To Alonso, the King of Naples, the roaring of the tempest becomes the voice of his own guilty conscience:

> O, it is monstrous, monstrous!
> Methought the billows spoke and told me of it,
> The winds did sing it to me, and the thunder,
> That deep and dreadful organ-pipe, pronounced
> The name of Prosper. It did bass my trespass.
> Therefore my son i' th' ooze is bedded, and
> I'll seek him deeper than e'er plummet sounded,
> And with him there lie mudded.   (III. iii. 95–102)

Nature speaks the name and *in* the name of Prospero. *Logos* and *nomos* become articulate in the voice of the thunder. But while this perfect godlike mastery of mind over matter ensures the plot's successful dynastic conclusion, it is far less successful in keeping the common animality of all the creatures of the island at bay, including his own. In the soundscape of *The Tempest* the voice of *nomos* is engulfed by the inarticulate voices of a teeming wildlife. In a non-vertical chain of being even the airy spirit Ariel is endowed with a body fully capable of creaturely pain, whose 'groans / Did make wolves howl and penetrate the breasts / Of ever-angry bears' (I. ii. 288–9). Caliban is the crucial link in this chain, with his acquired language of curses, his poetic idiom of non-rational experience, and his association with the cries, howls, and roars of the beasts of the forest. As such, he is also Shakespeare's final intimation of the link between the human stage and the animal-baiting arena, the link that will go missing after the Restoration.

V. A Severance and a Reunion: Descartes to Nietzsche

The rest of this chapter will examine what came after Shakespeare's engagement with the human–animal continuum and after the intermedial collusion that linked his stage with the stake and the scaffold. This is, of course, a wide-ranging topic which could easily fill another volume. What I offer instead is abridgement, turning, as it were, 'th'accomplishment of many years / Into an hourglass' (*Henry V*, Prologue 30–1). Straddling centuries across a radically condensed history of the afterlife of Shakespeare's Caliban, I will focus on two decisive turning points: the rift that separates the modern episteme from Shakespeare's universe of human–animal permeability, and the emergence of a counter-discourse which revoked that rift. This book, whose main concern has been with human–animal relations before the ascent of Cartesian rationality, thus ends with a glimpse at what comes after the crisis of the Cartesian paradigm. Set off by this crisis, the fundamental repositioning of humankind in relation to the other animals is a process that continues today, and it seems to me that in rediscovering the permeability of the divide that sets us apart from other species we are only beginning to catch up with the 'zoographic' imagination of Shakespeare.

★

When René Descartes's radical doubt comes to rest in the intuition of a single indubitable certainty—the 'I' that thinks, *cogito*— the animal ends up on the other side of the great divide: capable of movement, of sensation, perhaps even of some more complex emotions,[81] but categorically lacking what is exclusive to 'man': the ability to think:

> Nor will this appear at all strange to those who are acquainted with the variety of movements performed by the different automata, or moving machines fabricated by human industry, and that with the help of but few pieces compared with the great multitude of bones, muscles, nerves, arteries, veins, and other parts that are found in the body of an animal. Such persons will look upon this body as a machine made by the hands of God, which is incomparably better arranged, and adequate to movements more admirable than is any machine of human invention.[82]

'Incomparably better arranged', but ultimately just like any other 'moving machine', animals as Descartes conceives them are separated from man by the fundamental rift that marks the beginning of modern philosophy.[83] Like

---

[81] Whether Descartes denies the animals not only thought but also feeling, classing them with lifeless 'stones or machines or plastic dolls', as some modern critics have maintained, is a contested question. Descartes himself is somewhat inconsistent on this issue. The Letter to Newcastle (23 Nov. 1646) grants some animals even such complex affects as hope. The letter to Gibieuf, 19 Jan. 1642, seems to deny such faculties. The fifth part of *Principia philosophiae* on plants and animals might have clarified his position but remained unwritten. An excellent analysis of Descartes's views on animals and the critical discussion they have elicited is in Wild, *Die anthropologische Differenz*, 135–51.

[82] René Descartes, *A Discourse on Method*, trans. John Veitch (London and New York: Dent and Dutton, 1953), 44.

[83] 20th-c. philosophy has increasingly questioned the hegemony of the Cartesian tradition and advanced alternative strands of modernity, e.g. those deriving from Montaigne. Cf. Stephen Toulmin, *Cosmopolis: The Hidden Agenda of Modernity* (New York: The Free Press, 1990).

the human body, the animal—which in Descartes's view is all body—belongs to the world of objects, *res extensa*, which the thinking subject, *res cogitans*, contemplates from the vantage point of the rational soul which 'is of a nature wholly independent of the body'.[84] Indispensable though it is for the Cartesian 'disassociation of essential self from body',[85] more specifically for his attack on the Scholastic–Aristotelian conception of a three-tiered soul, the demotion of animals to self-propelled clockworks is hardly Descartes's main goal. It is also that part of his philosophy which was immediately challenged by his contemporaries as both absurd and morally reprehensible. Its direct influence on general attitudes towards animals and animal treatment must have been rather limited. Its historical significance is rather as harbinger of a new epistemic regime which placed man, no longer within, but opposite the natural world as observer, experimenter, manipulator.[86]

Of all the fanciful guises in which Caliban has appeared in his post-Jacobean career, it is the most fanciful of all that is, oddly enough, perfectly in keeping with Cartesian rationalism. The Polish-German artist Daniel Chodowiecki (1726–1801), best known as the chronicler of bourgeois domesticity in Frederician Prussia, cordoned off Caliban from the human in a Cartesian binary of absolute difference. His Caliban resembles a monster tortoise, looking somewhat like an evolutionary ancestor of the Teletubby (Fig. 12).

Begotten no doubt by literalizing Prospero's 'Come, thou tortoise, when?' (I. ii. 317), this 'strange thing as e'er I looked on' (V. i. 290) marks the furthest point of separation between master and slave, humanity and the bestial, in the pictorial history of Shakespeare's changeling. This creature is no longer liminal but a monster to be marvelled at, certainly not a dark mirror of the self. The bizarre image gives the human–animal dualism inscribed in the antagonistic relation between Prospero and Caliban a stability it does not have in Shakespeare's play. But the very impossibility of the figure makes it rationally acceptable as pure, unadulterated fantasy. This is enhanced through further distancing: Chodowiecki removes Shakespeare's figure of indeterminacy to a safely circumscribed dream world

---

[84] Descartes, *Discourse*, 46.
[85] Michael Schoenfeldt, *Bodies and Selves* (Cambridge: Cambridge University Press, 1999), 11.
[86] Cf. Hassan Melehy, 'Silencing the Animals: Montaigne, Descartes, and the Hyperbole of Reason', *symplokē*, 13 (2005), 263–82.

Figure 12. Daniel Nikolaus Chodowiecki, 'The Tempest', in *Goettinger Taschen Calender 1788*.

of exotic fabulation where simply everything is possible and nothing is real.[87] The potential of Shakespeare's Caliban to unsettle the very category of humanness to which he is persistently refused admittance has been effectively obliterated.

This holds true also for the dominant eighteenth- and nineteenth-century stage tradition which—while stopping short at the bizarrerie of Chodowiecki—used animal markers to keep the unruly creature 'stied', contained in clearly demarcated otherness. Not even when a popularized Darwinism claimed Caliban as the Bard's visionary anticipation of the missing link[88] did

---

[87] This fable world is reminiscent—as the turbaned Prospero suggests—of the recently famous *Tales of the Arabian Nights*. Their European success began with Antoine Galland's French edition of 1704, which was quickly followed by an anonymous English version in 1706 and Ambrose Philips's *The Thousand and One Days: Persian Tales* in 1714.

[88] Daniel Wilson, *Caliban: The Missing Link* (London: Macmillan, 1873).

Shakespeare's islander recover his subversive force. Unsettling though the Darwinian revolution proved for Western culture at large, the resulting 'anthropological anxiety'[89] seems to have been absent from late nineteenth- and early twentieth-century productions of *The Tempest*. These productions used Darwinist clichés to endorse, rather than undermine, anthropocentric humanism. If *The Descent of Man* animalized *homo sapiens*, popular appropriations (not without prompt from Darwin's own writings[90]) were quick to map man's evolutionary ascent onto the ethnic and social divisions within the species. With the Victorian gentleman at the top and the rest of humanity on lower rungs of the evolutionary ladder, ascription of animality, now authorized by pseudo-science, could serve its age-old purpose of denying full human status to the beggar, the serf, the barbarian—in Victorian terms: the undeserving poor, the working class, the natives in the colonies.

Self-congratulatory Anglocentric Darwinism, reinforcing an exclusivist notion of (Western) humanness instead of unsettling it, fuelled Frank Benson's 1891 ape impersonation just as it did Herbert Beerbohm Tree's Caliban of 1904, who 'crawl[ed] out' from his rock-sty 'with a fish in his mouth'.[91] A 'sort of Demon King', 'something between a monkey and a wild man of the woods',[92] this Caliban was given unprecedented prominence in Tree's production. Though Prospero (William Haviland) had the last word, Caliban had the last silence. He even appropriated the melancholy pathos of his artist-master in a visual epilogue all of Tree's own making:

> Caliban listens for the last time to the sweet air, then turns sadly in the direction of the departing ship. The play is ended. As the curtain rises again, the ship is seen on the horizon, Caliban stretching out his arms towards it in mute despair. The night falls, and Caliban is left on the lonely rock. He is a King once more.[93]

Tree's upgrading of Caliban to Prospero's rival king of the island (even if it had been prompted, as critics sneered, by the fact that he played the part)

---

[89] I borrow the term from Virginia Richter, *Missing Links*.

[90] See e.g. Charles Darwin, *The Descent of Man, and Selection in Relation to Sex* (1871) (London: Penguin, 2004), 85–6.

[91] Quoting from Tree's prompt-book, Mary M. Nilan, '*The Tempest* at the Turn of the Century: Cross-Currents in Production', *Shakespeare Survey*, 25 (1972), 113–23 at 120.

[92] R. Dickins, *Forty Years of Shakespeare on the English Stage, August 1867–August 1907: A Student's Memories* (London, 1907), 111–12, quoted in Brian Pearce, 'Beerbohm Tree's Production of *The Tempest*, 1904', *New Theatre Quarterly*, 11 (1995), 299–308 at 302.

[93] Quoted from a prompt-book in the Bristol University Theatre Collection in Pearce, 'Beerbohm Tree's Production of *The Tempest*', 304.

must be given credit as a remarkably innovative directorial decision.[94] But it is nonetheless firmly grounded in a Darwinist colonial imaginary, which is nowhere more apparent than in the final tableau. Translating key words of Prospero's epilogue (which according to the prompt-book was cut[95]) into dumb show, Tree presents a Caliban who has been 'set free' from his 'bands' and is yet all the more 'confined'; a Caliban whose 'ending is despair'— 'mute despair', a revocation of language—and whose 'hands' are stretched out towards his departing master in a gesture of 'prayer'. He may be 'King once more', but King of a 'bare island', a 'lonely rock' on which 'night falls' as the colonizer withdraws his 'charms', the gifts of enlightened civilization. This is the hirsute, clawed creature with mournful eyes that Charles A. Buchel captured in his painting of Tree's Caliban, the native of the White Man's Burden to whom the retreat of the colonizer means not liberation but loss, relapse into a primeval, subhuman form of life.

The contemporary descriptions of Tree's as well as Benson's Caliban all emphasize the liminal quality of the character, his 'half this/half that' nature, his inbetweenness, which had been supplanted by all-out monstrosity in Chodowiecki's image. But this liminality, 'half monkey, half coco-nut', 'something between a monkey and a wild man', does not infringe on the humanist certainties epitomized in Prospero, now by common consent regarded as the ghostly spokesman of the English national sage himself.[96] If the turn-of-the-century Calibans are perched on a threshold it is not one between 'above' and 'below', but between below and even further below, between *inferior* mankind and animality. 'Vulgar Darwinism' provides a buffer zone between gentleman and primate, an ample third to be surveyed and disciplined—and on occasion made fun of—from above.

★

From tortoise to ape to missing link, a cursory glance at the afterlife of Shakespeare's changeling signals a reopening of human–animal border

---

[94] Pearce, 'Beerbohm Tree's Production of *The Tempest*', 299, is I think right in claiming that 'Tree's production . . . , through the scholarship of G. Wilson Knight, influenced the main tradition of literary critical interpretation' in the 20th c.

[95] This goes for the prompt-book held by the Bristol University Theatre Collection.

[96] The identification of Prospero with Shakespeare, first suggested by Thomas Campbell in 1838, quickly caught on as one of the favourite fictions of biographical criticism. According to Michael Dobson, the identification can be traced back well into the 18th c., beginning with the inauguration of the Shakespeare statue in Westminster Abbey (1741) or, even earlier, with Charles Gildon's 'Shakespeariana' (1718). Michael Dobson, ' "Remember/First to possess his books": The Appropriation of *The Tempest*, 1700–1800', *Shakespeare Survey*, 43 (1991), 99–107 at 103–4.

traffic.[97] With the nineteenth century drawing to a close, the animal, though marginalized in an increasingly technological civilization, had returned to haunt and infiltrate the ambit of the human. Turn-of-the-century stage-Calibans register this. The Darwinist challenge to conventional anthropocentrism was making itself felt, but its pressure could still be contained, even as its stock image, the primeval ape-man, was being exploited for theatrical effect.

It is with Friedrich Nietzsche that Darwin's evolutionist 'dynamite' becomes a challenge to the foundations of rationalist modernity, the mainstream of Western philosophy inaugurated by Descartes's categorical separation of human from animal.[98] Darwin does not come off particularly well in Nietzsche's writings. Disapproval is unstinting, respect grudging, affiliation categorically denied.[99] But despite objections to specific aspects of Darwinian theory,[100] its fundamental importance shows in what Nietzsche describes as the crucial revolutionary thrust of his own philosophy: 'We no longer trace the origin of man in the "spirit," in the "divinity," we have placed him back among the animals.'[101]

'Animal nature is at the centre of Nietzsche's thought.'[102] If Descartes cut the cord of 'humanimality', Nietzsche's anti-metaphysical and 'Antichristian' project '[t]o translate humanity back into nature' marks the historical moment of its restitution. Though praising Descartes for his 'boldness . . . to

---

[97] For an excellent full survey see Vaughan and Vaughan, *Caliban*.

[98] Nietzsche says of himself 'I am not a man. I am dynamite'. Friedrich Nietzsche, *Ecce Homo: How One Becomes what One Is* (1908), trans. R. J. Hollingdale (London: Penguin, 1992), 96.

[99] Ibid. 41: 'Other learned cattle [Hornvieh] caused me . . . to be suspected of Darwinism.' But the 'learned cattle', for once, suspect right.

[100] Nietzsche's response to Darwin is captured in Margot Norris's formulation: 'Nietzsche misunderstands, rejects, and reappropriates an alienated version of Darwin's most radical thinking.' Margot Norris, *Beasts of the Modern Imagination: Darwin, Nietzsche, Kafka, Ernst and Lawrence* (Baltimore, Md. and London: Johns Hopkins University Press, 1985), 2. Norris calls Nietzsche's 'physiological, vitalistic approach' to his own biography 'itself inevitably derivative of Darwinian discoveries' (p. 74), notwithstanding his representing it as entirely of his own making or 'growing' within 'the natural etiology of his being' (p. 74).

[101] Friedrich Nietzsche, *Twilight of the Idols* (1889) and *The Antichrist* (1895), trans. R. J. Hollingdale (London: Penguin, 2003), 136. Commenting on this statement, T. J. Reed maintains: 'What he states as a conclusion has . . . , from his earliest essays on, been an axiom. To this extent Nietzsche is a Darwinian.' T. J. Reed, 'Nietzsche's Animals: Idea, Image and Influence', in Malcolm Pasley (ed.), *Imagery and Thought* (London: Methuen, 1978), 159–219 at 160.

[102] Reed, 'Nietzsche's Animals', 159. See also Ralph R. Acampora, 'Nietzsche's Feral Philosophy: Thinking through an Animal Imaginary', in Christa Davis Acampora and Ralph R. Acampora (eds.), *A Nietzschean Bestiary: Becoming Animal beyond Docile and Brutal* (Lanham, Md.: Rowman and Littlefield, 2004), 1–13, and Vanessa Lemm, *Nietzsche's Animal Philosophy: Culture, Politics and the Animality of the Human Being* (New York: Fordham University Press, 2009).

think of the animal as a *machine*',[103] Nietzsche sharply rejects the idealistic mind–body dualism which this boldness begets. Where Descartes needs the animal body-machine in order to detach from it the 'cogital'[104] core of the human subject, Nietzsche applauds the scientific rigour of the machine idea[105] but categorically rejects the detachment. ' "Pure spirit" ', he taunts, 'is pure stupidity: if we deduct the nervous system and the senses, the "mortal frame", *we miscalculate*—that's all!'[106] For Nietzsche, the human is not above but inescapably bound up with animal nature:

> When one speaks of *humanity*, underlying this idea is the belief that it is humanity that *separates* and distinguishes human beings from nature. But there is, in reality, no such distinction: the 'natural' qualities and those properly called 'human' grow inseparably. Human beings in their highest and noblest capacities are wholly nature and bear within themselves its uncanny dual character.[107]

Like Montaigne before him—and with a stab at popular Darwinism— Nietzsche deplores the delusion of anthropocentric exceptionalism, 'the vanity that man is the great secret objective of animal evolution. Man is absolutely not the crown of creation: every creature stands beside him at the same stage of perfection.'[108] But this recognition entails no easy 'return to nature', no comfortable all-embracing harmony, once the fallacies of ascetic idealism (Platonic, Judaeo-Christian) are exposed and rejected. Man cannot simply become animal precisely because he is no simple animal, but the most complex, most problematic one.[109] He cannot be

---

[103] Nietzsche, *Twilight* and *Antichrist*, 136.

[104] Friedrich Nietzsche, 'On the Use and Abuse of History [for Life]' (1874), trans. Adrian Collins, in *The Complete Works of Friedrich Nietzsche: The First and Complete and Authorised English Translation*, v: *Thoughts out of Season, Part II*, ed. Oscar Levy (New York: Russell and Russell, 1964), 1–100 at 94: 'I am permitted the empty *esse*, not the full green *vivere*. A primary feeling tells me that I am a thinking being but not a living one, that I am no "animal," but at most a "cogital." "Give me life, and I will soon make you a culture out of it"—will be the cry of every man in this new generation, and they will all know each other by this cry. But who will give them this life?'

[105] Nietzsche's idea of the natural animal body is not that of a machine (which inevitably entails notions of heterotelic instrumentality and of a 'divine watchmaker') but of autotelic organic growth, *physis* in the original Greek sense of the word.

[106] Nietzsche, *Twilight* and *Antichrist*, 137.

[107] Friedrich Nietzsche, 'Homer's Contest' (1871) ['Re/Introducing "Homer's Contest"': A New Translation with Notes and Commentary'], trans. Christa Davis Acampora, *Nietzscheana*, 5 (1996), pp. i–iv and 1–8 at 2.

[108] Nietzsche, *Twilight* and *Antichrist*, 136.

[109] Man is 'a fantastic animal', unique among species in his need 'to believe that he knows the reason for his existence'. He is 'the most endangered animal', 'an animal in the highest degree subject to fear', but also 'the bravest animal' and 'the cruellest', 'the not yet fixed animal', 'the sick animal' and 'the most interesting animal' (Nietzsche quotations in Reed, 'Nietzsche's Animals', 159).

dissevered from nature but cannot fully merge and cannot *want* to fully merge with nature either: 'According to nature you want to live? O you noble Stoics, what deceptive words these are!' Wasteful 'beyond measure' and 'indifferent beyond measure', nature cannot be the yardstick of human action. 'Living—', Nietzsche asks, 'is that not precisely wanting to be other than this nature?'[110]

There is an irreducible ambiguity in Nietzsche's conception of human animality, a dynamics of 'atavistic going-under' and 'noble overcoming'[111] defying systematic closure. The figure of the *Übermensch* is conceived as 'a centaur, half human, half animal'.[112] His heroic task is one of both 'cultivating and transforming animality'.[113] 'The human being is a rope, tied between the animal and the overhuman',[114] Nietzsche declares in the prologue of *Zarathustra*, couching his bid for the future of humanity in an image of unmistakably pre-Cartesian provenance. The 'rope' evokes both the continuum of 'ensouled' life envisaged as a Great Chain of Being and the 'in-betweenness' of Pico's self-creative Adam. '[T]he Antients', wrote Edward Tyson in 1699,

> were fond of making Brutes to be Men: on the contrary now, most unphilosophically, the Humour is, to make Men but meer Brutes and Matter. Whereas in truth Man is part a Brute, part an Angel; and is that Link in the Creation, that joyns them both together.[115]

This is a very late expression of faith in a continuum which had already begun to be torn apart by the disruptive forces of modernity. What Tyson called the 'Link in the Creation' was intended to mark the crucial position of man as the interface of heaven and earth in a model of cosmic harmony, but it turned out to be, quite contrary to intention, a point of extreme tension.[116] Nietzsche's *Übermensch*, of course, represents nothing like the

---

[110] Friedrich Nietzsche, *Beyond Good and Evil* (1886), trans. R. J. Hollingdale (London: Penguin, 2003), 39, § 9.

[111] Acampora, 'Nietzsche's Feral Philosophy', 6.

[112] Friedrich Nietzsche, *Human, All Too Human* (1878), trans. Marion Faber and Stephen Lehmann, ed. Marion Faber (London: Penguin, 2004), 149, §241.

[113] Acampora, 'Nietzsche's Feral Philosophy', 6.

[114] Friedrich Nietzsche, *Thus Spoke Zarathustra*, trans. and ed. Walter Kaufmann (New York: Modern Library, 1995), 4, 'Prologue'.

[115] Tyson, *Orang-Outang, sive Homo Sylvestris*, appendix, 55.

[116] The tension shows not least in Tyson's own, somewhat paradoxical position. As a comparative anatomist he was part of the development he deplores. His scientific—as opposed to theological—clarification of species distinction made an important contribution to the clearing out of the human-animal border zone compatible with the older *scala naturae*. Cf. the title of his

pure spirituality of an angel, nor is his animal 'mere brute and matter'.[117] Nietzsche adapts a key metaphor of pre-modern cosmology, but he rejects its metaphysics. The 'rope [between animal and overhuman] is never cut by Nietzsche—rather, the braiding of its strands is only tightened and celebrated.'[118] This sets Nietzsche apart from neo-Platonic eulogies on the spirit's triumph over beast and federates him with Shakespeare. Shakespeare's polyphonic texts can hardly be said to 'celebrate' the rope (or, for that matter, unconditionally deplore or condemn it) but, as we have seen, they pervasively affirm its tightness.

There is no explicit reference in Nietzsche to Shakespeare's insight into the animal condition of the human, but his praise for Shakespeare's rendering of the passions comes at least close to affirming such a connection. Under the heading 'Shakespeare the moralist', he writes:

> Shakespeare reflected a great deal on passions, and by temperament probably had very easy access to many of them (dramatists in general are rather wicked people). But, unlike Montaigne, he was not able to talk about them; rather he laid his observations *about* passions in the mouths of his passionate characters. Of course, this is unnatural, but it makes his dramas so full of thought that all other dramas seem empty and easily inspire a general aversion.[119]

There are unmistakable cues of affiliation. To have impassioned characters reason about their passions may be 'against nature' (in the sense of being, in conventional terms, 'unrealistic'). But this 'unnatural' technique does indeed render human nature so truthfully as to make 'all other drama seem empty', as is underscored by the parenthesis that has dramatists being 'rather wicked', by the term 'moralist' and by the mention of Montaigne. This evokes another, more famous observation from *Human, All Too Human* in which 'La Rochefoucauld and those other French masters of soul searching' are likened to 'accurately aimed arrows, which hit the mark again and again, the black mark of man's nature'.[120] If they are credited with hitting the

appendix: 'A Philological Essay concerning the Pygmies, the Cynocephali, the Satyrs and Sphinges of the Antients: Wherein it will appear that they were all either Apes or Monkeys; and not Men, as formerly pretended.'

[117] For useful clarification, see Lemm, *The Animal in Nietzsche's Philosophy*, 2: 'Rejecting a biologistic interpretation, I consider Nietzsche's thesis to be that every organic cell has spirit. In similar fashion, I reject the anthropocentric interpretation of life and consider Nietzsche's thesis to be that spirit is physiological.'

[118] Acampora, 'Nietzsche's Feral Philosophy', 6.

[119] Nietzsche, *Human, All Too Human*, 118, §176.

[120] Ibid. 40–1, §36.

'black mark' (*ins Schwarze*, literally 'into the black'), the Moralists, and by extension Shakespeare as moralist, must be hitting what Nietzsche takes to be the basic given of that nature, animality. 'The black' is not only the 'bull's eye' but also a darkness that requires hitting 'again and again', a depth that will never fully disclose itself.[121]

Being 'rather wicked' inoculates Nietzsche's Shakespeare against idealistic distortion. It enables him to see beyond civilized (that is, tamed) 'goodness' to conceive the transgressively 'overhuman' animality of a Coriolanus or a Macbeth. But it is the, at first glance much less formidable, figure of Julius Caesar that Nietzsche singles out as defining 'my highest formula for *Shakespeare*' in a passage of *Ecce Homo*, poignant for its desperate, megalomaniac exaltation, which he wrote only weeks before his final breakdown in the sobbing embrace of a cart horse that he saw being cruelly whipped by its driver in Turin's Piazza Carlo Alberto:

> When I seek my highest formula for *Shakespeare* I find it always in that he conceived the type of Caesar. One cannot guess at things like this—one is it or one is not. The great poet creates *only* out of his own reality—to the point at which he is afterwards unable to endure his own work . . . When I have taken a glance at my Zarathustra I walk up and down my room for half an hour unable to master an unendurable spasm of sobbing.—I know of no more heartrending reading than Shakespeare: what must a man have suffered to need to be a buffoon to this extent!—Is Hamlet *understood*? It is not doubt, it is *certainty* which makes mad . . . But to feel in this way one must be profound, abyss, philosopher . . . We all *fear* truth . . .[122]

Nietzsche's identification with Shakespeare, or rather his identification of Shakespeare as Nietzsche, could hardly be more total. The epitome of the dramatist's achievement is that 'he conceived the type of Caesar'—hardly the most impressive character in the Shakespearean canon, but that is beside the point.[123] At issue is not character but type, the perpetual idea, phantasm or, as the play puts it, the ghost of Caesar that set in motion not just a dynasty but the whole history of Western rulership, reaffirmed by the

---

[121] I am indebted for this to Karlheinz Stierle, 'Der Moralist als Bogenschütze: Nietzsche und Larochefoucauld', section I of his essay 'Was heißt Moralistik?', in Rudolf Behrens and Maria Moog-Grünewald (eds.), *Moralistik: Anthropologischer und ästhetischer Diskurs des Subjekts in früher Neuzeit und Moderne* (Munich: Fink, 2010) 1–22.

[122] Nietzsche, *Ecce Homo*, 28–9.

[123] See Scott Wilson, 'Reading Shakespeare with Intensity: A Commentary on Some Lines from Nietzsche's *Ecce Homo*', in John J. Joughin (ed.), *Philosophical Shakespeares* (London and New York: Routledge, 2000), 86–104.

investiture of the Prussian king Wilhelm as the first kaiser, or caesar, of Germany's 'Second Reich' in 1871.[124] But world history, the history of an assassinated Roman general who spawned empires, does not happen out there; it is acted out as personal psychodrama of the autobiographical author-subject of *Ecce Homo*. Shakespeare, Nietzsche declares, could not have made up a Caesar, could not have conceived the type unless he was of that type. That sort of thing (the type of Caesar) cannot be guessed (in the sense of imagined or invented)—'one is it or one is not. The great poet creates [or draws from; *schöpft*] only out of his own reality.' The poet-philosopher, one could thus say, must be able to conjure in himself the mindset, the drives, the energy of the conquering man of action. But this would still be just 'guessing', imagining oneself as Caesar rather than *being* him. The bolder, less 'reasonable' reading would transfer the poet-philosopher from the role of a reflector or recorder to that of an agent of history. This ambition seems much closer in spirit to the euphoric bravado of the opening announcement of *Ecce Homo*: 'Seeing that I must shortly approach mankind with the heaviest demand that has ever been made on it, it seems to me indispensable to say *who I am*.'[125]

What is that 'heaviest of demands' with which the ill and isolated, largely unread author proposes to shake the world? There is no telling. 'I will do such things—' exclaims the powerless Lear on the brink of madness; 'What they are, yet I know not; but they shall be / The terrors of the earth' (*Lear* vii. 439–41; (II. ii)). The beginning of *Ecce Homo* suggests that the writer means his imminent feat to be more than another piece of writing.[126] This would explain not only the crucial role attributed to Caesar in 'my ultimate formula for Shakespeare' but also the rather sudden apparition of Lord Bacon as the true begetter, behind the mask of 'Shakespeare', of both Caesar and the heart-rending buffoonery of Hamlet:[127]

> And, to confess it: I am instinctively certain that Lord Bacon is the originator, the self-tormentor [selbsttierquäler] of this uncanniest species of literature: what do *I* care about the pitiable character of American shallow-pates and muddle-

---

[124] Nietzsche found little to praise about the newly united Reich and its self-declared grandness. In 1888 he wrote: ' "German spirit": for eighteen years a *contradiction in adjecto*.' Nietzsche, *Twilight and Antichrist*, 35.

[125] Nietzsche, *Ecce Homo*, 3.

[126] To be sure, the concluding section of *Ecce Homo* suggests that the world-shaking task has already been accomplished in his writings, which the autobiography recapitulates one by one.

[127] Peter Holbrook, 'Nietzsche's *Hamlet*', *Shakespeare Survey*, 50 (1997), 171–86, compellingly traces Nietzsche's identificatory engagement with Shakespeare's prince.

heads? But the power for the mightiest reality of vision is not only compatible with the mightiest power for action, for the monstrous in action, for crime—*it even presupposes it*...We do not know nearly enough about Lord Bacon, the first realist in every great sense of the word, to know *what* he did, *what* he wanted, *what* he experienced within himself...[128]

The passage construes a double concatenation of doubles converging in the autobiographical subject of *Ecce Homo*: Hamlet is Shakespeare is Nietzsche; Caesar is Shakespeare is Nietzsche. For this double identification to work, Shakespeare must become Bacon, in whom reality of vision, the certainty that drives one insane, and the abyss that can only be endured by playing the fool conjoin with the mightiest force of action, the monstrous, the crime.

Deriding the Baconians, Nietzsche appropriates their biographical phantasm for his own phantasmal self-image as historical *force majeure*.[129] He concludes the section with a further ironic equation. What if he, Friedrich Nietzsche, like Lord Bacon had chosen to conceal his Zarathustra under the name of another imposturous 'Shakespeare'—Richard Wagner for example?

> And the devil take it, my dear critics! Supposing I had baptized my Zarathustra with another name, for example with the name of Richard Wagner, the perspicuity of two millennia would not have sufficed to divine that the author of 'Human, All Too Human' is the visionary of Zarathustra...[130]

Nietzsche's final work resembles Shakespeare's last play in that both are centred on the type of the artist-as-ruler. The magician Prospero who controls the *force majeure* of the elements and at whose command the dead wake from their sleep (V. i. 49) and the messianic, or anti-messianic, poet-philosopher of *Ecce Homo* whose exposure of Christian morality causes the 'catastrophe' that 'breaks the history of humanity into two parts'[131] are linked by the spectral presence of the precursor of modern science, Francis Bacon.

It is possible that King James's solicitor-general and later Lord Chancellor Bacon was actually present at one of the two recorded performances of *The Tempest* at court. Although—to borrow a favourite phrase of Shakespeare biographers—it would be tempting to think so, there is no need to venture

---

[128] Nietzsche, *Ecce Homo*, 29.
[129] Cf. the title of the last chapter of *Ecce Homo*: 'Why I am a Destiny'; 'The *unmasking* of Christian morality is an event without equal, a real catastrophe. He who exposes it is a *force majeure*, a destiny—'. Nietzsche, *Ecce Homo*, 103.
[130] Ibid. 29.
[131] Nietzsche, *Ecce Homo* 103.

such a claim. Baconian science is clearly part of the concoction of know-ledge cultures which the play cooks up on Prospero's laboratory island, an emergent historical force holding the promise of dominating nature with the 'vexations of art'. The Baconian instrumentalizing approach to nature heralded by *The Tempest* marks, as we have seen, a point of departure, the beginning of a trajectory away from the human–animal connectedness at the core of Shakespeare's early modern anthropology.

Launching a rebirth of the human *animal*, Nietzsche stages a surprise resurrection of Bacon. In Nietzsche's earlier writings, Bacon, as is to be expected, figures as the champion of anti-idealist, anti-ideological science. But in *Ecce Homo* he acquires the far more complex persona encapsulated in the striking Nietzschean coinage *Selbsttierquäler*. The German noun *Tierquäler*, tormentor of animals, is given a self-destructive twist which bends the outward-directed vexations of art back at the 'self-vexer', the tormentor of the animal that he is himself. Where Bacon's scientific utopia envisages man perched on an Archimedian control tower surveying nature, Nietzsche's Baconian alter ego is ineluctably placed within it. The *Selbsttierquäler* recalls a similar self-reflexiveness in the spectre of Bacon hovering behind the vexations, the pinching and racking of Prospero's art. Both hit again and again into the black, both are inescapably possessed of, and possessed by, the thing of darkness.

VI. Epilogue: Flesh Invisible

Charles and Mary Cowden Clarke's *Recollections of Writers* (1878) must be among the more unlikely places to come upon a scene of bear-baiting. It is a scene of bear-baiting mimicked by one of the principal subjects of Charles's recollections, whose 'entertainment with and appreciation of this minor scene of low life' produces an unforgettable performance:

> But his concurrent personification of the baiting, with his position,—his legs and arms bent and shortened till he looked like Bruin on his hind legs, dabbing his fore paws hither and thither, as the dogs snapped at him, and now and then acting the gasp of one that had been suddenly caught and hugged—his own capacious mouth adding force to the personation, was a remarkable and as memorable a display. I am never reminded of this amusing relation but it is associated with that forcible picture in Shakespeare, in *Henry VI*:

> . . . As a bear encompass'd round with dogs,
> Who having *pinch'd* a few and *made them cry*,
> The rest stand all aloof and bark at him.[132]

The animal impersonator who left such a vivid imprint on his friend's memory was none other than the young John Keats. Hard though it may be to reconcile with the tender youth memorialized in Shelley's 'Adonais', the scene is not incongruous with Keats's Shakespearean 'poetical Character' who 'lives in gusto, be it foul or fair' and 'has as much delight conceiving an Iago as an Imogen', the 'cameleon poet' who 'has no Identity' because he 'is continually in for—and filling some other Body', uncensored by the virtuous thoughtfulness of the 'wordsworthian or egotistical sublime'.[133] Biographical interest apart, Keats's animal impersonation offers an intriguing glimpse at the lingering afterlife of Renaissance bloodsports and the nexus between stake and stage. The 'hither and thither' movement of 'Bruin's' defence, for example, resembles the way in which an equally humanized bear ('a wight of great wizdom') fends off his attackers in the account of the Kenilworth bear-baiting in 1575: 'what shyft, with byting, with clawying, with roring, tossing and tumbling, he woold work too wynd himself from them'.[134] Both accounts follow a similar rhetorical pattern of cumulative intensification followed by a concluding summary of effect: '. . . was a matter of goodly relief' (Laneham), 'was a remarkable and as memorable a display' (Cowden-Clarke). While the Kenilworth chronicler relishes the 'the blud and the slaver about [the bear's] fiznamy', Cowden-Clarke's description is not only quite literally bloodless but studiously tones down the violence of the real-life event, from which the reader is distanced through a double filter of representation, histrionic and literary. Instead of 'byting' and 'clawying', there is mere 'snapping' and a none too dangerous 'hug' from the playfully ursine author of 'Endymion'.

---

[132] Charles Cowden Clarke and Mary Cowden Clarke, *Recollections of Writers* (1878; repr. Fontwell: Centaur Press, 1969), 145.

[133] Letter to Richard Woodhouse, 27 Oct. 1818, in *The Letters of John Keats*, ed. Hyder Edward Rollins (Cambridge: Cambridge University Press, 1958), i. 386–7. The bear-baiting imitation tallies with what other witnesses describe as Keats's extraordinary sensitivity to the natural world, be it 'the song of a bird . . . , the rustle of some animal, . . . the motions of the wind' or 'the wayfaring of the clouds'. This was so intense that it seemed to virtually transform him 'till he "would look sometimes like a wild fawn waiting for some cry from the forest depths," or like "a young eagle staring with proud joy before taking flight."' Sidney Colvin, *John Keats: His Life and Poetry, his Friends, Critics and After-Fame* (2nd edn., London: Macmillan, 1918), 79–80. Colvin cites 'paragraphs compiled by the late Mr William Sharp from many jotted reminiscences of [Keats's friend Joseph] Severn's.'

[134] Laneham, 'A Letter', 439–40.

Even more conspicuous, however, is the difference in social setting. What was a major scene of royal 'high life' in 1575 has become a 'minor scene of low life' in the nineteenth century. Not even in its Elizabethan heyday was bear-baiting an undisputedly respectable entertainment. But despite being denounced as base, coarse, vulgar, and irreligious, it was regularly frequented by the high-born, including the reigning monarch herself. By the end of the eighteenth century this cachet and clientele had given way to unambiguous disreputability and association with the 'riffraff' at the bottom end of society. Where Keats's contemporary Cowden-Clarke, looking back over the span of half a century, speaks frankly of 'low life', his later biographer Sidney Colvin, writing in 1917, cushions the episode in a frame of apologetic historicizing. To 'illustrate the wide and unfastidious range of [Keats'] contact with life', Colvin shows how the poet 'could enjoy and re-enact such a scene of brutal sport and human low-life as our refinement no longer tolerates',[135] though the First World War hardly seems the best of times for anyone to toast the advance of 'our refinement'.

Such distancing was already under way a century earlier, in what seems to have been one of the last, if not the last, account of animal baiting in English. 'There was a lion fight in the Amphitheatre at Vienna in the summer of 1790', *The Times* reported on 3 August 1825.[136] The event's having taken place three and a half decades previously and in another country marks it off from the news items on the same page. That this lion fight 'was almost the last permitted in that capital' further enhances the distance, and so does the venue, 'the Amphitheatre', which cannot but evoke the far-off Roman past. 'The lower part of the structure', the article explains, 'comprised the dens of the different animals. Above those dens, and about ten feet from the ground, were the first and principal seats, over which were galleries.'[137] The ensuing narrative, however, is not one of ancient cruelty and Christian martyrdom but of light-hearted travesty and comic relief:

In the course of the entertainment, a den was opened, out of which stalked, in free and ample range, a most majestic lion; and, soon after, a fallow deer was let into the circus from another den. The deer instantly fled, and bounded

[135] Colvin, *Keats*, 81.

[136] 'Lion Fight at Vienna', *The Times* (London), 3 Aug. 1825.

[137] The *Times* report is corroborated by contemporary Viennese sources. Cf. Felix Czeike, *Historisches Lexikon Wien*, 6 vols. (Vienna: Kremayr and Scheriau, 1992–7), iii. 175.

round the circular space, pursued by the lion; but the quick and sudden turnings of the former continually baulked the effort of its pursuer. After this ineffectual chase had continued for several minutes, a door was opened, through which the deer escaped; and presently five or six of the large and fierce Hungarian Mastiffs were sent in. The lion, at the moment of their entrance, was leisurely returning to his den, the door of which stood open. The dogs, which entered behind him, flew towards him in a body, with the utmost fury, making the amphitheatre ring with their barking. When they reached the lion, the noble animal stopped, and deliberately turned towards them. The dogs instantly retreated a few steps, increasing their vociferations, and the lion slowly resumed his progress towards his den. The dogs again approached; the lion turned his head; his adversaries halted; and this continued until, on his nearing his den, the dogs separated, and approached him on different sides. The lion then turned quickly round, like one whose dignified patience could brook the harassment of insolence no longer. The dogs fled far, as if instinctively sensible of the power of wrath they had at length provoked. One unfortunate dog, however, which had approached too near to effect his escape, was suddenly seized by the paw of the lion; and the piercing yells which he sent forth quickly caused his comrades to recede to the door of entrance at the opposite site of the area, where they stood in a row, barking and yelling in concert with their miserable associate. After arresting the struggling and yelling prisoner for a short time, the lion couched upon him with his forepaws and mouth. The struggles of the sufferer grew feebler and feebler, until at length he became perfectly motionless. We all concluded him to be dead. In this composed posture of executive justice, the lion remained for at least ten minutes, when he majestically rose, and with a slow step entered his den, and disappeared. The apparent corpse continued to lie motionless for a few minutes; presently the dog, to his amazement, and that of the whole amphitheatre, found himself alive, and rose with his nose pointed to the ground, his tail between his hind legs pressing his belly, and, as soon as he was certified of his existence, he made off for the door in a long trot, through which he escaped with his more fortunate companions.

In the course of the eighteenth century cruelty to animals had become a major issue of ethical concern and *The Times* report, published ten years before animal baiting was finally banned in Britain by Act of Parliament, reflects this concern. No doubt, King James would have been delighted at the lion's truly regal performance, which the Tower lions of his own day regrettably failed to deliver on more than one occasion. What would probably have pleased him less, though, is the failure of the royal beast at Vienna to achieve any maiming or killing. Like the account of Keats's bear pantomime, *The Times* carefully avoids any mention of bloodshed. The light

tone of the article and, it is safe to assume, the very existence of the text
depend on the comic relief that ensues when the seemingly dead dog turns
out to be alive. As other contemporary sources show, a less harmless
outcome invariably met with indignant disapproval and a call for the
abolishing of a barbarous sport.

Yet besides change, *The Times* article also bears witness to a remarkable
historical continuity. What we find is an unbroken chain of signification, a
semantic repertoire fully operative despite the changes of mentality that
caused the decline of, and would soon terminate, the practice that sustained and was sustained by this semantics. The lion, we note, is not just—
as he has been since time immemorial—'noble', 'most majestic', an aris-
tocratic being 'whose dignified patience' and 'power of wrath'[138] are
infinitely superior to the 'insolence' and noisy 'vociferations' of the (plebeian) dogs, but he also figures as the embodiment of 'executive justice',
performing the 'arrest' of a 'prisoner'. Thus, for all the reporter's studied
irony of genteel amusement, this late, studiously unsanguinary survival of
early modern blood-sports still preserves the elementary nexus between
animal baiting and the spectacle of punishment, the same nexus that shaped
Thomas Dekker's account of a bloodcurdling afternoon's entertainment on
Bankside in the early 1600s. With the blood, gore, and hellish noise
omitted, the spectacle takes on a typically nineteenth-century appearance.
In his 'composed posture', which the text freezes for the incredible span of
'at least ten minutes', the lion becomes a veritable emblem of power and
justice reminiscent of the well-nigh epidemic lions in the iconography of
European nationalism: rarely was Britannia or one of her Continental
sisters seen without one.

To the very last, then, the spectacle of animal baiting activates *synopsis*,
the double vision that enabled the intermedial collusion between stage,
stake, and scaffold in Shakespeare's London. The historically specific affinity
between the Shakespearean playhouse and the bear-garden did not outlast
the Restoration. But the perennial human habit of thinking with, and
meaning by, animals persisted after the theatre withdrew from this specific
historical configuration. Criminal justice continued to perform its gruesome
spectacles of public torture well into the second half of the eighteenth
century, though to a mounting chorus of abhorrence. The semiotics of

---

[138] 'Wrath', as we saw in *King Lear*, is the kind of anger associated with God or godlike
authority.

bestialization, inscribed in the ritual process of punishment and a fully functional part of its intended social message, became the principal argument against the juridical theatre of cruelty. The practice that sought to bestialize the culprit itself became regarded as bestial, a pattern of re-encoding we have encountered in Foxe's report of the burning of Huss. Symbolically downgraded to animal status, the tortured heretic reverses his doom into glorious martyrdom, while his tormentors turn into cruel butchers, cannibals, brutes. In Foxe's narrative, however, the enabling condition of this reversal is the heroic exceptionality of the martyr and his sacrifice. Not the penalty as such is condemnable, but its infliction on a confessor of the true faith. It is Huss's saintliness that makes the cruelty bestial, just as the bestiality of his punishment confirms his saintliness. In eighteenth-century campaigning for penal reform, by contrast, it is not the specific character of the condemned individual, but his most unspecific generic quality that makes his public torture intolerable. 'In the worst of murderers', Foucault writes, 'there is one thing, at least, to be respected when one punishes: his "humanity".'[139]

Formulated 'as a cry from the heart or from an outraged nature',[140] the crusade in the name of humanity did not stop at the borders of the human. The same sympathetic sentiments that motivated the campaign for penal reform and the anti-slavery movement[141] also fuelled the campaign for the prevention of cruelty to animals which led to the establishment of the SPCA in 1828.[142] As the sight of the tormented human body grew intolerable, so did the display of animals maiming and killing each other—especially when serving no other purpose than frivolous entertainment. The growing resistance to the sight of violated animals also reflected the changing material conditions of life brought about by the Industrial Revolution. In the transition from a predominantly rural to an urban civilization, the presence of animals in human experience declined and the majority of the population lost contact with livestock and forest animals. One upshot of this was the

---

[139] Foucault, *Discipline and Punish*, 74.

[140] Ibid.

[141] The Enlightenment demand for penal reform 'drew on the anti-slavery model', the 'iconic standing of the suffering slave' transferring 'easily to the suffering felon'. Gatrell, *The Hanging Tree*, 399.

[142] The SPCA was granted royal status in 1840. On the development of sympathetic attitudes to the suffering of animals, see Thomas, *Man and the Natural World*, 143–91; Harriet Ritvo, *Animal Estate: The English and Other Creatures in the Victorian Age* (Cambridge, Mass.: Harvard University Press, 1987), 125–66.

sentimentalizing of pets.[143] Another was the zoo, an artificial enclave of exotic fauna on display amidst a city environment. Clearly out of place and out of date was the older such urban enclosure of wildlife, the bear-garden.

The refinement of manners which Norbert Elias describes as a containment of man's animal body under the disciplinary regime of 'civility' increasingly applies to the non-human body as well.[144] What Hamlet refers to as 'country matters' passes from the animal-likeness of rustics to animals proper, and from offensive copulation to now equally offensive butchery.[145] Blood, formerly the very stamp of justice's authorization, becomes almost as private as semen, its shedding in public an obscenity. Tears, no longer 'womanish' but a sign of properly cultivated fine feeling, become the only socially acceptable body fluid. The occlusion of violence and of the violated body, whether human or animal, is part of the larger cultural work of eighteenth-century Sentimentalism. Laurence Sterne's hugely popular Yorick, travelling in France in quest of opportunities to wet his handkerchief, portrays this mentality and its concomitant role model, the man of feeling, to the verge of caricature. His encounter with the caged starling ('I can't get out')[146] shows that the moral imperative of philanthropic compassion now extends beyond ánthropos to man's non-human fellows.

'He prayeth well, who loveth well / Both man and bird and beast.'[147] Though it sits somewhat uneasily with the previously unfolded tale of arbitrary crime and punishment, this pious moral of Coleridge's Rime of the Ancient Mariner expresses a social consensus. What Montaigne had described as exceptional, his sensitivity to even the most everyday occurrence of physical cruelty ('a chickins necke puld off, or a pigge stickt'),[148] became the normative ethical response in nineteenth-century Britain.

---

[143] Cf. Kathleen Kete, The Beast in the Boudoir: Petkeeping in Nineteenth-Century Paris (Berkeley and London: University of California Press, 1994); Ritvo, Animal Estate, 82–121.

[144] Norbert Elias, The Civilizing Process: Sociogenetic and Psychogenetic Investigations, trans. Edmund Jephcott (rev. edn., Malden, Mass., and Oxford: Blackwell, 2000).

[145] Cf. Montaigne as discussed in Ch. 4 above: 'No man taketh delight to see wild beasts sport and wantonly to make much one of another: Yet all are pleased to see them tugge, mangle, and enterteare one an other.' Montaigne's Essays, ii. 122.

[146] Laurence Sterne, A Sentimental Journey through France and Italy (1768), ed. Graham Petrie (Harmondsworth: Penguin, 1967), 96.

[147] Samuel Taylor Coleridge, 'The Rime of the Ancient Mariner' (1797), in The Collected Works of Samuel Taylor Coleridge, Poetical Works, i: Poems (Reading Text), Part 1, ed. J. C. C. Mays (Princeton: Princeton University Press, 2001), 370–419 at 419, ll. 612–13.

[148] Montaigne's Essays, ii. 117.

At the same time, the likelihood of being confronted with a situation that would elicit this response decreased considerably. For a time—before the automobile made the last urban work animals redundant—the ill-treatment of carthorses was the most frequent cause of outrage among bourgeois animal-lovers.[149] After the ban on bear-baiting and cockfighting in Britain, bullfights abroad and fox-hunting at home gave cause for protest. But the pervasive, infinitely more momentous development is the invisibilizing of animal violation. Once more we find, as in the early modern examples, parallels in the treatment of animals and criminals, this time under a regime of concealment. In the case of the criminal, confinement and becoming unseen replace the public visibility of the theatre of execution. In the case of the animals, livestock and fowl, a common sight in rural communities, disappear for further processing behind the walls of the industrialized abattoir. The consumption of meat and the killing of animals come to inhabit hygienically disjunct spheres of awareness.

I want to close with two films—one early, one of recent date—in which this making invisible manifests itself despite being or rather precisely because it is temporarily suspended, making us see what is normally, and normatively, excluded from our field of cultural visibility.

My first example is a very brief (1′ 20″) one-reel 'actuality' film made in 1903. Produced by the Edison Company, it is a late product of the so-called 'war of currents' which was fought over what was to be the US standard electrical current.[150] Direct current (DC), patented by Thomas Alva Edison, had had a head start in the 1880s, but alternating current (AC), promoted by George Westinghouse and his partner Nikola Tesla, was catching up fast. AC would ultimately prove the superior system, but not without Edison's putting up fierce resistance. In 'a no-holds-barred smear campaign'[151] he aimed to convince the public of the dangers of alternating current, spreading false reports of AC-caused lethal accidents and arranging public killings of animals—stray dogs and cats, but also cows and horses—with alternating current. One product of the campaign was the AC-powered electric chair,

---

[149] Middle-class outrage rarely fails to vent its indignation at the 'brutishness' of the cab drivers. One typical example of many is Henry Curling, 'An Exposition of the Cruelties Practised upon the Cab and Omnibus Horses of London, Being a Chapter that All who Ride Should Read', in his *Recollections of the Mess-Table and the Stage* (London: Bosworth, 1855), 195–215.

[150] My source for this section is Tom McNichol, *AC/DC: The Savage Tale of the First Standards War* (San Francisco: Jossey-Bass, 2006).

[151] Craig Brandon, *The Electric Chair: An Unnatural American History* (Jefferson, NC: McFarland & Co., 1999), 72.

constructed by Harold P. Brown, an engineer secretly paid and instructed by Edison.[152] When the new invention was tried out on a human victim in 1890, the first jolt badly injured the condemned man but failed to kill him, so that the procedure had to be repeated. It was 'an awful spectacle, far worse than hanging', one witness reported, and Westinghouse declared: 'They would have done better using an axe.' Edison even attempted to popularize the term 'Westinghousing' as a synonym for electrocution. In 1903,[153] when the owners of a circus at Coney Island's Luna Park were looking for a way to put down a dangerous elephant, Edison, the wizard from Milan (Ohio),[154] suggested Westinghousing the creature and also had the event recorded on celluloid.

The elephant was called Topsy, a name suggestive of clumsy cuddliness, but Topsy had killed three men, the third supposedly having given the six-ton 36-year-old female a lighted cigarette to eat.[155] Considering Topsy an incalculable risk, the owners of Luna Park decided to have her destroyed. The method first thought of was hanging, but this raised protest from the American Society for the Prevention of Cruelty to Animals. It was then that Edison suggested electrocution. To make doubly sure, Topsy was administered a pound of potassium cyanide with her last meal of carrots. Then a 6,600-volt current was sent through her body and killed her within seconds. The execution took place in the Coney Island amusement park and was witnessed by an estimated 1,500 spectators. Edison's film of the event, released under the title *Electrocuting an Elephant*, was shown all over the United States.[156]

What the film shows in the noiseless drizzle of its faded images is the animal being led, criminal-like, in shackles to the place of execution, then, after a jump cut, the killing itself filmed in one long shot. After 'smoke erupt[ing] from her feet (which had been placed in special devices that introduced the current into her body)',[157] we see her going suddenly limp and collapsing.

---

[152] Ibid. 70.

[153] By this time the battle was over, the victory of alternating current no longer in doubt.

[154] Thomas Alva Edison was born in Milan, Ohio, in 1847. His popular sobriquet was 'The Wizard of Menlo Park', while Nikola Tesla, the Serbian inventor, was known as 'The Wizard of the West'.

[155] Some reports give Topsy's age as 28.

[156] *Electrocuting an Elephant*, dir. Jacob Blair Smith and Edwin S. Porter (Edison Manufacturing Company, 1903).

[157] Akira Mizuta Lippit, 'The Death of an Animal', *Film Quarterly*, 56 (2002), 9–22 at 12.

What follows is perhaps the most macabre moment of the film: In what appears to be a temporal lapse, the camera stops, then resumes filming. The interruption is registered by a slight jump cut. When the scene of the dying elephant resumes, a human figure returns with it, fading into the background behind the lifeless elephant's body. As the film ends, this human figure exits to the left. . . . It is as if the human being is there to accompany the elephant to the other world, an agent of the transition from one existential state to another. Or, the spirit of the elephant appears to transfer to the man. The human figure hovers on the surface of the shot, never fully absorbed—an ectoplasmic manifestation of the anthropomorphosis that infuses the electrocution.[158]

Accustomed as we are to the shock of ever more realistic simulations of blood and gore in modern films, this sequence of flickering images scarcely registers as a record of a real killing. It comes to us muffled in the haze of time-worn celluloid: instead of Dolby-sensurround, silence; instead of the plasticity of full-colour body texture, a pale grey silhouette, hardly more than a shadow. Before we realize what is happening, it is over. Yet the thick layer of obstructive mediality interposing between us and this death creates its own kind of intensity, owing perhaps to our sense of being witness to a scene of annihilation which seems to annihilate itself even as we are watching it: a glimpse of something close to pure temporality.[159]

Across the gulf of the centuries, the electrocution of Topsy the elephant pairs up weirdly with the medieval practice of hanging pigs for murder. It is a travesty of archaic category confusion, an act of antiquated mock-justice absurdly replayed with modern technology. Virtually point by point, element by element, it parallels the configurations linking animal baiting, criminal justice, and theatre that I have explored in the chapters of this book. If Coney Island (an island by name only) seems light years apart from Prospero's island, its analogies with Shakespeare's Southwark are unmistakable: a popular entertainment district, semi-respectable perhaps, located at a distance from the city. On the threshold of a new media age, film takes the place of the stage, and the scaffold gives way to the electric chair. Instead of 'Monsieur Hunks' being tied to the stake, an elephant named Topsy has 'a hawser . . . put around her neck', one end of which is

---

[158] Ibid.

[159] Akira Mizuta Lippit, *Electric Animal: Toward a Rhetoric of Wildlife* (Minneapolis: University of Minnesota Press, 2000), 197, sees Edison's film as emblematic: 'The advent of cinema is thus haunted by the animal figure, driven, as it were, by the wildlife after the death of the animal.' Cf. also Tom Gunning, 'The Cinema of Attractions: Early Film, Its Spectator, and the Avant-Garde', in Thomas Elsaesser (ed.), *Early Cinema: Space, Frame, Narrative*, (London: BFI, 1990), 56–62.

'attached to a donkey engine and the other to a post', while electrodes placed in copper-lined 'wooden sandals [are] attached to her feet'.[160] Just as the shows on Shakespeare's Bankside and in the early modern theatre of justice, the public execution of an elephant effects a slippage of human–animal distinction, an intermedial exchange of signifiers across a permeable species boundary. Interviewed by the *New York Times* in 2003, the proprietor of the Coney Island Museum is quoted as saying: ' "Coney Island, which was at the forefront of popular culture at the turn of the century, brought together electricity and film and entertainment and cruelty to animals... It's a seminal moment." '[161] Less seminal (if this implies future-directedness) than untimely, I would argue. For despite the deployment of cutting-edge killing equipment and media technology, the electrocution of an elephant is, more than anything else, a moment of glaring anachronism. What distinguishes it from its historical precedents is its cultural location. Stage, stake, and scaffold may have occupied similarly marginal spaces in the cultural topography of the early modern city, but they generated an exchange of meanings that spoke to that culture's central concerns. By contrast, the public electrocution of an elephant in 1903 is distinctly at odds with the cultural normality of twentieth-century modernity. It would have been normal, for example, to shoot the elephant; it would have been normal not to invite spectators, let alone a film crew. But the entrepreneurial logic that made the execution happen capitalized precisely on the *abnormality* of the event, of allowing us to see what our rules of propriety keep concealed. It draws on the calculated sensation of a freak show.

My second film is *Unser täglich Brot* (*Our Daily Bread*), a documentary about food production by the Austrian filmmaker Nikolaus Geyrhalter released in 2007.[162] It also discloses what is otherwise culturally invisible. But its approach is decidedly non-voyeuristic. Abruptly alternating between various scenes and modes of food production all over Europe, the film shows the industrialized processes that fabricate what we eat: the spraying of a field with insecticides, the machine-harvesting of olive trees, an endless stream of newly hatched chicks carried along, incessantly

---

[160] 'Bad Elephant Killed: Topsy Meets Quick and Painless Death at Coney Island', *Commercial Advertiser* (New York), Monday, 5 Jan. 1903.

[161] Tom Vanderbilt, 'City Lore; They Didn't Forget', *New York Times*, Sunday, 13 July 2003.

[162] *Unser täglich Brot* (*Our Daily Bread*, 2005), dir. Nikolaus Geyrhalter (Alive Productions, 2007), DVD.

chirping, on a conveyor belt, production lines of cows being milked, piglets castrated, oxen serially slaughtered and their bodies cut up and disembowelled in a smoothly efficient, fully automated process. Unlike other treatments of the subject,[163] *Our Daily Bread* abstains from campaigning. There are no interviews, no explanations, there is no exposure of culprits, indeed no commentary at all and no music either. But there is no lack of noise—from the soft hum or deafening roar of machines to the squealing, screeching, lowing of animals and the voices of workers engaged in mostly unintelligible conversations. The effect of the sound track is radically alienating, like a very noisy silent movie. The visual style is equally disconcerting, each scene captured by the calm gaze of an almost stationary camera. A succession of moving stills, the film develops an almost meditative rhythm as it shifts in calm detachment from cascading pig offal to a slaughterhouse worker quietly eating her lunch. The force and conviction of the film derive from its abstention from 'normal' language, from any 'normal' cinematic idiom—the idiom, for example, with which food commercials seek to persuade us of the naturalness of their products. The mechanical abruptness jolts us, arbitrarily it seems, from greenhouse to slaughterhouse to battery farming and back and mirrors the mechanized production processes we are made to witness. What the film shows is not so much dehumanization as 'de-animalization'. The workers come across as ordinary people doing their job. But precisely because there is nothing gratuitously brutal or callous in the calmly efficient way they handle the animals, the mere object status of the creatures we produce for our consumption becomes all the more devastatingly clear.

Unlike *Electrocuting an Elephant*, *Our Daily Bread* exposes no freakish anomaly but rather a normality that is not normally seen. In making visible what is culturally invisible, both films, each in its way, illustrate our distance from the early modern theatres of human–animal border traffic I have explored here.

There are parts of the world where bear-baiting is practised to this day, and it takes but a mouse-click to get there and watch. But appalling though this and other forms of voyeuristic cruelty to animals unquestionably are, they dwindle to near-insignificance beside the structural cruelty to animals

---

[163] *Darwin's Alptraum* (*Darwin's Nightmare*), dir. Hubert Sauper (Sunfilm Entertainment, 2005), DVD; *We Feed the World*, dir. Erwin Wagenhofer (Universum Film, 2006), DVD.

built into the Western consumer food supply system. 'We feed the world'—though parts of it appallingly less than others—but prefer not to see how. The parallels with the change of the penal system described by Foucault are too obvious to miss, except that for the animals the '*disappearance* of torture'[164] does not mean that it no longer exists. What the food industry shows—or rather what it does *not* show—is an object lesson in the dialectic of enlightenment, a stealthy triumph of instrumental reason, of the knowledge 'which is power' and 'knows no limits...in its enslavement of nature';[165] it is the fulfilment of Bacon's dream and of Descartes's 'to render ourselves masters and possessors of nature'.[166]

The bear-garden has been described as 'the most explicit and spectacular site of anthropocentrism in the early modern period, but...also the most explicit and spectacular site of humanity's confusion about itself'.[167] We lack such sites (or sights) and could no longer tolerate them, though we can hardly claim to have overcome either the anthropocentrism or the confusion. The collusion between stage, stake, and scaffold whose traces we have tracked in Shakespeare's theatre thus draws us with renewed urgency to what it means to be an animal that considers itself human.

---

[164] Foucault, *Discipline and Punish*, 7 (my italics).

[165] Theodor W. Adorno, with Max Horkheimer, *Dialectic of Enlightenment*, trans. Edmund Jephcott (Stanford: Stanford University Press, 2002), 2 'Enlightenment, understood in the widest sense as the advance of thought, has always aimed at liberating human beings from fear and installing them as masters. Yet the wholly enlightened earth is radiant with triumphant calamity.'

[166] Descartes, *Discourse*, 49.

[167] Fudge, *Perceiving Animals*, 19.

Bibliography

QUOTED SHAKESPEARE EDITION

Shakespeare, William, The Complete Works, ed. Stanley Wells and Gary Taylor, (2nd edn., Oxford: Clarendon Press, 2005).

OTHER EDITIONS USED

Coriolanus, ed. Lee Bliss, The New Cambridge Shakespeare (Cambridge: Cambridge University Press, 2000).

2 Henry VI, ed. Roger Warren (Oxford: Oxford University Press, 2002).

3 Henry VI, ed. John Dover Wilson (Cambridge: Cambridge University Press, 1952).

Hamlet, ed. G. R. Hibbard (Oxford: Oxford University Press, 1994).

The History of King Lear, ed. Stanley Wells, The Oxford Shakespeare (Oxford: Clarendon Press, 2000).

King Lear 1608 (Pied Bull Quarto), Shakespeare Quarto Facsimiles, 1 (Oxford: Clarendon Press, 1964).

King Lear, ed. R. A. Foakes, Arden, 3rd ser. (Walton-on-Thames: Thomas Nelson and Sons, 1997).

King Richard III, ed. Janis Lull (Cambridge: Cambridge University Press, 1999).

The Tempest, ed. Morton Luce (London: Methuen, 1901).

The Tempest, ed. Virginia Mason Vaughan and Alden T. Vaughan, Arden, 3rd ser. (Walton-on-Thames: Thomas Nelson and Sons, 1999).

The Third Part of Henry VI, ed. Michael Hattaway (Cambridge: Cambridge University Press, 1993).

Titus Andronicus, ed. John Dover Wilson (Cambridge: Cambridge University Press, 1948).

Titus Andronicus, ed. Eugene M. Waith, The Oxford Shakespeare (Oxford: Oxford University Press (1984).

Titus Andronicus, ed. Jonathan Bate, Arden, 3rd ser. (London: Thomson Learning, 2006).

The Tragedy of Macbeth, ed. Nicholas Brooke (Oxford: Oxford University Press, 1990).

The Winter's Tale, ed. Sir Arthur Quiller-Couch and John Dover Wilson (Cambridge: Cambridge University Press, 1959).

The Winter's Tale, ed. Stephen Orgel (Oxford: Oxford University Press, 1996).

The Winter's Tale, ed. Susan Snyder and Deborah T. Curren-Aquino (Cambridge: Cambridge University Press, 2007).

PRE-1700 WORKS

Aristotle, *On the Parts of Animals*, trans. with a commentary by James G. Lennox (Oxford: Clarendon Press, 2001).

—— *De Anima*, Books II and III (with passages from Book I), ed. and trans. D. W. Hamlyn (Oxford: Clarendon Press, 1968).

—— *Politics. Books I and II*, trans. with a commentary by Trevor J. Saunders, Clarendon Aristotle Series (Oxford: Clarendon Press, 1995).

Augustine, *The City of God*, trans. Marcus Dods (New York: The Modern Library, 1993).

—— *The Confessions of Saint Augustine*, trans. Edward B. Pusey (Teddington, Middlesex: Echo Library, 2006).

—— *De vera religione liber unus*, ed. William M. Green (Vienna: Hoelder-Pichler-Tempsky, 1961).

Bacon, Francis, *The Essays or Counsels Civil and Moral*, ed. Brian Vickers, Oxford World's Classics (Oxford: Oxford University Press, 1999).

—— 'The New Atlantis', in *Francis Bacon: A Critical Edition of the Major Works*, ed. Brian Vickers (Oxford: Oxford University Press, 1996), 457–89.

Bernini, Gian Lorenzo, *Fontana di Trevi*, ed. Cesare d'Onofrio (Rome: Staderini, 1963).

Bodin, Jean, *The Six Bookes of a Commonweale*, trans. Richard Knolles (London: G. Bishop, 1606; facs. repr., ed. Kenneth Douglas McRae. Cambridge, Mass.: Harvard University Press, 1962).

Boorde, Andrew, *Compendious Regiment or a Dietary of Health* (London: Wyllyam Powell, 1547).

Bullein, William, *A New Book Entitled the Government of Health* (London: John Day, 1558).

Caius, Iohannes, *Of English Dogges*, trans. Abraham Fleming (London: Rychard Johnes, 1576; facs. repr., Amsterdam and New York: Da Capo Press, 1969).

Capella, Galeazzo, *L'anthropologia di Galeazzo Capella secretario dell'illustrissimo signor duca di Milano* (Venice: Aldo Manuzio eredi and Andrea Torresano eredi, 1533).

Casas, Bartolomé de las, *The Devastation of the Indies. A Brief Account*, trans. Herma Briffault (Baltimore, Md.: Johns Hopkins University Press, 1992).

Casmann, Otto, *Psychologia anthropologica*, 2 vols. (Hanau: Fischer, 1594–6).

Cicero, *Brutus*, With an English translation by G. L. Henderson, Loeb Classical Library (London: William Heinemann; Cambridge, Mass.: Harvard University Press, 1952).

Cromwell, Oliver, *Oliver Cromwell's Letters and Speeches: With Elucidations*, ed. Thomas Carlyle, vol. 4 (London: Chapman and Hall, 1845).

—— *The Writings and Speeches of Oliver Cromwell*, ed. W. C. Abbott, 4 vols. (Cambridge, Mass.: Harvard University Press, 1937–47).

Davies, John, *The Poems of Sir John Davies*, ed. Robert Krueger (Oxford: Clarendon Press, 1975).

Dekker, Thomas, *The Non-Dramatic Works*, ed. Alexander B. Grosart, vol. 4 (1885; repr. New York: Russell and Russell, 1963).

Descartes, René, *A Discourse on Method*, trans. John Veitch, Everyman's Library (London and New York: Dent and Dutton, 1953).

—— *Philosophical Letters*, ed. and trans. Anthony Kenny (Oxford: Blackwell, 1981).

Donne, John, 'Hymne to God my God, in my sicknesse', in *The Metaphysical Poets*, ed. Helen Gardner (Harmondsworth and Middlesex: Penguin, 1957), 89.

—— *Selected Prose*, ed. Neil Rhodes (Harmondsworth: Penguin, 1987).

Döpler, Jacob, *Theatrum Poenarum, Suppliciorum et Executionum Criminalium, oder Schau-Platz derer Leibes und Lebens-Straffen* (Sondershausen: L. H. Schönermarck, 1693).

Elyot, Thomas, *The Castle of Health* (London: T. Berthelet, 1539).

England as Seen by Foreigners in the Days of Elizabeth and James the First, ed. William Brenchley Rye (London: John Russell Smith, 1865).

Fletcher, Giles, and Fletcher, Phineas, *Poetical Works*, ed. Frederick S. Boas, 2 vols. (Cambridge: Cambridge University Press, 1909).

Foxe, John, *Actes and Monuments of Matters Most Speciall and Memorable* (1583), facs. edn. on CD-Rom, ed. David G. Newcombe and Michael Pidd (Oxford: Oxford University Press, 2001).

Gauden, John, *The tears, sighs, complaints, and prayers of the Church of England* (London: Royston, 1659).

The Geneva Bible. A Facsimile of the 1560 Edition. With an introduction by Lloyd E. Berry. (Madison, Wis., Milwaukee, and London: University of Wisconsin Press, 1969).

Gesner, Conrad, *Historia Animalium*, 4 vols. (Zürich: Froschauer, 1551–8).

Gower, John, *Confessio Amantis*, ed. Russell A. Peck (Kalamazoo: Medieval Institute Publications, 2004).

Hakluyt's Voyages, vii: *The Principal Navigations, Voyages, Traffiques & Discoveries of the English Nation*, ed. John Masefield (London: Dent, 1927).

Harsnett, Samuel, *A Declaration of egregious Popish Impostures, to withdraw the harts of her Maiesties Subiects from their allegeance, and from the truth of Christian Religion professed in England, vnder the pretense of casting out deuils* (London: James Roberts, 1603).

Henslowe Papers, ed. W. W. Greg (London: A. H. Bullen, 1907).

Hentzner, Paul, *Paul Hentzner's Travels in England, during the Reign of Queen Elizabeth*, trans. Horace Walpole (London: Edward Jeffery, 1797).

Herodotus, *The History*, trans. David Grene (Chicago: University of Chicago Press, 1987).

Hobbes, Thomas, *Leviathan, or, The Matter, Forme and Power of a Commonwealth Ecclesiastical and Civil*, ed. Michael Oakeshott (Oxford: Blackwell, 1960).

Holinshed, Raphael, *Shakespeare's Holinshed: An Edition of Holinshed's Chronicles (1587). Source of Shakespeare's History Plays*, King Lear, Cymbeline, and Macbeth, ed. Richard Hosley (New York: G. P. Putnam's Sons, 1968).

[Homer], *Batrachomyomachia*, ed. T. W. Allen (Oxford: Oxford University Press, 1946).

Hugh of St-Victor, *Didascalion. De Studio Legendi*, ed. Charles Henry Buttimer (Washington, DC: Catholic University Press, 1939).

Hundt, Magnus, *Antropologium de hominis dignitate, natura et proprietatibus, de elementis, partibus et membris humani corporis* (Leipzig: Wolfgang Stöckel, 1501).

Isidore of Seville, The Etymologies, ed. W. M. Lindsay (Oxford: Oxford University Press, 1911).

James VI and I, *Basilikon Doron* (Edinburgh, 1599; repr. London: Westheimer, Lea, and Co., 1887).

—— 'Basilikon Doron', in *Selected Writings*, ed. Neil Rhodes, Jennifer Richards, and Joseph Marshall (Aldershot: Ashgate, 2003).

—— *Daemonologie* (1597), *Newes from Scotland* (1591), ed. G. B. Harrison (London: John Lane, The Bodley Head; New York: E. P. Dutton, 1924).

Jonson, Ben, *The Complete Plays of Ben Jonson*, ed. G. A. Wilkes (Oxford: Clarendon Press, 1982).

Knox, John, *The first blast of the trumpet against the monstrous regiment of women* (Geneva: J. Poullain and A. Rebul, M.D.LVIII [1558]).

Laneham, Robert, 'A Letter: Whearin, part of the Entertainment, untoo the Queenz Majesty, at Killingworth Castl, in Warwik Sheer, in this Soomerz Progress, 1575, iz signified . . .', in *The Progresses and Public Processions of Queen Elizabeth*, ed. John Nichols, 3 vols. (London: J. Nichols and Son, 1823), i. 420–84.

Léry, Jean de, *History of a Voyage to the Land of Brazil*, trans. Janet Whatley (Berkeley: University of California Press, 1990).

Ligon, Richard, A true & exact history of the island of Barbados (London: Humphrey Moseley, 1657).

Locke, John, *TheSecond Treatise of Government*, ed. with an Introduction by Thomas F. Peardon (New York: Liberal Arts Press, 1952).

Livy, *Ab urbe condita libri*, ed. W. Weissenborn and M. Müller (Leipzig: Bibliotheca Teubneriana, 1932).

Lucian, *The Works of Lucian of Samosata*, trans. and ed. H. W. Fowler and F. G. Fowler, 4 vols. (Oxford: Clarendon Press, 1905).

Macchiavelli, Niccolò, *The Art of War, 1560* (London: David Nutt, 1905).

Mandeville, John, *The Travels of Sir John Mandeville*, trans. and ed. C. W. R. D. Moseley (Harmondsworth: Penguin, 1983).

Markham, Gervaise, *Countrey contentments . . .* (London: R. Jackson, 1615).

Marlowe, Christopher, *Marlowe's Doctor Faustus 1604–1616: Parallel Texts*, ed. W.W. Greg (Oxford: Clarendon Press, 1950).

—— *The Jew of Malta*, ed. Roma Gill, *The Complete Works of Christopher Marlowe*, 4 (Oxford: Clarendon Press, 1995).

Marvell, Andrew, *The Poems of Andrew Marvell*, ed. Nigel Smith (rev. edn., London: Pearson Longman, 2007).

Milton, John, *The Prose Works of John Milton*, ed. Rufus Wilmot Griswold, vol. 2 (Philadelphia: John W. Moore, 1847).

Montaigne, Michel de, *Montaigne's Essays*, trans. John Florio, 3 vols., Everyman's Library (London: Dent, 1965).

More, Thomas, *English Poems, Life of Pico, The Last Things*, ed. Anthony S. G. Edwards, Katherine G. Rogers, and Clarence H. Miller, *Complete Works of St. Thomas More*, i (New Haven and London: Yale University Press, 1997).

Münster, Sebastian, *Cosmographei* (1550), ed. Ruthardt Oehme (Amsterdam: Theatrum Orbis Terrarum, 1968).

Narrative and Dramatic Sources of Shakespeare, v: *The Roman Plays*, ed. Geoffrey Bullough (London: Routledge and Kegan Paul; New York: Columbia University Press, 1964).

Pepys, Samuel, *The Diary of Samuel Pepys*, ed. Robert Lanham and William Matthews, 11 vols. (Berkeley and Los Angeles: University of California Press, 1970–83).

Physiologus, trans. Michael J. Curely (Austin: University of Texas Press, 1979).

Pico della Mirandola, Giovanni, *Oration on the Dignity of Man*, trans. A. Robert Caponigri (Washington, DC: Regnery Publishing, 1999).

Plato, *The Symposium*, trans. M. C. Howatson, ed. M. C. Howatson and Frisbee C. C. Sheffield (Cambridge: Cambridge University Press, 2008).

Pope, Alexander, *The Poems of Alexander Pope*, ed. John Butt (London: Methuen, 1963).

The Progresses and Public Processions of Queen Elizabeth, ed. John Nichols, 3 vols. (London: J. Nichols and Son, 1823).

Puttenham, George, *The Arte of English Poesie*, ed. Gladys Doige Willcock and Alice Walker (Cambridge: Cambridge University Press, 1936).

Rainolds, John, *Th'overthrow of stage plays* (Middelburg: Schilders, 1599).

Sahagún, Bernardino de, *Historia general de las cosas de la Nueva España* (c.1540–1585), Engl.: Bernardino de Sahagun, *Florentine Codex: General History of the Things of New Spain*, trans. and ed. Charles E. Dibble and Arthur J. O. Anderson, 13 vols. (Santa Fe, NM and Salt Lake City: School of American Research/University of Utah Press, 1950–82).

Scot, Reginald, *The Discoverie of Witchcraft* (1584) (Arundel: Centaur Press, 1964).

Sophocles, *Antigone*, ed. Mark Griffith (Cambridge: Cambridge University Press, 1999).

Spon, Jacob, *Italiänische, Dalmatische, Griechische und Orientalische Reise-Beschreibung* (Nuremberg: Andreas Knorzen, 1681).

Stradanus, Johannes, *Venationes Ferarum* (Antwerp, 1578; repr. Hildesheim: Georg Olms, 2000).

Stubbes, Phillip, *The Anatomy of Abuses* (London: William Wright, 1583).

Taylor, John, *All the Workes of John Taylor the Water Poet* (London: James Boler, 1630).

—— *Bull, Beare, and Horse* (1638), in *The Works of John Taylor the Water Poet Not Included in the Folio Volume of 1630*, iii (Manchester: Spenser Society, 1876).

Thevet, André, *The new found vvorlde, or Antarctike [. . .]*, trans. Thomas Hacket (London: Thomas Hacket, 1568).

Thomas Aquinas, *Summa Theologiae*, lviii: *The Eucharistic Presence (3a. 73–8)*, trans. and ed. William Barden (London: Blackfriars, 1965).

Topsell, Edward, *The historie of foure-footed beastes . . .* (London: William Jaggard, 1607).

—— *The Historie of Serpents. Or, The second Booke of liuing Creatures* (London: William Jaggard, 1608).

Tyson, Edward, *Orang-outang: sive Homo-Sylvestris, Or, the Anatomy of a Pygmie: Compared with that of a Monkey, an Ape, and a Man* (London, Printed for Thomas Bennet at the Half Moon in St. Paul's Churchyard, 1699).

Waldstein, Zdeněk, Baron, *The Diary of Baron Waldstein: A Traveller in Elizabethan England*, trans. and annot. G. W. Groos (London: Thames and Hudson, 1981).

Walpurger, Christoph, *Hussus Combustus* (Gera, 1624).

Wedel, Lupold von, *Lupold von Wedels Beschreibung seiner Reisen und Kriegserlebnisse 1561–1606*, ed. Max Bär, Baltische Studien, 45 (Stettin: Gesellschaft für Pommersche Geschichte und Alterthumskunde, 1895).

William of St-Thierry, *De natura corporis et animae libri duo*, in *Opera omnia*, iii: *Opera didactica et spiritualia*, ed. Paul Verdeyen (Turnhout: Brepols, 2003).

Willis, Thomas, *Two Discourses concerning the Soul of Brutes, Which is that of the Vital and Sensitive of Man*, Englished by S. Pordage (London: Thomas Dring, 1683).

POST-1700 WORKS

Acampora, Ralph R., 'Nietzsche's Feral Philosophy: Thinking through an Animal Imaginary', in Christa Davis Acampora and Ralph R. Acampora (eds.), *A Nietzschean Bestiary: Becoming Animal beyond Docile and Brutal* (Lanham, Md.: Rowman and Littlefield, 2004), 1–13.

Adams, Joseph Quincy, *Shakespearean Playhouses: A History of English Theatres from the Beginnings to the Restoration* (Boston and New York: Houghton Mifflin, 1917; repr. Gloucester, Mass.: Smith, 1960).

Adelman, Janet, *Suffocating Mothers: Fantasies of Maternal Origin in Shakespeare's Plays, 'Hamlet' to 'The Tempest'* (New York and London: Routledge, 1992).

Adorno, Theodor W., with Horkheimer, Max, *Dialectic of Enlightenment*, trans. Edmund Jephcott (Stanford: Stanford University Press, 2002).

Aebischer, Pascale, *Shakespeare's Violated Bodies* (Cambridge: Cambridge University Press, 2004).

Agamben, Giorgio, *Homo Sacer. Sovereign Power and Bare Life*, trans. Daniel Heller-Roazen (Stanford: Stanford University Press, 1998).

—— *The Open: Man and Animal*, trans. Kevin Attell (Stanford: Stanford University Press, 2004).

Albanese, Denise, *New Science, New World* (Durham, NC, and London: Duke University Press, 1996).

Amussen, Susan Dwyer, 'Punishment, Discipline, and Power: The Social Meanings of Violence in Early Modern England', *Journal of British Studies*, 34 (1995), 1–34.

Archer, Jayne, and Turley, Richard Marggraf, 'Lear in the "High-grown fields": Landscape, Politics, Performance', paper presented at the autumn meeting of the Deutsche Shakespeare Gesellschaft, Cologne, 27–8 Nov. 2009.

Arens, William, *The Man-Eating Myth: Anthropology and Anthropophagy* (Oxford: Oxford University Press 1979).

'Bad Elephant Killed: Topsy Meets Quick and Painless Death at Coney Island', *Commercial Advertiser*, New York, Monday, 5 Jan. 1903.

Baker, Steve, *Picturing the Beast: Animals, Identity, and Representation* (Urbana, Ill. and Chicago: University of Illinois Press, 1993).

Balme, Christopher B., *The Cambridge Introduction to Theatre Studies* (Cambridge: Cambridge University Press, 2008).

—— 'Intermediality: Rethinking the Relationship between Theatre and Media', *TheWis: Zeitschrift der Gesellschaft für Theaterwissenschaft*, 01/2004 (online at <http://www.theaterwissenschaft.uni-muenchen.de/mitarbeiter/professoren/balme/balme_publ1/balme_publ_aufsaetze/intermediality.pdf> accessed 13 December 2010).

Barber, C. L., *Shakespeare's Festive Comedy* (Cleveland, Ohio, and New York: World Publishing, 1959).

—— and Wheeler, Richard P., *The Whole Journey: Shakespeare's Power of Development* (Berkeley: University of California Press, 1986).

Barker, Francis, 'Treasures of Culture: *Titus Andronicus* and Death by Hanging', in Miller, O'Dair, and Weber (eds.), *The Production of English Renaissance Culture*, 226–61.

——, Hulme, Peter, and Iversen, Margaret (eds.), *Cannibalism and the Colonial World* (Cambridge: Cambridge University Press, 1998).

Barroll, Leeds, 'A New History for Shakespeare and his Time', *Shakespeare Quarterly*, 39 (1988), 441–64.

Bataille, Georges, *Eroticism, Death and Sensuality*, trans. Mary Dalwood (San Francisco: City Light Books, 1986).

Bate, Jonathan, *Shakespeare and Ovid* (Oxford: Clarendon Press, 1993).

Baumbach, Sibylle, *Let me behold thy face: Physiognomik und Gesichtslektüren in Shakespeares Tragödien* (Heidelberg: Winter, 2007).

Beckerman, Bernard, *Shakespeare at the Globe 1599–1609* (New York: Macmillan, 1962).

Beecher, D. A., 'Gianlorenzo Bernini's *The Impresario:* The Artist as the Supreme Trickster', *University of Toronto Quarterly*, 53 (1984), 236–47.

Belsey, Catherine, *The Subject of Tragedy: Identity and Difference in Renaissance Drama* (London: Methuen, 1985).

Benjamin, Walter, *The Origin of the German Tragic Drama*, trans. John Osborne (London: New Left Books, 1977).

Bentley, Gerald Eades, *The Jacobean and Caroline Stage*, 7 vols. (Oxford: Clarendon Press, 1941–68).

Berger, Harry, Jr., *Imaginary Audition: Shakespeare on Stage and Page* (Berkeley and Los Angeles: University of California Press, 1989).

Berry, Edward, *Shakespeare and the Hunt* (Cambridge: Cambridge University Press, 2001).

—— *Shakespeare's Comic Rites* (Cambridge: Cambridge University Press, 1984).

Berry, Ralph, *Shakespeare and the Awareness of the Audience* (London: Macmillan, 1985).

Betteridge, Tom, 'Truth and History in Foxe's Acts and Monuments', in Christopher Highley and John N. King (eds.), *John Foxe and his World* (Aldershot: Ashgate, 2002), 145–59.

Bloom, Harold, *Shakespeare: The Invention of the Human* (New York: Riverhead Books, 1998).

Blumenberg, Hans, *The Genesis of the Copernican World* (1970), trans. Robert M. Wallace (Cambridge, Mass.: MIT Press, 1987).

—— *The Legitimacy of the Modern Age* (1966), trans. Robert M. Wallace (Cambridge, Mass.: MIT Press, 1983).

—— *Die Lesbarkeit der Welt* [The Legibility of the World] (Frankfurt am Main: Suhrkamp, 1979).

—— *Shipwreck with Spectator: Paradigm of a Metaphor for Existence* (1979), trans. Steven Rendall (Cambridge, Mass.: MIT Press, 1997).

—— *Work on Myth* (1979), trans. Robert M. Wallace (Cambridge, Mass.: MIT Press, 1985).

Boehrer, Bruce, *Shakespeare among the Animals: Nature and Society in the Drama of Early Modern England* (Houndmills, Basingstoke: Palgrave, 2002).

Boehrer, Bruce (ed.), *A Cultural History of Animals in the Renaissance* (Oxford and New York: Berg, 2007).

Bono, James J., 'Science, Discourse and Literature: The Role/Rule of Metaphor in Science', in Stuart Peterfreund (ed.), *Literature and Science: Theory and Practice* (Boston: Northeastern University Press, 1990), 59–89.

—— *The Word of God and the Languages of Man: Interpreting Nature in Early Modern Science and Medicine* (Madison, Wis.: University of Wisconsin Press, 1995).

Booth, Stephen, *King Lear, Macbeth, Indefinition and Tragedy* (New Haven: Yale University Press, 1983).

Brandon, C., *The Electric Chair: An Unnatural American History* (Jefferson, NC: McFarland & Co., 1999).

Brecht, Bertolt, *Gesammelte Werke*, ed. Elisabeth Hauptmann and Herta Ramthun, vol. 18 (Frankfurt am Main: Suhrkamp, 1967).

Bredekamp, Horst, *Thomas Hobbes: Der Leviathan. Das Urbild des modernen Staates und seine Gegenbilder 1651–2001* (Berlin: Akademie Verlag, 2003).

—— 'Thomas Hobbes's Visual Strategies', in Patricia Springborg (ed.), *The Cambridge Companion to Hobbes's Leviathan* (Cambridge: Cambridge University Press, 2007), 29–60.

Breight, Curt, ' "Treason doth never prosper": *The Tempest* and the Discourse of Treason', *Shakespeare Quarterly*, 41 (1990), 1–28.

Bremmer J. M., and Norsfall, N. M., *Roman Myth and Mythography*, Bulletin Supplement 52 (London: University of London, Institute of Classical Studies, 1987).

Briley, John, 'Of Stake and Stage', *Shakespeare Survey*, 8 (1955), 106–9.

The Broken Spears: The Aztec Account of the Conquest of Mexico, ed. Miguel León-Portilla (Boston: Beacon Press, 1962).

Bronfen, Elisabeth, *Over her Dead Body: Death, Femininity and the Aesthetic* (Manchester: Manchester University Press, 1992).

Brown, John Russell, *Shakespeare's Plays in Performance* (London: Edward Arnold, 1966).

Brown, Keith, 'The Artist of the Leviathan Title-Page', *British Library Journal*, 4 (1978), 24–36.

Brownlow, F. W., *Shakespeare, Harsnett, and the Devils of Denham* (Newark, Del.: University of Delaware Press, 1993).

Brownstein, Oscar Lee, 'Stake and Stage: The Baiting Ring and the Public Playhouse in Elizabethan England' (Ph.D. diss., University of Iowa, 1963; Microfilm, CDI #64–03353, Ann Arbor, Mich., Microfilms).

—— 'Why Didn't Burbage Lease the Beargarden? A Conjecture in Comparative Architecture', in Herbert Berry (ed.), *The First Public Playhouse* (Montreal: McGill-Queen's University Press, 1979), 81–96.

Brunner, Bernd, *Bears: A Brief History*, trans. Lori Lantz (New Haven: Yale University Press, 2007).

Bruster, Douglas, 'Local *Tempest*: Shakespeare and the Work of the Early Modern Playhouse', *Journal of Medieval and Renaissance Studies*, 25 (1995), 33–53.

Bülow, Gottfried von, 'Journey through England and Scotland made by Lupold von Wedel in the Years 1584 and 1585', *Transactions of the Royal Historical Society*, NS 9 (1895), 223–70.

Burckhardt, Jacob, *The Civilization of the Renaissance in Italy* (1860), trans. S. G. C. Middlemore (London: Penguin, 2004).

Burke, Kenneth, 'Coriolanus—and the Delights of Faction', in id. (ed.), *Language as Symbolic Action: Essays on Life, Literature, and Method* (Berkeley and Los Angeles: University of California Press, 1966).

Burkert, Walter, *Savage Energies: Lessons of Myth and Ritual in Ancient Greece*, trans. Peter Bing (Chicago and London: University of Chicago Press, 2001).

Calderwood, James L., *If It Were Done: Macbeth and Tragic Action* (Amherst, Mass.: University of Massachusetts Press, 1986).

Callaghan, Dympna, and Kyle, Chris R., 'The Wilde Side of Justice in Early Modern England and *Titus Andronicus*', in Constance Jordan and Karen Cunningham (eds.), *The Law in Shakespeare* (Houndmills, Basingstoke: Palgrave, 2007), 38–57.

Campbell, John, 'The Seminoles, the "Bloodhound War", and Abolitionism, 1796–1865', *Journal of Southern History*, 62 (2006), 259–302.

Campbell, Joseph, *The Hero with a Thousand Faces* (1949; 2nd rev. edn., Princeton: Princeton University Press, 1968).

Campbell, Mavis C., *The Maroons of Jamaica, 1655–1796: A History of Resistance, Collaboration and Betrayal* (Granby, Mass.: Bergin and Garvey 1988).

Campe, Rüdiger, 'Der Befehl und die Rede des Souveräns im Schauspiel des 17. Jahrhunderts', in Armin Adam and Martin Stingelin (eds.), *Übertragung und Gesetz: Gründungsmythen, Kriegstheater und Unterwerfungstechniken von Institutionen* (Berlin: Akademie Verlag, 1995), 55–71.

Cartwright, Kent, *Theatre and Humanism: English Drama in the Sixteenth Century* (Cambridge: Cambridge University Press, 1999).

Cassirer, Ernst, *Individuum und Kosmos in der Philosophie der Renaissance* (1926; Darmstadt: Wissenschaftliche Buchgesellschaft, 1969).

Cavell, Stanley, *Conditions Handsome and Unhandsome: The Constitution öof Emersonian Perfectionism* (Chicago: University of Chicago Press, 1990).

—— *Disowning Knowledge. In Seven Plays of Shakespeare* (updated edn., Cambridge: Cambridge University Press, 2003).

—— *Philosophy and Animal Life* (New York: Columbia University Press, 2008).

Cavell, Stanley, Diamond, Cora, McDowell, John, Hacking, Ian, and Wolfe, Cary, *Philosophy and Animal Life* (New York: Columbia University Press, 2008).

Cerasano, S. P., 'Edward Alleyn: 1566–1626', in Aileen Reid and Robert Maniury (eds.), *Edward Alleyn: Elizabethan Actor, Jacobean Gentleman* (London: Dulwich Picture Gallery, 1994), 5–16.

—— 'The Master of the Bears in Art and Enterprise', *Medieval and Renaissance Drama in England*, 5 (1991), 195–209.

Certeau, Michel de, *Heterologies: Discourse on the Other*, trans. Brian Massumi (Minneapolis and London: University of Minnesota Press, 2000).

Chambers, Edmund K., *The Elizabethan Stage*, 4 vols. (Oxford: Clarendon Press, 1923).

—— *William Shakespeare: A Study of Facts and Problems*, 2 vols. (Oxford: Clarendon Press, 1930).

Chapple, Freda, and Kattenbelt, Chiel (eds.), *Intermediality in Theatre and Performance* (Amsterdam and New York: Rodopi, 2006).

Clegg, Arthur, 'Craftsmen and the Origin of Science', *Science and Society*, 43 (1979), 186–201.

Clemen, Wolfgang, *The Development of Shakespeare's Imagery* (London: Methuen, 1951).

Clubb, Louise G., 'The Tragicomic Bear', *Comparative Literature Studies*, 9 (1972), 17–30.

Coghill, Nevill, *Shakespeare's Professional Skills* (Cambridge: Cambridge University Press, 1964).

—— 'Six Points of Stage-Craft in *The Winter's Tale*', *Shakespeare Survey*, 11 (1958), 31–41.

Cohen Esther, 'Law, Folklore and Animal Lore', *Past and Present*, 110 (1986), 6–37.

Coleridge, Samuel Taylor, *The Collected Works of Samuel Taylor Coleridge, Poetical Works*, i: *Poems (Reading Text), Part 1*, ed. J. C. C. Mays (Princeton: Princeton University Press, 2001).

Colvin, Sidney, *John Keats: His Life and Poetry, his Friends, Critics and After-Fame* (2nd edn., London: Macmillan, 1918).

Copenhaver, Brian P., 'Magic and the Dignity of Man: De-Kanting Pico's Oration', in *The Italian Renaissance in the Twentieth Century: Acts of an International Conference. Florence, Villa I Tatti, June 9–11, 1999*, ed. Allen J. Grieco, Michael Rocke, and Fiorella Gioffredi Superbi (Florence: Leo S. Olschki Editore, 2002), 295–320.

Coward, Barry, *Oliver Cromwell* (London and New York: Longman, 2000).

Cowden Clarke, Charles, and Cowden Clarke, Mary, *Recollections of Writers* (1878; Fontwell: Centaur Press, 1969).

Crane, Mary Thomas, *Shakespeare's Brain: Reading with Cognitive Theory* (Princeton and Oxford: Princeton University Press, 2001).

Curling, Henry, *Recollections of the Mess-Table and the Stage* (London: T. Bosworth, 1855).

Czeike, Felix, *Historisches Lexikon Wien*, iii (Vienna: Kremayr and Scheriau, 1994).

Daigl, Christoph, *'All the world is but a bear-baiting': Das englische Hetztheater im 16. und 17. Jahrhundert* (Berlin: Gesellschaft für Theatergeschichte, 1997).

Danby John F., *Shakespeare's Doctrine of Nature: A Study of 'King Lear'* (London: Faber and Faber, 1949).

Darwin, Charles, *The Descent of Man, and Selection in Relation to Sex* (London: Penguin, 2004).

Darwin's Alptraum (*Darwin's Nightmare*), dir. Hubert Sauper (Sunfilm Entertainment, 2005), DVD.

Daston, Lorraine, and Mitman, Gregg, 'Introduction: The How and Why of Thinking with Animals', in Lorraine Daston and Gregg Mitman (eds.), *Thinking with Animals: New Perspectives on Anthropomorphism*, ed. (New York: Columbia University Press, 2005), 1–14.

—— and Park, Katharine, *Wonders and the Order of Nature 1150–1750* (New York: Zone Books, 1998).

Davidson, Clifford, and Seiler, Thomas H. (eds.), *The Iconography of Hell* (Kalamazoo: Medieval Institute Publications, 1992).

Dawson, Giles E., 'London's Bull-Baiting and Bear-Baiting Arena in 1562', *ShakespeareQuarterly*, 15 (1964), 97–101.

Defaux, Gérard, 'Un Cannibale en haute de chausses: Montaigne, la différence et la logique de l'identité', *Modern Language Notes*, 97 (1982), 919–57.

De Grazia, Margreta, *Hamlet without Hamlet* (Cambridge: Cambridge University Press, 2007).

Dekoven, Marianne, 'Guest Column: Why Animals Now?', *PMLA* 124 (2009), 361–9.

Derrida, Jacques, *The Animal that Therefore I Am*, trans. David Wills, ed. Marie-Louise Mallet (New York: Fordham University Press, 2008).

—— *The Beast and the Sovereign*, trans. Geoffrey Bennington, ed. Michel Lisse, Marie-Louise Mallet, and Ginette Michaud (Chicago and London: The University of Chicago Press, 2008).

—— 'Geschlecht II: Heidegger's Hand', trans. John P. Leavey, Jr., in *Deconstruction and Philosophy: The Texts of Jacques Derrida*, ed. John Sallis (Chicago: University of Chicago Press, 1986), 161–96.

Diamond, Cora, *The Realistic Spirit: Wittgenstein, Philosophy, and the Mind* (Cambridge, Mass., and London: MIT Press, 1991).

Dickey, Stephen, 'Shakespeare's Mastiff Comedy', *Shakespeare Quarterly*, 42 (1991), 255–75.

Diehl, Huston, 'Horrid Image, Sorry Sight, Fatal Vision: The Visual Rhetoric of *Macbeth*', *Shakespeare Studies*, 16 (1983), 191–204.

Dillon, Anne, *The Construction of Martyrdom in the English Catholic Community 1535–1603* (Aldershot: Ashgate, 2002).

Dillon, Steven, *Derek Jarman and Lyric Film: The Mirror and the Sea* (Austin, Tex.: University of Texas Press, 2004).

Dobson, Michael, ' "Remember/First to possess his books": The Appropriation of *The Tempest*, 1700–1800', *Shakespeare Survey*, 43 (1991), 99–107.

Dollimore, Jonathan, *Radical Tragedy: Religion, Ideology and Power in the Drama of Shakespeare and his Contemporaries* (Brighton: Harvester Press, 1984).

Drakakis, John, 'Yorick's Skull', paper read at the 'Gothic Renaissance' conference, organized by Beate Neumeier and Elisabeth Bronfen, Cologne, 3–4 Dec. 2009.

Eccles, Christine, *The Rose Theatre* (London: Routledge, 1990).

Electrocuting an Elephant, dir. Jacob Blair Smith and Edwin S. Porter (Edison Manufacturing Company, 1903).

Elias, Norbert, *The Civilizing Process. Sociogenetic and Psychogenetic Investigations*, rev. edn., trans. Edmund Jephcott (Malden, Mass., Oxford, and Victoria, BC: Blackwell, 2000).

—— *What Is Sociology?*, trans. Stephen Mennell and Grace Morrissey (New York: Columbia University Press, 1978).

Eliot, T. S., *Selected Prose of T. S. Eliot*, ed. Frank Kermode (London: Faber and Faber, 1975).

—— *The Waste Land: A Facsimile and Transcript of the Original Drafts Including the Annotations of Ezra Pound*, ed. Valerie Eliot (London: Faber and Faber, 1971).

Elliot, John H., *The Old World and the New, 1492–1650* (Cambridge: Cambridge University Press, 1970).

Engels, Friedrich, 'Der Antheil der Arbeit an der Menschwerdung des Affen' (= 'The Part Played by Work in the Transition from Ape to Man'), in Karl Marx and Friedrich Engels, *Werke*, xx (Berlin: Dietz, 1962), 444–55.

Enright, D. J., '*Coriolanus*: Tragedy or Debate?' *Essays in Criticism*, 4 (1954), 1–19.

The European Magazine and London Review, 42 (July–Dec. 1802).

Evans, E. P., *The Criminal Prosecution and Capital Punishment of Animals*. (1906; repr. London: Faber and Faber, 1987).

Evans, Malcolm, *Signifying Nothing: Truth's True Contents in Shakespeare's Texts* (Hemel Hempstead: Harvester Wheatsheaf, 1989).

Evans, Richard J., *Rituals of Retribution: Capital Punishment in Germany 1600–1987* (Oxford: Oxford University Press, 1996).

Evans, Robert J. W., and Marr, Alexander (eds.), *Curiosity and Wonder from the Renaissance to the Enlightenment* (Aldershot and Burlington, Vt.: Ashgate, 2006).

Felperin, Howard, *Shakespearean Representation: Mimesis and Modernity in Elizabethan Tragedy* (Princeton: Princeton University Press, 1977).

Fischer, Joachim, 'Exploring the Core Identity of Philosophical Anthropology through the Works of Max Scheler, Helmuth Plessner and Arnold Gehlen', trans. Christina Harrison, in *Iris: European Journal of Philosophy and Public Debate* (Florence: Florence University Press, 2009), 153–70.

Fisher, Philip, 'The Aesthetics of Fear', *Raritan*, 18 (1998), 40–72.

Fitzpatrick, Joan, 'Apricots, Butter, and Capons: An Early Modern Lexicon of Food', *Shakespeare Jahrbuch*, 145 (2009), 74–90.

Foakes, R. A., *Illustrations of the English Stage, 1580–1642* (London: Scolar Press, 1985).

—— *Shakespeare and Violence* (Cambridge: Cambridge University Press, 2003).

Foucault, Michel, *Discipline and Punish: The Birth of the Prison*, trans. Alan Sheridan (New York: Vintage, 1995).

—— *Madness and Civilization*, trans. Richard Howard (London: Tavistock, 1987).

—— *The Order of Things: An Archaeology of Human Sciences, trans. Alan Sheridan* (New York: Pantheon Books, 1970).

Fraser, Antonia, *Mary Queen of Scots* (10th edn., London: Weidenfeld and Nicolson, 1975).

Frye, Northrop, 'The Argument of Comedy', in *English Institute Essays, 1948*, ed. D. A. Robertson, Jr. (New York: Columbia University Press, 1949), 58–73.

Fudge, Erica, *Brutal Reasoning: Animals, Rationality, and Humanity in Early Modern England* (Ithaca, NY, and London: Cornell University Press 2006).

—— *Perceiving Animals: Humans and Beasts in Early Modern English Culture* (Houndmills, Basingstoke: Macmillan, 2000).

—— (ed.), *Renaissance Beasts: Of Animals, Humans, and Other Wonderful Creatures* (Urbana, Ill. and Chicago: University of Illinois Press, 2004).

—— Gilbert, Ruth, and Wiseman, Susan (eds.), *At the Borders of the Human: Beasts, Bodies and Natural Philosophy in the Early Modern Period* (Houndmills, Basingstoke: Macmillan, 1999).

Fuss, Diana, 'Introduction: Human, All Too Human', in ead. (ed.), *Human, All Too Human* (New York and London: Routledge, 1996), 1–7.

Gabrieli, Vittorio, 'Giovanni Pico and Thomas More', *Moreana*, 15–16 (1967) 43–57.

Galinsky, Karl G., *Ovid's Metamorphoses: An Introduction to the Basic Aspects* (Berkeley: University of California Press, 1975).

Gardner, Helen, *King Lear*, The John Coffin Memorial Lecture 1966 (London: Athlone Press, 1967).

Gatrell, V. A., *The Hanging Tree: Execution and the English People 1770–1868* (Oxford: Oxford University Press, 1994).

Gehlen, Arnold, *Man: His Nature and Place in the World*, trans. Clare McMillan and Karl Pillemer (New York: Columbia University Press, 1988).

——, *Man in the Age of Technology*, trans. Patricia Lipscomb (New York: Columbia University Press, 1980).

Gent, Lucy, 'The Self-Cozening Eye', *Review of English Studies*, NS 34 (1983), 419–28.

Gottschalk, Paul A., 'The Universe of Madness in *King Lear*', *Bucknell Review*, 19/3 (1971), 51–68.

Greenblatt, Stephen, *Hamlet in Purgatory* (Princeton: Princeton University Press, 2001).

—— *Learning to Curse: Essays in Early Modern Culture* (New York and London: Routledge, 1990).

—— *Marvelous Possessions: The Wonder of the New World* (Oxford: Clarendon Press, 1991).

—— *Shakespearean Negotiations* (Oxford: Clarendon Press, 1988).

Gregory, Brad S., *Salvation at Stake: Christian Martyrdom in Early Modern Europe* (Cambridge, Mass.: Harvard University Press, 1999).

Grene, Nicholas, *Shakespeare's Serial History Plays* (Cambridge: Cambridge University Press, 2002).

Gumbrecht, Hans Ulrich, *Production of Presence: What Meaning Cannot Convey* (Stanford: Stanford University Press, 2004).

Gunning, Tom, 'The Cinema of Attractions: Early Film, its Spectator, and the Avant-Garde', in Thomas Elsaesser (ed.), *Early Cinema: Space, Frame, Narrative* (London: BFI, 1990), 56–62.

Gurr, Andrew, 'Bears and Players: Philip Henslowe's Double Acts', *Shakespeare Bulletin* 22 (2004), 31–41.

—— *The Shakespearean Stage 1574–1642* (2nd edn., Cambridge: Cambridge University Press, 1980).

Hahn, Daniel, *The Tower Menagerie* (London and Sydney: Simon and Schuster, 2004).

Haller, William, *Foxe's Book of Martyrs and the Elect Nation* (London: Jonathan Cape, 1963).

Halpern, Richard, ' "The picture of Nobody": White Cannibalism in *The Tempest*', in Miller, O'Dair, and Weber (eds.), *The Production of English Renaissance Culture*, 262–92.

Hanafin, Patrick, Gearey, Adam, and Brooker, Joseph (eds.), *Law and Literature* (*Journal of Law and Society*, 31/1) (Oxford: Blackwell 2004).

Hapgood, Robert, 'Shakespeare and the Ritualists', *Shakespeare Survey*, 15 (1962), 111–24.

Haraway, Donna J., *The Companion Species Manifesto: Dogs, People, and Significant Otherness* (Chicago: University of Chicago Press, 2003).

—— *When Species Meet* (Minneapolis and London: University of Minnesota Press, 2008).

Harmon, A. G., *Eternal Bonds, True Contracts: Law and Nature in Shakespeare's Problem Plays* (Albany, NY: State University of New York Press, 2004).

Harris, Bernice, 'Sexuality as a Signifier for Power Relations: Using Lavinia, of Shakespeare's *Titus Andronicus*', *Criticism*, 38 (1996), 383–406.

Hartog, François, *Le Miroir d'Hérodot: Essai sur la représentation de l'autre* (Paris: Gallimard, 1980).

Haser, Verena, *Metaphor, Metonymy, and Experientialist Philosophy: Challenging Cognitive Semantics* (Berlin and New York: Mouton de Gruyter, 2005).

Hawkes, Terence, 'Harry Hunks, Superstar', in id. (ed.), *Shakespeare in the Present* (London: Routledge, 2002), 83–106.

Heidegger, Martin, *Holzwege* (4th edn., Frankfurt am Main: Klostermann, 1963).

—— *Was heisst Denken?* (Tübingen: Niemeyer, 1954).

Heilman, Robert B., *This Great Stage: Image and Structure in* King Lear (Baton Rouge, La.: Louisiana State University Press, 1948).

Herkommer, Hubert, 'Die Geschichte vom Leiden und Sterben des Jan Hus als Ereignis und Erzählung', in Ludger Grenzmann and Karl Stackmann (eds.), *Literatur und Laienbildung im Spätmittelalter und in der Reformationszeit* (Symposium Wolfenbüttel 1981) (Stuttgart: Metzler, 1984), 114–46.

Higgins, Dick, 'Intermedia', *Something Else Newsletter*, 1/1 (n.p., 1966); repr. in id., *Horizons: Poetics and Theory of the Intermedia* (Carbondale, Ill.: Southern Illinois University Press, 1984), 18–21.

Hillman, David, '*Homo Clausus* at the Theatre', in Bryan Reynolds and William N. West (eds.), *Rematerializing Shakespeare: Authority and Representation on the Early Modern English Stage* (Houndmills, Basingstoke: Palgrave/Macmillan, 2005), 161–85.

—— *Shakespeare's Entrails: Belief, Scepticism and the Interior of the Body* (Houndmills, Basingstoke: Palgrave Macmillan, 2007).

Hockey, Dorothy C., 'The Trial Pattern in *King Lear*', *Shakespeare Quarterly*, 10 (1959), 389–95.

Hodgen, Margaret, *Early Anthropology in the Sixteenth and Seventeenth Centuries* (Philadelphia: University of Pennsylvania Press, 1964).

Höfele, Andreas, '*Bestiarium Humanum*: Lear's Animal Kingdom', in Christa Jansohn (ed.), *German Shakespeare Studies at the Turn of the Twenty-First Century* (Newark, Del.: University of Delaware Press, 2006), 84–98.

—— 'The Place of the Human: Shakespeare's Stage and the Bear Garden', in Virginia Mason Vaughan, Fernando Cioni, and Jacquelyn Bessell (eds.), *Speaking Pictures: The Visual/Verbal Nexus of Dramatic Performance* (Madison and Teaneck, NJ: Fairleigh Dickinson University Press, 2010), 46–59.

Höfele, Andreas 'Sackerson the Bear', in Herbert Grabes (ed.), *Literary History/ Cultural History: Force-Fields and Tensions = Yearbook of Research in English and American Literature (REAL)*, 17 (2001), 161–77.

—— 'Stages of Martyrdom: John Foxe's *Actes and Monuments*', in Susanne Rupp and Tobias Döring (eds.), *Performances of the Sacred in Late Medieval and Early Modern England* (Amsterdam and New York: Rodopi, 2005), 81–93.

—— ' "What have we here—a man or a fish?" Animalität und Alterität in Shakespeares *Sturm*', in Christopher Balme (ed.), *Das Theater der Anderen* (Tübingen: Francke, 2001), 55–76.

—— and Laqué, Stephan, 'Introduction', in Andreas Höfele, Stephan Laqué, Enno Ruge, and Gabriela Schmidt (eds.), *Representing Religious Pluralization in Early Modern Europe* (Berlin: Lit, 2007), pp. ix–xviii.

Holbrook, Peter, 'Nietzsche's *Hamlet*', *Shakespeare Survey*, 50 (1997), 171–86.

Honigmann, E. A. J., *Myriad-Minded Shakespeare* (Basingstoke: Macmillan, 1989).

Hotson, J. Leslie, 'Bear Gardens and Bear-baiting during the Commonwealth', *PMLA* 40 (1925), 276–88.

Hulme, Peter, 'Introduction: The Cannibal Scene', in Barker, Hulme and Iversen (eds.), *Cannibalism and the Colonial World*.

Hunt, Albert, and Reeves, Geoffrey, *Peter Brook* (Cambridge: Cambridge University Press, 1995).

Hunt, John, 'A Thing of Nothing: The Catastrophic Body in *Hamlet*', *Shakespeare Quarterly*, 39 (1988), 27–44.

Hutcheon, Linda, *A Theory of Adaptation* (New York and London: Routledge, 2006).

Hyde, W. W., 'The Prosecution of Animals and Lifeless Things in the Middle Ages and Modern Times', *University of Pennsylvania Law Review*, 64 (1916), 696–730.

Ives, E. W., 'The Law and the Lawyers', *Shakespeare Survey*, 17 (1964), 73–86.

Jacobson, Norman, 'The Strange Case of the Hobbesian Man', *Representations*, 63 (1998), 1–11.

James, Susan, *Passion and Action: The Emotions in Seventeenth-Century Philosophy* (Cambridge: Cambridge University Press, 1997).

Jancsó, Daniella, *Excitements of Reason: The Presentation of Thought in Shakespeare's Plays and Wittgenstein's Philosophy* (Heidelberg: Winter, 2007).

Jardine, Lisa, *Erasmus, Man of Letters: The Construction of Charisma in Print* (Princeton: Princeton University Press, 1993).

Johnson, Samuel, *Johnson on Shakespeare*, ed. Arthur Sherbo, The Yale Edition of the Works of Samuel Johnson, viii (New Haven and London: Yale University Press, 1968).

Jones, Norman, *God and the Moneylenders* (Oxford: Basil Blackwell, 1989).

Joyce, James, *Ulysses*, ed. Hans Walter Gabler with Wolfgang Steppe and Claus Melchior (London: The Bodley Head, 1986).

Kaeuper, Richard W., 'The King and the Fox: Reactions to the Role of Kingship in Tales of Reynard the Fox', in Anthony Musson (ed.), *Expectations of the Law in the Middle Ages* (Woodbridge: Boydell Press, 2001), 9–21.

Kahn, Coppélia, 'Excavating "those dim Minoan Regions"': Maternal Subtexts in Patriarchal Literature', *Diacritics*, 2 (1982), 32–41.

—— *Roman Shakespeare: Warriors, Wounds, and Women* (London and New York: Routledge, 1997).

Kahn, Paul W., *Law and Love: The Trials of 'King Lear'* (New Haven and London: Yale University Press, 2000).

Kalof, Linda, and Resl, Brigitte (eds.), *A Cultural History of Animals*, 6 vols. (Oxford and New York: Berg, 2007).

Kastan, David Scott, 'Proud Majesty Made a Subject: Shakespeare and the Spectacle of Rule', *Shakespeare Quarterly*, 37 (1986), 459–75.

Keast, W. R., 'The "New Criticism" and *King Lear*', in R. S. Crane (ed.), *Critics and Criticism* (Chicago: University of Chicago Press, 1952), 108–37.

Keats, John, *The Letters of John Keats*, ed. Hyder Edward Rollins, 2 vols. (Cambridge: Cambridge University Press, 1958).

Keeton, George, *Shakespeare's Legal and Political Background* (London: Pitman, 1967).

Kennedy, John S., *The New Anthropomorphism* (Cambridge: Cambridge University Press, 1992).

Kermode, Lloyd Edward, 'Introduction', in *Three Renaissance Usury Plays*, ed. Lloyd Edward Kermode (Manchester and New York: Manchester University Press, 2009), 1–78.

Kerridge, Eric, *Usury, Interest and the Reformation* (Aldershot: Ashgate, 2002).

Kersting, Thomas, *Thomas Hobbes* (Hamburg: Junius, 1992).

Kete, Kathleen, *The Beast in the Boudoir: Petkeeping in Nineteenth-Century Paris* (Berkeley and London: University of California Press, 1994).

Kilgour, Mary, *From Communion to Cannibalism: An Anatomy of Metaphors of Incorporation* (Princeton: Princeton University Press, 1990).

Knight, G. Wilson, *The Imperial Theme* (1931) (London: Methuen, 1963).

—— *The Wheel of Fire: Interpretations of Shakespearean Tragedy* (4th edn., London: Methuen, 1962).

Kolentsis, Alysia, ' "Mark you / His absolute shall?"': Multitudinous Tongues and Contested Words in *Coriolanus*', *Shakespeare Survey*, 62 (2009), 141–50.

Kolnai, Aurel, 'Der Ekel', in *Jahrbuch für Philosophie und phänomenologische Forschung*, ed. Edmund Husserl, vol. 10 (Halle/Saale: Niemeyer, 1929), 515–69.

Koslow, Susan, *Frans Snyders: The Noble Estate. Seventeenth-Century Still-Life and Animal Painting in the Southern Netherlands* (Antwerp: Fonds Mercator Paribas, 1995).

Kott, Jan, *Shakespeare our Contemporary* (London: Methuen, 1964).

Kövecses, Zoltán, *Metaphor and Culture: Universality and Variation* (Cambridge: Cambridge University Press, 2005).

Kuriyama, Constance Brown, *Hammer or Anvil: Psychological Patterns in Christopher Marlowe's Plays* (New Brunswick, NJ: Rutgers University Press, 1980).

Lakoff, George, and Johnson, Mark, *Metaphors We Live By* (Chicago and London: University of Chicago Press, 1980).

Lamb, Mary Ellen, 'The Red Crosse Knight, St. George, and the Appropriation of Popular Culture', *Spenser Studies*, 18 (2003), 185–208.

Lansbury, Coral, *The Old Brown Dog: Women, Workers and Vivisection in Edwardian England* (Madison, Wis. and London: University of Wisconsin Press, 1985).

Laqué, Stephan, *The Metaphysics of Isolation: Delimitation, Knowledge and Identity in 20th-Century Literature* (postdoctoral thesis, Ludwig-Maximilians-Universität, Munich, 2009; publ. forthcoming).

Laqueur, Thomas W., 'Crowds, Carnival and the State in English Executions, 1604–1868', in A. L. Beier, David Cannadine and James Rosenheim (eds.), *The First Modern Society: Essays in English History in Honour of Lawrence Stone* (Cambridge: Cambridge University Press, 1989), 305–55.

—— *Making Sex: Body and Gender from the Greeks to Freud* (Cambridge, Mass., and London: Harvard University Press, 1990).

Largier, Niklaus, *In Praise of the Whip: A Cultural History of Arousal*, trans. Graham Harman (New York: Zone Books, 2007).

Latour, Bruno, *We Have Never Been Modern* (Cambridge, Mass.: Harvard University Press, 1993).

Leacroft, Richard, *The Development of the English Playhouse* (London: Eyre Methuen, 1973).

Lear, Jonathan, *Aristotle: The Desire to Understand* (Cambridge: Cambridge University Press, 1988).

Ledwon, Lenora, *Law and Literature: Text and Theory* (New York: Garland, 1996).

Lemm, Vanessa, *Nietzsche's Animal Philosophy: Culture, Politics and the Animality of the Human Being* (New York: Fordham University Press, 2009).

Lemon, Rebecca, *Treason by Words: Literature, Law, and Rebellion in Shakespeare's England* (Ithaca, NY, and London: Cornell University Press, 2006).

León-Portilla, Miguel, *Bernardino de Sahagún: First Anthropologist*, trans. Mauricio J. Mixco (Norman, Okla.: University of Oklahoma Press, 2002).

Lestringant, Frank, 'Catholiques et cannibales: Le thème du cannibalisme dans le discours protestant au temps des guerres de religion', in Jean-Claude Margolin and Robert Sauzet (eds.), *Pratiques et discours alimentaires à la Renaissance* (Paris: G.-P. Maisonneuve et Larose, 1982), 233–45.

Lévi-Strauss, Claude, *Totemism*, trans. Rodney Needham (London: Merlin, 1964).

—— *Tristes tropiques*, trans. John Weightman and Doreen Weightman (New York: Atheneum Books, 1974).

Liebler, Naomi Conn, 'Bully St. George: Richard Johnson's *Seven Champions of Christendom* and the Creation of the Bourgeois National Hero', in ead. (ed.), *Early Modern Prose Fiction: The Cultural Politics of Reading* (New York and London: Routledge, 2007), 115–29.

'Lion Fight at Vienna', *The Times* (London), 3 Aug. 1825.

Lippit, Akira Mizuta, 'The Death of an Animal', *Film Quarterly*, 56 (2002), 9–22.

—— *Electric Animal: Toward a Rhetoric of Wildlife* (Minneapolis: University of Minnesota Press, 2000).

Lobsien, Verena, 'Multi pertransibunt, oder: das versprochene Ende — Inszenierungen frühneuzeitlicher Apokalyptik in Shakespeares *King Lear*', in Maria Moog-Grünewald and Verena Lobsien (eds.), *Apokalypse: Der Anfang im Ende* (Heidelberg: Winter, 2003), 103–27.

Lockhart, Adrienne, 'The Cat is Grey: *King Lear's* Mad Trial Scene', *Shakespeare Quarterly*, 26 (1975), 469–71.

Losse, Deborah N., 'Rewriting Culture: Montaigne Recounts New World Ethnography', *Neophilologus*, 83 (1999), 517–28.

Lotman, Yuri, *The Structure of the Artistic Text* trans. Gail Lenhoff and Ronald Vroon (Ann Arbor: University of Michigan, Department of Slavic Languages and Literatures, 1977).

—— *Universe of the Mind: A Semiotic Theory of Culture*, trans. Ann Shukman, introd. Umberto Eco (London and New York: Tauris, 1990).

Lovejoy, Arthur O., *The Great Chain of Being: A Study in the History of Ideas* (1936; Cambridge, Mass.: Harvard University Press, 1961).

Lupton, Julia Reinhard, 'Creature Caliban', *Shakespeare Quarterly*, 51 (2000), 1–23.

Lynch, Kathryn L., ' "What hands are here?": The Hand as Generative Symbol in *Macbeth*', *Review of English Studies*, 39 (1988), 29–38.

McCoy, Richard, ' "The Grace of Grace" and Double-Talk in *Macbeth*', *Shakespeare Survey*, 57 (2004), 27–37.

McDonald, Russ, *Shakespeare and the Arts of Language* (Oxford: Oxford University Press, 2001).

MacGregor, Arthur, *Curiosity and Enlightenment: Collectors and Collections from the Sixteenth to the Nineteenth Century* (New Haven and London: Yale University Press, 2007).

McHugh, Susan. 'Literary Animal Agents', *PMLA* 124 (2009), 487–95.

Mack, Maynard, *King Lear in our Time* (London: Methuen, 1966).

McLuskie, Kathleen. 'The Patriarchal Bard: Feminist Criticism and Shakespeare: *King Lear* and *Measure for Measure*', in *Political Shakespeare*, eds. Jonathan Dollimore and Alan Sinfield (Manchester: Manchester University Press, 1985), 88–108.

McNichol, Tom. *AC/DC: The Savage Tale of the First Standards War* (San Francisco: Jossey-Bass, 2006).

Madden, Frederic, trans. 'Narrative of the Visit of the Duke de Nájera to England, in the Year 1543–4', *Archaeologia*, 23 (1831), 344–57.

Marcus, Leah S., *Unediting the Renaissance: Shakespeare, Marlowe, Milton* (London and New York: Routledge, 1996).

Marshall, Cynthia, ' "I can interpret all her martyr'd signs": *Titus Andronicus*, Feminism, and the Limits of Interpretation', in Carole Levin and Karen Robertson (eds.), *Sexuality and Politics in Renaissance Drama* (Lewiston, NY, Queenston, Ont., and Lampeter, Wales: The Edwin Mellen Press: 1991), 193–213.

Mastromarino, Mark A., 'Teaching Old Dogs New Tricks: The English Mastiff and the Anglo-American Experience', *The Historian*, 49 (1986), 10–25.

Melehy, Hassan, 'Silencing the Animals: Montaigne, Descartes, and the Hyperbole of Reason', *symploke*, 13 (2005), 263–82.

Menninger, Karl, *The Crime of Punishment* (New York: Viking Press, 1968).

Menninghaus, Winfried, *Ekel: Theorie und Geschichte einer starken Empfindung* (Frankfurt am Main: Suhrkamp, 1999).

Miller, David Lee, O'Dair, Sharon, and Weber, Harold (eds.), *The Production of English Renaissance Culture* (Ithaca, NY, and London: Cornell University Press, 1994).

Miller, William Ian, *The Anatomy of Disgust* (Cambridge, Mass.: Harvard University Press, 1997).

Monta, Susannah B., *Martyrdom and Literature in Early Modern England* (Cambridge: Cambridge University Press, 2005).

Moretti, Franco, 'The Great Eclipse: Tragic Form as the Deconsecration of Sovereignty', in *Signs Taken for Wonders: Essays in the Sociology of Literary Form*, trans. Susan Fischer, David Forgacs, and David Miller (London and New York: Verso, 1988), 42–82.

Morse, Ruth, 'Unfit for Human Consumption: Shakespeare's Unnatural Food', *Shakespeare Jahrbuch West* (1983), 125–49.

Mowat, Barbara, 'Prospero, Agrippa, and Hocus Pocus', *English Literary Renaissance*, 11 (1981), 281–303.

—— 'Prospero's Book', *Shakespeare Quarterly*, 52 (2001), 1–33.

Muir, Kenneth, 'Image and Symbol in *Macbeth*', *Shakespeare Survey*, 19 (1966), 45–54.

Mullaney, Steven, *The Place of the Stage: License, Play, and Power in Renaissance England* (Chicago and London: University of Chicago Press, 1988).

Neill, Michael, 'Heroic Heads and Humble Tails: Sex, Politics, and the Restoration Comic Rake', *Literature Criticism from 1400 to 1800*, 140 (2008), 287–301.

—— *Issues of Death: Mortality and Identity in English Renaissance Tragedy* (Oxford: Clarendon Press, 1997).

—— 'Shakespeare's Halle of Mirrors: Play, Politics, and Psychology in *Richard III*', *Shakespeare Studies*, 8 (1975), 99–129.

Nelle, Florian, *Künstliche Paradiese: Vom Barocktheater zum Filmpalast* (Würzburg: Königshausen und Neumann, 2005).

Nietzsche, Friedrich, *Beyond Good and Evil*, trans. R. J. Hollingdale (London: Penguin, 2003).

—— *The Complete Works of Friedrich Nietzsche: The First and Complete and Authorised English Translation*, v: *Thoughts out of Season, Part II*, ed. Oscar Levy (New York: Russell and Russell, 1964).

—— *Ecce Homo: How One Becomes What One Is*, trans. R. J. Hollingdale (London: Penguin, 1992).

—— *The Gay Science*, trans. Thomas Common (1882; Mineola, NY: Dover, 2006).

—— 'Homer's Contest' (1871) ['Re/Introducing "Homer's Contest": A New Translation with Notes and Commentary'], trans. Christa Davis Acampora, *Nietzscheana*, 5 (1996).

Nietzsche, Friedrich, *Human, All Too Human*, trans. Marion Faber and Stephen Lehmann, ed. Marion Faber (London: Penguin, 2004).

—— *Sämtliche Werke*, 15 vols., ed. Giorgio Colli and Mazzino Montinari. (Munich: Deutscher Taschenbuch Verlag; Berlin and New York: de Gruyter, 1980).

—— *Thus Spoke Zarathustra*, trans. and ed. Walter Kaufmann (New York: Modern Library, 1995).

—— *Twilight of the Idols* and *The Antichrist*, trans. R. J. Hollingdale (London: Penguin, 2003).

Nilan, Mary M., '*The Tempest* at the Turn of the Century: Cross-Currents in Production', *Shakespeare Survey*, 25 (1972), 113–23.

Nørgaard, Holger, 'Never Wrong but with Just Cause', *English Studies*, 45 (1964), 137–41.

Norris, Margot, *Beasts of the Modern Imagination: Darwin, Nietzsche, Kafka, Ernst and Lawrence* (Baltimore, Md. and London: The Johns Hopkins University Press, 1985).

Nowottny, Winifred M., 'Lear's Questions', *Shakespeare Survey*, 10 (1957), 90–7.

Nussbaum, Martha, 'Animal Rights: The Need for a Theoretical Basis', *Harvard Law Review*, 114 (2001), 1506–49.

—— 'Facing Animal Complexity', talk given at a panel entitled *Facing Animals*, Harvard University, 24 Apr. 2007 (online at <http://www.hcs.harvard.edu/~hrp/lecture/facing_ animals-nussbaum.pdf>; accessed 23 July 2010).

Oldridge, Darren, *Strange Histories: The Trial of the Pig, the Walking Dead, and Other Matters of Fact from the Medieval and Renaissance Worlds* (London and New York: Routledge, 2005).

Olson, Greta, and Kayman, Martin, 'From "Law-and-Literature" to "Law, Literature and Language": A Comparative Approach', *European Journal of English Studies*, 11 (2007), 1–15.

—— 'Richard III's Animalistic Animal Body', *Philological Quarterly*, 82 (2003), 301–24.

Orgel, Stephen, 'Making Greatness Familiar', *Genre*, 15 (1982), 41–8.

Orrell, John, *The Human Stage: English Theatre Design, 1567–1640* (Cambridge: Cambridge University Press, 1988).

Pagden, Anthony, *The Fall of Natural Man: The American Indian and the Origins of Comparative Ethnology* (Cambridge: Cambridge University Press, 1982).

Palmer, D. J., '"A New Gorgon": Visual Effects in *Macbeth*', in John Russell Brown (ed.), *Focus on 'Macbeth'* (London: Routledge/Kegan Paul, 1982), 54–69.

—— 'The Unspeakable in Pursuit of the Uneatable: Language and Action in *Titus Andronicus*', *Critical Quarterly*, 14 (1972), 320–39.

Park, Katharine, 'The Organic Soul', in Charles B. Schmitt, Quentin Skinner, and Eckhard Kessler (eds.), *The Cambridge History of Renaissance Philosophy* (Cambridge: Cambridge University Press, 2000), 464–84.

—— and Daston, Lorraine, 'Introduction: The Age of the New', in *The Cambridge History of Science*, iii: *Early Modern Science* (Cambridge: Cambridge University Press, 2006), 1–17.

Paster, Gail Kern, *The Body Embarrassed: Drama and the Disciplines of Shame in Early Modern England* (Ithaca, NY: Cornell University Press, 1993).

—— *Humoring the Body: Emotions and the Shakespearean Stage* (Chicago and London: The University of Chicago Press, 2004).

—— Rowe, Katherine, and Floyd-Wilson, Mary (eds.), *Reading the Early Modern Passions: Essays in the Cultural History of Emotions* (Philadelphia: University of Pennsylvania Press, 2004).

Pearce, Brian, 'Beerbohm Tree's Production of *The Tempest*, 1904', *New Theatre Quarterly*, 11 (1995), 299–308.

Peters, Edward, *Torture* (Philadelphia: University of Pennsylvania Press, 1996).

Pfister, Manfred, 'Animal Images in *Coriolanus* and the Early Modern Crisis of Distinction between Man and Beast', *Shakespeare Jahrbuch*, 145 (2009), 141–57.

—— '"Man's Distinctive Mark": Paradoxical Distinctions between Man and his Bestial Other in Early Modern Texts', in Elmar Lehmann and Bernd Lenz (eds.), *Telling Stories: Studies in Honour of Ulrich Broich on the Occasion of his 60th Birthday* (Amsterdam: Grüner, 1992), 17–33.

Preece, Rod, *Awe for the Tiger, Love for the Lamb: A Chronicle of Sensibility to Animals* (Vancouver and Toronto: University of British Columbia Press, 2002).

Quint, David, 'A Reconsideration of Montaigne's *Des cannibales*', in Karen Ordahl Kupperman (ed.), *America in European Consciousness, 1493–1750* (Chapel Hill, NC, and London: University of North Carolina Press, 1995), 166–91.

Quiring, Björn, *Shakespeares Fluch: Die Aporien ritueller Exklusion im Königsdrama der englischen Renaissance* (Munich: Fink, 2009).

Raffield, Paul, *Images and Cultures of Law in Early Modern England: Justice and Political Power, 1558–1660* (Cambridge: Cambridge University Press, 2004).

Ravelhofer, Barbara, ' "Beasts of Recreacion": Henslowe's White Bears', *English Literary Renaissance*, 32 (2002), 287–323.

Reed, T. J., 'Nietzsche's Animals: Idea, Image and Influence', in Malcolm Pasley (ed.), *Imagery and Thought* (London: Methuen, 1978), 159–219.

Rhodes, Kimberly, *Ophelia and Victorian Visual Culture: Representing Body Politics in the Nineteenth Century* (Aldershot: Ashgate, 2008).

Rice, Raymond J., 'Cannibalism and the Act of Revenge in Tudor-Stuart Drama', *Studies in English Language*, 44 (2004), 297–316.

Richter, Virginia, 'Missing Links: Anthropological Anxiety in British Imperial Discovery Fiction 1870–1930' (postdoctoral thesis, Ludwig-Maximilians-Universität, Munich, 2005; publ. forthcoming).

Riebling, Barbara, 'Virtue's Sacrifice: A Machiavellian Reading of *Macbeth*', *Studies in English Literature 1500–1900*, 31 (1991), 273–86.

Ritvo, Harriet, *Animal Estate: The English and Other Creatures in the Victorian Age* (Cambridge, Mass.: Harvard University Press, 1987).

Ritvo, Harriet, 'Border Trouble: Shifting the Line between People and Other Animals', in Arien Mack (ed.), *Humans and Other Animals* (Columbus, Ohio: Ohio State University Press, 1995), 67–86.

Robels, Hella, *Frans Snyders: Stilleben- und Tiermaler, 1579–1657* (Munich: Deutscher Kunstverlag, 1989).

Roberts, Mark S., *The Mark of the Beast: Animality and Human Oppression* (West Lafayette, Ind.: Purdue University Press, 2008).

Romm, James S., *The Edges of the Earth in Ancient Thought: Geography, Exploration, and Fiction* (Princeton: Princeton University Press, 1992).

Ronan, Clifford, *'Antike Romans': Power Symbology and the Roman Play in Early Modern England, 1585–1635* (Athens, Ga., and London: University of Georgia Press, 1995).

Rosand, David, 'Rubens's Munich "Lion Hunt": Its Sources and Significance', *Art Bulletin*, 51 (1969), 29–40.

Rosenberg, Marvin, *The Masks of King Lear* (Berkeley, Los Angeles, and London: University of California Press, 1972).

Rowe, John Howland, 'The Renaissance Foundations of Anthropology', *American Anthropologist*, 67 (1965), 1–20.

Rozett, Martha Tuck, 'Drowning Ophelias and Other Images of Death in Shakespeare's Plays', in Holger Klein and James L. Harner (eds.), *Shakespeare and the Visual Arts* (Lewiston, NY, Queenston, Ont., and Lampeter, Wales: Edward Mellen Press, 2000), 182–96.

Runciman, W. G., 'The Sociologist and the Historian' (= review of Keith Hopkins, *Death and Renewal* (Cambridge: Cambridge University Press, 1983)), *Journal of Roman Studies*, 76 (1986), 259–65.

Rushdie, Salman, *The Satanic Verses* (Dover, Del.: The Consortium, 1992).

Ryan, Kiernan, *Shakespeare* (Hemel Hempstead and Atlantic Highlands, NJ: Harvester Wheatsheaf, 1989).

Salisbury, Joyce E., *The Beast within: Animals in the Middle Ages* (New York: Routledge, 1994).

Die Sammlung der Herzog August Bibliothek in Wolfenbüttel, Wolfgang Harms with Michael Schilling and Andreas Wang, vol. 2 (Munich: Kraus International Publications, 1980).

Sawday, Jonathan, *The Body Emblazoned: Dissection and the Human Body in Renaissance Culture* (London and New York: Routledge, 1995).

Scarry, Elaine, *The Body in Pain: The Making and Unmaking of the World* (Oxford: Oxford University Press, 1985).

Schaefer, David Lewis, *The Political Philosophy of Montaigne* (Ithaca, NY, and London: Cornell University Press, 1990).

Schiller, Johann Christoph Friedrich von, *Schillers Werke. Nationalausgabe*, ed. Norbert Oellers, 42 vols. (Weimar: Böhlau, 1943–2006).

Schmidt, Gabriela, 'Representing Martyrdom in Post-Reformation England', in Höfele, Laqué, Ruge, and Schmidt (eds.), *Representing Religious Pluralization*, 63–90.

Schmitt, Carl, *Glossarium: Aufzeichnungen der Jahre 1947–1951*, ed. Eberhard Freiherr von Medem (Berlin: Duncker & Humblot, 1991).

—— *Hamlet or Hecuba: The Intrusion of the Time into the Play*, trans. David Pan and Jennifer R. Rust (1956; New York: Telos, 2009).

Schmitt, Carl, *The Leviathan in the State Theory of Thomas Hobbes: Meaning and Failure of a Political Symbol*, trans. George Schwab and Erna Hilfstein (1938; Westport, Conn., and London: Greenwood Press, 1996).

—— *Political Theology: Four Chapters on the Concept of Sovereignty*, trans. George Schwab (1922; Chicago and London: University of Chicago Press, 2005).

Schoeck, R. J., 'Shakespeare and the Law: An Overview', *The Shakespearean International Yearbook* 1999, 219–39.

Schoenfeldt, Michael, *Bodies and Selves* (Cambridge: Cambridge University Press, 1999).

Scott-Giles, C. W., *Shakespeare's Heraldry* (London: J. M. Dent and Sons, 1950).

Scott-Warren, Jason, 'When Theatres Were Bear-Gardens; or, What's at Stake in the Comedy of Humours', *Shakespeare Quarterly*, 54 (2003), 63–82.

Serres, Michel, *Rome: The Book of Foundations*, trans. Felicia McCarren (Stanford: Stanford University Press, 1991).

Shannon, Laurie, 'The Eight Animals in Shakespeare; or, Before the Human', *PMLA* 124 (2009), 472–9.

—— 'Poor, Bare, Forked: Animal Sovereignty, Human Negative Exceptionalism, and the Natural History of King Lear', *Shakespeare Quarterly*, 60 (2009), 168–96.

Shapiro, James, *1599: A Year in the Life of William Shakespeare* (London: Faber and Faber, 2005).

Sharpe, J. A., ' "Last Dying Speeches": Religion, Ideology and Public Execution in Seventeenth-Century England', *Past and Present*, 107 (1985), 144–67.

Shklar, Judith, *Ordinary Vices* (Cambridge, Mass.: Belknap Press, 1984).

Shupack, Paul M., 'Natural Justice and *King Lear*', *Cardozo Studies in Law and Literature*, 9 (1997) 67–105.

Singer, Peter, *Animal Liberation: A New Ethics for our Treatment of Animals* (London: Jonathan Cape, 1976).

Sisson, C. J., 'Justice in *King Lear*', repr. in Frank Kermode (ed.), *Shakespeare: King Lear*. (London: Macmillan, 1969), 228–44.

Skura, Meredith Anne, *Shakespeare the Actor and the Purpose of Playing* (Chicago and London: University of Chicago Press, 1993).

Smith, Bruce, *The Acoustic World of Early Modern England: Attending to the O-Factor* (Chicago: University of Chicago Press, 1999).

Smith, Pamela H., *The Body of the Artisan: Art and Experience in the Scientific Revolution* (Chicago: University of Chicago Press, 2004).

Sokol, B. J., and Sokol, Mary, 'Shakespeare and the English Equity Jurisdiction: The Merchant of Venice and the Two Texts of *King Lear*', *Review of English Studies*, 50/200 (1999), 417–39.

Sokol, B. J., and Sokol, Mary, *Shakespeare's Legal Language: A Dictionary,* (London and New Brunswick, NJ: Athlone, 2000).

Spiller, Elizabeth, 'Shakespeare and the Making of Early Modern Science: Resituating Prospero's Art', *South Central Review*, 26 (2009), 24–41.

Spinoza, Charles, ' "The name and all th'addition": *King Lear's* Opening Scene and the Common-Law Use', *Shakespeare Studies*, 23 (1995), 146–86.

Spurgeon, Caroline F. E., *Shakespeare's Imagery and what It Tells Us* (Cambridge: Cambridge University Press, 1935).

Sterne, Laurence, *A Sentimental Journey through France and Italy*, ed. Graham Petrie (Harmondsworth: Penguin, 1967).

Stewart, Alan, *Shakespeare's Letters* (Oxford: Oxford University Press, 2008).

Stierle, Karlheinz, 'Was heißt Moralistik?', in Rudolf Behrens and Maria Moog-Grünewald (eds.), *Moralistik: Anthropologischer und ästhetischer Diskurs des Subjekts in früher Neuzeit und Moderne* (Munich: Fink, 2010).

Strauss, Leo, *The Political Philosophy of Hobbes: Its Basis and its Genesis*, trans. Elsa M. Sinclair from German manuscript (Oxford: Clarendon Press, 1936).

Sturgess, Keith, *Jacobean Private Theatres* (London: Routledge and Kegan Paul, 1987).

Styan, J. L., *The English Stage: A History of Drama and Performance* (Cambridge: Cambridge University Press, 1996).

—— *Shakespeare's Stagecraft* (Cambridge: Cambridge University Press, 1967).

Surya, Michel, *Humanimalité: L'inéliminable animalité de l'homme* (Paris: Néant, 2001).

Tayler, Edward W., '*King Lear* and Negation', *English Literary Renaissance*, 20 (1990), 17–39.

Taylor, Charles, *The Sources of the Self: Making of the Modern Identity* (Cambridge, Mass.: Harvard University Press, 1989).

Taylor, Gary, 'Feeling Bodies', in *Shakespeare and the Twentieth Century. The Selected Proceedings of the International Shakespeare Association World Congress, Los Angeles, 1996*, ed. Jonathan Bate, Jill Levenson, and Dieter Mehl (Newark, Del.: University of Delaware Press, 1998), 258–79.

—— '*King Lear* and Censorship', in Taylor and Warren (eds.), *The Division of the Kingdoms*, 75–119.

—— and Warren, Michael (eds.), *The Division of the Kingdoms: Shakespeare's Two Versions of 'King Lear'* (Oxford: Clarendon Press, 1983).

Tennyson, Alfred, *In Memoriam,* LV, 4, ed. Susan Shatto and Marion Shaw (Oxford: Clarendon Press, 1982).

Thomas, Keith, *Man and the Natural World: Changing Attitudes in England 1500–1800* (London: Allan Lane, 1983).

Thompson, Ann, and Thompson, John O., *Shakespeare: Meaning and Metaphor* (Brighton: Harvester Press, 1987).

Toulmin, Stephen, *Cosmopolis: The Hidden Agenda of Modernity* (New York: The Free Press, 1990).

Tricomi, Albert H., 'The Aesthetics of Mutilation in *Titus Andronicus*', *Shakespeare Survey*, 27 (1974), 11–19.

Trinkaus, Charles E., *In Our Image and Likeness: Humanity and Divinity in Italian Humanist Thought*, 2 vols. (London: Constable, 1970).

Unser täglich Brot (*Our Daily Bread*, 2005), dir. Nikolaus Geyrhalter (Alive Productions, 2007), DVD.

Vanderbilt, Tom, 'City Lore; They Didn't Forget', *New York Times*, Sunday, 13 July 2003.

Vaughan, Alden T., and Vaughan, Virginia Mason, *Shakespeare's Caliban: A Cultural History* (Cambridge: Cambridge University Press, 1991).

Verma, Rajiva, *Myth, Ritual, and Shakespeare: A Study of Critical Theory and Practice* (New Delhi: Spantech, 1990).

Waith, Eugene M., *The Herculean Hero in Marlowe, Chapman, Shakespeare and Dryden* (London: Chatto and Windus, 1962).

Wallace, C. W. W., 'The Children of the Chapel at Blackfriars, 1597–1603', *University of Nebraska Studies*, 8 (1908), 103–321.

Ward, Ian, 'Law and Literature: A continuing Debate', in *Law and Literature: Possibilities and Perspectives*, ed. Ian Ward (Cambridge: Cambridge University Press, 1995).

Warner, Marina, 'Fee fie fo fum: The Child in the Jaws of the Story', in Barker, Hulme, and Iversen (eds.) *Cannibalism and the Colonial World*, 158–82.

Warren, Roger, 'The Folio Omission of the Mock Trial: Motives and Consequences', in Taylor and Warren (eds.), *The Division of the Kingdoms*, 45–57.

—— 'Rough Magic and Heavenly Music: *The Tempest*', in Virginia Mason Vaughan and Alden T. Vaughan (eds.), *Critical Essays on Shakespeare's The Tempest* (New York: Hall, 1998), 152–89.

Watson, Robert N., 'As You Liken It: Simile in the Wilderness', *Shakespeare Survey*, 56 (2003), 79–92.

—— *Back to Nature: The Green and the Real in the Late Renaissance* (Philadelphia: University of Pennsylvania Press, 2006).

—— *The Rest is Silence. Death as Annihilation in the English Renaissance* (Berkeley, Los Angeles, and London: University of California Press, 1994).

We Feed the World, dir. Erwin Wagenhofer (Universum Film, 2006), DVD.

Weber, Harold, *The Restoration Rake-Hero: Transformations in Sexual Understanding in 17th-Century England* (Madison, Wis.: University of Wisconsin Press, 1986).

Weimann, Robert, *Author's Pen and Actor's Voice: Playing and Writing in Shakespeare's Theatre* (Cambridge: Cambridge University Press, 2000).

—— *Shakespeare and the Popular Tradition in the Theater: Studies in the Social Dimension of Dramatic Form and Function* (Baltimore, Md.: Johns Hopkins University Press, 1978).

Wells, Robin Headlam, *Shakespeare's Humanism* (Cambridge: Cambridge University Press, 2005).

Wertheimer, Jürgen, 'Im Blutstrom blättern: Das elisabethanische Theater der Grausamkeit', in Peter Gendolla and Carsten Celle (eds.), *Schönheit und Schrecken: Entsetzen, Gewalt und Tod in alten und neuen Medien* (Heidelberg: Winter, 1990), 39–53.

West, William N., *Theatres and Encyclopedias in Early Modern Europe* (Cambridge: Cambridge University Press, 2002).

Westerhoff, Jan C., 'A World of Signs: Baroque Pansemioticism, the *Polyhistor* and the Early Modern *Wunderkammer*', *Journal of the History of Ideas*, 62 (2001), 633–50.

Wickham, Glynne, *Early English Stages 1300–1660*, 2 vols. (London and Henley: Routledge and Kegan Paul, 1959–72).

Wild, Markus, *Die anthropologische Differenz: Der Geist der Tiere in der frühen Neuzeit bei Montaigne, Descartes und Hume* (Berlin and New York: De Gruyter, 2006).

Wiles, David, *Shakespeare's Clown: Actor and Text in the Elizabethan Playhouse* (Cambridge: Cambridge University Press, 1987).

—— 'William Kemp and Harry Hunks: Play as Game, Actor as Sign—A Theoretical Conclusion', in id., *Shakespeare's Clown*, 164–81.

Willbern, David, 'Rape and Revenge in *Titus Andronicus*', *English Literary Renaissance*, 8 (1978), 159–82.

Willson, Robert F., Jr., 'Gloucester and Harry Hunks', *Upstart Crow*, 9 (1989), 107–11.

Wilson, Daniel, *Caliban: The Missing Link* (London: Macmillan, 1873).

Wilson, Scott, 'Reading Shakespeare with Intensity: A Commentary on Some Lines from Nietzsche's *Ecce Homo*', in John J. Joughin (ed.), *Philosophical Shakespeares* (London and New York: Routledge, 2000), 86–104.

Wise, Steven M., *Rattling the Cage: Toward Legal Rights for Animals* (Cambridge, Mass.: Perseus Books, 2000).

Wiseman, Susan J., 'Hairy on the Inside: Metamorphosis and Civility in English Werewolf Texts', in Fudge (ed.), *Renaissance Beasts*, 50–69.

Wittreich, Joseph, ' "Image of that horror": The Apocalypse in *King Lear*', in C.A. Patrides and Joseph Wittreich (eds.), *The Apocalypse in English Renaissance Thought and Literature: Patterns, Antecedents and Repercussions* (Manchester: Manchester University Press, 1984), 175–206.

Wofford, Susanne L., 'The Body Unseamed: Shakespeare's Late Tragedies', in ead. (ed), *Shakespeare's Late Tragedies* (Upper Saddle River, NJ: Prentice Hall, 1996), 1–21.

Wolf, Werner, *The Musicalization of Fiction: A Study in the Theory and History of Intermediality* (Amsterdam: Rodopi, 1999).

Wolfe, Cary, 'In the Shadow of Wittgenstein's Lion', in id. (ed.), *Zoontologies*, 1–57.

—— *Philosophy and Animal Life* (New York: Columbia University Press, 2008).

—— *What Is Posthumanism?* (Minneapolis: University of Minnesota Press, 2009).

—— (ed.), *Zoontologies: The Question of the Animal* (Minneapolis: University of Minnesota Press, 2003).

Woolf, Virginia, 'Character in Fiction' (1924), in *Selected Essays*, ed. David Bradshaw (Oxford and New York: Oxford University Press, 2009), 37–54.

Wynne-Davies, Marion, ' "The Swallowing Womb": Consumed and Consuming Women in *Titus Andronicus*', in Valerie Wayne (ed.), *The Matter of Difference: Materialist Feminist Criticism of Shakespeare* (Ithaca, NY, and New York: Cornell University Press, 1991), 129–51.

Yates, Frances A. 'Magic in Shakespeare's Last Plays—On *The Tempest*', *Encounter*, 44 (1975), 14–22.

—— *Shakespeare's Last Plays* (London: Routledge, 1975).

—— *Theatre of the World* (Chicago: University of Chicago Press, 1969).

Young, Alan R., Hamlet *and the Visual Arts, 1709–1900* (Newark, Del.: University of Delaware Press; London: Associated University Presses, 2002).

Zimmerman, Susan, *The Early Modern Corpse and Shakespeare's Theatre* (Edinburgh: Edinburgh University Press, 2005).

Ziolkowski, Theodore, *The Mirror of Justice: Literary Reflections of Legal Crisis* (Princeton: Princeton University Press, 1997).

Index

Actaeon 146
actor (*also* player) 12, 49, 161–2, 216,
    237, 245
    and (baited) animal 6–7, 15, 34, 98,
        231
    as 'shadow' 75
    king as a. 72, 78, 81
Adam 18, 54, 89, 166, 247, 249, 261
adaptation 13
Adelman, Janet 79–80
Agamben, Giorgio 54–5, 58, 112, 166,
    179–80, 246
Alexander the Great 118 n. 4, 159, 164
Alleyn, Edward 7, 36, 83
anatomy 202–3
Anaxagoras 56–7
angel 165, 188, 217, 261
anima 25, 165, 228
animal, animals (*also* beasts)
    capable of own thoughts 121, 166
    cruelty to 116–7, 129 n. 39, 269,
        276–7
    disappearance from the scene of
        punishment 9–10
    disavowal of 23
    domestication/taming of 11, 37, 92,
        94, 140
    electrocution of 273–6
    figure of inversion 135
    as figure of the Other 120
    heraldic 83, 87, 183–4
    as machine 22, 254–5, 260
    as performers 34, 95, 97–8, 209
    physical presence on Shakespeare's
        stage 30
    semantic range of term 24–7, 173
    sympathy with 210, 271–2
    thinking with 20, 101
    ape (*also* monkey) 235, 244–5, 257–9

anthropogenesis of 57
    on horseback 10–11
ass 35, 133 n. 48
bear (*see also* bear-baiting) 10, 31–2,
    50, 79, 229
bird (*see separate entry*)
boar 79, 83
bull (*see also* baiting) 273
butterflies 224
cat 52, 121, 180, 199, 241, 273
chameleon (*also* man as) 18, 90, 160,
    213, 267
cow x, 273, 277
crocodile 160, 177
deer/doe/stag 92, 97, 151, 152, 268
dog (*see separate entry*)
dolphin 216
dragon 106, 107 n. 41, 113, 131,
    177–9, 183–8, 190, 200, 206,
    211, 214, 219
elephant 273–7
fish 164, 241–2, 245
fox 66, 90, 180, 200, 208, 224,
    225 n. 156
    she-fox 189, 198–201, 208, 217
frog 175, 213, 240
hare 116
hedgehog 88, 147, 235
horse 34, 43, 114, 133 n. 48, 145, 191,
    216, 226, 228, 263, 273
jackal 101–2
lamb 65, 82, 88, 102–3, 134–5, 147
leopard 83
lion 66, 82–85, 90, 101–2, 169, 180,
    183, 199, 268–70
maggot 158, 164
monkey (*see* ape)
mouse 175
mule 132, 133 n. 48

animal, animals (*cont.*)
  ox 108, 277
  oyster 165–6
  paddock 52
  pig 116, 129, 194–5, 199–200, 272,
      275–7
  pony 11
  rat 100, 105, 213, 228
  serpent (*also* snake, adder) 131, 147,
      177, 188–90, 222, 235
  spider 88
  stallion 160
  tadpole 213
  tiger 167, 169, 189
  toad 88, 131, 147, 213, 222
  tortoise 241, 255, 258
  whale 177, 217
  wolf 88, 90, 102, 110–13, 131, 135,
      188, 213–14, 217, 223, 253
    she-wolf 108, 112–13
  worm 131, 157, 159, 164
animal baiting (*see* baiting)
animal fable 48, 173
animal imagery (*also* metaphor, simile)
    28–9, 50, 86, 101, 103–4, 171,
    224–5
animal impersonation 30, 267
animal sacrifice 135
animal trials 194–5, 200, 202, 274–6
animality (*also* human animality) 3, 20–1,
    23, 38, 40, 55, 63, 88, 90,
    103, 130, 133, 136, 156, 171–3,
    178–9, 189–90, 199, 208–9,
    216, 235, 243, 253, 257–9,
    261, 263
anthropomorphism 11, 35, 38, 48, 63,
    98–9, 210, 275
anthropocentrism 21, 38, 40, 121, 166,
    257, 259, 278
anthropology 16, 19
  Aristotelian 27, 104–6, 130, 173, 236
  Cartesian 3, 22, 25, 27, 167–8, 173,
      254, 259–60
  Christian 25, 58
  cultural 16–18, 20
  humanist (*see also* humanism) 89, 166,
      191, 249, 250
  Nietzschean 259–6
  philosophical 17–20

political 167
Shakespearean 3, 15, 22, 28, 38–40,
    51, 173, 249, 254, 266
Antichrist 177
anti-slavery movement 271
Saint Antony 200, 207 n. 108
Apocalypse 220–21, 227
Aristotle 18, 24, 56, 104, 106, 130, 173,
    168 n. 139
audience 11, 34–5, 46, 110
  as many-headed monster 77, 82,
      111–12, 231
  complicit 118
  dangerous unpredictability of 78
  fascination with violence 119, 131
St Augustine 27, 57, 136
authority (paternal, royal) 182, 219

Bacon, Francis 91, 127, 187, 205,
    239–40, 250–1, 264–6, 278
baiting (*see also* bear-baiting),
  of animals 269
  of ape 10–11
  of bull 4–7, 10, 12, 34, 45, 59, 83
  Christian *ur*-scene of 79
  of humans 12, 80, 114
  of lion 83–4, 268–70
  and criminal justice 12, 14,
      173, 270–1
Bataille, George 158 n. 113
bear-baiting 10, 36–7, 39, 42–8, 59–61,
    63–4, 83–7, 95, 97, 99, 101,
    116, 174–5, 209–10, 232, 234–5,
    266–8, 273, 277
bear garden (*also* bear pit, baiting ring)
    6–7, 10, 30, 32–8, 46, 60, 62, 64,
    85, 96, 100, 173, 208–10, 228–33,
    253, 270–2, 278
bear hunt 93–100
Benjamin, Walter 246
Benson, Frank 245, 257–8
Bernini, Gian Lorenzo 237
bestialization 23, 46, 58, 63, 100, 105,
    131–2, 137–8, 173–4, 185,
    187–94, 209, 211, 226
  of criminal 9–10, 12, 36, 63, 115, 133,
      219, 271
  as tool of colonialism 243, 257
bestiary 48, 173

Beuckelaer, Joachim 133
Bible
    Isaiah (6,3) and (13,6) 227
    Job 176
    Judges (15,4–5) 224 n. 155
    Luke (12,1–3) 77–9
    Matthew (27,28–30) 79
bird 167, 188, 217, 223–4, 272
    capon 160
    chicken 83 n. 36, 116, 272, 276
    cuckoo 188–9
    fowl 160
    nightingale 199, 217, 225
    owl 213–14, 217, 223
    pelican 188–9
    starling 272
    swallow 225
    vulture 189
Blackfriars Theatre 233
Bloom, Harold 2
Bodin, Jean 177–82
body 45–6, 56, 102, 115, 118, 138, 148,
        159, 165, 191, 216, 245, 255, 273
    eye 56–7, 60, 207
    face 201
    hand 56–8, 61
    heads (severed) 64–5, 68–70, 72, 74,
        76, 80–1, 139
    heart 201, 203
    humoral 27–28
    as machine 168
    mouth 150
    tongue 111, 113
    vagina 147
    womb 80, 88, 114, 147–48,
body fluids 272
body politic 39, 98–9, 138, 185, 251
body-soul dualism 168
Boeckhorst Jan 93
Booth, Stephen 53
Bosch, Hieronymus 200
Bosse, Abraham 176 n. 20
Bovillus, Carolus 55–6
Brecht, Bertolt 14, 108 n. 45
Bredekamp, Horst 176 n. 20
Brook, Peter 172, 197
Brown, Harold P. 274
Brownstein, Oscar Lee 4, 6

Brueghel, Pieter the Younger 93, 200
Buchel, Charles A. 258
Burbage, James 3, 5 n. 10
Burckhardt, Jacob 18, 54
butchery (also slaughter) 10, 57, 76, 131,
        133–5, 138, 141, 161, 203, 272,
        277–8

Cacus 108
Campbell, Joseph 212, 218
cannibalism 40, 113, 115–16, 120–33,
        146, 148, 150, 157, 165–7,
        186–7, 271
    idealization of 121–4, 126
    relationship to revenge (see also
        punishment) 115, 124–5, 127–9,
        133, 141–2, 149–56, 160, 162–3,
        167, 169, 170
    as social hygiene 169
    symbolic 131, 142, 153
    universal 164–5, 167, 186
Capella, Galeazzo 17
Casas, Bartholomé de las 17 n. 51, 233
Casmann, Otto 17
Cassirer, Ernst 55
Cecrops 179–80
censorship 195–96
centaur 120, 191–2, 261
    female c. 192
Cerberus 132
Chambers, Edmund 3
Charles I 72
Charles II 83
Charles V of Spain 233
Chodowiecki, Daniel 255–58
Clemen, Wolfgang 87, 171
Coghill, Nevill 30
Coleridge, Samuel Taylor 272
colonialism 17, 20, 240, 243, 246, 248,
        258
Columbus, Christopher 169
Colvin, Sidney 268
Cortés, Hernán 233
Cowden Clarke, Charles and Mary
        266–8
Crane, Mary 252
Crane, Ralph 244
Cranmer, Thomas 41–5

criminal justice (*see also* execution, punishment, torture, whipping) 14, 63, 117, 128, 131, 137, 173, 203, 205, 235, 270–1, 275
Cromwell, Thomas 41–4, 46, 233
cruelty 119–20, 123, 125–6, 273
  of punishment 118, 129, 138, 141, 205–6, 208–9, 270–1

Danby, John 187
Darwin, Charles 256–7, 259
Darwinism 256–60, 261
decapitation (*see also* body, heads) 68, 70, 76, 78, 85
Deianira 112
Dekker, Thomas 59–63, 173–75, 209–10, 270
Derrida, Jacques 36, 58 n. 31, 92
Descartes, René 22, 25, 27, 167–68, 254–5, 259–60, 278
Devil 59, 62, 132, 177, 184, 196
Diamond, Cora x
Diana (goddess of the hunt) 97, 146
disgust 157–58, 165, 168
dissecting theatres 202
dog (*also* hound) 6, 10–11, 30, 34–5, 42, 47, 50, 59–60, 83–4, 88, 91–101, 105–6, 116, 129, 145–6, 158, 174, 189, 199, 210 n. 114, 213, 216, 219, 228, 233–5, 266–7, 269–71, 273
  bandog 97–9, 106, 235
  bloodhound 232
  execution (hanging) of dogs 84 n. 37
  hell-hound 59, 88, 91
  hound (hunting dog) 93–7, 231
  mastiff 1, 7, 30, 83, 84 n. 37, 231–3, 269
Dollimore, Jonathan 172
Donne, John 45
Dorset Garden 230
Drury Lane 230
Dudley, Robert, 1. Earl of Leicester 97
Duke of Mecklenburg 170

Edison, Thomas Alva 273–5
Edward the Confessor 58
Elias, Norbert 10, 272
Elizabeth I 47, 73, 83, 97, 138, 146
electrocution 273–7

Engels, Friedrich 57
Enlightenment 10, 278
Erasmus, Desiderius 238
ethnocentrism 121, 166, 243
Eucharist 48
Evander 108
exceptionalism 173
execution 73, 128, 133, 168

Fennor, William 61
Fletcher, Phineas 185, 251
Foakes, R. A. 206
food 131, 160–1, 213, 226, 276–7
Foucault, Michel 9, 14, 21, 128, 168, 251, 271, 278
Foxe, John 40–8, 115, 129, 132–37, 151, 164–66, 271
Freud, Sigmund 146
Fudge, Erica 15, 24, 278

Gardiner, Stephen, Bishop of Winchester 135
Gauden, John 162
gaze (*see also* audience) 12, 77, 81–2, 110, 121, 246
Geertz, Clifford 243
Gehlen, Arnold 19 n. 59
Genet, Jean 196
St George 183–4
Gérard, Balthazar 234
Gesner, Conrad 26
Geyrhalter, Nikolaus 276
Gillbert, William 239
Globe theatre 6, 8, 30, 32, 34–5, 64, 229–30
God 54, 70, 77, 89, 104, 106, 165, 222, 247, 254
  as privileged spectator 77–8
Gower, John 161
Granville-Barker, Harley 197
Greenblatt, Stephen 215, 243
Grünewald, Matthias 200
Gumbrecht, Hans Ulrich 48–50, 52
Gurr, Andrew 3, 7

Halpern, Richard 236
hanging 62, 274
  of pigs 194, 200, 275
Haraway, Donna 217–18
Harsnett, Samuel 215, 224

Haviland, William 257
Harry Hunks (bear) 1, 60–1, 63, 209, 275
Hawkes, Terence 12
Hecate 181
Hector 111 n. 53
Hecuba 111 n. 53, 161
Heidegger, Martin 44 n. 10, 58 n. 31
Heilman, Robert B. 171–2, 189
Hegel, Georg Friedrich Wilhelm 67
hell (and hell-mouth) 59–60, 62, 131–2, 146, 155
Henry II 83
Henry III 83
Henry VII 84
Henry VIII 41–2, 47, 233
Henry Frederick Stuart, Prince of Wales 77, 83, 182
Henslowe, Philip 6–7, 30, 32
Hentzner, Paul 11, 68
Hercules 107–08, 112, 130, 132
heretic (see also martyr) 45
Herodotus 16–17, 20, 120, 123, 125
Hillman, David 165
Hobbes, Thomas 176–80, 185, 187, 203, 206, 221
Holinshed, Raphael 80
Holland, Philemon 104
Hollar, Wenceslaus 8, 35, 176 n. 20
Homo-humus 165
Hope theatre (see also bear garden) 7, 61–2
hospitality 204
hubris 252
human,
    as defective being 19 n. 59
    dignitas xi, 18, 91, 106, 250
    h. Other 17, 122, 142, 242–3, 258
    as political animal 104
human and animal as fellow creatures 209–15, 272
human nature xi, 19, 21, 22, 64, 87, 106, 165, 173, 211, 216, 242, 259–63, 266
human-animal distinction (and its blurring) ix–xi, 3, 15, 22, 24–5, 34–6, 53, 63, 65, 90, 103, 112–3, 137, 167, 173, 175, 179, 203, 209, 214–6, 223, 226, 241, 252, 254–5, 275–6

humanimality 217, 259
humanism x, 19, 40, 58, 171, 211, 257
humanity 17, 93, 243
humiliation 110–11, 207
Hundt, Magnus 17–18
hunting 36–7, 39, 79, 95, 101, 145–6, 149, 151, 156, 213, 231–2, 234, 273
    and animal-baiting 92–3, 96
    metaphor for wooing 149
    prerogative of nobility 94
Huss, Jan (John) 40, 129–33, 137, 271
hybridization 132 n. 45, 179, 191–193
Hydra 78, 82, 105, 112, 132
Hyperion 166

Icarus 252
industrial revolution 271
Innocent III 18
interiority 75
intermediality (see also media) 13–15, 64, 82, 115, 208, 234, 253, 270, 276
invisibilization (of punishment, slaughter) 9, 10, 40, 273, 276–8
Isidore of Seville 165
Ixion 193

James I 30, 39, 47, 72–8, 81–3, 138, 182, 250, 265, 269
St Jerome 238
Jesus Christ 49, 79–82, 135, 203
Johnson, Mark 28
Johnson, Richard 184
Johnson, Samuel 89, 223
Joyce, James ix

Keats, John 267–70
Kenilworth entertainment (1575) (see Laneham, Robert)
Knight, G. Wilson 101–2, 171–2
Kott, Jan 172

Lacan, Jacques 152
Lakoff, George 28
Laneham, Robert 97–9, 173–5, 234–5, 267
La Rochefoucauld, François de 262
law 175, 185, 206
Le Brun, Charles 15–16

Leviathan 176–79, 217
Lévi-Strauss, Claude 101, 120, 123
Ligon, Richard 231
Livy 104, 108–9, 113
Locke, John 180, 206
Lotman, Yuri 13, 46
Luce, Morton 241
Lupton, Julia 246–7, 248
Luther, Martin 27, 177, 210

Machiavelli, Niccolò 59 n. 34, 66, 76,
    90, 206
McLuskie, Kathleen 192
Mandeville, John 120
Manetti, Gianozzo 18
Markham, Gervase 94
Marlowe, Christopher 236
Mars 108
martyr 9, 44–6, 129, 130–3, 137, 151,
    268, 271
    imitatio Christi 81
    theatre of martyrdom 136
Mary Stuart, Queen of Scots 15, 72–3
master-slave dialectics 247–8, 255
media,
    early modern media environment 3
    new 275
    as technical devices 13, 276
Messina, Antonella da 238
metamorphosis (also translation) 35, 90,
    149, 209, 216, 224–5
metatheatricality 237
microcosm 27–8
Milton, John 233
mind 236–8
misanthropy 165
misogyny 189–92
missing link 256, 258
monster 176, 255
    female 191
    royal 187, 219
    as sign 91
monstrous 242, 258
    beasts 132
    birth 191
    hybrids 112
Montaigne, Michel de 17 n. 51, 115–48,
    162, 166–9, 210 n. 114, 251,
    260–2, 272

More, Sir Thomas 24 n. 78
Mullaney, Steven 91
Münster, Sebastian 169–70
Mystery cycles 79, 131

natural law 172
nature 172, 187
    control over 239, 266, 278
    -culture divide 213
    as 'ensouled' 27
    fraternity with 212–13
    immersion in 218
    as life process 158, 163
    as sanctuary 212–13
    state of 124–5, 180, 203, 209
    wild 94, 128
Nessus 112
Nietzsche, Friedrich 40, 165, 259–66
Norden, John 3–4
Nowottny, Winifred 187

order (and its disruption),
    civil 175, 178–9, 203, 209, 226, 248
    cosmic 14, 172, 186
    epistemic 239
    feudal 87
    legal 128, 167
    moral 172
    patriarchal 142, 147, 150, 154
    political 187, 198
    social 93, 94, 107, 172, 189, 219
    symbolic 228
Orrell, John 4
Ovid 123, 136, 146, 148–9, 224–5

pain 36–7, 117, 138, 149, 227, 243, 252–3
panopticism 168
Paris garden ix, 6 n. 12, 43
passions 27–8, 137, 185, 187, 262
Paster, Gail Kern 27
pastoral 211–12
penal system 9, 170, 205, 278
    reform of 10, 271
Pepys, Samuel 230
Philip IV of Spain 93
Physiologus 48
Pico della Mirandola, Giovanni 18, 54–5,
    89–91, 166, 191, 261
Plato 176, 251

Platter, Thomas 34, 68
pluralization 14, 19, 24
poetic justice 223
Polo, Marco 16
Pope, Alexander 22
posthumanism 218
postcolonial criticism 235
Pride, Thomas 229
Primadaye, Pierre de la 26
print revolution 14
Proteus 76, 90, 213
public (*see also* audience) 77–8,
    109–110
punishment (*see also* execution, torture,
    whipping) 12, 63, 122–3, 137,
    173, 235, 252, 270–1
  and revenge (*see also* cannibalism) 129,
    141, 154, 169–70, 205
Puttenham, George 29 n. 98
Pyrrhus 161–3

Quiller-Couch, Arthur 30
Quint, David 124, 148

Rainolds, John 35
rape 145–50
Ravelhofer, Barbara 30–1
reason 105, 165, 167, 185, 216, 218,
    251, 254
Rembrandt van Rijn 203
representation 83, 103, 123, 125, 127,
    162–3, 208, 216, 244
  and presence 48–51, 60
Restoration 230, 253
revenge (*see also* cannibalism) 40, 115,
    120, 127–8, 136–7, 143, 149–51,
    156, 161–2, 167, 205
Richenthal, Ulrich von 132–3
rites of passage 218
Roman amphitheatre 136, 268
Romanitas 104, 109, 140
Rome
  cannibalistic R. 141–2
  founding of R. 108, 113
  headless R. 139
Romulus and Remus 108, 113
Rosenberg, Marvin 197
Rose Theatre 1 n. 1, 6
Rubens, Peter Paul 93

Sackerson (bear) ix, x, 1
Sahagún, Bernadino de 17
Satan 132 n. 45
satyr 157, 166
Saunders, Laurence 45
Sawter, Lollard William 130 n. 40
Scarry, Elaine 36–7
Schmitt, Carl 73 n. 13, 162,
    176–9, 246
Schiller, Friedrich 222
Scofield, Paul 172, 197
Scot, Reginald 250
semiosphere 13, 231
Serres, Michel 108–9
Shakespeare, William,
  1 Henry VI 92
  2 Henry VI 86–7
  3 Henry VI 69, 73, 75–6, 79–81, 84–5,
    88–91, 234–5
  Antony and Cleopatra 112
  As You Like It 38
  Coriolanus 82, 92, 98–114, 263
  Hamlet 18, 49, 51, 75, 115, 143,
    155–69, 185, 263–4, 272
  Henry V 184, 244
  Julius Caesar 10, 34, 71, 107, 263–5
  King Lear 27, 61, 144, 151, 171–3, 176,
    181–228, 264
  Macbeth 22, 51–67, 71, 74,
    90, 263
  A Midsummer Night's Dream 35,
    144–5, 217
  Richard II 82
  Richard III 70–6, 87–9, 91, 212
  The Tempest 115, 124, 233–59, 265–6
  Titus Andronicus 64, 115, 137–155,
    162, 166–7
  Twelfth Night 38
  The Two Gentlemen of Verona 30, 49
  The Winter's Tale 30–3
shaming rituals 11, 62, 133
Shannon, Laurie 25
Shelley, Percy Bysshe 267
Singer, Peter x, 38 n. 126
siren 192
Skura, Meredith Anne 12
Snyders, Frans 93–8
Sophocles 67
soul 24, 165

sovereignty 73, 77, 179–80, 185, 190,
    198, 246, 250
    and anger 165, 181–3, 187, 205–6
Spenser, Edmund 184
sphinx 192
Spiller, Elizabeth 239
Spon, Jacob 179
Spurgeon, Caroline F. E. 171
Sterne, Laurence 272
Stradanus, Johannes (Jan van der
    Straet) 95–6
Strauss, Leo 178
Stubbes, Phillip 37

Taylor, Charles 25
Taylor, Gary 195–8
Taylor, John (the Water Poet) 11,
    61–2, 82
Tesla, Nikola 273
theatre 229, 238
    and bear-baiting ix, 1, 3–8, 12, 27,
        32–4, 62, 64–5, 208–9, 229, 231,
        253
    and bear-baiting and punishment 2–3,
        9, 12–15, 39–40, 45, 63–4, 68–9,
        81–2, 93, 116, 118–19, 136, 173–4,
        230, 234–5, 253, 266–8, 270, 276, 278
    and kingship 72–3, 76–82
    and litigation 174–5
    and punishment 72–4, 76, 78, 122–3,
        131, 137–8, 168
    and science 240
    and violence 64, 119
theatricality 9, 91, 94
theatrum mundi 77–8
theriomorphism 38, 176, 200
Thomas, Keith 20
Throckmorton, Francis 234
Topsell, Edward 26, 184, 190–1
torture 137–8, 204, 234
Tower menagerie 83
travesty 175, 207, 231, 268, 275
treason 70–1, 75, 86, 185, 205, 221,
    234, 251
Tree, Herbert Beerbohm 257–8
trial by combat 221
Tyson, Edward 191, 203, 261

Übermensch 261

Van Dyck, Anthonis 93
violence 36, 88, 109, 121,125–6, 151,
    159, 203, 205, 208, 241,
    273
    of baiting 87
    congruence of law and 206
    and counter violence 85, 126
    domestic 207–8
    exploitation of violence 119
    imagined acts of 208
    juridical 190
    media violence 116
    meta-violence 119
    representation of 37, 119
    of representation 119
    retributive 148
    sovereign 188
    as spectacle 72, 234
Virginius 151
Vitruvius 4, 5 n. 10
vivisection 203
Vos, Cornelis de 93

Wagner, Richard 265
Waith, Eugene M. 107
Waldstein, Baron Zdeněk 68
Warren, Roger 196–98
Watson, Robert 133, 135, 203
Webster, John 64
Wedel, Lupold von 33, 35
Weimann, Robert 49–50
Wells, Stanley 187, 198, 206
werewolf 112–13
Westinghouse, George 273–4
whipping 9, 11–12, 47, 60, 62, 70,
    209, 263
Wilhelm I, German Emperor 264
Willbern, David 146
William the Conqueror 194
William of Orange 234
Wilson, John Dover 137, 148
Wiseman, Susan 113
Wolfe, Cary x
wonder-cabinet (also Wunderkammer)
    91, 238, 250
wrath 107, 182–3, 206–7, 211, 214,
    219, 270
Wyclif, John 130 n. 40, 177
Wynne-Davies, Marion 147

Yates, Frances 239

Zeuxis 192
Zinzerling, Justus 6
zoo 272

zoographic 254
zoology 40, 48, 173, 190
zoomorphism 38, 99 n. 25,
    101, 211
zôon politikón 104

Lightning Source UK Ltd.
Milton Keynes UK
UKHW020638190223
417171UK00003B/200